COLLECTED WORKS OF ERASMUS

VOLUME 28

COLLECTED WORKS OF
ERASMUS

LITERARY AND EDUCATIONAL WRITINGS 6

CICERONIANUS / NOTES / INDEXES

edited by A.H.T. Levi

University of Toronto Press

Toronto / Buffalo / London

The research and publication costs of the
Collected Works of Erasmus are supported by the
Social Sciences and Humanities Research Council of Canada.
The publication costs are also assisted by
University of Toronto Press.

Canadian Cataloguing in Publication Data
Erasmus, Desiderius, d. 1536.
[Works]
Collected works of Erasmus
Partial contents:
v. 27. Literary and educational writings,
5. Panegyricus. Moria. Julius exclusus.
Institutio principis christiani. Querela pacis.
– v. 28. Literary and educational writings,
6. Ciceronianus. Notes. Index.
ISBN 0-8020-5602-4 (v. 27–28)
1. Erasmus, Desiderius, d. 1536. I. Title.
II. Title: Collected works of Erasmus.
PA8500 1974   876'.04   C74-6326-x rev.

Collected Works of Erasmus

The aim of the Collected Works of Erasmus
is to make available an accurate, readable English text
of Erasmus' correspondence and his
other principal writings. The edition is planned
and directed by an Editorial Board, an Executive Committee,
and an Advisory Committee.

Contents

VOLUME 28

THE CICERONIAN:
A DIALOGUE ON THE IDEAL LATIN STYLE

Dialogus Ciceronianus

translated and annotated by
BETTY I. KNOTT

The *Ciceronianus*, subtitled 'The Ideal Latin Style,' presents itself at first sight as a challenge to the Ciceronians, those contemporaries of Erasmus who claimed this title as a sign of their devotion and obedience to Cicero as the supreme Latin stylist, the one and only 'parent of the Latin tongue.' For them, Cicero was the only model of correct and stylish Latinity, the only prose author to be imitated by those who wished to use Latin for civilized communication. Some went so far as to hold that no Latin word or phrase was to be employed unless it had actually been used by Cicero, and that the competent stylist must be able to deploy Cicero's every construction, idiom, mannerism, and rhythmical cadence. Extreme supporters of this doctrine, we are told, not content with aping Cicero's style in their own writings, rejected as 'unciceronian,' and therefore not worth reading, any person, whatever his merits as writer, who showed a more eclectic taste in modelling his own Latin style or indeed chose to develop a different style of Latinity altogether. As Erasmus and his friends jokingly remarked, not to be Ciceronian was, in the eyes of these persons, worse than being a heretic.[1] The term 'Ciceronian,' however, covered a wide range of opinion and practice, and many a 'Ciceronian' was by no means as rigid and doctrinaire as these extremists caricatured by Erasmus.

The idea that every form of literary activity presupposed the setting up of a model for imitation had been inherited from the classical world, and had acquired a new prominence in fifteenth-century Italy when classical Latin usage, especially as manifested in the rediscovered and reassembled *opus* of Cicero, had been set up as the proper linguistic and stylistic norm by certain of the Italian humanists. As Cicero gradually acquired a uniquely exalted position, Italian Ciceronianism came into being, but at the same time the whole question of imitation became the subject of passionate debate. The main points of disagreement were the admissibility of using Cicero in conjunction with other models and the extent to which a writer could diverge from his chosen model(s). On these questions extreme positions were taken up, and violent antipathies generated.

Ciceronianism remained primarily an Italian phenomenon, and at the time of this dialogue there were strong centres of the movement in Rome, Padua, and Bologna.[2] Disciples appeared in other countries, especially France, as young men returned to their native lands converted to Ciceronianism of various degrees by their Italian tutors; but the extreme Italian Ciceronians claimed that they alone of all nations had the true gift of the Latin tongue, and that all but Italians were automatically precluded from writing Latin of a quality fit to be called 'Ciceronian.'

A considerable part of the *Ciceronianus* is concerned with Christophe de Longueil (1488–1522),[3] who represents for Erasmus a gifted man spoiled by adherence to Ciceronianism. Longueil was a native of Brabant,[4] but he was sent to France at the age of nine, and received most of his education in Poitiers. His sympathies were in consequence French. After the usual school course in which rhetoric played a large part he studied chiefly law, and indeed taught it for a year or two, but after his arrival in Paris about 1514–15 he was induced by his friends Guillaume Budé, François Deloynes, Louis Ruzé, and others to abandon law for more literary studies, including Greek. Before long he departed for Rome with Lazare de Baïf in order to study Greek under Marcus Musurus and Janus Lascaris. After a year or two there (c 1517–18) he was taken up by Pietro Bembo and Jacopo Sadoleto,[5] the most distinguished representatives of Ciceronianism in Italy at the time. He was led by them to change course and devote his energies to the pursuit of the Ciceronian ideal.

Soon Bembo sought to have Longueil's abilities as man of letters and Latin orator acknowledged by the grant of honorary Roman citizenship and other distinctions; but these favours to a non-Italian aroused furious opposition, especially when a youthful speech of Longueil's was brought into the matter. In this speech, made some ten years or so before, Longueil had innocently praised France at the expense of Italy. In 1519 Longueil's antagonists launched a violent onslaught on him as a foreigner and one unworthy in every way of the honours accorded him. Longueil countered the attack by writing two long speeches in his own defence, speeches which demonstrated his complete mastery of the Ciceronian idiom, but he dared not stay in Rome to deliver them. He fled from the city, leaving the speeches in the hands of his friends, who published them. In the eyes of his supporters the speeches vindicated their protégé and discomfited the opposition.[6] Nonetheless Longueil, who had gone as far as Venice, did not feel it wise to return to Rome immediately but went on to northern Europe, where he visited friends and relations and also called on Erasmus in Louvain.

When young, Longueil had admired Erasmus, but even before leaving Paris he had adopted an independent and critical stance towards him.[7] This was strengthened by his association in Rome with circles which were finding fault with Erasmus on various grounds, both theological and literary. In January 1519, he had written from Rome to Jacques Lucas, dean of Orléans, making a comparison between Budé and Erasmus, generally to Erasmus' detriment, especially in the matter of style.[8] This letter was eventually communicated to Erasmus via Ruzé, and Longueil must have been disconcerted to receive in April a letter from Erasmus himself in which he countered Longueil's criticisms.[9] The tone of the letter is one of outward modesty and courtesy, though Erasmus' wounded pride is evident. To Longueil's annoyance, in October Erasmus published this letter sent to Lucas in a collection of letters written and received by himself. The relationship between Erasmus and Longueil thus moved in an unpromising direction.

When Longueil went to Louvain in October 1519 to make Erasmus' personal acquaintance, he no doubt expected to be welcomed as an equal and congratulated on his literary achievement by his eminent fellow-countryman, but he also wanted to take up the matter of the letter to Lucas. The meeting was not a success. Longueil's criticisms obviously rankled,[10] and Erasmus was not predisposed to like this young Ciceronian who was questioning his standing in the world of letters. In his much later account of the visit he describes him as lacking in openness and totally humourless.[11] Erasmus, it seems, did not make any great effort to conceal either his lack of enthusiasm for this unwanted visitor who took up three days of his time or his failure to be impressed by the long account he was given of the two Ciceronian speeches and the supposed Roman triumph.[12]

In spite of the protestations of his French friends, Longueil soon returned to Italy, and after a winter spent studying at Bembo's house near Venice, settled in Padua. His lack of any reliable and permanent source of income meant that his few remaining years were dogged by poverty, and in 1522 he died there at the early age of thirty-three in the house of Richard Pole. Erasmus, in keeping with his reserve towards Longueil, made proper but uneffusive comments on his death.[13] His later correspondence shows, however, that he did not forget him.

Longueil's conversion to ardent Ciceronianism must have been an obstacle to any close understanding with Erasmus. Like many others, Erasmus respected Cicero as a Latin stylist; in his early educational writings he urges the young to have him constantly in hand – and he is still saying the same thing in the *Ciceronianus* (ASD I-2 708:5–7). But he also declared that he himself had come to esteem Cicero rather as an exemplar of cultured sensitivity and nobility of thought, an opinion voiced for example in the preface to his edition of Cicero's *Tusculan Disputations* of 1523.[14] His own style had indeed never been cramped by rigid conformity to Ciceronian or any other usage, but the fact is that Erasmus was in these years developing an increasingly hostile stance to Ciceronianism as a stylistic ideal as part of his antipathy towards certain aspects of contemporary Italian scholarship and culture as he saw them, an antipathy reciprocated by a number of Italians. In spite of the friends he had made in Italy, Erasmus had never returned there after his visit of 1506–9, and his relations with Rome became increasingly uncomfortable as his stand with regard to Luther became more suspect. One finds him and his friends jeering at the Ciceronians for years before the *Ciceronianus* was written. By 1526 there was an idea about that

Erasmus (or one of his friends) would soon involve himself directly in the Ciceronian debate with some form of literary challenge to the Ciceronians.[15]

In 1524 Pole had seen to the posthumous publication in Florence of Longueil's collected writings,[16] and Erasmus was sent a copy the following year.[17] It is clear that Erasmus had read the book by the time he came to write the *Ciceronianus*, and he must have been thinking again in these years of Longueil's early death and the waste of the undoubted talents of his countryman on the Ciceronian ideal propagated by Italians. Furthermore, throughout this period, and especially in 1527, Erasmus was receiving reports of Italians who were criticizing his style as unciceronian, labelling him *barbarus* and *Batavus*, and holding the most eloquent of northerners to be not Erasmus but the deceased Longueil.[18] All this must have brought Erasmus' opposition to a head at this point and determined the content of the work when he finally did put pen to paper.

What emerged after eighteen months or so of gestation was a lively dialogue well exemplifying Erasmus' dramatic skill and power of characterization. The argument is presented in leisurely and flexible fashion, but in spite of its length the dialogue holds the reader's attention by the skilful changes of tone, by the wealth of ideas presented through the interweaving conversation of the three very different characters, and by Erasmus' earnest sincerity as he warms to themes on which he feels deeply. Above all, the wit, the satirical approach, and the deliberately provocative remarks give vividness and individuality to what could have been a fairly uncontroversial contribution to a long-standing literary debate. It is a piece of writing well repaying the effort Erasmus says it cost him.[19]

The basic plot of the drama is as follows: Nosoponus (Mr Workmad), through whom Erasmus satirizes the Italian opposition to himself, is hoping by determination and unremitting effort, no matter what the cost, to learn to imitate Cicero so successfully that he will one day be hailed as a true Ciceronian, even by Italians. This is the sole aim of his life. The other two characters, Bulephorus (Mr Counsellor, who is the main carrier of Erasmus' views) and his supporter Hypologus (Back-up) endeavour by their arguments to cure Nosoponus of his mental aberration and point him to a nobler ideal. In this they succeed.

The opening scene is one of pure amusement, designed to introduce the misguided Nosoponus in all his folly. Before long, the name of Longueil is casually dropped into the conversation when Nosoponus mentions him as a unique example of a northerner granted the glorious title of Ciceronian by the very Italians, and an inspiration to himself in his own pursuit of the title. The other two immediately question the value of Longueil's achievement, but after a brief discussion Longueil is apparently forgotten for the time being. The fun continues as Nosoponus is induced to describe the laborious methods by which he sets about imitating Cicero, a caricature of the principles and methods of real Ciceronians so exaggerated as to amuse by its very absurdity.

The tone becomes more serious as we are gradually led into the second section, where we are presented with a wide-ranging discussion which touches on various debatable topics connected with imitation: whether the model should be one or many, whether Cicero is really the best model, especially for Christians, what features one should imitate, and what imitation is seeking to achieve. Erasmus attacks at length the superficial verbal imitation of Cicero, which he accuses the Ciceronians of practising to the exclusion of every other consideration, representing it as not only ludicrous but time-wasting and ineffective. More importantly, however, he turns the tables on the opposition by accusing them of a neopaganism which he claims to see as a consequence of whole-hearted Ciceronianism. (By this he seems to mean that the misplaced adulation of Cicero causes the mind to occupy itself excessively with the classical world and its ideas and ideals, so that it imbibes pagan concepts rather than Christian ones, and through admiration for that world accepts its philosophy of life as equal or superior to the Christian one.) Erasmus claimed to have been made aware of this 'paganism' during his visit to Italy in 1506–9, and in the years before the writing of this dialogue he frequently accused the literary circles of Rome of being particularily guilty of it.[20] He deliberately contrasts this paganism with his concept of the fusion of the best in the classical heritage with sincere Christian faith. He makes a fervent appeal for an approach to the world of letters informed by true Christian devotion, for a genuine faith, not a nominal one, and urges an attitude of mind that understands and cares for the Christian topics which are of contemporary importance and desires to write about them eloquently without trying to cramp them into the distorting mould of a narrow stylistic canon derived from the writings of a pagan Roman of the first century BC. For him Ciceronian Latin is an inappropriate vehicle for the writings of a Christian world, and apart from anything else its employment on topics for which it is not suited breaks the fundamental ancient law of *decorum*.

Nonetheless, he professes still to admire Cicero as a supreme exponent of artistic Latin. For him, however, the object of imitation should be not Cicero's words but his oratorical virtues, and the end product should be, not a veneer of mechanically copied Ciceronian mannerisms, but a new synthesis reflecting each writer's own personality and concerns.

Erasmus seems to be proposing a sort of Christian Ciceronianism, that is, a Ciceronianism subservient to Christian thinking and responding to

Christian needs. What this means in reality is a style so moulded to Christian thought that it cannot be considered Ciceronian in a way that would be recognized by the Ciceronians. It may be that on the stylistic level the usage of Cicero makes a large contribution to it, but so do many other sources. The important thing is that it is free from preconceptions and rules. All the talk of imitating Cicero's oratorical virtues – his sensitivity, his flexibility, his feeling of appropriateness – means that the ideal style is one in which the writer himself responds to the demands of each topic as he judges best. It is in fact a charter of freedom, and a justification and defence of Erasmus' own chosen and characteristic style, eloquent, rich but above all eclectic. In particular, in dealing with Christian material, it can if necessary draw on the resources of centuries of Christian writing in Latin.

The main arguments have now been set out, but the cure of Nosoponus, who is only partly convinced, continues in a third section which provides a survey of scores of persons who had written in Latin from classical times down to Erasmus' own day. This fails to produce one whom Nosoponus is prepared to accept as a real Ciceronian: as Bulephorus proposes each name, Nosoponus rejects it, usually with scorn, sometimes with faint praise, (or in the case of friends, real praise), but not one measures up to his ideal. This ideal is thus shown to be quite unrealistic, and one that had no influence on many men of great distinction who had been quite happy to write elegantly and clearly in a non-Ciceronian style.

At the end of this review of writers in Latin comes a lengthy assessment of the most distinguished of contemporary or recent Italian classicizers – Bembo, Sadoleto, Pontano, Sannazaro – and here the tone is more generous. Erasmus gives praise where praise is due, especially to Bembo and Sadoleto, whom he respected. But the main discussion is devoted to Longueil, whose writings are now submitted to a detailed investigation. It is quite possible that Erasmus meant the portrait of Nosoponus in the early part of the dialogue to present a caricature of Longueil, as Longueil's admirers certainly took it to be. There are one or two marked similarities with details given in Pole's life of Longueil – for example, Longueil's confining his reading to Cicero for five years. But the assessment given at the end of the dialogue seems fair enough. Longueil, as a whole-hearted Ciceronian, must necessarily be criticized by Erasmus as an exponent of all that he considered foolish and misguided, all that he had been arguing against in the earlier part of the dialogue, but the tone of the criticism is here eminently reasonable. Erasmus certainly speaks his mind; he expostulates, he is ironic, but he is not mocking or cruel. During his visit in 1519, Longueil had asked Erasmus to mention his Ciceronian triumph in Rome somewhere in his writings. It is perhaps a little malicious of Erasmus to 'mention' it six years later like this, and to present the whole incident of the accusation and Longueil's self-defence as a much less serious business than Longueil or his supporters took it to be. Even so, in spite of, or perhaps because of, his uncomfortable relations with Longueil, Erasmus seems to be going out of his way to be fair to him in this assessment. It bears some resemblance to Longueil's remarks to Lucas about Erasmus – a frank assessment addressed to a third party and therefore not toned down by the requirements of courtesy or affection. Erasmus, it seems, had not felt any need to write a tribute to Longueil as a man of letters at the time of his death. The dialogue could be considered a belated tribute to him, but it is a mixed one.

Erasmus' criticism of Longueil is then reinforced by a restatement of his own views on the proper method of imitation, culminating in a close summary and discussion of the letters on the subject exchanged by Angelo Poliziano and Paolo Cortesi. Erasmus makes plain here his agreement with the anti-Ciceronian views of Poliziano, especially his characterization of those who in his own day copied Cicero in a slavish and mechanical manner as 'apes of Cicero.' The 'Ciceronian apes' are jeered at eleven times in all in the course of the dialogue. (Though he picks these out for special mention, Erasmus was familiar with other contributions to the controversy and assigns to Bulephorus at various points arguments and analogies which, starting in the ancient world, had become commonplace in the literature on the subject). Finally all the arguments put forward in the dialogue are drawn together and summarized, and Nosoponus declares himself practically cured.

Erasmus expected, even intended, the *Ciceronianus* to offend the Italians,[21] and it certainly did so. There was a, to modern eyes, surprisingly furious reaction: Italians saw in the dialogue not only the rejection of Ciceronianism and the vicious ridiculing of its most distinguished supporters but an attempt to discredit Cicero totally as a model of Latin style and to show the whole concept of stylistic imitation as misconceived – in short, a belittling of decades of Italian scholarship and literary achievement. Some indignantly accused Erasmus of proposing himself and his own style as a better model than Cicero. Above all, the accusation of paganism gave great offence.

Erasmus may well have observed all this at first with amused satisfaction from Basel, but there was a reaction he had not expected. A furore was caused in Paris by the passage (ASD I-2 672:5–673:1) in the list of 'failed Ciceronians' where Nosoponus finds Guillaume Budé inferior to Josse Bade as an aspirant after the Ciceronian style. Frenchmen were incensed that Budé, the glory of French scholarship and letters, should be even thought of in the same context as the worthy printer Bade, who, for all his claims to scholarship, was primarily a businessman and by no means in the same intellectual class as Budé. Louis de Berquin, in a letter not extant, and Germain de Brie[22] wrote immediately to comment on Erasmus' indiscretion, de Brie, who was a friend of Budé as well as of Erasmus, suggesting[23] various ways of undoing the apparent insult. Erasmus replied to Berquin, and sent a copy of the letter to de Brie, but it leaked out to a wider audience[24] and only made things worse by spreading talk of the affair. More and more people came to believe that Erasmus had deliberately set out to insult French scholarship in the person of Budé, and at the same time take revenge on Budé for accusing Erasmus of a persistently derogatory attitude towards the French nation.[25] Other remarks put in Nosoponus' mouth in this section of the dialogue were taken as the direct expression of Erasmus' own views and interpreted as showing that he despised the whole community of contemporary men of letters for having tried to attain the Ciceronian ideal and having failed.[26]

The indignation gathered momentum: defamatory epigrams attacking Erasmus circulated in Paris, written by Budé's supporter Jacques Toussain[27] and by the Greek Janus Lascaris,[28] and the quarrel even reached the ears of the king. Erasmus was taken aback by the vehemence of the storm raised by his ill-considered remark. In September he wrote again to Berquin[29] and replied at length to de Brie,[30] protesting that he meant no insult to Budé and at the same time defending other points in the dialogue. He also set about having de Brie's original letter together with this reply printed in both Basel[31] and Paris. He wrote as well to Budé,[32] repeating what he had said to de Brie: that the comparison with Bade, coming from Nosoponus, was not to be taken seriously, and that Budé himself would not wish to be called a Ciceronian on Nosoponus' terms; but Budé, though he professed to make light of the affair, was seriously offended,[33] and indeed neither replied to this letter nor corresponded with Erasmus thereafter. The offending passage was somewhat modified in the second edition of March 1529, though Erasmus would not change the essential tenor of his argument and allow Budé even to approximate to the ranks of Nosoponus' Ciceronians.

The list of unciceronian writers on which Erasmus had so incautiously embarked succeeded in giving offence also because the names of certain contemporaries were not included. This was taken to show that Erasmus did not consider them worthy of mention. Some people complained on their own account at being omitted,[34] some on behalf of others: very soon after the appearance of the work, round about June 1528, Ursinus Velius wrote from Prague to point out the omission of various men of letters, including Haio Herman and Juan Luis Vives, the well-known Spanish humanist. In reply to Velius,[35] Erasmus protested that he could not include everyone, that there was little point in mentioning people who, like Haio, had published nothing (though in fact Erasmus had mentioned several persons whose publications were meagre or non-existent), and that some scholars, like Rhenanus and Vives, took offence too easily to be mentioned lightly. A certain restraint seems to have developed between Erasmus and Vives at this time,[36] and the omission was probably not an oversight as he professed it to be in his rather abrupt apology to Vives.[37] Vives' reply[38] shows that he had been hurt by the omission, but he remained on friendly terms with Erasmus.

None the less, in the second edition, Erasmus bowed to criticism and inserted paragraphs on Herman (ASD I-2 683 apparatus) and on Vives (ASD I-2 691 apparatus). He also added Peter Schade (ASD I-2 675 apparatus), and a brief reference to Jakob Spiegel (ASD I-2 685 apparatus). In the third edition, further thoughts prompted him to add Claudius Cantiuncula and Cornelis de Schepper (ASD I-2 674–5), and Ulrich Zasius (ASD I-2 687).

Erasmus' survey of writing in Latin was indeed a strange one if taken as a serious and well-considered review. In the section on past writers distinguished figures such as Anselm jostle with Claudius of Turin (ASD I-2 660: 33–4), Guarino Guarini with the little known Antonio Pasini (ASD I-2 662:11). The space allotted to each person mentioned does not accord with his intrinsic merits as man of letters and writer: Leo the Great, Poggio, Lorenzo Valla, Pico della Mirandola, and Gaguin are briefly dismissed, being granted very little more space in the discussion than the brothers Fernand (ASD I-2 672:3). The list as a whole is heavily overweighted on the side of Italian scholarship, both past and present (though of course Italy, with its longer tradition of humane culture, had far more names to offer, and the long list of their fellow-countrymen who had not apparently achieved the ideal was in itself an argument against the Italian Ciceronians). Other countries were patchily and unevenly represented, and the selection of names often seems arbitrary.

It was of course not meant to be taken all that seriously. The list of names is part of a dramatic dialogue (Erasmus may have got the idea for it from the survey of Roman oratory in Cicero's *Brutus*), and in the interests of verisimilitude Erasmus makes his interlocutors digress, backtrack, and forget certain names at the appropriate moment, recalling them only later. It was supposed to be a casual conversation, not a definitive work of reference, and Erasmus, writing fluently and rapidly, did not apparently weigh his words too much. In any case, if Gregory the Great, Ficino, Gaguin and others are dismissed in a word by Nosoponus, this is all part of the characterization of the blinkered Ciceronian.

But beyond Nosoponus and the dramatic intent, the responsibility for the list is Erasmus' – these are the names he chose, for whatever reason, for inclusion, and his readers took it so. While no one minded the survey of the dead and gone, rapid and uneven as it is and influenced by Erasmus' personal predilections, the list of contemporaries was a different matter. The basic fact was that Erasmus could not include everybody, and his selection ultimately depended on feeling rather than dispassionate judgment.[39] Most of the contemporary persons mentioned appear simply because they were friends or acquaintances of Erasmus whose names sprang to mind whether or not their literary eminence warranted their inclusion. For example, Erasmus' friend Goclenius, who wrote hardly anything, merits not a line or two but a short bantering paragraph (ASD I-2 683:14), and Paolo Bombace and William Latimer were anything but prolific writers (ASD I-2 669:4, 678:11). Erasmus also included some antagonists doubtless because they were prominent in his thoughts at this period: Aleandro, Pio, Hutten, Zúñiga. So the omission of certain people was all the more noticeable. Whatever overt justification Erasmus produced when challenged, one suspects that he genuinely forgot the person or that there was some undercurrent of personal feeling which he later, as so often, wished to disclaim. In either case the disappointment of those omitted was understandable – to have been mentioned in the *Ciceronianus* became an accolade. Consequently this section of the work, originally an appendage to the main argument, came to have undue importance attached to it and occasioned Erasmus a great deal of trouble. He soon felt it had been mistaken generosity to include more than one or two representative names, or indeed to mention the living at all.[40]

At the same time what he actually wrote about some persons who were included[41] also gave scope for resentment. While some of the 'thumb-nail sketches' contain effusive tributes, others damn with faint praise or include quite uncomplimentary remarks. The blame for this cannot be laid entirely on the characterization of Nosoponus. At this point in the dialogue[42] Nosoponus has explicitly changed roles with Bulephorus, and we are never quite sure how far he is speaking in his own dramatic persona and how far he is voicing Erasmus' own thoughts. He certainly seems to be speaking for Erasmus in the enthusiastic remarks about friends like Bombace and More, to name but two, so Erasmus was not entirely honest in trying to dissociate himself from Nosoponus' remarks where they caused resentment. They could often have been expressed more tactfully. Though one point made in the dialogue is that no sensible person would want to be hailed as a Ciceronian by Nosoponus, not everyone was capable of understanding Erasmus' irony, if that is what it was (the teasing is sometimes quite hurtful), and it is not surprising that only a few people expressed positive pleasure at what was said about them here.

For years after the appearance of this dialogue, Erasmus found himself obliged to write letters of protest and self-justification, for the various causes of offence were never either forgiven or forgotten. In particular, there was war between Erasmus and the Ciceronians for the remainder of his life, and attacks were launched by various adversaries. For example, J.C. Scaliger in 1531 published in Paris his *Oratio pro Marco Tullio Cicerone contra Desiderium Erasmum Roterodamum*, a vitriolic attack in which Erasmus professed to see the hand of his old antagonist Aleandro.[43] Ortensio Lando, a Ciceronian enemy of long standing, in 1534 published his *Cicero relegatus et renovatus* (Lyons: Gryphius, and Venice: Sessa), while in 1535 Gaudenzio Merula was meditating a *Bellum civile inter Ciceronianos et Erasmicos*. In the same year Pietro Corsi produced a *Defensio pro Italia ad Erasmum Roterodamum* (Rome: Bladus), to which Erasmus wrote a reply printed in Allen as Ep 3032. Scaliger produced a second oration in 1537, the year after Erasmus' death, and even then did not drop the matter, but produced a third, which, however, did not appear in print. (These orations his son, J.J. Scaliger, regretted and endeavoured to suppress.) In the general Ciceronian debate, which continued for the rest of the century, various persons rose to the defence of Longueil, notably Dolet, who in 1535 issued his *Dialogus de imitatione Ciceroniana*, an enthusiastic apologia for Longueil, as well as a vehement criticism of Erasmus and the *Ciceronianus*.[44]

In one of the last letters he wrote[45] Erasmus, clearly wearied by the continuing hostility, names several of these persons who had been attacking him. His last word on the subject is to describe them as 'limbs of Satan' and to declare that Satan would prefer to have everyone Ciceronian rather than Christian.[46]

The *Ciceronianus* was first published by the firm of Froben in March 1528 in a fat volume where it was preceded by an edition of *De recta pronuntiatione* and followed by a considerable number of very minor pieces in Greek and Latin by various hands. Five of these commemorated Johann Froben, the head of the firm, who had died the previous year. Erasmus provided three of them, together with a six-line Latin verse tribute to Bruno Amerbach, who died in 1519. There were also thirteen verse and prose epitaphs on Maarten van Dorp, the Louvain theologian who had died in 1525, including seventeen lines of Latin iambic trimeters from Erasmus. At the end were two rather more substantial works: Rodolphus Agricola's *Oratio in laudem Matthiae Richili*, and Erasmus' *Epistola consolatoria in adversis* of 1528, addressed to the nuns of Denny, near Cambridge.

The *Ciceronianus* was dedicated to Johann von Vlatten, and the dedicatory epistle was printed as the third piece in the volume, immediately before the text of the dialogue.[47] Vlatten was a friend of long standing to whom Erasmus had dedicated his edition of Cicero's *Tusculan Disputations* five years earlier. Although his own studies were primarily in law, Vlatten was an appropriate enough recipient of two works dealing with a central figure of Latin literature, as he had been 'scholaster' at St Mary's, Aachen since 1517. He wrote immediately to express his appreciation, sending a silver cup in return,[48] whereupon Erasmus felt obliged to apologize[49] for dedicating to him a work that had not been printed separately, a situation which he blamed on the printers.

The *Ciceronianus* in fact does not seem to have been considered long enough or weighty enough by printers to merit separate issue,[50] although there was considerable demand for it, no doubt due to the notoriety occasioned by Erasmus' unfortunate *obiter dicta*.[51] Apart from the fresh editions authorized by Erasmus, which followed quickly in March 1529, October 1529, and March 1530, there were several printings between 1528 and 1531, emanating from Paris, Lyon, Alcalá, and Cologne, in which, as in the first edition, it was combined with *De recta pronuntiatione* and minor pieces.

For the second authorized edition, Erasmus wrote a second letter of dedication to Vlatten in which he defended his motives in the various passages which had given offence and maintained a generally unrepentant stand.[52] He was, however, induced to modify some of the offending sections (see 331–2 above). At the same time he took the opportunity of changing the word order and making minor improvements to the Latinity in numerous places. In this edition, published in Basel by Hieronymus Froben and Johann Herwagen, the *Ciceronianus* was combined with an edition of the *Colloquia* and a different selection of minor works: the chief changes were the omission of the epitaphs on Dorp and the insertion of more memorials to Johann Froben and three epitaphs on Jakob Wimpfeling, who had died in November the previous year. There were also some appendages to the *Colloquia* (scholia, Erasmus' *De utilitate colloquiorum* of 1526, and an index).

The third edition authorized by Erasmus was published in Basel by Hieronymus Froben, Johann Herwagen, and Nicolaus Episcopius in October 1529. It combined the dialogue with an improved edition of *De recta pronuntiatione* and with the same selection of minor works as in the second edition, except for the addition of a Hebrew epitaph on Johann Froben and a letter by Erasmus to Karel van Uutenhove (Ep 2209). Erasmus introduced some further changes into the text (see 332 above) and made more minor corrections. The fourth edition (March 1530) reproduced the third almost unchanged: it is in reality not a fourth edition but a reissue of the third, utilizing the identical sheets, except that the last sheet was reset and redated and carried a longer list of errata.[53]

There is a full critical edition of the text with introduction in ASD I-2 599–710. ASD prints the text of the first, March 1528, edition, showing the changes in subsequent editions in the apparatus criticus. This translation is based on a collation of the ASD text with LB (I 973–1026), which gives the latest and fullest version. A good many of Erasmus' changes in the later editions were simple insertions which involved hardly any alteration of the surrounding text. These insertions have been incorporated into the translation for continuity in reading, and, if significant, their existence is indicated by a footnote. Where passages were substituted, the first version is translated in the body of the text, the later version in a footnote. Minor changes and unimportant variations have not been noted, since details are available in ASD; in these cases the clearest and most satisfactory version of the Latin has been translated.

B I K

DESIDERIUS ERASMUS OF ROTTERDAM TO THE HONOURABLE JOHANN
VON VLATTEN, GREETING

My honourable friend,[1] to prosper the state by wise and honest counsel is a
noble task, and one especially appropriate to kingship. Homer for this
reason calls[2] the person in his poem who wielded supreme authority
boulephorus 'the giver of counsel.' Men of this kind do the highest service to
cities and countries at all times, and especially in our own age when some
fated upheaval has thrown everything into total confusion – the Christian
faith, kingdoms and republics, and the world of scholarship and letters.
Everything is in such turmoil that the Greek proverb 'counsel is of god' is
truer than it ever was.

So it may seem irresponsible, criminal even, to claim your attention
when you are engaged in this noble activity, which you perform with such
honesty, alertness, and ability. But Horace rightly, I think, told his friend,
'Amidst your schemes and planning find frivolity a place,'[3] so here is a little
book from Erasmus to distract you with its nonsense from your gloomy and
important preoccupations – though, to quote Horace again,[4] this nonsense
is something that has a serious outcome. Far from having nothing to do with
matters of public concern, it is particularly relevant to you as director of
education in Aachen.

Good letters, which had begun to flourish and make some healthy
growth, are now, as a result of general indifference combined with low moral
standards, everywhere on the verge of extinction; and as if this were not
enough, there have been in existence for some time now persons who are
trying to foist upon us what is more or less a new sect – 'Ciceronians' is the
name they have taken, and they reject with intolerable arrogance any literary
work which does not reproduce Cicero's stylistic characteristics. They keep
the young from reading other writers and restrict them to the meticulous
imitation of Cicero as their only model, yet no one reproduces Cicero's
manner less effectively than these very persons who make such ostentatious
claims for themselves by brandishing this insubstantial title.

But what a disaster it would be for scholarship if it were accepted that
no one but Cicero was to be read or imitated! There is, however, a suspicion
of something else afoot under cover of this name, and that is to make us
pagans instead of Christians – though I believe our prime object is to ensure
that good letters proclaim the glory of Christ our Lord and God, with all the
richness, brilliance, and magnificence that Cicero displayed in speaking of
things pagan. Moreover, I observe that a number of young men returning to
us from Italy, especially from Rome, have been considerably infected by
these attitudes.

So it seemed to me that I would be doing something to serve religion and to aid the studies of our young people if I contributed some small work to the subject – not to dissuade young persons who are learning to write and speak from imitating Cicero (what could be stupider than that?), but to show how we can genuinely represent Cicero, and combine his supreme powers of expression with the faith of Christ.

This is the work I am now sending you. I have written it in dialogue form so that it will hold the reader's attention better and make more of an impression on the attitudes of students. Farewell.

Basel, 14 February 1528

DESIDERIUS ERASMUS OF ROTTERDAM TO THE HONOURABLE JOHANN VON VLATTEN, GREETING

My dear Vlatten,[5] is it fate or some power interfering in our lives that puts this unpleasant streak in human affairs, so that the very things that many people like rouse violent antipathies in others? I recently published two books at the same time, both at the one birth so to speak, one on pronunciation,[6] the other on the imitation of Cicero. The former offended no one, but did not find many friends; the second was eagerly bought up, but also gave considerable offence to quite a number of people. They complain that some persons were passed over in silence who should not have been, that others were not treated with proper respect, that some received less than their due and others more.

For the point I was making, seven examples taken from ancient literature would have been enough, so far was I from intending to make a methodical survey of every known writer, especially when this section was secondary to my main argument. If I had wanted to expand my material to the full at such a point, I could very properly have had quoted against me the Greek adage 'The extras are bigger than the basic load.'[7] I could with more justification be thought a fool for naming so many than for leaving out a few, and I should have been much more of a fool if I had tried to assess the style of every person who has published anything, when there are so many young men now in Germany, France, England, Hungary, and Poland who can both speak and write in good Latin. If only my kindness had produced some benefit to match!

The fact that I made no mention of some close friends whom I see every day shows that I did not omit anyone through ill will or forgetfulness. I knew that some were so maidenly modest that they could not bear to have their names mentioned in a publication – a thing as bad as having them proclaimed from the stage, for sending a book out into the world is definitely a kind of histrionic activity; some are so fastidious that one wouldn't know how they should be treated, and some so cantankerous and touchy that they jump however you handle them.

Now if I had only praised the people whose names I mention, and if I had praised them without exception, I would have spoiled the fruits I wanted this work to produce – the young learn a great deal from critical assessments like the ones here, as they get into the habit of reading always with discrimination and recognizing what to avoid and what to try to do. There is a vast difference between criticism and eulogy.

The reason I included the review was to make my meticulous pursuer of the Ciceronian turn of phrase deny the honour of the title 'Ciceronian' to every one of them. This was done in the character of Nosoponus, who in this area displays a judgment far from sound. However, I did not want the refusal of the title to offend anyone, so I added quite a dash of praise to what was said about various individuals, apportioning it so that no one could find me deficient in generosity, and everyone would recognize that each man had been given his due – which was done so ungrudgingly that I don't suppress the names even of enemies like Hutten and Zúñiga, or deprive them of the praise that they deserve. As for the people who took offence at Budé's being treated insultingly, I imagine they now regret the attitude they took. Others with equal effrontery muttered that I was jealous of Longueil, when hardly anyone has made more frank and honourable mention of him – though he interspersed various remarks in his writings which make one suspect he didn't have a particularly high opinion of my abilities. But I never take offence at freely expressed opinions in men of learning. If they are right, one can learn from them; if not, it's a human enough failing and nothing to justify the breakup of a friendship between good men. I wish there were many Longueils to joke about the Dutch word-spinner, provided they did good service to Christian learning and Christian faith – which he would have done nobly, in my opinion, if he had been granted longer life.

Moreover, to make sure the words of praise bestowed on the various literary men were not discounted as having no weight, I invented a character who was a considerable scholar and a man of sense, apart from the silliness of his excessive admiration of Cicero.

But how transient is the life of man! The tide of mortal things flows out fast as the Euripus,[8] or faster, if any faster tide there is. Even as we speak, the hour is gone, as the satirist[9] says; even as we review our friends, we find we have lost one, and not one we valued least – I refer to Jakob Wimpfeling of Sélestat. He could have been counted happy if his old age had not coincided with these very troubled times. From his earliest years onwards he was educated in the noblest subjects, first at Sélestat under Ludwig Dringenberg of Westphalia; later on at Freiburg and then at Heidelberg he acquired skill in canon law, to which he happily added knowledge of theology, but was besides versed in every good discipline. As for literary skills, he demonstrated in both poetry and prose all that one could ask of a theologian or a man living at that period. He was appointed to an ecclesiastical office at Speyer in which he performed his duties admirably.

While there, this pious man on fire with love of heavenly things grew weary of this world which, as John[10] says, lies totally in wickedness, and determined to retreat from it. He had as his companion in this intention Christoph von Utenheim,[11] a man both scholarly and of the purest personal integrity. That he might 'flee with nothing to the Christ who has nothing'[12] Wimpfeling resigned what income he had from the church – it was indeed enough to provide a decent livelihood. Christoph however went no further with the plan but was drawn back to his office of bishop,[13] for his friends put forward the view that if his holiness of mind were combined with authority he would win more men for Christ than if he hid himself away. But Wimpfeling, rejoicing in his poverty, persevered in the course he had begun.

Returning to Heidelberg, he expounded the text of Jerome and other sacred authors. He also published books which were a means of instructing the young and inspiring priests to seek piety and chastity. Because of his concern for spiritual growth he was prepared to act as tutor to a number of young persons for whom the future held great promise. Outstanding among this noble group in learning, integrity, openness, and wisdom is at the present time the noble Jakob Sturm, to whose counsel not only the famous city of Strasbourg but almost the whole of Germany owes the greatest debt.

His spiritual outspokenness did not fail to arouse hostility. A tired old man suffering from hernia, he was summoned to Rome, thanks to the efforts of the Augustinian monks, for writing somewhere[14] that Augustine was not a monk – or certainly not like the accepted idea of an Augustinian monk today: the Augustinians themselves represent the saint in pictures and booklets with a long beard, a black habit and a leather belt. The fire started by this tiny spark was on the point of developing into a great conflagration, but Julius II intervened to extinguish it, with the approval of all good men.

Besides other conflicts that made trial of his virtue, he was much grieved by this fatal division of the whole church, which all but destroyed his desire to live. So, after his unsuccessful attempts at solitude and withdrawal, when his years began to weigh upon him, he went to live at Sélestat with his sister Magdalena. His two nephews, her sons, whom he had always loved like a father, he left at his death well set up in both mind and morals. One of them, Jakob Spiegel, became well known as a lawyer and has acted as counsellor first to the emperor Maximilian and then to King

Ferdinand. The younger, Johannes Maius, recently succeeded his brother[15] in the service of King Ferdinand, and made himself very popular at court by his civilized mind and sociable manners.

I have not yet made up my mind whether rejoicing or sorrow is the proper response to Wimpfeling's death: he reached almost his eightieth year, and would have lived longer if he had been prepared to take any account of his failing physical powers; he was given his release from the present age, which is the wickedest one can imagine; and I have no doubt that he now enjoys with those in heaven the rewards of a virtuous life.

But to return to the subject. Some time after the publication of the *Ciceronianus*, I discovered that this very topic had been discussed in three letters[16] exchanged between Gianfrancesco Pico della Mirandola and Pietro Bembo. Pico lets his argument range over a considerable number of topics; Bembo holds much the same views as myself, for he says he is only speaking of intellects of outstanding ability. Nor does he dissuade people from reading good authors, but he does urge that Cicero be taken as the only model for imitation, and indeed, a much more difficult thing, for emulation. I am taking issue only with those who are so committed to this irrational creed that they reject with incredible disgust anything that does not conform.

I have gone over the book and emended a few passages, and have also added a few names. For when it was first going through the press, a noisy troublemaker[17] suddenly turned up who considerably distracted my attention and interrupted its progress. Some persons are born for nothing except to cause trouble to people trying to do something decent, while they have nothing to fill their own time except gambling, whoring, guzzling, and boasting. Farewell.

Basel, 24 January 1529

THE CICERONIAN:
A DIALOGUE ON
THE IDEAL LATIN STYLE[1]

Bulephorus[2] Who's that I see strolling about down there at the end of the arcade? Unless[3] my eyes have lost their sharpness, it's our old friend and fellow student, Nosoponus.

Hypologus Nosoponus? the fellow who once used to be the life and soul of our set, rosy-cheeked, a bit on the plump side, diffusing charm and amiability in every direction?

Bulephorus The very same.

Hypologus But whatever has made him look so different? He's more like a ghost than a human being. Is he suffering from some disease?

Bulephorus Yes, a very serious one.

Hypologus Whatever is it? Surely not dropsy?

Bulephorus No, it's a malady that goes deeper than the skin.

Hypologus You don't mean that new sort of ulcerating disease, the scab,[4] as people euphemistically call it nowadays?

Bulephorus No, this is eating him away deeper than that.

Hypologus He's not spitting blood?

Bulephorus This illness has got a hold somewhere further in than the lungs.

Hypologus Not tuberculosis or jaundice?

Bulephorus It's something more deep-seated than the liver.

Hypologus Perhaps he's got a fever affecting his veins and heart?

Bulephorus Yes, it is a fever, but then it isn't: it's something that burns deeper down than any fever raging in the veins and heart – something with its source in the brain, in the depths of the mind.[5] But stop making wrong guesses, it's a new sort of illness.

Hypologus Hasn't it got a name yet then?

Bulephorus Not a Latin one; the Greeks call it *zelodulea*, 'style-addiction.'

Hypologus Did he catch it recently, or has he had it a long time?

Bulephorus It's had the poor fellow in its grip for more than seven years. I say, we've been spotted. It looks as if he's coming this way. You'll get a better idea what's wrong from the man himself. I shall play Davus[6] to begin with – you see that you follow my lead in the conversation and act your part in the charade.

Hypologus Yes, I'll join in wholeheartedly – if I know what you're giving me to do.

Bulephorus What I really want is to deliver our poor old friend from his great affliction.

Hypologus Do you understand medicine[7] as well, then?

Bulephorus There's a form of madness, you know, which doesn't take away the wits entirely; it damages just one part of the mind, but with remarkable effect – I mean cases like the ones where people are convinced they have bull's horns growing on their heads,[8] or that they're afflicted with an enormously long nose, or have a huge pottery head balanced on a spindly neck, which must smash as soon as they make the slightest movement. Some of them even believe they are dead, and are terrified of any contact with the living.

Hypologus Say no more, I know that sort of illness.

Bulephorus The most effective way of healing people like that is to pretend that you suffer from the same disease yourself.

Hypologus So I've often heard.

Bulephorus That's what we're going to do.[9]

Hypologus Then I'll be delighted to take a supporting role and not just watch the play, as I really do wish the man well.

Bulephorus Very well then, look serious and start acting your part. He musn't get any inkling that we're in collusion.

Hypologus All set.

Bulephorus Greetings, Nosoponus, and how are you? I do sincerely hope you're well.

Hypologus And greetings from me – I'm Hypologus – I hope you're well too.

Nosoponus And the same to both of you. But it would be nice if I had that health you wish me.

Bulephorus You would, if we could give it as easily as wish it. But do tell us what's wrong. That look, that emaciated face, suggest something ominous. You have all the signs of something wrong with your liver.

Nosoponus No, my dear fellow, with my heart.

Hypologus Say not the word! – That's an incurable disease.

Bulephorus Can the doctors give you no hope?

Nosoponus I can hope for nothing from human resources. Some god has got to help me.

Bulephorus You must be dreadfully ill. But whatever god do you think can help you?

Nosoponus There's a divinity whose name in Greek is Peitho.[10]

Bulephorus Yes, I know that goddess who charms away the soul.[11]

Nosoponus I am desperately in love with her, and I shall die if I don't win her.

Bulephorus Then I'm not surprised you're wasting away, Nosoponus. I know what a violent thing desire is, and what it is to be enraptured by a nymph.[12] But how long is it since love seized upon you?

Nosoponus For about ten years now I've been pushing at this rock[13] and getting nowhere. I'm quite determined, you see, to win what I love eventually or die in the attempt.

Bulephorus That's a tenacious passion you're suffering from, as well as an unhappy one. It hasn't grown any weaker in all these years, and it hasn't given you possession of the thing you've set your heart on either.

Hypologus Possibly our friend would suffer more from possessing[14] his nymph than from being deprived of her.

Nosoponus No, no, it's because I don't possess her that I'm worn away with misery.

Bulephorus How can that be? Until now you've been quite without rival in the art of speaking – people used to say of you, as was once said of Pericles,[15] 'Persuasion is seated upon your lips.'

Nosoponus To put it in a few words, all eloquence revolts me, apart from the Ciceronian sort. That's the nymph for love of whom I'm melting away.

Bulephorus Now I understand the state you're in. You're out to win that lovely, splendid title of 'Ciceronian.'

Nosoponus Yes. I want it so much that if I don't achieve it, I shall consider my whole life bitter and wasted.

Bulephorus I'm no longer puzzled – you've set your heart on the finest thing of all. But the Greek proverb is only too true: nothing fine comes easy.[16] I join my prayers with yours and entreat some god to look mercifully on us, because I am praying for myself too.

Nosoponus What do you mean?

Bulephorus I'll tell you if you can brook a rival.

Nosoponus What are you getting at?

Bulephorus I'm tormented by love of the same nymph.

Nosoponus What? You feel the same anguish?

Bulephorus Yes, as much as anyone ever could, and the flames rise higher every day.

Nosoponus That makes you dearer to me than ever, Bulephorus. I have always been particularly fond of you,[17] but after this I shall really love you, now that we are kindred spirits.

Bulephorus Maybe you wouldn't want to be delivered from this sickness of yours, even if someone promised relief through herbs, precious stones, and magic spells?

Nosoponus That would be killing, not curing. I must either die or possess, there is no middle course.

Bulephorus How easy it was for me to guess your feelings from my own!

Nosoponus Then I shall conceal nothing from you – you are an initiate in the same mysteries.[18]

Bulephorus You can do so without fear, Nosoponus.

Nosoponus It's not only the glory of the beautiful title that gives me an incentive; it's also the brazen arrogance of some Italians, who won't approve any Latin style at all unless it's Ciceronian and think it's the height of disgrace for someone to be described as not Ciceronian, and at the same time brag that the honour of this title has never since the world began lighted upon any one living north of the Alps – the only exception being Christophe de Longueil,[19] who lately departed this life. I wouldn't like to give the impression that I grudge him this renown, so I'll be bold to say of him what Quintilian[20] wrote of Calvus: death coming untimely, did him an injustice.

Hypologus More than that – Longueil's premature death was unjust not only to the man himself, but to scholarship in general. What couldn't he have done for us by way of restoring good letters, if the powers above had added a normal length of life to such intellect and such industry?

Bulephorus But if one person has succeeded, what's to prevent lots of other people, if the Muses favour them, from managing it as well?[21]

Nosoponus Longueil died just when he had achieved this marvellous success, and I consider him to have died happy. What can be finer, nobler, grander, than for a man born north of the Alps to be voted a Ciceronian by Italians?[22] And I think we should be glad at his good fortune in dying at the best moment for him, while his Ciceronian glory was still undimmed by any little cloud. He might have developed an enthusiasm for Greek literature, as he had begun to study that,[23] or he might not have been able to abstain totally from Christian authors, if he had enjoyed a longer life.

Hypologus Yes, as you say, it was granted him to die while the glory of his achievement was still fresh. I hope that we, however, may survive the achievement, not die at the moment of success.

Nosoponus I hope so too. May I drop dead if I wouldn't rather have that than be numbered among the saints.

Bulephorus But of course. Who wouldn't prefer to be celebrated by posterity as a Ciceronian rather than as a saint? But since a love like ours is a stranger to jealousy, I beg you, by the pains and by the hopes familiar to us both, to tell your fellow lover at least your plan of campaign, the means you use to win your mistress. Perhaps we shall both arrive at our goal sooner, if each of us helps the other.

Nosoponus The Muses know no envy, much less their companions, the Graces. A comrade in studies should be denied nothing, and friends should have all things in common.[24]

Bulephorus You really will do me a great favour.

Hypologus Would you receive me into your brotherhood? The same prick has long been goading me too.

Nosoponus We will[25] indeed. And so, in the presence of initiates of the same god, I will reveal the mysteries.[26] For seven whole years now I have touched no books but Ciceronian ones, abstaining from all the rest as religiously as a Carthusian from meat.[27]

Bulephorus Why so?

Nosoponus In case some alien phrase should attach itself from somewhere or other and besmirch the pure sheen of my Ciceronian diction. And so, to prevent myself sinning by accident, I have shut up all my other books in boxes and put them out of sight; there is absolutely no place in my library for anyone else at all but Cicero.

Bulephorus How slapdash I am! I have never worshipped Cicero with such scrupulous devotion.

Nosoponus I have a picture of him, nicely painted, not only in my private chapel[28] and in my study, but on all the doors too;[29] and I carry his portrait about with me, carved on gems,[30] so that all the time he's present to my thoughts. I never see anything in my dreams but Cicero.

Bulephorus I'm not surprised.

Hypologus What I've done is give Cicero a place in my calendar among the apostles.

Bulephorus That's not surprising – he used to be called the presiding deity of eloquence.

Nosoponus I've been so assiduous in thumbing over Cicero's works from end to end and back again that I know practically the whole of him by heart.

Bulephorus That's industry indeed.

Nosoponus Now I'm all ready to start imitating him.

Bulephorus How much time have you allocated for that?

Nosoponus As much as I did for reading.

Bulephorus It's not long for such a difficult task. I'd be glad to win the honour of such a glorious title by the time I was seventy.

Nosoponus But wait – I'm not relying just on my reading. There isn't the smallest word in all the works of our divine author which I haven't classified and put into my alphabetical lexicon.[31]

Bulephorus It must be a huge volume.

Nosoponus Two strong pack-horses with proper saddles could hardly carry it on their backs.

Bulephorus Fancy that! And I've seen some in Paris that could have carried an elephant.

Nosoponus But volume two is even bigger. In it I've noted down all Cicero's characteristic expressions in alphabetical order.

Bulephorus Now I really do feel ashamed of the way I yawned through my early years.

Nosoponus There's a third one as well.

Bulephorus What – a third one?

Nosoponus Yes, a third one was essential. In it I've collected all the rhythmical patterns Cicero uses to begin or end his phrases, clauses, and periods,[32] and the measures he employs for the units in between, also which variation he associates with which sentence-type, so that not the smallest possible detail can escape my notice.

Bulephorus But how does it come about that your first index volume is so much bigger than the whole of Cicero?

Nosoponus Just listen, and you will stop being surprised. Perhaps you think I am content with merely noting down separate words?

Bulephorus Well, that's what I did think. Is there more to it than that?

Nosoponus Why, what we've mentioned is hardly anything.

Bulephorus How is that?

Nosoponus See how far you are off the mark. The same word isn't always used in the same way. To take an example, the verb *refero* 'bring back' has a different force according to whether Marcus Tullius[33] uses it in the phrase *referre gratiam* 'to return thanks,' or in *liberi parentes et forma corporis et moribus referunt* 'children recall their parents in physical features and in character,' or in *refero me ad intermissa studia* 'I am taking myself back to my interrupted studies,' or in *si quid erit quod mea referat scire* 'if there is anything which it would be to my advantage to know,' or *non ignota referam* 'what I shall recount is not unknown.' *Orare* likewise means one thing in *orare Lentulum* 'entreat Lentulus,' and another in *orare causam* 'plead a case.' Then *contendit* 'contends' has different meanings depending on whether it is used of a man who *strives* with somebody else, or who *demands* something insistently, or *makes great efforts* to achieve something, or *sets* two things *against* each other and compares them.

Hypologus Phew, that really is compiling an *index verborum*.

Bulephorus It's only now I appreciate that you've been wide awake while I've been dozing.

Nosoponus And I don't put down separate words in isolation – I include what comes before and after. And I'm not satisfied with recording one or two occurrences, which is what other people do, but every time I come across a usage in Cicero, however similar it is to other examples, without fail I make a note of page, recto or verso,[34] and line, adding a sign to indicate whether it occurs in the middle, beginning, or end of the line. All of which, as you can see, makes one word occupy several pages.

Bulephorus Goodness, what could such attention to detail not achieve?

Nosoponus Just wait, Bulephorus. You've heard nothing yet.

Bulephorus Can there be more to come?

Nosoponus What's the good of knowing a word, if you're uncertain or slip up when it comes to its modifications, derivatives, and compounds?

Bulephorus I don't quite follow what you're saying.

Nosoponus I'll explain. What is there more ordinary and everyday than the verbs *amo, lego, scribo*[35] 'love, read, write'?

Bulephorus Do even these raise problems?

Nosoponus Or than the nouns *amor, lectio, scriptor* 'love, reading, writer'?

Bulephorus Nothing.

Nosoponus But you may be assured that I find it absolutely essential – in fact it's necessary for anyone contending with real dedication for the exalted title of Ciceronian – not to use even the most ordinary words like these without consulting an index; unless maybe you think it safe to trust the grammarians, who give complete lists of verb inflections through all moods, persons, voices, and tenses, and of noun, pronoun, and participle inflections through all cases and numbers, when it's not right for us to use any of these forms that Cicero didn't use. It's no great thing[36] to talk grammatically, but it's something more than ordinary human achievement to talk Ciceronially.[37]

Bulephorus Please explain a bit more.

Nosoponus Let's take *amo, amas, amat* 'I love, you love, he loves.' These forms I find in Cicero. But perhaps I don't find *amamus, amatis* 'we love, you love.' Likewise, I find *amabam*[38] 'I used to love' but not *amabatis* 'you used to love.' Again I find *amaveras* 'you had loved' but not the form *amaras*. On the other hand, I do find the form *amasti*[39] 'you loved,' but no sign of *amavisti*. Suppose you discover *legeram, legeras, legerat* 'I, you, he had read,' but not *legeratis* 'you had read'? *scripseram* 'I had written,' but not *scripseratis* 'you had written'? You can make similar inferences about all the verbal inflections. And the same applies to the cases. I can find the noun *amor* 'love' in Cicero in the forms *amor, amoris, amorem, amori*, but not *o amor, hos amores, horum amorum, his amoribus, o amores*, Likewise *lectio* 'reading' occurs in the forms *lectio, lectionis, lectioni* and *lectionem*, but not in the forms *lectiones, lectionibus, lectionum, has lectiones, o lectiones*. In the same way I can discover the agent noun *scriptor* 'writer' in the forms *scriptorem, scriptores*, but not in the form *scriptor*[40] or *scriptorum*. I am quite prepared for you to find all this ridiculous, if you are bold enough to take upon your lips such forms as *stultitias, stultitiarum, vigilantias, vigilantiarum, speciebus, specierum, fructuum, ornatuum, cultuum, vultuum, ambitibus, ambituum*,[41] and countless others of the same sort. These are just a few examples, but you can deduce from them how things stand with all the other nouns that are declined in the same way.

Hypologus 'Slight the theme on which my toil is spent.'

Bulephorus 'But rich renown I hope to win thereby.'

Nosoponus And I'll go on with the next line: 'If to any man the grudging spirits yield / And Apollo bends an ear when on his name we call.'[42] Let's go on to derivatives. I am quite happy to use *lego* 'I read,' but I wouldn't dare to say *legor* 'I am read.' I would say *nasutus*[43] 'witty,' but never *nasutior*, *nasutissimus* 'wittier, wittiest.' I have no misgivings about using *ornatus* 'distinguished' and *ornatissimus* 'most distinguished,' *laudatus* 'honorable' and *laudatissimus* 'most honorable,' but unless I actually find the forms *ornatior*, *laudatior* 'more distinguished, more honorable,' I would feel scruples about using them. Because I come across the words *scriptor* 'writer' and *lectio* 'reading' in Cicero, I don't imagine that immediately entitles me to use the forms *scriptorculus* 'scribbler' and *lectiuncula*[44] 'browsing.'

Bulephorus I can see there's a vast supply of material here.

Nosoponus Now for compounds. I will say *amo, adamo, redamo* 'love, fall in love, love in return,' but I will not say *deamo* 'love passionately.' I will say *perspicio* 'perceive,' but not *dispicio*[45] 'investigate.' I will say *scribo, describo, subscribo, rescribo, inscribo* 'write, write down, sign, write back, inscribe,' but not *transcribo* 'transcribe,' unless I come across it in the works of Marcus Tullius Cicero.

Bulephorus Don't wear yourself out going through it all, Nosoponus. You've made it as clear as a reflection in a mirror.

Nosoponus This is what the smallest of the index volumes contains.

Bulephorus It's a load for a camel's back.

Hypologus And a full load at that.

Bulephorus How do you avoid making mistakes with all this different material?

Nosoponus First of all I don't rely at all on grammarians or other authorities, however respected, or on instructions, rules, or analogies, which mislead a good many people. In my index I note down the inflections, derivatives, and compounds of each separate word, in that order. Then I put a little red mark against the ones which are in Cicero, and a black one against those that are not. And so it's quite impossible for me to be mistaken.

Bulephorus Will you put a black mark against a form found in Terence[46] or some other equally good author?

Nosoponus I make no exceptions. No one will be Ciceronian if even the tiniest word is found in his works which can't be pointed to in Cicero's *opus*. I shall judge a man's entire mode of expression spurious and like counterfeit money if even a single word which doesn't bear Cicero's stamp finds a lodging there. Heaven granted to no one but him, the prince of eloquence, the right to strike the coin of Roman speech.

Bulephorus This law of yours is more severe than the Draconian code,[47] if a whole book is condemned for one little tiny word which isn't quite Ciceronian, when it's otherwise stylish and eloquent.

Hypologus But it's quite fair. You must see that a vast amount of money is called out of circulation because of a single bad penny, and one wart, however tiny, ruins a girl's beauty, perfect though it may be everywhere else.

Bulephorus I grant you that.

Nosoponus If you consider all the implications of what I've been telling you, you must have a good idea of the labour involved in putting together a structure like that index volume; so just think how much more is involved in the one in which I've covered idioms, metaphorical usages, rhetorical figures, aphorisms, epiphonemata,[48] witticisms, and all similar felicities of expression. And in the third one, which contains all the rhythms and metrical feet with which Cicero begins, develops, and closes his various sentence units. There isn't a place in the whole of Cicero where I haven't worked out the rhythmical pattern.

Bulephorus A structure like that would need an elephant to carry it.

Hypologus Rather call it the proverbial wagon-load.[49]

Nosoponus Every word is true.

Bulephorus Well, you haven't spent the last seven years at all badly. But now you're so well set up with indexes, it remains for you to tell us, as a friendly gesture to your fellow initiates, how you set about turning all this splendid equipment to good use in writing and speaking.

Nosoponus I don't want to give the impression of keeping anything back. I'll speak about writing first, since it was truly said[50] that the pen is the best teacher of speaking.

First of all, I never get down to writing except at dead of night when it's absolutely quiet and deep silence reigns over all, or, if you'd rather have a poetic description out of Virgil:[51]

> When weary bodies lie in quiet sleep
> Over all the earth; the woods, the cruel seas
> Have sunk to rest, while stars in mid-course
> Go wheeling on, every field lies hushed,
> And all the beasts and speckled birds are still;[52]

in short, when there's such complete peace that if Pythagoras[53] were alive he would be able to hear the music of the spheres quite clearly. At such a time gods and goddesses delight to hold converse with pure minds.

Hypologus At that time of night we outsiders are usually afraid of meeting ghosts.

Nosoponus But to us the Muses have given the gift of ignoring ghosts and all their menace – and 'the crowd with its envy'[54] as well.

Bulephorus But some nights are so peaceful that in them gusts from south and north play at blowing down houses and wrecking poor ships.

Nosoponus I know that, but I pick the most peaceful ones. I think Ovid[55] knew what he was saying when he wrote: 'There is a god within us: his impulse fires our hearts.' If the mind of man does possess anything that is divine, it's in that profound silence that it reveals itself.

Bulephorus Yes, I am well aware that the most famous men have always sought out that kind of solitude whenever they were labouring at something worthy of immortality.

Nosoponus I have a shrine of the Muses[56] in the innermost part of the house, with thick walls and double doors and windows, and all the cracks carefully sealed up with plaster and pitch, so that hardly any light or sound can penetrate even by day, unless it's a very loud one, like quarrelling women or blacksmiths[57] at work.

Bulephorus True, the sudden boom of human voices and workshop crashes destroy one's concentration.

Nosoponus I won't even allow anyone to use any of the nearby rooms as a bedroom, because I don't want the voices even of sleepers, or their snorts, breaking in on the sanctuary of my thoughts – some people talk in their sleep, and a good many snore so loudly they can be heard quite a long way off.

Hypologus When I'm trying to write at night I'm often troubled by mice as well.

Nosoponus In my house there's no place even for a fly.

Bulephorus You're very wise, Nosoponus; and you're lucky too, if you can shut out the clamourings of inward cares as well. If these accompany us into our secret refuge even when it's night, what shall we gain[58] by achieving silence?

Nosoponus You're right to mention that, Bulephorus. I understand that other people often find that sort of tumult more troublesome than the bellows and hammers of a neighbouring smithy.

Bulephorus Well then, does the voice of love, hate, spite, hope, fear, jealousy, never break in on your thoughts?

Nosoponus Not to beat about the bush, you can take it as a fact, Bulephorus, that people who suffer from love,[59] jealousy, ambition, greed for money, and other such diseases, are wasting their time in aspiring to this honour for which we have entered our names. A sacred vocation like this requires a heart not only pure from all sin but free from all care, just like the esoteric disciplines of magic, astrology, and so-called alchemy. In any case, comparatively superficial concerns such as you mentioned soon retreat before a purpose as intense and serious as this. Still, if any of them are present, I do dispel them before entering the shrine – I've accustomed my mind to do this by long practice. This is the main reason I've decided to remain a bachelor, though I'm well aware what a holy state matrimony is. It's inevitable that wife, children, and relations bring with them plenty to worry about.

Bulephorus That was wise of you, Nosoponus. If I were to start giving that amount of attention at night to Cicero, my wife would break down the door, tear up my indexes, and burn all my papers with my Cicero exercises on them. Worse than that, while I was giving my attention to Cicero, she would invite in a substitute husband to give her a little attention in place of me. And so, while I was aiming to make myself the image of Cicero, she would produce a child who was anything but the image of Bulephorus.

Nosoponus I know that that has actually happened to some people, so I've taken warning from others' peril[60] and looked out for myself in good time. For the same reason, I've refused to undertake any public office or ecclesiastical dignity, for fear that they might be the source of some disturbance to my mind.

Bulephorus But other people strive with might and main to acquire those very things!

Nosoponus They are welcome to them. As far as I'm concerned, being a Ciceronian and being acknowledged as one is preferable to being even head of state or sovereign pontiff with all his power.

Hypologus Ah yes, a man who's really in love can love only one girl.

Nosoponus Next, if I am projecting anything of this sort, I refrain from dinner in the evening, and have only a light lunch as well, to prevent any gross substance from invading the seat of the limpid mind, and to make sure no dampness steaming up from the stomach weighs down and 'nails to earth the fragment of the breath of God.'[61]

Bulephorus That's the state Hesiod[62] was in, I imagine, when the Muses spoke with him.[63]

Hypologus But 'Great father Ennius never except well oiled / Rushed out to sing of arms.'[64]

Nosoponus And that's why he wrote tipsy poetry.

Bulephorus Besides, 'Horace was full when he cried / "Hurrah for the god Dionysus!" '[65]

Nosoponus The antics of poetic frenzy are nothing to do with us. It's a sober thing to be a Ciceronian.

Hypologus My head swims if I go without food.

Nosoponus I don't go without food altogether. I take ten very small raisins, the Corinthian sort. They are not really food or drink, but yet they are in a way.

Bulephorus I understand – they exude moisture slowly, and stimulate brain and memory.

Nosoponus I add three sugared coriander seeds.

Bulephorus Splendid – that prevents any dampness from the ten raisins flying up into the seat of the mind.

Nosoponus I don't use just any night for work of this sort.

Bulephorus You don't? You've excluded the ones when there's a gale from north or south. Perhaps you avoid winter nights because it's so cold?

Nosoponus A blazing fire easily removes that disadvantage.

Hypologus But meantime the smoke and crackling are a nuisance.

Nosoponus I have fires that don't smoke.[66]

Bulephorus What nights do you choose then?

Nosoponus There aren't many that are lucky for this sort of business. So I choose the propitious ones.

Bulephorus How do you do that?

Nosoponus By means of astrology.

Bulephorus Cicero takes you up more than entirely, so how did you find time to become proficient in astrology?

Nosoponus I bought myself an almanac from an expert in the art. I work it out from that.

Hypologus From what I've heard, many people have been misled by almanacs of that sort, whenever the writer has made a mistake in a number.

Nosoponus I bought a tried and tested one.

Bulephorus Heavens above, that really is writing. I'm not surprised any more, Hypologus, if the stuff we write is rough and unpolished. But when you've got yourself settled like this, do you turn your thoughts first to subject-matter or to expression?

Nosoponus Each of them comes both first and second.

Bulephorus That's a riddle, not an answer.

Nosoponus I'll solve it for you. Generically, one thinks about subject-matter first; specifically, one thinks about it second.

Bulephorus It's still not quite clear what you mean.

Nosoponus I'll explain by means of an example. Imagine I've decided to write to John Doe or Richard Roe, [67] telling him to see that the books I lent him are sent back at once if he wants us to go on being friends; something has happened to make me need them urgently. If he does so, there is nothing of mine he may not consider his own; but if not, I return to him the token of our long-standing friendship and proclaim a state of enmity. These first thoughts deal with content, obviously, but in a general way.

Bulephorus I follow you.

Nosoponus After this comes consideration of the expression. I read over as many letters of Cicero as I can; I consult all my lists. I pick out some characteristic Ciceronian idioms, and some figures of speech and phrases; then some rhythms; finally, when I've got myself thoroughly fitted up with this sort of equipment, I look to see what stylistic niceties I can slip in, and where. Then I go back to the actual content. It's a matter of real skill to find ideas to fit these nice expressions.

Hypologus It's exactly like a craftsman preparing a dress of splendid material and a whole lot of necklaces, rings, and jewels, and then making a wax statue to put all the ornaments on, or rather moulding the statue to fit the ornaments.

Bulephorus Quite so. But tell me, Nosoponus, surely you don't spend the whole night on one letter?

Nosoponus What do you mean, one letter? I feel the Muses have accepted my devotions if a winter's night produces one single period.[68]

Bulephorus So you write a great long letter on this rather insignificant topic?

Nosoponus No, indeed, I write a very short one, you can be sure of that, not longer than six periods.

Bulephorus So naturally six nights will be enough to complete it?

Nosoponus As if it were enough to write things once! You must reshape what you've written ten times, check it against your word-lists ten times, in case some tiny illegitimate word has slipped past your guard. Then you have to check it again for figures of speech and idioms, and finally for rhythms and word order.

Bulephorus That really is doing the job thoroughly.

Nosoponus My dear fellow, even that's not enough. When you've worked it over as carefully as you can, you must put it aside[69] for several days so that in the interval your affection for your brain-child may cool off, and you read your own words as if they were somebody else's. It's at this point that you exercise really severe criticism. This is where we have that strict impartial judgment, ἀδέκαστος 'immune to bribery,' as the Greeks call it, where the author ceases to be a parent and becomes an Areopagite.[70] At this point one very often takes one's eraser and rubs it all out.

Bulephorus Your letter will certainly be a model of industry, but meantime the other fellow goes on enjoying the books you need.

Nosoponus I would rather suffer that inconvenience than have anything emanate from me that wasn't Ciceronian. Everyone must judge for himself. I would rather write intensively than extensively.

Bulephorus Now we know how you set about writing. What kind of mental preparation do you make for speaking?

Nosoponus First of all, I take care not to speak to anyone in Latin, in so far as I can avoid it.

Bulephorus Not in Latin? But they tell us[71] that speaking makes us good speakers. It's a new sort of exercise if we learn to speak by keeping silent.

Nosoponus No, speaking makes us ready speakers; it certainly doesn't make us speak in a Ciceronian way. The riders in a horse-race keep their thoroughbreds from galloping about beforehand so that they come to the serious business vigorous and fresh; the huntsman doesn't unleash his hounds till the quarry is sighted. And if I want to chatter about something or other unimportant, I'm quite content with French or Dutch; I don't contaminate the sacred tongue with common, everyday talk. If some pressing need arises so that I have to speak Latin, I say very little, and I don't do that without due forethought. I keep a number of ready-made phrases for that kind of situation.

Bulephorus What sort of phrases do you mean?

Nosoponus Ones for greeting a learned friend or replying to his greeting if you meet him accidentally, or for returning compliments to someone who has complimented you, or for congratulating someone who has returned from a long voyage or recovered from a serious illness, or thanking someone who has done you a service, or wishing well to someone who has just got married, or sympathizing with someone who has lost his wife. For contingencies of this sort I've provided myself with phrases extracted from Cicero, which I've put in order and then learned by heart, so that I can produce them as if on the spur of the moment. If ever a situation arises where I can't avoid talking at some length, I go in for a long course of reading afterwards to remove any contamination my lips have suffered. I'm well aware what a lot of offences I'm committing in this very conversation[72] I'm having with you now, and what a set-back it will be to me in attaining my ambition. A month's reading will hardly undo the damage.

Bulephorus What do you do if you've got time for preparation?

Nosoponus I work something out over the midnight oil in the way I've described to you, and then I learn it by heart; to make sure I don't forget it, I recite it over to myself several times, and so when the occasion comes, I speak as fluently as if I were reading it.

Bulephorus Suppose some unavoidable situation demands an extempore speech?

Nosoponus How could such a situation arise, seeing I don't do anything public? Even if I did perform some public function, I don't claim to be better than Demosthenes,[73] and he was never willing to rise[74] and speak unless he'd had time to prepare, however insistent public demand was. I wouldn't consider it anything to feel ashamed of, when the chief of Greek orators was praised for it. Nor would I mind the censure if someone said my words stank of lamp oil.[75]

Bulephorus Really, Nosoponus, I can't say how much I admire your purpose and respect your determination. I would envy you as well, if that poisonous feeling could arise in studies of our sort, or between such close friends and companions as we are. Still, our goal is not an easy one to reach, and the road to it is not only long and rough going, but difficult to be sure of as well. If you were the only one in danger, I should still feel I owed it to our close and long-standing relationship to be concerned for my friend and to be generous in advising him, for fear he should undertake so much anxious care, so many sleepless sessions endangering both health and wealth, and should keep them up so relentlessly, all to no avail. I wouldn't like him to experience what happens all too often in human affairs, and instead of the treasure he has been looking for so long and so hard, to find in the end only dust and ashes.[76] But the fact is, we are all led by a similar desire, we are all possessed by love of the same nymph – for Hypologus here is of the same mind – so a decent fellow like yourself will naturally take in good part any advice we offer, and will also freely share[77] with his friends any better suggestions of his own.

Nosoponus A fair request, Bulephorus. So I will neither hear you with bad grace, nor be mean in contributing to the common store any ideas I may have.

Bulephorus First of all we are agreed, I think, that the man who seeks fame as speaker or writer must first study and get a thorough grasp of the theory of rhetoric and then, out of all the acknowledged great writers, choose some outstanding one to imitate and take as his model.

Nosoponus Absolutely.

Bulephorus We are also agreed that no one, among the Latin writers at any rate, excels in more of the virtues of eloquence than Marcus Tullius. He was justly likened to Apelles,[78] who combined in himself the individual excellencies of all other painters.

Nosoponus No one would question that.

Bulephorus You must forgive me, Nosoponus, if I make my points in a rather laboured and clumsy fashion, as I am not experienced in dialectic.

Nosoponus Among friends everything should be taken in good part. Though in general it seems to me that a man argues shrewdly enough if he draws sound conclusions.

Bulephorus Well then, what is your opinion of Zeuxis[79] of Heraclea?

Nosoponus Why, the opinion that one must have of a most distinguished practitioner of the art of drawing and painting.

Bulephorus Is that because you think he had judgment as well as genius?

Nosoponus How could such art be devoid of judgment?

Bulephorus A proper reply. Now when he was going to paint that picture of Helen for the city of Croton, he wanted to make it a demonstration of his powers as an artist. The ancient writers tell us he was supreme as a painter of women, and he was determined to produce an absolutely lifelike representation of perfect feminine beauty in which every known charm could be discovered. So why did he decide not to take one particularly beautiful girl as his model? Instead, out of all those offered him, he picked out several who stood out from the rest, and then proceeded to select from each girl her loveliest feature. And that was how he produced his masterpiece.[80]

Nosoponus He acted as a conscientious artist should.

Bulephorus Then consider whether we are right in thinking that we should seek our model of eloquence in Cicero and no one else, even if Cicero does surpass the rest.

Nosoponus If Zeuxis had found a girl as supreme in beauty as Cicero is in eloquence, possibly he would have been content to use one figure as a model.

Bulephorus But how could he have come to a decision on this point, without inspecting lots of figures?

Nosoponus Take it that he did decide somehow.

Bulephorus So you are of the opinion that there is no virtue worthy of imitation in other orators which doesn't appear at its finest in Cicero?

Nosoponus That is what I think.

Bulephorus And that any blemishes in Cicero are far worse in all the rest?

Nosoponus That too.

Bulephorus I could well bring in Brutus[81] at this point, since he rejected in its entirety the style of oratory which Cicero thought the best. In any speech, the definition of the point at issue and the exposition of the main line of argument are the columns on which the whole case rests and are its most important part. Yet in the speech *Pro Milone*,[82] which everyone admires so much, the same Brutus did not agree with the primary and secondary definitions adduced by Cicero, and himself treated the same case[83] quite differently. I could bring in against you Atticus,[84] who used nail-marks[85] and little red pencils to indicate the passages in Cicero's writings which he took objection to (marks which Cicero says in his letters he was afraid of); or Cato,[86] who called Cicero a comic[87] when he fancied he was being a great wit. These were all men whose opinion carried weight and who were friends of Cicero's. I could add to them Gallus,[88] Lartius, Licinius,[89] Cestius,[90] Calvus,[91] and Asinius;[92] I could add Caelius[93] and Seneca[94] and many others besides who didn't have a particularly high opinion of Cicero's ability and condemned his style of oratory as well. Some of them called him[95] dry, jejune, dessicated, bloodless, disjointed, sloppy, soft, and lacking in virility, while others called him turgid, Asiatic,[96] and awash with superfluities. If I do bring them in, you will reply that these are the judgments of enemies, or of the envious[97] who, once Cicero himself had been struck down in the proscriptions[98] of the triumvirate,[99] endeavoured to dim his glory if they could not extinguish it.

Nosoponus You're quite right. That's just what I was going to say, and I think it would have been justified.

Bulephorus We may put judgments like this down to hate or jealousy; yet you will, I think, allow, with all the literary world, that wit and laughter are a part of the art of rhetoric?

Nosoponus Yes, otherwise what need was there for orators to write so much on the subject?[100]

Bulephorus No one denies that Cicero went in for jokes a great deal; some say he did so to excess, and at inappropriate moments, and went beyond the limits of decency. The general consensus of opinion among the learned is that he lacked discrimination in this, whereas Demosthenes lacked facility.[101] Quintilian protests mildly at this view of Cicero, but lays the blame for it on Tiro,[102] who was too ready to increase the number of Cicero's *bons mots*, and displayed more enthusiasm in collecting than discrimination in selecting from them – though this charge against Tiro redounds upon his master. But whatever may be the truth of the matter, who ever gave first prize to Cicero in this sphere? The chief praise here belongs to the Dorians, and after them to the Athenians.[103] Consequently, though humour and wit are the main attractions of both pastoral poetry and comedy,[104] the Latin writers never came anywhere near[105] that Greek charm in their own literature. So there is one oratorical virtue which you would do better to look for in people other than Cicero.

Nosoponus We are talking about speakers of Latin.

Bulephorus Well, then, shall we be bold enough to compare Cicero's witticisms with Julius Caesar's or Augustus'?[106]

Nosoponus I would hardly be bold enough to do what no scholar has dared to do as yet.

Bulephorus So if the occasion requires a humorous touch, will it not be right for me to reproduce one of Augustus' witticisms?

Nosoponus Not if you want to be thought Ciceronian.

Bulephorus I have another question for you. Do you think aphorisms are ornaments of style?

Nosoponus Far from wanting to exclude them from the art, I consider them the jewels and highlights.

Bulephorus Now give me your opinion on this. Does Cicero surpass everyone else in this stylistic virtue?

Nosoponus I am well aware that Seneca preferred[107] the mime writer Publius[108] to everyone else here. But we don't have to take as a divine pronouncement what Seneca thought – Seneca was without self-discipline in his own use of aphorisms, and often couldn't resist quite vacuous ones.

Hypologus That was a criticism of Seneca voiced by Quintilian,[109] but we can dismiss it, together with Aulus Gellius' strictures,[110] on the grounds that both of them seem to have disliked Seneca, one out of rivalry, the other because of the very similarity of their minds and styles.

Bulephorus But Gellius, though prejudiced, does admit[111] that among Seneca's aphorisms are some that couldn't be bettered. Besides, one wouldn't expect all aphorisms to be equally successful in a passage composed of nothing else. Even so you are more likely to find something to imitate in such a passage than in one where aphorisms are neither frequent nor striking. Now another thing. Doesn't the subject on occasion demand brevity?

Nosoponus Possibly.

Bulephorus Would you do better to look for an example of this in Sallust[112] or Brutus,[113] or in Cicero?

Nosoponus Cicero wasn't interested in brevity.

Bulephorus Demosthenes' style is admired for its forcefulness,[114] that is, a certain vigorous natural quality. So to which one shall we go for this?

Nosoponus We were talking about Latin speakers.

Bulephorus But these are features common to all languages. Again, the situation sometimes requires a severe style. Shall we go for this to Cicero, or to Brutus[115] and Pollio?[116]

Hypologus Let me answer for him – to those who were known for precisely this feature.

Bulephorus When we have to set out a complicated case using division into heads,[117] shall we go to Cicero, or to Hortensius[118] and his like?

Nosoponus How can we go to someone of whom nothing is extant but the memory?

Bulephorus For the sake of argument, let's suppose he were extant.

Nosoponus We don't need any supposing. Let's keep to the real and the known.

Bulephorus Everyone is agreed that credibility[119] is of prime importance to the orator. This is generated by a belief in the speaker's honesty and seriousness of approach, destroyed by suspicion of artificiality or lack of self-control. Let us take it that Cicero was a good man – though Quintilian,[120] in spite of his championship of Cicero, does have doubts on this score – but it can't be denied that he makes more of a display of artifice, indulges more in boasting[121] about his own achievements, and allows himself greater licence in attacking other people than do Cato and Brutus, or Caelius, whose integrity was acknowledged by Quintilian.[122] For these features, will we not do better to look for a model to Aristides, Phocion,[123] Cato, and Brutus, rather than to Cicero?

Nosoponus You seem to have come here determined to find fault with Cicero.

Bulephorus Not at all, my dear Nosoponus. If you wait patiently until I've finished what I have to say, you will see that I am pleading not only Cicero's case, but ours too: Cicero's, in that I hope to prevent us producing a bad copy of him that will give him a bad name, just as a portrait by an incompetent painter who cannot reproduce the features properly makes the sitter an object of ridicule; and ours, in that I want to save us from misplacing our affections, and suffering a fate as humiliating and miserable as Ixion's,[124] who, according to the story, embraced an empty cloud-form instead of his desired Juno; or Paris', who fought a war for ten years for the Helen he had carried off and all the time was embracing a false image of Helen, because the real Helen had of course been carried off to Egypt by a stratagem of the gods.[125] What could be more miserable and humiliating for us, if after all our efforts we found ourselves in possession of nothing but an empty counterfeit semblance of Cicero?

Nosoponus Heaven preserve us!

Bulephorus Amen to that. Our purpose in all this is to prevent any such thing happening.

Nosoponus But if we are going to imitate Cicero, it does help to have the highest possible opinion of Cicero.

Bulephorus A modern form of generosity to have a higher opinion of Cicero than he had himself! Even if we attribute his own disclaimers[126] about his abilities simply to modesty on his part, did anyone in the ancient world ever have such an admiration for Cicero as to think that every feature of stylish writing was to be looked for in him alone?

Nosoponus But today there are very many people who do think just that.

Bulephorus I don't care how many there are of them – not one of them is, I think, a person of perception and true learning. What mortal man has ever been so blessed by nature, even in one single discipline, as to excel everyone else[127] in every aspect of it? Hasn't nature always left him with some deficiency, made it possible for others to be his superiors sometimes? Such perfection would be even less credible in oratory, which consists of practically all the other disciplines together,[128] and which requires so many other qualities which no one can transmit by instruction. Suppose that Cicero were alive today, and that there were someone like Trachalus.[129] Would you go to Cicero for modulation of the voice, or to Trachalus? I imagine you would go to the one who was held to be preeminent in this aspect of the art. For an example of discretion and control would you prefer to go to Crassus,[130] if he were alive, or to Cicero? Not to labour the point, wouldn't you choose from each individual speaker the feature in which he surpassed all the rest?

Hypologus Everyone would of course select the superior example, unless he couldn't tell the difference, or wanted to make things difficult for himself.

Bulephorus That's why I approve of Zeuxis' procedure on that occasion, and Quintilian agrees with it too, since he tells the student[131] who is learning by imitation that he must not read just one author, nor all authors, nor any and every author, but must select from among the best authors a number of particularly outstanding ones; and among these Quintilian awards Cicero first place,[132] but not in isolation. He wants him to be chief among the princes, not a solitary figure with everyone else excluded.

Nosoponus If we listen to Quintilian, the same thing will happen to us as happened to him.

Bulephorus What's that?

Nosoponus We shall finish up unciceronian. And that is not the destination we have in mind.

Bulephorus Now, you mean that something is unciceronian if it has anything incorporated in it which is not derived from Cicero?

Nosoponus Yes. That's the idea.

Bulephorus Even if the feature derived from someone else is better, or if the thing is completely missing from Cicero?

Nosoponus But of course.

Bulephorus But just consider, my dear Nosoponus, what a large proportion of the Ciceronian corpus has disappeared, including that inspired work *De* *republica.*[133] The fragment that has survived by some quirk of fate merely tantalizes our minds with desire for the rest, for we can divine from it what the other books were like. You can tell a lion by his claws, as the proverb[134] says. What about all those books of letters, all those speeches which succumbed to the ravages of time, the three volumes in which Tiro, we are told,[135] assembled Cicero's jokes and witticisms, and the shattered remains of the rest of his writings? How can you be a complete and entire Ciceronian when there is so much of his work you haven't read? Besides, Cicero didn't deal with all subjects. If by some chance we have to speak on subjects he didn't touch, just where are we going to find the basic stuff of our speech? Shall we go off to the Elysian fields[136] and ask the man what words he would have used for these topics?

Nosoponus I shall only handle subjects that suit Ciceronian vocabulary.

Bulephorus But I thought you considered Cicero supreme among orators?

Nosoponus More than supreme.

Bulephorus And Apelles? He's the finest of painters, don't you think?

Nosoponus So they say, and I believe it.

Bulephorus Well then, would you say a painter was a true follower of Apelles if he couldn't draw a picture of any and every subject, but only of those which Apelles had painted before? Especially if he hadn't even seen all the pictures which Apelles had actually painted?

Hypologus Of course not. Nobody could, unless he approved of the painter that Horace[137] makes fun of – the one who accepted a commission to paint a shipwreck and then painted a cypress tree, and when his client was furious, asked him if maybe he would like something added sticking out of the tree.

Bulephorus But what is being Ciceronian if it is not being as like as possible to Cicero?

Nosoponus Nothing.

Bulephorus Are we then to consider a person like Cicero if he can only speak on certain subjects?

Nosoponus Well?

Bulephorus I wouldn't consider he deserved the name even of orator. Cicero could make a splendid speech on any subject whatsoever, so to my mind a speaker will be Ciceronian only if he too can speak effectively on any and every topic; just as we saw that only an artist who can use his brush to depict gods, men, living creatures, in short, anything, shows any real affinity with Apelles.

Nosoponus Well, I consider it a finer thing to write three letters in Ciceronian idiom than a hundred volumes in a style as polished as you like, but quite different from Cicero's.

Bulephorus Once we begin to think like that, Nosoponus, I am afraid that we shall not only fail to finish up as Ciceronians, but that Cicero himself would think us out of our minds. Now give me a frank answer. Do you believe we should represent the whole Cicero, or a fragmentary one?

Nosoponus The whole of him in his entirety, and him alone.

Bulephorus How can it be the whole of him, when he didn't reveal himself wholly? And even in the places where he did give us a chance to observe him, he's fragmented and hardly half there. Besides, in the works that are extant, he was not satisfied with himself on occasion – he more or less rejected *De inventione*[138] by writing *Orator* to replace it. And he called the speech *Pro Deiotaro* a flimsy piece of work.[139] Furthermore, in the things he wrote but didn't revise Cicero himself is unciceronian, as for example in *De legibus*,[140] and many other works besides. How can we imitate him whole and in his entirety, when we have him in a fragmentary and mangled state, and in lots of places rough-hewn and unlike himself? Unless of course you will applaud the approach of someone who thinks he will turn out a second Apelles or Lysippus[141] by imitating Apelles' preliminary sketches or Lysippus' roughed-out statues. Surely, if Apelles himself saw such a thing, being, we are told, a candid and outspoken person,[142] he would cry out 'What are you doing, you undiscriminating fellow? There's no Apelles in that'? If someone set out to copy a famous statue by Lysippus, where the mouth and chin had been corroded by rust or left without the finishing touches[143] by the artist, would he object to taking a model for that section from some other artist? Or would he prefer to reproduce it, damaged and imperfect as it was, instead of supplying the missing bit from another artist's statue, in order not to desert his chosen prototype?

Nosoponus As the saying[144] goes, we must do as we are able, when we can't do as we wish.

Bulephorus That remark, Nosoponus, would come better from others, from people who do take things from other writers to patch the holes in Cicero. They would of course prefer to have everything from the one author, either because it's simpler, or because he puts things better than anyone else; but since that isn't possible, they borrow from others. Then the Cicero we have is not only defective and mutilated, but so distorted that if he were to come to life again, he wouldn't, I think, recognize his own writings, nor would he be able to restore the text where it has been corrupted by the audacity, carelessness, and ignorance of scribes and persons with half-knowledge – an iniquity which Poliziano[145] lays mainly at the door of the Germans. Without wishing to defend the Germans, I do consider that just as many disfigurements have been introduced by certain audacious Italians with a smattering of scholarship. While we are on this subject, I could well mention the works foisted upon Cicero and falsely claiming his parentage, like the four books of the *Rhetorica ad Herennium*,[146] whose author was himself by no means incompetent, but a mere stammerer compared with Cicero.[147] Among the speeches too there are some apparently not written by Cicero but composed by various literary figures as rhetorical exercises. A speech *Pro Marco Valerio*[148] was recently added to the corpus – far from having any claim to being considered Ciceronian, it bristled with solecisms. There are people who read Porcius Latro's[149] invective against Catiline as a Ciceronian oration. So if we devoutly dedicate ourselves to the imitation of Cicero alone with the intention of blindly reproducing whatever we find in him, surely we shall be running a great risk of making ourselves miserable for years, only in the end to seize upon German words and Teutonic solecisms and to imitate them as if they were Ciceronian felicities.

Nosoponus May the Muses preserve us from that!

Bulephorus I'm afraid this is what often happens to us, Nosoponus, while the Muses are taking forty winks. We've seen more than one such farce.[150] A fragment extracted from Cicero was attributed to some German or other, and how those who considered themselves real Ciceronians laughed at it and called it barbarous. Another time, something made up only the day before was put out under Cicero's name, with the story that a copy had been found in an ancient library. How they loved it, how they worshipped the divine, inimitable Ciceronian diction!

Then of course scholars don't deny that inexcusable solecisms are found in Cicero's writings, such as literary men always have and still do let slip when they are thinking of several things at once and remember the sense of the preceding expression rather than the actual words, with the result that the end of the sentence doesn't agree with the earlier part. An example might be: 'Staying rather longer at Athens because the wind did not allow of sailing, my intention was to write to you.' The writer's first thought was 'I wanted' or 'I had decided,' but then he settled on 'it was my intention,' which means the same but doesn't fit with the preceding words. Again, Aulus Gellius[151] in book 6, chapter 15 quotes a passage out of Cicero's *De gloria* book 2, where Cicero has obviously made a slip, attributing to Ajax some lines from Homer's *Iliad* book 7 which are actually spoken by Hector. Shall we endeavour to emulate this also? That is what we ought to do if we are going to reproduce him in his entirety. Furthermore, we have literary testimony[152] to the fact that Cicero said some things that no scholar has ever thought should be imitated, such as saying *in potestatem esse*[153] instead of *in potestate esse* 'to be in the power of.' It is, of course, possible that the notorious *-tem* ending instead of *-te* appeared in his original manuscript through a slip of the pen or some other mischance or was introduced into later copies by some half-asleep scribe.

On another occasion[154] Cicero tears apart the form *piissimus*, the superlative of *pius* 'loyal,' used in an edict of Mark Antony, as a barbarism never heard by Latin ears, although the form can be found in the most respectable Latin writers. He also picks on Antony[155] for committing a solecism in writing *facere contumeliam* 'inflict an insult,' just as we say *facere iniuriam* 'inflict an injury,' though in Terence, who is, I believe, the highest authority for correct, idiomatic Latin, we find the character Thais[156] saying *nam si ego digna hac contumelia / sim maxime, at tu indignus qui faceres tamen* 'Though I be most worthy such insult to receive, / Yet you it becomes not to inflict,' where presumably *contumeliam* 'insult' is understood after *faceres* 'inflict.' Again Cicero avoided[157] as un-Latin the forms *novissime* 'in the last place, recently,' and *novissimus*[158] 'latest, last,' although Cato and Sallust[159] had no misgivings about them. Gellius[160] records that our Marcus Tullius showed the same over-sensitiveness with regard to many other words which good Latin authors, both before and after him, employed frequently. We are also told that he wrote -ss- when preceded by a long vowel, as in *caussa*, *visse, remissi*,[161] instead of *causa, vise, remisi* 'for the sake of, observe, I have sent back.' So, if we are imitating the whole Cicero, are we going to refrain from writing things which every man of letters, apart from Cicero alone, found perfectly satisfactory, and are we going to follow things in him which no person with any knowledge has wanted to imitate and has not even been able to excuse?

Hypologus But that's what lovers do – they adore even the warts on the beloved![162]

Bulephorus Well then, if he is to be reproduced in his entirety, are we to follow his example in writing verse over which 'breathed no Muse or Apollo'?[163]

Nosoponus I exclude the verse.

Bulephorus Good gracious, you exclude a large part of his erudition if you exclude the verse. Besides, what's to prevent us making the same kind of exception anywhere where Cicero is surpassed by others, even in some of his strong points, not just in the verse, where he is altogether inferior[164] to most other, not to say all other, people? What a lot of verse he introduces into his writings, translated from Homer, Sophocles, and Euripides, and not very successfully translated at that, because in iambic verse he doesn't follow Greek practice, but allows himself to imitate the liberties taken with the metre by the writers of Latin comedy. If you want to quote Greek verse in your own translation, will you be afraid of producing a neater translation, if you can, or one in better verse, in case it makes you unciceronian? Surely Cicero disfigures his prose by introducing these incongruous scraps of verse, which he makes his own by the act of translation? Again, Cicero liberally sprinkles his works with lines out of Ennius, Naevius, Pacuvius, and Lucilius,[165] all of them bringing with them an aura of the crude, uncouth, primitive era to which they belonged. Will this inhibit you from introducing similar quotations from Virgil, Horace, Ovid, Lucan, and Persius[166] – or rather I should say dissimilar quotations, as the work of these poets has lost the rough finish of that earlier age, and is polished and sophisticated by comparison? Will you be afraid of seeming unlike Cicero in this?

Nosoponus We should certainly find we'd diverged quite a bit from the model we're endeavouring to reproduce in every possible way.

Bulephorus But what need is there always and in every way to be identical, when it would often be preferable to be as good but different, and would sometimes be easier to surpass[167] than to equal, that is, to write something better rather than something similar?

Nosoponus Not even the Muses in my view could produce things better than Cicero's.

Hypologus Perhaps they could if they really exerted themselves, went without dinner, and spent the night writing by candlelight.

Bulephorus Don't get angry, Nosoponus, I did stipulate that we should be free to say what we thought. Now, if a person is as devoted and dedicated to Cicero as we have been hitherto, isn't there some danger that he will be blinded by his affection for Cicero and will either admire the faults as if they were virtues, or will even copy them in full knowledge that they are faults?

Nosoponus Heracles![168] Faults in Cicero?

Bulephorus Why no, of course not, unless maybe a solecism is a fault in other people but not in Cicero. As we've said, scholars do point to solecisms in the works of Marcus Tullius. Or perhaps a slip of the memory isn't a fault. That sort of thing has been pointed out by the experts too. Or don't you think it a fault to become an embarrassment even to the person you are defending by excessively singing your own praises? Asconius[169] says that happened in Cicero's defence of Milo; and this habit does tend to make Cicero something of a perpetual bore, priding himself, as Seneca[170] neatly puts it, 'not without cause, but without end.' I don't know whether he goes to greater extremes in boasting about himself or in vilifying others. On whatever showing we defend all this, we cannot deny that here at any rate an example could be better looked for in others.

Nosoponus Let's cut out discussion of character – it's the virtues and strengths of eloquence we're debating.

Bulephorus I would gladly cut it out, if the teachers of rhetoric did not themselves contend that no one can be a good orator without also being a good man.[171] Still, tell me whether you think it a faulty arrangement[172] if the second word begins with the same syllables as the previous word ends with, producing a kind of silly echo. Like saying *ne mihi dona donata, ne voces referas feras, ne mihi per imperitos scribas scribas*[173] 'Don't give me second-hand hand-outs, don't make your answer surly, see that your secretaries write right to me.'

Nosoponus Yes, I accept that it is stupid and ridiculous to put words like that next to each other.

Bulephorus But people produce exactly that sort of thing out of our precious Cicero: *O fortunatam natam me consule Romam*[174] 'O Roman state, so fortunate – Thy natal day dates from my consulate!'

Nosoponus I've already excluded the verse once.

Bulephorus That's all right by me, provided you also exclude the idea of 'Cicero in his entirety.' But you've not escaped yet. Here's a piece of equally bad wording quoted by Quintilian[175] from Cicero's prose: *res mihi invisae visae sunt Brute* 'The outlook looked nasty, Brutus.' Or if you prefer a Ciceronian sound, we'll spell it with double -ss-, *invissae vissae sunt*! While we're at it, I could take exception to the double molossus[176] at the end of the phrase, but I'll refrain.

Nosoponus It slipped out in a letter to a friend.

Bulephorus I'm not objecting, I merely ask whether you think it should be imitated. You surely admit that it could be better expressed.

Nosoponus I don't know.

Bulephorus Need I mention the frequent collocation of vowels, which makes what he's saying jerky and unattractive? Isn't this too spotted by the experts in Cicero? He was careless, you will say, and again I don't object, so long as we admit that there are things which either don't occur in other writers or are done better in other writers. Now I would like to ask you this. Have you ever known any writer vigilant enough and lucky enough not to nod[177] occasionally?

Nosoponus Of course not. They were only human.

Bulephorus Do you count Cicero then as human?

Nosoponus Sometimes.

Bulephorus Well then, which do you think more sensible, to imitate Cicero when he is nodding, or Sallust, Brutus, or Caesar when wide awake?

Hypologus Who wouldn't prefer to have a wide-awake model?

Bulephorus Didn't Virgil imitate Homer at his finest moments? Consequently, he improved on Homer in many places, but there are also numerous passages which he ignored. Didn't he imitate Hesiod[178] only at his best, and wasn't that how he surpassed him constantly? Didn't Horace set out to imitate the Greek lyric poets[179] in the same way? Wasn't it by culling the finest features from each one of them that he left them all far behind? As he says:[180]

> Like the Apulian bee
> Harvesting with toil the scented thyme
> Round many a grove, along the river banks
> By spray-drenched Tivoli,
> I too ply a humble task, and
> With care and effort mould my verse.

In imitating Lucilius,[181] didn't he deliberately omit quite a number of features, with the intention of taking from other writers anything in them that deserved imitation more? Need I mention others? Did Cicero himself derive his wonderful eloquence from one single source?[182] Didn't he rather scrutinize philosophers, historians, and rhetoricians, comic, tragic, and lyric poets, Greek as well as Roman, in short, did he not from all writers of every kind assemble, fashion, and bring to perfection his own characteristic and divine idiom? If we choose to imitate Cicero in every respect, let us imitate his example here.

Hypologus What Bulephorus is saying seems not unreasonable to me, Nosoponus.

Bulephorus Didn't Cicero himself teach[183] that the highest form of art was the concealment of art? Indeed, a speech that gives an impression of artifice is received coldly, viewed with suspicion, and feared as deceptive. For who would not be on his guard against someone setting out by the use of false glitter to get a hold over our minds?[184] And so, if we want to be successful in our imitation of Cicero, the first thing must be to conceal our imitation of Cicero. But take someone who never departs from Cicero's guidelines, who collects his vocabulary, figures of speech, and rhythms out of Cicero, even imitating some things that should not be imitated, the way some of Plato's pupils rounded their shoulders in order to look like their master and Aristotle's students copied the slight lisp[185] we are told he had. Such a person makes no secret of his determination to reproduce his model, and so who will believe he speaks with sincerity? And what kind of approbation will he get in the end? Only the sort acquired by those people who write patchwork poems[186] – who possibly give pleasure, but only for a short while and only if one has nothing better to do; and they neither impart information, nor stir the emotions, nor rouse to action.[187] The best you can say of them is that they know their Virgil, and have put a lot of effort into constructing their mosaic.

Nosoponus The more obvious my imitation, the easier my acceptance as a Ciceronian. And that's all I pray for.

Bulephorus Fair enough, if we are preparing our eloquence for display rather than practical use. But there's a lot of difference between an actor and an orator. An actor is satisfied with giving pleasure, but an orator wants to be of some use as well, provided he is a good man; and if he isn't,[188] he will not be able to keep the title of orator either.

Well, I think we have now shown that there are in Cicero some features which should be avoided, some which are missing, and some which are present only in such measure that Cicero is there surpassed by those more richly gifted. But even if we grant that there is no species of oratorical effect or stylistic ornament in which Cicero is not the equal or superior of the rest, certainly various felicities stand out more clearly in other writers simply because they don't occur all at once,[189] whereas in Marcus Tullius they are obscured by their very concentration. To take an analogy: it's easier to identify individual stars where they are few and far between than in a section of the sky studded with numbers of equally brilliant ones; and when you see a dress entirely covered with jewels you are less likely to notice individual stones.

Nosoponus Anyone who has absorbed the whole Cicero cannot express anything but Cicero.

Bulephorus Ah, we've got back to that point again.[190] Very well, I will accept as eloquent a man who successfully reproduces Cicero, the whole Cicero, excluding his early efforts; to show I'm not biased, it can be Cicero faults and all, provided it is the whole Cicero. We will put up with that little streak of vanity he mentions,[191] that habit of stroking the chin[192] with the left hand, a rather long and scraggy neck,[193] a tendency to shout[194] all the time, a discreditable and cowardly nervousness when starting to speak,[195] an excessive indulgence in humorous remarks,[196] and any other characteristics which were criticized either by Cicero himself or by other people. We will put up with the faults provided the speakers also reproduce the features by which Cicero concealed the faults[197] or made up for them.

Nosoponus If only I could reproduce the whole Cicero before my dying day!

Bulephorus That, Nosoponus, is just what we are trying to bring about by our present activity. But just think what a lot is implied in a few words when one says 'the whole Cicero.' Yet, ye Muses above, what a tiny portion of Cicero is offered by those Ciceronian apes[198] who scrape up a few phrases, idioms, figures, and rhythmical patterns from here and there and then exhibit just a top surface or veneer of Cicero. In ancient times there were people who tried to reproduce the Attic style[199] of speaking, and only managed to be dessicated, pinched, and lifeless, always keeping their hand carefully tucked inside their gown, as the great teacher[200] himself describes it, and came nowhere near the uncluttered, lithe elegance of Greek speakers. Quintilian[201] with good reason laughs at certain characters who saw themselves as genuine Ciceros, when they finished off their sentences from time to time with the rhythmical ending *esse videatur*[202] 'would seemingly be so,' simply because Cicero happened to do the same once or twice; or if they had constructed a long sweeping period, as Cicero did on occasion, especially in his opening paragraphs. And today there is no shortage of people like them, who pat themselves on the back and see themselves as Ciceros come to life again if they make the first word of their speech *quanquam* 'although,' *etsi* 'even though,' *animadverti* 'I have observed,' *quum* 'when, since, though,' or *si* 'if' – all because Cicero begins his *De officiis* with the words *Quanquam te, Marce fili* 'Although, Marcus my son ...' (and hardly brings his first period to an end inside nine lines). And he begins the speech *Pro lege Manilia* with *Quanquam mihi semper* 'Although I have always found ...' That highly admired speech of his in defence of Milo starts with *Etsi vereor, iudices* 'Even though I fear, gentlemen of the jury ...' And the twelfth *Philippic* begins with *Etsi minime decere videtur* 'Even though it seems highly inappropriate ...' And the *Pro Rabirio* with *Etsi, Quirites* 'Even though, citizens of Rome ...' Quite a lot of the letters have the same sort of beginning too. Maybe those characters attribute the *Ad Herennium*[203] to Cicero because it starts off with *etsi*! Then he starts the fifth book of *De finibus bonorum* with *Quum audivissem Antiochum Brute* 'When I had been to one of Antiochus' lectures, Brutus ...' He launches his *Tusculan Disputations* with *Quum defensionum laboribus* 'When from my labours on behalf of clients ...,' and begins the fourth book of the same work with *Quum multis in locis nostrorum hominum ingenia* 'While the intellectual brilliance of my countrymen in many places ...' The *Pro Flacco* begins with *Quum in maximis periculis* 'At a time when, amidst the gravest perils ...,' the speech *Pro domo sua*, delivered before the priests, with *Quum multa divinitus* 'While much by divine inspiration ...,' and the *Pro Plancio* with *Quum propter egregiam* 'Since, because of his remarkable ...' Moreover, he begins the first book of *De natura deorum* with *Quum multae res in philosophia* 'While many topics in philosophy ...' and the *Somnium Scipionis* with *Quum multae res in Africa* 'When many African interests ...' In his speech *Pro Rabirio*[204] he starts off *Animadverti iudices* 'I have observed, gentlemen of the jury ...,' and in his work *De paradoxis Stoicorum*, dedicated to Brutus, he begins *Animadverti Brute* 'I have observed, Brutus ...' The speech *Pro Lucio Cornelio Balbo* begins *Si autoritas patronorum* 'If the prestige of the advocate ...,' the one *Pro Publio Sestio* begins *Si quis antea iudices* 'If anyone hitherto, gentlemen of the jury ...,' the *Pro*

Caecina, Si quantum in agro 'If, as much as out in the wilds ...,' the *Pro Archia poeta, Si quid est in me ingenii* 'If there is in me any ability ...,' the speech *In Vatinium testem, Si tua tantummodo Vatini* 'If, Vatinius, I had merely ...,' the speech he made to the knights[205] before going into exile, *Si quando inimicorum* 'If ever my enemies ...,' and the one to the senate on his return (*Oratio post reditum in senatu*), *Si P.C.*[206] *vestris* 'If, members of this august house, your favours ...,' the *Pro Caelio, Si quis iudices* 'If anyone, gentlemen of the jury ...,' and the speech *De provinciis consularibus, Si quis vestrum P.C.* 'If any of you, honourable members of this house ...'

But what could be more ridiculous and less like Cicero than to have nothing of Cicero's except some paltry words of this sort right at the beginning of a speech? If anyone were to ask Cicero why he began with these words in particular, I imagine he would give the same answer as Homer gave to Lucian[207] in the Islands of the Blest, when he asked why he had decided to make the first word of the *Iliad* μῆνιν 'wrath' – a question which had vexed grammarians for centuries. 'It was the first word,' he said, 'that happened to come into my head.'

Equally impudent are those people who see themselves as more than Ciceronian because they push in every so often an *etiam atque etiam* 'again and again' instead of *vehementer* 'urgently,' *maiorem in modum* 'to a considerable degree' instead of *valde* 'very,' *identidem* 'over and over again' instead of *subinde* 'often,' or use *quum ... tum* 'while ... yet at the same time' to link two ideas, one of which is subordinate to the other, or *tum ... tum* 'at the one time ... at the same time' for two co-ordinate ideas, or push in the phrase *tuorum in me meritorum* 'of the services you have rendered me.' *Quid quaeris?* 'what would you?' (equivalent to *in summa* 'in short' or *breviter* 'to sum up'), *non solum peto, verum etiam oro contendoque* 'I do not merely ask, but even entreat and demand,' *ante hac dilexisse*[208] *tantum, nunc etiam amare mihi videor* 'hitherto I feel I have merely respected, now I actually love,' *valetudinem tuam cura et me ut facis ama* 'take care of yourself, and continue to love me,' *non ille quidem vir malus sed parum diligens* 'not a bad man to be sure, but one who wasn't sufficiently careful' – such expressions are so typical of Cicero, they think, that you find them repeated several times on the same page. The same thing is true of Cicero's use of the pronoun *illud* 'that' to refer not to what has preceded, but to what is about to come next. In the *Letters* he wrote maybe once or twice *cogitabam in Tusculanum* 'I was intending for my estate at Tusculum'; and so a man thinks himself Ciceronian if he's constantly saying *Romam cogitabam* 'I was intending for Rome,' meaning 'I had in mind' or 'I had decided to go to Rome.' Cicero doesn't put the number of the year at the end of his letters, only the day of the month. So I suppose a man won't be Ciceronian if he gives the year AD, which is often necessary, and always

useful. These same characters cannot bear it if someone, out of respect, puts
the name of the person he is writing to before his own, as for example *Carolo
Caesari Codrus Urceus salutem* 'To the Emperor Charles, from Codro Urceo,[209]
greetings.' They consider it an equal crime to add some phrase to a proper
name to indicate rank or honour, like *inclyto Pannoniae Bohemiaeque regi
Ferdinando Velius s.d.*[210] 'To the illustrious Ferdinand,[211] king of Hungary
and Bohemia, Velius[212] sends greetings.' Nor can they forgive the younger
Pliny for putting *suus*[213] 'my dear ...' when writing to a friend, when there is
no example in Cicero of this procedure. A man will be rejected as non-Tullian
if he puts at the top of his letter a summary of the one he is replying to – a
practice adopted recently by scholars from the administrative offices of rulers
– because this was nowhere done by Marcus Tullius Cicero. I have known
men censured as writers of bad Latin for putting in their salutation *s.p.d.*
(that is, *salutem plurimam dicit*[214] 'sends much greeting'), instead of *s.d.*,
because, they say, the former can't be found in Cicero. Some people think it's
also Tullian to put the salutation not on the front but on the back of the letter,
because this practice in Cicero's day served to tell the bearer which letter was
for which person, as well as greeting the recipient. What a tiny thing will
cause us to miss the prize we're after! Much less will anyone be Ciceronian
who formulates his greeting like this: 'Hilarius Bertholf[215] wishes Lieven
Algoet[216] the salvation (or the everlasting salvation), of the whole man.' And
it will fall even further short of the Ciceronian ideal to begin a letter as
follows: 'Grace, peace, and mercy from God the Father and our Lord Jesus
Christ.'[217] Likewise, instead of saying 'Keep well'[218] at the end of a letter, to
put 'May the Lord Jesus preserve you' or 'May the Lord, the author of all
salvation, keep you unharmed.' How the Ciceronians will hoot with
laughter when they see this! But what sin has been committed? Are the
words not Latin, neat, euphonious, even noble? If you consider the
meaning, how much more there is here than in 'sends greetings' or 'best
wishes.' What is more trite than to 'send greetings'? A master 'sends
greetings' to his servant, and people who are on bad terms 'send greetings'
to each other. In any case, who would believe that the phrases *dicit illi
salutem* 'speaks greeting to' and *iubet illum salvere* 'bids be well' were real
Latin expressions, if they were not authorized by the practice of the
Ancients?

That deals with the beginning of a letter. As for the end, we put 'best
wishes' even to people we wish ill to. How much better the implications of
the phrases used among Christians, if indeed we are truly and genuinely
Christian; 'grace' proclaims the free forgiveness of sins, 'peace' the quiet joy
of the conscience, since God is well-disposed towards us instead of angry,
'mercy' the various gifts of mind and body which the bounty of the secret

spirit richly bestows on those who are his; and to make more confident our hope that these blessings will be ours forever, we have those added words 'from God the Father and from our Lord Jesus Christ.' When you hear the word 'Father' you lay aside the fear proper to a servant, for you are adopted as a son, and that status implies love; when you hear 'Lord' you are made strong to face the might of Satan, for Christ will not desert what he has redeemed at such great price, and he alone is mightier than all the squadrons of the devil. What more welcome words than these to a man who already feels all this in his heart, what more salutary reminder to one who has not yet entered into this state of love? And so, as far as words go, we are not inferior to Cicero, in fact we are superior; in sentiment we easily have the upper hand.

To take the doctrine of the fitting and appropriate,[219] which is a matter of primary importance whatever we are saying, how much more suited are such sentiments to a Christian man than 'sends greetings' or 'take care of yourself'? Let's not have that puerile objection, 'Cicero did not speak like that.' Hardly surprising that he did not, when the idea was unknown to him. There are thousands of things we have to speak about often, that Cicero never even dreamed of. But if he were alive now, he would say the same things as we do. Don't those imitators of Cicero look feeble when they mimic Cicero by noting petty details like these and, turning a blind eye to so many of the inspired orator's virtues, employ his rhythms, figures, phraseology, and characteristic little phrases, copying only the things which Cicero liked using, whether consciously or unconsciously? I don't mean you when I say this, Nosoponus, but since the conversation has turned to Cicero's imitators, I thought it was not out of place to make these remarks. Imitators of this kind ought to be equally odious to us and to Cicero himself – to us, who are genuinely trying to follow Cicero's example, because thanks to them we are made a laughing-stock and a joke, as people look at their stupidity and judge us to be the same; and to Cicero, since people receive a bad impression of him, as we said earlier,[220] from imitators of this sort, just as unsatisfactory pupils spoil the reputation of a good teacher, bad children of a good man, an incompetent painter of a beautiful woman. This is the point Quintilian[221] was making when he complained that Seneca was brought into bad repute by the excessive enthusiasm of certain people who imitated only his faults, with the result that anyone who had not actually read Seneca judged Seneca's style from the writings of these other persons.[222] It is ignorant pupils and bad sons who make a great show and try to impress by dropping the names of teachers and family, using this as bait to hook a favourable opinion since they can't win one by their own good qualities. In the same way, it is the people who are least like Cicero who confidently make free with Cicero's name. I have known doctors[223] who were impressively ignorant of the art they professed, who, in order to increase their takings, boasted that they were the students of some distinguished medical man whom they had hardly seen; and if they were asked why they used this or that unconventional treatment, angrily replied, 'Are you more knowledgeable on the subject than the great Dr x? I learnt this from him.' Yet they copied practically nothing of the famous man whose name they used, apart from things that would be better avoided than emulated – the great man may for example have been bad-tempered and disagreeable when interviewing his patients or harsh in exacting his fee. How do you think our distinguished doctor will view pupils such as these?

Hypologus Obviously he will view them very coldly, unless he is quite indifferent to his own reputation.

Bulephorus And what about the great doctor's other students, the true and genuine ones?

Hypologus They will feel the same way towards the arrogant quack, because the experience the public have of him makes them think all the great doctor's students alike. But if you'll allow me to interrupt the flow of your argument, I'll give you an illustration.

Bulephorus Please do.

Hypologus A certain person once saw Erasmus writing with a pen he'd fixed to a piece of wood because it was too short, so this man started tying sticks to his pens, and fancied that like this he was writing Erasmian fashion. But please go on.

Bulephorus An amusing story, and not 'irrelevant to Dionysus.'[224] But to return to our subject.[225] Don't we hear fathers scolding their sons when they behave badly, and saying to them, 'You are giving me a bad name and making me unpopular in the town; you are disgracing the family, which has been respected for generations; I'm ashamed to have such children, and if you continue like this, I shall disown you.' Likewise we hear men remonstrating with their brothers at times, because their own reputation is being damaged by their brothers' bad behaviour. This is the way Cicero would probably feel towards those ridiculous apes, and this is the way we ought to feel, we who are eager to be known as his true and worthy sons.[226]

Nosoponus When the glory is so great, it's quite something to achieve even a faint reflection of the original.

Bulephorus Let those people find it something who are content to be called faint reflections of Cicero. Personally I wouldn't want to be called even Apollo's reflection. I would rather be a genuine living Crassus[227] than a reflected Cicero. But to go back to the point we started discussing earlier. Suppose that we do have someone who can reproduce the whole Cicero, in vocabulary, in rhetorical figures, in rhythms – and I don't know that many could do that – how little of Cicero he will succeed in capturing! Let us assume that this person is as adept in recreating Cicero as Zeuxis was in representing the female form. Zeuxis was able to depict his subject's features, complexion, age, even a suggestion of the feelings. It is this that demonstrates his supreme artistry – he could show grief, joy, anger, fear, attention, or boredom. Now the man who could offer all this surely realized the full potential of his art? As far as was possible, he transferred the form of the living person to the mute image. Nor can we ask anything more of a painter. You recognize the physical characteristics of the woman painted, you observe her age and feelings, possibly her state of health as well; some artists, we are told, made it possible for a physiognomist[228] to read off the character, habits, and life-span. But what an enormous amount of the real person is missing from the portrait! We find represented everything it is possible to ascertain from the outermost layer, the skin.[229] Yet man consists of soul as well as body, and we have very little even of one constituent part, and the inferior one at that. Where are the brain, the flesh, the veins, the sinews and bones, the bowels, blood, breath, humours? Where are life, movement, feeling, voice, and speech? Where finally are man's special characteristics, mind, intelligence, memory, and understanding? The painter in fact finds it impossible to represent the most distinctive features of a person. Likewise, no mere attempt to reproduce an effect[230] is going to develop the real oratorical virtues. We have to produce them from within ourselves. Nothing more is asked of the artist if he has provided the one thing his art claims to offer; something very different is required of us if we wish to represent the whole Cicero. If the picture we paint of Marcus Tullius is devoid of life, movement, feeling, sinew, and bone, our representation of him will be completely unconvincing; worse than that, our picture will be ridiculous, if we put in bumps and warts and scars and other physical deformities to make quite sure our reader recognizes that we have read Cicero.

Hypologus We all had a laugh not so long ago at a painter who did that sort of thing. He'd undertaken to paint our friend Murius[231] to the life, and since he couldn't produce a true likeness of the man, he looked around for something distinctive in his body or his clothes. He started painting in summer, and had already largely completed the picture. He'd painted the ring he wore, his money-bag, his belt, and did a very detailed drawing of his hat. He observed that he had a scar on the index finger of his left hand, so he carefully put that in. On the right wrist there was a lump, an obvious one, so that wasn't left out either. On his right eyebrow he faithfully represented a few hairs that stuck out in the wrong direction, and he also drew in a mark on the left cheek, the scar from an old wound. Once when he went back to his sitter – which he was always doing – he saw that Murius had cut off his beard, so he gave the portrait a new chin. Later, when he saw that Murius had let his beard grow a bit because he preferred it that way, he changed the chin again. In the mean time Murius caught a slight fever, which as usual, when it began to get better, erupted onto his lip. The painter put the pimple in. At length winter came. The sitter changed his hat, the painter his picture. The sitter put on a winter robe lined with fur, the artist painted in a new robe. The harsh weather changed the sitter's colour, and as it so often does, made his skin look drawn, so the painter changed the whole skin. Murius caught a cold in the head which spoilt the look of his left eye and made his nose a bit bigger and a lot redder from continually being wiped – so he gave him a new eye and a new nose. If ever he saw his model when he hadn't combed his hair, he painted in the rumpled look; if he had combed it, he straightened up the locks. Murius happened to nod off while he was being painted, so he represented him asleep; he took some medicine on his doctor's advice which made him look and feel years older, so he changed the face. If he had been able to depict the really characteristic features of the man, he would not have resorted to these incidentals. If we imitate Cicero like that, we shall deserve to have Horace[232] cry out: 'How often, you copiers, you slavish rabble, / Have I laughed or mocked at your mindless gabble!'

But even supposing we managed to portray, in our presentation of Cicero, as much of the personality as a supreme artist is capable of portraying, where would be Cicero's sensitivity, his rich and happy gift of invention, his skill in arrangement, his development of propositions,[233] his judgment in handling arguments, his effectiveness in stirring the emotions, the charm that captivated his audience, his quick, efficient memory, his grasp of so much material, in short that mind that still breathes through his writings, that genius endowed with its own mysterious energy? If these are missing, the image resulting from our imitation will carry no conviction at all.
Nosoponus That's all very eloquent, Bulephorus,[234] but what's the intention, if not to deter the young from modelling themselves on Cicero?
Bulephorus Perish the thought! The intention is rather to ensure that we ignore the irrelevant chatter of the apes and proceed to imitate Cicero as far as we may, in his entirety, and with success.
Nosoponus In that at any rate we are agreed.
Bulephorus Unless emulation is skilful as well as painstaking it will not succeed, and we shall finish up very unlike Cicero. Aspiring to be like Cicero has its dangers, I assure you – the giants[235] came to a bad end for aspiring to the throne of Jove, and several persons were destroyed by their desire[236] to see the gods face to face. It is 'a task with hazard and danger fraught'[237] to

copy that inspired, superhuman tongue. Possibly someone may be born a
Cicero, no one can become one.

Nosoponus What are you getting at now?

Bulephorus I mean that his virtues, because they are great, approximate to
faults.[238] It's inevitable that imitation falls short when it tries only to follow a
model, not surpass it. Consequently, the more determinedly you aim to copy
Cicero, the nearer you come to a fault.

Nosoponus I don't quite see what you mean.

Bulephorus I'll explain. Don't doctors hold the theory[239] that the best state
of health is the least secure, because it's closest to sickness?

Nosoponus So I've heard. What then?

Bulephorus And isn't supreme monarchy very close to tyranny?

Nosoponus So they say.

Bulephorus Yet nothing is better than supreme monarchy, provided there is
no sign of tyranny. And supreme generosity is very close to the fault of
extravagance, isn't it, and extreme severity to positive brutality?

Nosoponus Certainly.

Bulephorus And great gaiety and wit come very near to frivolity and
scurrility?

Nosoponus You needn't go through the list. Take it that I've said yes to all
of them.

Bulephorus Let me quote some Horace:[240]

> If I strive to be concise, my meaning is not plain;
> And power fails and passion's gone, should smoothness be the aim;
> And one who seeks the style sublime, mouths empty words and vain.

So those who aim at the Attic style become bald[241] instead of clear and
elegant; those who aim at the Rhodian style become flabby; the Asiatic[242]
style, bombastic. Now in Sallust's case,[243] terseness of expression was a
virtue, but if anyone tried to imitate it too rigidly, wouldn't he be in danger of
becoming abrupt and jerky?

Nosoponus Possibly.

Bulephorus In Demosthenes people commended an economy of word and
argument from which nothing could be subtracted as superfluous.

Nosoponus So Quintilian thought[244] at any rate.

Bulephorus But if someone tries over-anxiously to emulate this praisewor-
thy quality in hopes of appearing Demosthenic, he may well fall into the trap
of saying less than the occasion demands. Isocrates[245] is applauded for
arrangement and rhythm – anyone who pursues this goal too far will be in

danger of becoming tedious because of his obsessive concern with word order and will lose the confidence of his hearers by his obvious artificiality. Seneca is praised[246] for his rich, inventive style. The industrious but incautious imitator risks finishing up with a style that is flashy and overdone instead. If you meticulously copy Brutus' seriousness,[247] you may turn out harsh and gloomy. The feature praised in Crispus[248] is charm. The man who imitates this is likely to become silly and superficial instead of pleasant to listen to. I have known men who attempted to reproduce that wonderful fluency of Ovid's and merely spouted verses devoid of any substance and force. If I go on mentioning individual writers by name, I'll bore you, so I'll put the rest in general terms. Some speakers are noted for close, detailed argument. The man who aims determinedly at this virtue is in danger of boring his audience or bewildering them. In others we admire a happy disregard of theory. Anyone who tries this may possibly fall into an over-colloquial style, chatting rather than speaking. Another is successful because he follows every rule in the book; copy him, and you will become stagey and histrionic. Next door to Attic economy lies poverty of speech; a rich flowing style is near neighbour to verbosity. The impassioned presentation[249] of facts that works up an audience's emotions moves into a kind of mad extravagance, magisterial becomes pompous, confident becomes brazen.

Nosoponus You're preaching to the converted here!

Bulephorus Some of these features are indeed so pronounced that they would have to be considered faults if the writers didn't compensate by combining them with virtues. Seneca for example is characterized[250] by jerkiness and excessive use of aphorisms, but these faults are excused by many virtues, including the high tone of his moral precepts, the brilliance of expression and content, and the general attractiveness of his writing. Isocrates' harmonious word order is admirable only because it is supported by clarity of diction and loftiness of sentiment.

Nosoponus This is all perfectly true so far, but I don't see yet what point you are making.

Bulephorus Why, this, of course. Cicero's style displays not one but many features like this, so it seems to me dangerous to emulate him in a hidebound, slavish fashion, because we are unable to emulate the virtues which either set such features in a good light or make them unobtrusive.

Nosoponus But what features do you mean?

Bulephorus His style of oratory is so fluid that it could at times be thought slack and flabby; his expression so exuberant that it could be thought long-winded; he follows textbook procedure more like a professor of rhetoric than a practising counsel, and is prepared to throw his credibility away for the sake of demonstrating his mastery of oratorical techniques. He was so outspoken in attack that one could consider him slanderous, and was always ready to indulge in banter – he even made Cato smile on one occasion during his consulship. He was sometimes so ingratiating as to be crawling; so smooth as to be called feeble and effeminate by sterner minds.[251] We may agree that in Cicero these are not faults because of that singular felicity of personality which makes everything he does seem right. As for their being actual virtues, they lie so close to faults that they look like faults to an unsympathetic critic. All the same, he has many remarkable virtues to counterbalance the things that can be criticized, so that any attack on Cicero's style will be generally regarded as deliberate, provocative disparagement. But these virtues are not what we try to reproduce. In any case, if we believe Quintilian,[252] they don't lend themselves to imitation and it's no use seeking them via example or precept; they come only from one's own natural genius. But without them, what will our imitation of the other features we have mentioned be like? So our conclusion is that there are more opportunities for disaster in imitating Cicero than anyone else, not just because, as the greatest of orators, he himself rises superior[253] to all the hazards involved in any exercise of mental ability – Horace[254] on the same grounds warns against any attempt to emulate Pindar, and quotes the example of the fall of Icarus – but also because most of his great characteristics become great only by approximating to faults.[255] This is why it is easy to tip over the edge of the precipice.

Nosoponus But earlier we were all accepting that the most outstanding characteristics are the most readily imitated, so that even if you fall short to some extent of what you're trying to copy, you still get the credit of writing good stuff.[256]

Bulephorus Reproducing exactly and producing something like are different things. So are imitating one's exemplar and being a slave to it, always following behind it. And it's falling short of one's model not to reproduce the features that forestall criticism. Yet Quintilian says these features are hardly capable of imitation even by gifted minds.

Nosoponus I am not allowing any to compete unless they are extremely outstanding minds of superhuman ability. If they are also blessed with tireless enthusiasm, then there is some hope of their successfully recapturing the Ciceronian idiom.

Bulephorus Maybe, but there are not enough of them to be counted. Now some acute people distinguish imitation from emulation.[257] The goal of imitation is being like, of emulation, being better. If in setting up as your model Cicero entire and Cicero alone your intention is not merely to reproduce him but to outdo him, you will not just have to run past him, but get away from him altogether. Otherwise, if you choose to add to his fullness, you will become prolix; if to his free tongue, insolent; if to his wit, scurrilous; if to his euphonious arrangement of words, you will be singing a song[258] rather than delivering a speech. This is the situation; if your aim is to equal Cicero, you are in danger of speaking less well, for the very reason that the superhuman virtues of the man, which made up for his faults or near faults, you cannot reproduce, while of course reproducing the rest; whereas if you try to get ahead of him, even supposing you manage something equivalent to those features which you cannot really reproduce however hard you try, any development of Cicero's other characteristics will become a fault. What was said about him[259] is absolutely true: nothing can be added to his eloquence, just as nothing can be subtracted from Demosthenes'. You see the danger, Nosoponus.[260]

Nosoponus I'm not frightened by the danger, provided that one day I achieve the glory of being called a Ciceronian.

Bulephorus If all that makes no impression on you, there's another uneasiness which grates even more on my mind, if you're prepared to hear about it.

Nosoponus Please yourself what use you make of our agreement.

Bulephorus Well then, do you think anyone deserves the title of eloquent if he does not speak in a manner in keeping with his subject?

Nosoponus Not at all. It's a particular virtue of the orator to speak appositely.

Bulephorus And this quality of appositeness is judged partly according to the subject-matter, partly according to the persons involved, including both speakers and audience, partly according to place, time, and other circumstances?

Nosoponus Certainly.

Bulephorus Now surely you want your Ciceronian to be an outstanding orator?

Nosoponus Of course I do.

Bulephorus So a person won't be a Ciceronian if he holds forth on Stoic paradoxes[261] or Chrysippus'[262] sophistries in the theatre; or indulges in facetiousness during a murder trial in the court of the Areopagus;[263] or talks about cooking in the language and imagery of tragedy?

Nosoponus An orator of that sort would be as much a laughing-stock as someone who performed an extract from an Atellan farce[264] dressed like a tragic hero; or, as the proverb has it, gave a cat a saffron robe[265] or royal purple to an ape,[266] or dressed Bacchus[267] or Sardanapalus[268] in the lion-skin and club of Hercules. A thing deserves no praise, however intrinsically splendid, if it's inappropriate.

Bulephorus A true and proper reply. Well then, Cicero spoke in the best possible way in the age he lived in. Would he still have spoken in the best possible way if he had adopted the same style in the age of Cato the Censor,[269] Scipio,[270] or Ennius?[271]

Nosoponus No. The ears of his audience would have rejected that polish and rhythm of his, being accustomed of course to a more rugged form of speech. Their language matched the customs of the age they lived in.

Bulephorus Would you say then that language is a sort of dress[272] to subject-matter?

Nosoponus Yes, I would, unless you prefer to call it a kind of painting.[273]

Bulephorus Well, the dress that suits a child is not appropriate to an old person; what is suitable for a woman would not be right for a man; the clothes for a wedding would not be proper for a funeral; and what was admired a hundred years ago wouldn't be acceptable now.

Nosoponus No indeed, everyone would laugh and boo. Just look at pictures that aren't all that old, painted, say, sixty years ago, and see what was being worn by those of the fair sex belonging to prominent families or living at court. If a woman went out in public dressed like that now, the village idiots and street-urchins would pelt her with rotten fruit.

Hypologus Only too true. Who would put up now with a decent married woman wearing those huge horns and pyramids and cones sticking out from the top of the head, and having her brow and temples plucked so that nearly half her head is bald; or with men wearing those hats stuffed like a cushion with a great tail hanging down, coats with scalloped borders and enormous padded shoulders, hair shaved off an inch above their ears, tunics far too short to reach the knees, hardly covering their private parts, slippers with a long pointed beak sticking out in front, and silver cross-gartering from knee to ankle? And the people of those days would have found the clothes we think perfectly respectable just as monstrous as we find theirs.

Nosoponus We're of one mind on the subject of clothes.

Bulephorus Now take painters. Suppose that Apelles,[274] who was the supreme portrayer of gods and men of his age, by some chance returned to life in our time. If he now painted Germans as he once painted Greeks, and monarchs as he once painted Alexander, since people are not like that any more, wouldn't he be said to have painted badly?

Nosoponus Yes, because he had not painted them in an appropriate manner.

Bulephorus If someone painted[275] God the Father with the attributes Apelles gave to Jove, and Christ looking like Apelles' representations of Apollo, would you consider it a good picture?

Nosoponus Certainly not.

Bulephorus Suppose someone today represented the Blessed Virgin the way Apelles long ago portrayed Diana,[276], or the virgin Agnes[277] with the form he gave his Aphrodite Anadyomene[278] in the famous painting that all the writers talk about, or St Thecla[279] looking like his Lais,[280] would you say he was a painter like Apelles?

Nosoponus I don't think so.

Bulephorus And if someone decorated our churches with the sort of statues that Lysippus[281] made in ancient times to adorn the temples of the gods, would you say he was like Lysippus?

Nosoponus I wouldn't.

Bulephorus And why not?

Nosoponus Because the statues would not fit the things they represented. I would say the same if someone painted an ass looking like an ox, or a hawk like a cuckoo, even if the painting was otherwise done with the greatest care and skill.

Hypologus I wouldn't even call a man a good painter if he represented an ugly person as handsome.

Bulephorus But suppose he displayed the greatest skill, apart from that?

Hypologus I wouldn't say the painting showed lack of skill, but lack of integrity. He could have painted differently if he had wanted, but he preferred to flatter his sitter, or else dupe him. But come, surely you wouldn't think such a man a good artist?

Nosoponus Even if he were, he certainly hasn't shown himself one in these circumstances.

Bulephorus But you think him a good man?

Nosoponus Neither a good artist nor a good man, considering that the essence of art is to represent the object as it actually is.[282]

Bulephorus One doesn't need Ciceronian eloquence for that sort of thing. On the contrary, your rhetorical theorists[283] allow the orator on occasion to misrepresent the truth, to magnify the unimportant and make the splendid look small, which is a kind of conjuror's trick, to infiltrate the hearer's mind by deception, and finally to carry his intelligence by storm through rousing his emotions, which is putting a kind of spell on him.

Nosoponus So they do, where the hearer deserves to be deceived.

Bulephorus This has really 'nothing to do with Dionysus,'[284] so let's leave it for the moment. It's enough for me that you don't approve of clothes which aren't suitable for the wearer and don't think much of a painting which isn't appropriate to the subject the artist professes to be representing.

Nosoponus What's all this Socratic introduction[285] of yours leading up to?

Bulephorus This is the point I was working towards, my dear Nosoponus. We are agreed that Cicero is the best of all orators.

Nosoponus We are.

Bulephorus And that no one deserves the fair title of Ciceronian unless he can speak as Cicero does.

Nosoponus Quite so.

Bulephorus And moreover that a man doesn't speak well, if he doesn't speak appositely.[286]

Nosoponus That too.

Bulephorus And that we only speak appositely if what we say is appropriate to present persons and circumstances?

Nosoponus Certainly.

Bulephorus Well then, do you think the world as it is now has anything in common with the situation at the time when Cicero lived and delivered his speeches? Everything has been completely altered – religion, empire, government, constitution, law, customs, pursuits, even men's physical appearance.

Nosoponus Yes, indeed.

Bulephorus What effrontery then on the part of anyone to demand that we speak in a totally Ciceronian manner! He must first give us back the Rome of long ago, the senate[287] and the curia,[288] the conscript fathers,[289] the equestrian order,[290] the people distributed into tribes and centuries;[291] he must restore the colleges of augurs and haruspices,[292] the pontifices maximi,[293] the flamens[294] and vestals,[295] the aediles, praetors, tribunes of the people, consuls, dictators,[296] Caesars,[297] the voting in the comitium,[298] the laws, the decrees of the senate, the resolutions of the people, the statues, triumphs, ovations,[299] the supplications,[300] the temples and shrines, the feasts of couches,[301] the religious rites, the gods and goddesses, the Capitol[302] and the sacred fire;[303] he must restore the provinces, colonies, municipalities and allies[304] of the city that was mistress of the world. Since the entire scene of human activity has been transformed, the only speaker who can respond to it appropriately is one who is very different from Cicero. This view, quite the opposite of yours, is the one to which our discussion has led, as it seems to me. You say that no one can speak well unless he reproduces Cicero; but the very facts of the matter cry out that no one can speak well unless he deliberately and with full awareness abandons the example of Cicero. Wherever I turn I see everything changed, I stand on a different stage, I see a different theatre, a different world. What am I to do? I am a Christian and I must talk of the Christian religion before Christians. If I am going to do so in a manner befitting my subject, surely I am not to imagine that I am living in the age of Cicero, and speaking in a crowded senate before the conscript fathers on the Tarpeian height,[305] and scrounge a few poor words, figures and rhythms from speeches which Cicero delivered in the senate?

Suppose I have to give an address to a mixed audience including young girls, married women, and widows; my subjects are the value of fasting, penitence, the effectiveness of prayer, the benefit of almsgiving, the sanctity of marriage, contempt for the transient world, zeal for the Holy Scriptures. What help will Cicero's eloquence be to me here? The subjects I have to speak about were unknown to him, so he could not have employed the words for them: they came in after his time as new words to express new ideas. If our orator tacks patches filched from Cicero on to this sort of subject, his speech will surely fall completely flat.

I'll tell you a story – not a bit of hearsay, but something I saw with my own eyes,[306] heard with my own ears. In Rome at the time the two men with the most distinguished reputation as speakers were Pietro Fedra[307] and Camillo.[308] Camillo was younger and in actuality the more powerful speaker, but the older man had occupied the citadel first. Neither of them though, unless I'm mistaken, was actually Roman by birth. Now a certain person had been appointed to speak on the death of Christ, on the holy day known as the Day of Parasceve,[309] in the presence of the pontiff himself. A few days before the event I received an invitation from the literary community to go and hear the speech. 'Be sure to be there,' they said. 'Now you will really hear how the language of Rome sounds in the mouth of a Roman.' I was there, full of expectation. I stood as close to the platform as I could, so as to miss nothing. Julius II was present himself, and that doesn't happen very often, because of his health,[310] I think. There were rows of cardinals and bishops and, besides the common crowd, quite a number of scholars who were staying in Rome. I won't tell you the name of the speaker, then no one will think it my intention to damage the reputation of an honest scholar. He held the same views as you do, Nosoponus, that is, he was an aspirant after Ciceronian eloquence. His preface and his peroration – which was almost longer than the entire speech – were taken up with singing the praises of Julius II, whom he called Jupiter Optimus Maximus, describing him as grasping and hurling with his omnipotent right hand the three-forked, unerring thunderbolt and with a mere nod performing whatever is his will. All that had been done in the preceding years in France, Germany, and Spain, in Portugal, Africa, and Greece had come about, he maintained, by the nod of his will and his alone. In all of which to be sure, he spoke as a Roman in Rome, using Roman speech and a Roman accent. But what had all this to do with Julius as the high priest of the Christian religion, the vicar of Christ and successor of Peter and Paul? What had it to do with the cardinals and bishops who act in the stead of the other apostles? As for the subject he had undertaken to treat, what could be more sacred, more real, more wonderful, more sublime, more fitted to stir the feelings? What speaker, even one endowed with quite ordinary gifts of expression, could fail to wring tears even from men of stone on such a theme? The general plan of his speech was first to represent the death of Christ as piteous, and then, swinging his oratory onto the other tack, to show it as glorious and triumphant, no doubt in order to give us a demonstration of that Ciceronian power of impassioned presentation which enabled him to swing the emotions of his audience in any direction he chose.[311]

Hypologus Well, did he succeed?

Bulephorus To tell you the truth, when we were in the thick of his tragic emotions – the ones the rhetoricians[312] call πάθη 'passions' – I wanted to laugh. Nor did I see anyone in all that assembly showing the slightest sign of sorrow when he deployed his every oratorical gift in a harrowing description of the unjust sufferings of the entirely innocent Christ; nor for that matter did anyone look one jot gladder when he was straining every nerve to present that death to us as triumphant, admirable, and glorious. He spoke of the Decii[313] and Quintus Curtius[314] who dedicated themselves to the spirits of the dead to save the republic, and of Cecrops,[315] Menoeceus,[316] Iphigenia,[317] and several others who had set the safety and honour of the fatherland above their own lives. With a sob in his throat he bemoaned the fact that the heroes who came to the aid of the republic of Rome by putting themselves in peril received the thanks of the nation by official proclamation: some were awarded a gold statue in the forum, others became the recipients of divine honours; but Christ, in return for his benefits, received from the thankless Jewish race not a reward but the cross, horrible sufferings, and utter degradation. And there he was, rousing our pity for that good, innocent man, who deserved nothing but gratitude from his people, as if deploring the deaths of Socrates[318] and Phocion,[319] who were sentenced by their ungrateful fellow-citizens to drink hemlock, though innocent of all crime; or Epaminondas,[320] who, in return for his distinguished public career, was made to stand trial for his life by his own countrymen; or Scipio,[321] who went into exile after all he had done for the Roman republic; or Aristides,[322] whom the Athenian people voted into exile by the procedure of ostracism[323] because they could not stand his nickname 'the Just,' given him because of his outstanding integrity of character. I ask you, could anything be more tedious and irrevelant? And yet he emulated Cicero to the best of his ability. But never a word about the hidden plan of the supreme Godhead, who willed by this incredible means to redeem the human race from the tyranny of the devil through the death of his only Son, not a word of those mysteries, of what it means to die with Christ, to be buried with him, to rise with him again.[324] He wept for his innocence, trounced the ingratitude of the Jews; but never a tear for our wickedness, our ingratitude – ours who have been thus redeemed, granted so many blessings, summoned by unheard-of

generosity to partake of such bliss, and who, as far as in us lies, crucify him
again, turning back of our own choice to the tyranny of Satan, slaves of
avarice, indulgence, pleasure, ambition, more in thrall to this world than
ever the pagans were, to whom God had not yet revealed this heavenly
philosophy.

In the other part of his speech, where he was making great efforts to fill
us with exultation, I felt more like crying, when I heard the triumphs[325] of
Scipio,[326] Aemilius Paulus,[327] and Julius Caesar[328] and the apotheosis[329] of
Roman emperors compared with the triumph of the cross. Anyone who
wanted to do justice to the glory of the cross ought to have taken the Apostle
Paul as his model rather than Cicero. How Paul[330] exults on this theme, how
he gets carried away, how he glories, lords it, triumphs, looks down on all
earthly things with contempt as if from the heights of heaven, once he starts
preaching the cross. In short, this Roman spoke so Romanly that I heard
nothing about the death of Christ. Yet this eager aspirant after the
Ciceronian idiom was judged by the Ciceronians to have spoken marvellous-
ly; though he said practically nothing on the subject, which he seemed
neither to understand nor care for, said not a thing that was appropriate,
and stirred no feelings. The only thing he could be praised for was for
speaking in Roman fashion and recalling something of Cicero. One could
approve of a speech like this as being a demonstration of ability and
intelligence if it were delivered by a schoolboy before his fellow pupils in
class, but what connection, I ask you, did it have with such a day, such an
audience, such a theme?

Nosoponus And is this man without a name?

Bulephorus As I said, I prefer to leave the name to be inferred, as it is not my
present purpose to cast aspersions on anyone's name. What I am doing is to
point out an error that should be avoided, one that under the shadow of a
mighty name[331] leads a good many people astray these days. This is what
concerns us, Nosoponus; the name of the man[332] in my story does not matter.
But the story has its implications also for the fame of Cicero, for which I see
you are so very concerned, for which every scholar anywhere in the world is
rightly concerned. The fact is that those apes not only create obstacles for the
young in their studies and in their moral development, but also darken
Cicero's name by putting themselves forward under the title of Ciceronian
when that is the last thing they are. Benedict, a man of great holiness, is
defamed by people who profess themselves Benedictines in dress and name
and live lives bearing more resemblance to Sardanapalus[333] than to Benedict;
and that least malicious of all men, Francis, is defamed by those who make a
great parade of his name, though their behaviour recalls the Pharisees rather
than Francis; and Augustine,[334] by those who style themselves Augustin-

ians, though they are far removed from both the doctrine and the spirituality of that great man; and maybe Christ is too, by those who have nothing of him but his name. In the same way, Cicero's name is sullied by those who constantly have on their lips 'Cicero' and 'Ciceronian,' when they are further than anyone from the eloquence of Cicero. It's wonderful how they turn up their noses in disgust at the barbaric language of Thomas,[335] Scotus,[336] Durandus,[337] and their fellows; yet if the matter is called into strict account, they, who made no profession of being either eloquent or Ciceronian, are more Ciceronian than these creatures who expect to be considered not just Ciceronian but veritable Ciceros.

Nosoponus What a monstrous[338] statement!

Bulephorus Truth can't be monstrous – only lies can be that. You do agree, don't you, that the man who most resembles Cicero is one who speaks in the best possible way on any subject whatsoever?

Nosoponus I do.

Bulephorus Now good speaking has two main sources: a thorough understanding of the subject to be treated, and sensitivity and passion to generate the words.

Nosoponus So Horace[339] and Quintilian[340] tell us; in any case it's obviously true without quoting authorities, so I won't try to deny it.

Bulephorus Then how will anyone acquire the name of Ciceronian, that is, of a man who speaks in the best possible way, if he talks about subjects he does not thoroughly understand, in which his feelings are not involved, which I might even say he has no time for and positively dislikes?

Hypologus It would be very difficult. How could a painter, however good technically, produce a portrait of a man he had never looked at carefully, or maybe never even seen? In fact, it's difficult to get an artist in this line to produce a clever likeness unless he actually finds his subject congenial.

Bulephorus So the first concern of the Ciceronians should have been to understand the mysteries of the Christian religion, and to turn the pages of the sacred books with as much enthusiasm as Cicero devoted to the writings of philosophers, poets, experts in law and religion, and historians. With all this did the great Cicero equip himself. So how shall we ever be Ciceronians when we never touch – when we positively despise and recoil from – the laws, prophets, histories, and commentators that belong to what we profess?

Well then, a speech has to be made before a Christian audience, but on a non-religious subject, say on an election, or a marriage, or the signing of a treaty, or the declaration of war. Shall we as Christians, before other Christians, discuss these topics in exactly the same way as the pagan Cicero did before pagans? Shouldn't every action of our lives be referred to the standard of Christ? If your speech departs from that you will prove neither a good orator nor a good man.

But suppose our speaker is one who utters no word unless it is recorded in his lists. The complete change that has occurred in the lives of men has introduced words that are new, so what will the Ciceronian do, faced with these, when he won't be able to find them either in Cicero's works or in his own word list? Any word which can't be pin-pointed in Cicero's writings is to be rejected; but since so many of his writings have not survived, just think how many things we shall avoid as barbarisms which Cicero did in fact write; and how many we shall avoid which he would have used if he had had to talk about our sort of subject. Nowhere in Cicero do we find the expressions 'Jesus Christ,' 'word of God,' 'Holy Spirit,' 'Trinity,' or 'evangel,' 'evangelist,' 'Moses,' 'prophet,' 'Pentateuch,' 'psalms,' 'bishop,' 'archbishop,' 'deacon,' 'subdeacon,' 'acolyte,' 'exorcist,' 'church,' or 'faith, hope and charity,' or 'the one essence of three persons,' or 'heresy,' or 'symbol,'[341] or 'the seven sacraments of the church,' or 'baptism,' 'Baptist,' 'confirmation,' 'Eucharist,' 'extreme unction,' 'penance,' 'sacramental confession,' 'contrition,' 'absolution,' 'excommunication,' 'church burial,' 'mass,' and innumerable other things of which the life of Christians is wholly made up. These constantly rise up in our path, whatever subject we try to talk about; they thrust themselves upon us even against our will. What shall our meticulous Ciceronian do? Where shall he turn? Shall he for Father of Christ say 'Jupiter Optimus Maximus,'[342] for the Son, 'Apollo' or 'Aesculapius'?[343] Shall he for Queen of Virgins say 'Diana';[344] for church, 'sacred assembly' or 'state' or 'republic'; for pagan, 'foeman';[345] for heresy, 'faction'; for schism, 'sedition'; for the Christian faith, 'the Christian persuasion'; for excommunication, 'proscription';[346] for excommunicate, 'consign to the spirits of dread'[347] or, as some prefer, 'debar from fire and water';[348] for apostles, 'ambassadors' or 'couriers'; for the Roman pontiff, 'flamen Dialis';[349] for the conclave of cardinals, 'conscript fathers';[350] for general synod, 'senate and people of the Christian republic';[351] for bishops, 'superintendents of provinces'; for the election of bishops, 'comitia';[352] for a synodal resolution, 'decree of the senate'; for the sovereign pontiff, 'supreme governor of the state'; for Christ the head of the church, 'supreme president of the republic'; for the devil, 'denouncer';[353] for prophet, 'soothsayer' or 'seer'; for prophecies, 'oracles of the gods'; for baptism, 'dipping'; for mass, 'victim'; for the consecration of the body of Christ, 'all-holy bread-offering'; for the Eucharist, 'sanctifying cake';[354] for the priest, 'sacrificer' or 'conductor of rites'; for deacon, 'assistant' or 'curio';[355] for the grace of God, 'the generous gift of the divine power'; for absolution, 'manumission'?[356] Obviously I have touched on only a small proportion of the vast number of words involved. What is our aspirant after the Ciceronian turn of phrase going to do here? Is he going to say nothing, or is he going to make the kind of substitution I've suggested for established Christian vocabulary?

Nosoponus And why shouldn't he?

Bulephorus Very well, let's invent an example: Jesus Christ, the Word and the Son of the eternal Father, according to the prophets came into the world, and having been made man, of his own free will surrendered himself to death and redeemed his church; he turned aside from us the wrath of the Father whom we had offended, and reconciled us to him so that, being justified by the grace of faith and delivered from tyranny, we might be ingrafted into the church, and persevering in the communion of the church, might after this life attain the kingdom of heaven. The Ciceronian will express it like this: The interpreter and son of Jupiter Optimus Maximus, our preserver and king, according to the oracles of the seers winged his way from Olympus to the earth and, assuming the shape of man, of his own free will consigned himself to the spirits of the dead to preserve the republic; and thus asserting the freedom of his assembly or state or republic, quenched the thunderbolt of Jupiter Optimus Maximus, directed at our heads, and renewed our good relations with him, in order that, being restored to innocence by the generous gift of our persuasion, and manumitted from the lordship of the denouncer, we might be co-opted into citizenship of the state and, persevering in the society of the republic, might, once the fates summon us to depart this life, achieve the sum total of all things in the company of the gods.

Nosoponus You are being facetious, Bulephorus.

Bulephorus As I hope for the love of our Peitho,[357] I am in earnest. Now suppose it happens that I have to discuss one or other of the difficult questions raised by our doctrines. How much light will be generated by my argument, if the words of my mouth strut out dressed up in fripperies like this? I shall only add smoke to the existing darkness of the subject-matter, and my reader will be constantly brought up short against these obstacles in his road. However, granted that we play about with copying Cicero up to this point, what are we going to do when the context demands scriptural evidence? When I have to cite something from the Ten Commandments, shall I merely insert the words, 'Read out the law'? When I have to announce 'synodal resolution,' shall I insert 'Read out the decree of the senate'? When I have to bring in something from the prophets or apostles, will it be enough to write in 'Read the witness's deposition'? For that's just what Cicero does.[358] And shall I thus avoid contaminating my Ciceronian diction with non-Ciceronian words?

Nosoponus What's the alternative? Are you urging us to speak the way Thomas and Scotus[359] wrote?

Bulephorus If the better speaker is the one who speaks more appropriately to the subject, then to speak as they did on sacred subjects was certainly preferable to copying Cicero in such a context – though there is something in between the extremes of the Scotuses and Cicero's apes. If something doesn't occur in Cicero it's not inevitably bad Latin, since Cicero, as I have said several times, is not extant in his entirety; and even if he were, he did not deal with all subjects; and even if he had dealt with all the subjects of his own times, he neither dealt with nor knew of the subjects of ours. Moreover, where correctness and precision of language are concerned, Varro[360] is not inferior to Cicero, and Caesar ranks higher.[361] Nor was Marcus Tullius the originator and begetter of the Roman tongue[362] – he was its finest orator, and the one with the most dazzling reputation in civil cases; in other types of case he was inferior to quite a number of speakers; in poetry he was lame; in translating from Greek not particularly happy; what he would have been in other spheres we cannot tell. If I have to speak about marriage, which is now very differently constituted from what it was in ancient times, and is a subject on which Cicero didn't write, shall I hesitate to draw ideas and words from Aristotle,[363] Xenophon,[364] Plutarch,[365] the Bible, Tertullian,[366] Jerome,[367] and Augustine,[368] for fear of someone thinking me unciceronian? If I have to lecture on agriculture, will it not be right to cull suitable material from Virgil,[369] Cato,[370] Varro,[371] and Columella?[372]

If whatever is new and recently come into the world is considered barbarous, every word must have been at one time barbarous. How many new words will you find even in Cicero – especially in the works where he is dealing with rhetoric or philosophy? Who before Cicero ever heard the words *beatitas, beatitudo*[373] 'happiness'? What would Latin speakers understand by *finis bonorum*[374] 'delimitation of the good'? He uses it to mean the ultimate good, or that wherein lies supreme happiness, according to the various theories. What do we make of *visum, visio, species*[375] 'mental picture,' *praepositum* and *reiectum*[376] 'thing advanced, thing relegated'? What would speakers of Latin make of *occupatio* 'forestalling of argument,' *contentio* 'antithesis,' *superlatio* 'hyperbole,' *complexio* 'résumé,' *traductio* 'transference,' *frequentatio* 'condensed recapitulation,' *licentia* 'speaking plainly,' *gradatio* 'climax,' *status, constitutio*, and *iudicatio* 'point at issue, or definition,' *continens, firmamentum* 'central argument or foundation,' *demonstrativum genus* 'epideictic type,' *inductio* 'arguing from analogy,' *propositum* 'premise,' *aggressio* 'rhetorical syllogism,' *insinuatio* 'indirect approach,' *acclamatio* 'clinching remark,' and innumerable other words which were either unknown hitherto in Latin and boldly invented out of the blue by Cicero or given a meaning by him which was not recognized by the Roman man in the street? Cicero was not afraid to do this when passing on the doctrines of Greek philosophers to a Latin-speaking audience, in spite of the outcry of his contemporaries; and when he wished to expound the teaching of the rhetorical theorists, he used the special vocabulary developed for the requirements of the subject and admitted quite a number of foreign words to Roman citizenship.[377] Are we then to think it a dreadful sin if we use a few new words to fit a new situation?

Every sphere of human activity is allowed[378] the right of employing its own technical terms: we permit grammarians to say 'supine' and 'gerund,' mathematicians to say 'three over two' and 'five over three';[379] farmers and smiths have words belonging to their particular skills. Shall we be bringing the sky down[380] on our heads if we use the proper words to expound the mysteries of our religion? Some of these were words imported at the same time as the things they signified. A few were Hebrew in origin, many were Greek, since the philosophy of Christ first came to us from Palestine, Asia Minor, and Greece. I mean words like hosanna, amen, ecclesia, apostle, bishop, catholic, orthodox, heretic, schism, charisma, dogma, chrism, Christ, baptize, Paraclete, evangel, evangelize, evangelist, proselyte, cate- chumen, exorcism, Eucharist, symbol,[381] anathema. Others of these words were brought into use by the early teachers of the Christian religion to facilitate discussion of such transcendent themes, words like ὁμοούσιος, which we translate into Latin as consubstantialis 'consubstantial,' and fides, gratia, Mediator 'faith, grace, Mediator,' etcetera, which were either un- known to speakers of Latin before or used in a different sense. Shall we set such store by the name of Ciceronian that we either hold our tongues on the only subjects it has ever been our duty to talk about or else reject the words handed on by the apostles or introduced by our founding fathers, received up to this very day by the consensus of all the intervening centuries, and instead think up something or other to take their place as the fancy moves us? The Greeks, followed by the Romans, adopted the native names for honey, pepper, and mustard when they introduced the substances. Shall we by contrast turn up our noses at a group of expressions which we have received together with that marvellous heavenly philosophy, transmitted to us from hand to hand via Christ, the apostles, and the Fathers on whom the Holy Spirit breathed, and instead go running to Cicero in order to raise words from him? That's putting 'sweet oils on lentils,'[382] as the Greek proverb says.

If anyone took strict issue with us on this, he would be more likely to say that the majesty of the philosophy of Christ was defaced by words, figures, and rhythms from Cicero. Not that I would agree – I like grace and attractiveness of style, whatever the subject. But I won't have it that a man is speaking in Ciceronian manner, if, being a Christian, he speaks to Christians on a Christian subject in the way that Cicero, being a pagan, once spoke to pagans on non-Christian subjects; but only if he speaks as Cicero would be likely to speak if he were living today as a Christian among Christians, endowed with his original native ability and his oratorical experience, possessed of the same understanding of our concerns that he once had of pagan ones, inspired, finally, with love and loyalty for the Christian world as he was once fired with pride and passion for the city of Rome and the honour of the Roman name. Let anyone who can proffer all this step forward, and we shall without argument allow him to be named a Ciceronian, if it really matters to him so much to have this title. If Marcus Tullius himself were living in our world, he would consider the name God the Father no less felicitous than that of Jupiter Optimus Maximus and would think his style no less enhanced by constant reference to Jesus Christ than by the naming of Romulus, Scipio Africanus, Quintus Curtius, or Marcus Decius.[383] He would think 'Catholic church' no less grand than 'conscript fathers'[384] or 'Quirites'[385] or 'senate and people of Rome.'[386] He would join us in saying 'faith in Christ,' he would say 'infidels' for those alienated from Christ, he would say 'the Spirit, the Paraclete' and 'Holy Trinity.' One can find good evidence to support what I say. Did an overriding concern for choice diction prevent him from using words in the *Philippics*[387] that were hallowed by custom rather than good Latin, when he recited the formula for a decree of the senate? Doesn't he, in the *Topica*,[388] use legal terminology quite irreconcilable with rhetorical polish? Would such a man have scorned the words proper to our philosophy?

Nosoponus You seem to me at any rate to be making a very good speech yourself.

Bulephorus Furthermore, doesn't the attractiveness of a passage depend to a large extent on the flavour given it by allusions? And where does Marcus Tullius get his flavourings from, if not from Homer,[389] Euripides,[390] Sophocles,[391] Ennius,[392] Lucilius,[393] Accius,[394] Pacuvius,[395] Naevius,[396] and the philosophers and historians?

Nosoponus I quite agree. Without ornaments of this sort speech is mean and banal. They make a passage striking, like jewels and trimmings woven into fabric.

Bulephorus Suppose we were to look for ours in Virgil,[397] Horace, Ovid, Seneca,[398] Lucan,[399] and Martial.[400] We shan't be counted different from Cicero on that score, surely?

Nosoponus It's passable, but only just. After all, Cicero does get a touch of grandeur from quoting authors of such antiquity.

Bulephorus Well then, Cicero, being a pagan, gets his flavourings from pagans. So how does it come about that we consider we've polluted the whole speech if we derive ours from the most ancient prophets, from Moses, the Psalms, the Gospels, and the Letters of the apostles? We think we've added a marvellous jewel if we incorporate into our speech some dictum of Socrates'. Why do we think it's a blot if we introduce one of Solomon's proverbs? Do we find Solomon repellent compared with Socrates? Our words light up if we throw in some line from Pindar[401] or Horace, are dull and mean if we weave in an apt quotation from the Psalms. Weight and dignity are added if we insert some pronouncement of Plato's, but the moment we add one of Christ's sayings from the Gospels the passage ceases to please. What's the reason for this preposterous opinion? Do we feel greater admiration for Plato's wisdom than for Christ's? Are the books written under the inspiration of the heavenly Spirit contemptible beside Homer, Euripides, Ennius? But let's not speak of the Holy Spirit here, so that we don't seem to compare the human with the divine. Take history. If the author is not to be trusted, it doesn't deserve even the name of history. So just compare, if you please, Herodotus,[402] that teller of tales, with Moses; compare the account of the creation of the world and the departure from Egypt with the fables of Diodorus;[403] compare the books of the Judges and the Kings with Livy,[404] who doesn't even write a consistent account of Rome's exploits, let alone a true one; compare Plato with Christ, Socrates' 'irony'[405] with Christ's heavenly pronouncements; compare the Psalms,[406] breathing nothing of man, with Pindar's flatteries;[407] compare the song of Solomon with Theocritus' trifles.[408] Whether you consider the authors or their subjects, there is no point of comparison. The divine wisdom has its own special eloquence, nor is it surprising that it is very different from Demosthenes' or Cicero's, since one garb suits the consort of a great king, another a swaggering soldier's mistress. If anyone were to start comparing the words of one group with the other, the figures, the rhythms, I would probably say: Does 'Thessalian Tempe'[409] really sound more delightful in our ears than 'Mount Sion'? Is 'the gift of the immortal gods' really more majestic than 'the gift of God the Father'?[410] Is 'Socrates, son of Sophroniscus' really more pleasing to our ears than 'Jesus, Son of God, and God'? Why do our ears get more pleasure from 'Hannibal,[411] commander-in-chief of the Carthaginians' than from 'Paul, teacher of the gentiles'? If you weigh the two persons, one worked to destroy the Roman world, while the other brought it the philosophy of salvation. But if you compare the words, is there anything, I ask you, to make one group superior to the other?

Hypologus To be honest, only the thing which carries more weight with people than anything else – prejudice, some idea that has really got into our systems. We have accepted the belief, we have let it take root in our minds, that one set of words is polished and brilliant, and the other ugly and uncivilized.

Bulephorus You've hit the nail on the head.[412] But whatever gave us such an idea in the first place?

Hypologus I don't know.

Bulephorus Perhaps it really is so?

Hypologus I don't think so.

Bulephorus Would you like me to speak frankly, to tell the complete and utter truth?

Hypologus Certainly, as far as I'm concerned.

Bulephorus I'm waiting to hear what Nosoponus says.

Nosoponus Claim the rights we conceded when you made your conditions.

Bulephorus But I'm afraid that what I'm going to say won't seem very Ciceronian.

Nosoponus That doesn't matter.

Bulephorus It's paganism,[413] believe me, Nosoponus, sheer paganism, that makes our ears and minds accept such an idea. The fact is we're Christians only in name. Our bodies may have been dipped in the holy water, but our minds are unbaptized. The sign of the cross may have been put on our brows, but the cross itself is repudiated by the mind within. We have Jesus on our lips, but it's Jupiter Optimus Maximus and Romulus that we have in our hearts. Otherwise, if we really were what we are said to be, what name underneath the sun should we hear or think of with more delight than the name of Jesus? He it is who has snatched us from disaster, his free generosity calls us to high honour and invites us to eternal bliss; wicked spirits, the implacable foes of the human race, tremble at the sound of his name; spiritual intelligences bow the neck and knee. So mighty is it that, as soon as it is invoked, demons flee, incurable diseases yield, the dead are restored to life; so gentle and kind is it that no calamity, however bitter, is not comforted and alleviated if you name Jesus from your heart. And do we really convince ourselves that his name dims the lustre of a speech while Hannibal[414] and Camillus[415] are pure spots of light? We must destroy this paganism, tear it out, expel it from our minds, bring a truly Christian heart to our reading, and then we shall see the name of Jesus as a brilliant star whenever it appears; the name of the Virgin Mother or of Peter and of Paul will seem a splendid jewel; we shall feel that beauty has been added when we find incorporated some saying drawn from the sanctuary of the sacred books, from the Holy Spirit's storehouse of oils and perfumes – provided it is brought in at the right moment, provided it is brought in with sincerity. That, we shall feel, makes the writer's style far more impressive than if he quoted ten thousand of Ennius' and Accius'[416] finest sayings.

Hypologus By quoting them, at least one avoids being accused of heresy by the theologians!

Bulephorus As for style, insofar as it depends on the employment of rhetorical tropes and figures, we are there on a level with Cicero; in faith and grandeur of subject-matter we are his superiors by far. But when it comes to vocabulary, our pagan way of thinking imposes on us; because our affections are not sufficiently Christian we judge falsely. We find what is essentially beautiful unattractive because we don't love it. Indeed I suspect that we hate it. To the eye of love even what is not beautiful becomes beautiful, as Theocritus[417] said, so it can't find hateful what isn't ugly in the first place.

Let's turn now to allusions. If you do away with these, as you yourself know, speech loses much of its attractiveness. Why should we get so much more pleasure from someone writing 'vetch among the vegetables'[418] to mean someone embarrassingly in the wrong social group rather than 'Saul among the prophets'?[419] or saying 'sweet oils on lentils'[420] rather than 'gold ring in a pig's snout'[421] for something done or said in an inappropriate place; or, to mean that one should trust to a clear conscience rather than good luck, saying 'put your trust in your sheet-anchor'[422] rather than 'stand on the solid rock'?[423] Suppose someone wants to express the idea that the duty of a good man is to consider the well-being of others rather than his own personal advantage. Is he to say 'nothing is more unchristian than doing what the Aspendian lyre-player[424] did,' or is he to allude to the verse in Paul's epistle[425] and say 'one should consider what is lawful rather than what is expedient'? If I were to deal with this topic thoroughly there would be enough material for a whole book, so I'll be content just to have given an idea of it.

How we gasp and gaze in admiration if we get hold of a statue of one of the gods of the ancient world, even a bit of a statue; but the images of Christ and his saints get hardly a glance from our prejudiced eyes. How we enthuse over some inscription, some epitaph discovered on a crumbling stone: 'To my splendid wife Lucia who perished before her time. Set up by Marcellus and dedicated to the spirits of the dead. Alas, why do I yet live?' This sort of thing is usually full of foolish pagan ideas, and dreadful grammar mistakes besides; yet we love it, we adore and practically worship its antiquity. What the apostles have left us we treat with contempt. If anyone were to produce a bit of the Twelve Tables,[426] wouldn't we all set it up in a holy of holies? But which of us adores, which of us worships the laws written on tables[427] by the finger of God? Our prize possessions are coins stamped with the image of Hercules, Mercury, Fortune, Victory, Alexander the Great, or one of the Caesars; and we laugh at the superstition of those who treasure the wood of the cross or pictures of the Trinity and the saints. If you have ever observed those museums[428] of the Ciceronians at Rome, just recollect whether you have ever noticed in any of them a crucifix or a representation of the Trinity or the apostles. No, everything is full of the monuments of paganism. In paintings our gaze is held more by Jupiter coming down through the roof into Danaë's lap[429] than by Gabriel announcing[430] the heavenly conception to the holy Virgin; we get far more delight from Ganymede[431] snatched up by the eagle than from Christ ascending into heaven; our eyes dwell on representations of the festivals of Bacchus[432] and Terminus,[433] full of vice and obscenity, rather than on Lazarus[434] recalled to life or Christ baptized[435] by John. These are the mysteries which lurk under the veil of Cicero's name. Believe you me, under cover of a fair-seeming label snares are laid for our young persons, who are unsuspecting and vulnerable to misrepresentation. We dare not profess paganism openly, so we camouflage it with the name of Ciceronian. Surely it would be better to be dumb than to get into this state of mind?

Nosoponus I thought you were going to help our endeavours, but you've somehow moved on to another question, and you're undermining my resolution instead.

Bulephorus I've already said, and I now repeat it, that I am not trying to deflect your mind from its noble undertaking, but to point it to what really is the best; and I never meant to suggest that you yourself show any sign of the attitude I've been describing. What I am really trying my hardest to do is make sure that our pursuit of Ciceronian eloquence is successful, to prevent us going about it on wrong principles, so that, in spite of our application to the task, in spite of all our determination to be recognized as Ciceronians, that is the last thing we are in the end – provided of course that you allow what you conceded earlier to stand, namely that the real mark of Cicero is speaking in the way that is best, that no one can even speak well if he does not speak in a manner appropriate to his subject, and that any speech that does not come from the heart is cold and dead.

Nosoponus Well then, how are we going to be made genuinely Ciceronian? I've no objections to following a plan of yours if you've got a better one than mine.

Bulephorus I have something I can wish for all of us, something I can suggest to you, but beyond that not much. I can wish that we had the ability and natural gifts of Cicero, but I can't give them to us. Every one of us has his own personal inborn characteristics, and these have such force that it is useless for a person fitted by nature for one style of speaking to strive to achieve a different one. As the Greeks say, no one ever succeeded in battling with the gods.[436]

Nosoponus Quintilian,[437] I know, emphasizes that point.

Bulephorus So the first thing I would say is that no one should endeavour to copy Cicero if his natural bent is totally different from Cicero's. Otherwise he will finish up as some kind of monstrosity, having lost his own natural form and not having acquired anyone else's. It is essential to ask yourself first of all what style of speaking you are fitted for by nature, for, if we have any faith in the astrologers, no one finds it easy to succeed in anything which his horoscope says is not in his stars. The natural musician will not be successful as a soldier; the natural soldier will never write satisfactory poetry; the man who is fitted by nature for marriage will never be a good monk; the one who enjoys farming will never get on at court, and vice versa.

Nosoponus All the same, there is no difficulty which can't be surmounted by unremitting toil.[438] We see human ingenuity turning stones to water, lead to silver, bronze to gold, human care making plants throw off their wild nature. What is to prevent a man's nature being transformed by skill and practice?

Bulephorus The care of man assists nature where it is already going in the right direction, adjusts it when it is slightly astray, corrects it when faulty; but you will meddle in vain,[439] my dear Nosoponus, with a nature which is totally out of harmony and fitted for something quite different. You can teach a horse to go round in circles and step in time, but it is no good taking an ox to the wrestling school,[440] or expecting a dog to pull a plough, or a buffalo to take part in a horse-race. Water possibly turns to air, and air to fire, if fire is indeed an element; but earth never turns to fire, nor fire to water.[441]

Nosoponus Still, what's to prevent us applying Cicero's phraseology to any subject?

Bulephorus I quite agree that Cicero has some general characteristics which can be applied whatever the subject matter, things like lucidity, clarity, correctness of language, good arrangement, and so on; but this isn't enough for Cicero's apes, they must have total similarity in the very wording. This is indeed possible in certain subjects not too remote from Cicero, but it just will not work in those which are absolutely and entirely different. You would be prepared, I imagine, to allow that Virgil holds first place[442] among Latin poets, as Cicero does among orators?

Nosoponus I would.

Bulephorus Well then, if you were setting about writing a lyric poem, would you take as your model Horace or Virgil?

Nosoponus Why, Horace – he's the greatest in that branch[443] of poetry.

Bulephorus And if you were writing satire?

Nosoponus Horace even more.

Bulephorus Suppose you were thinking of a comedy?

Nosoponus Then I'd look to Terence for my example.

Bulephorus Obviously because of the vast difference in subject.

Nosoponus All the same, Cicero's way of expressing things has a certain something – I don't know what it is – an effect of being just right that you don't find in anyone else.

Bulephorus And I could reply in as many words: I don't know what it is. Many people are misled by their excessive adulation of Cicero – applying Cicero's phraseology to quite unciceronian subject-matter means not being like him at all.[444]

Besides, it isn't necessary to aim at being identical if one can manage to be equal, or at any rate not far behind, even if different. The emerald and ruby are very different, yet they are equally valued and admired. The rose is totally unlike the lily, and has a different perfume, yet neither flower is superior to the other. You must often have seen two girls who were quite different to look at, but both so pretty that it would be difficult to choose between them if you were asked to. As we started saying earlier, the closest copy of Cicero isn't automatically the best. No animal is more like man in all its physical features than the ape; if it had the power of speech in addition, it could be taken for a man. Nothing is less like a man than a peacock or a swan; but you would, I imagine, prefer to be a swan or a peacock rather than an ape.

Hypologus Personally, I'd rather be a camel or a buffalo than the handsomest of apes.

Bulephorus Tell me, Nosoponus, would you rather be given the voice of the nightingale or the cuckoo?

Nosoponus The nightingale.

Bulephorus Yet the cuckoo sounds more like a human voice. Would you rather sing with the lark or croak with the crow?

Nosoponus Sing with the lark.

Bulephorus Yet the crow's voice is more like a man's. Would you rather bray with the ass,[445] or neigh with the horse?

Nosoponus Neigh with the horse, if I were forced to do one or the other.

Bulephorus Yet the ass makes a sort of effort to talk like a human being.

Nosoponus But I don't think my natural genius does run in a direction all that different from Cicero's. Besides I shall make up by thought what is lacking in nature. So produce that advice you promised.

Bulephorus You do well to recall me to our main line of argument, as I was about to digress again. The crux of the whole matter is that we want genuinely to achieve our object and reproduce Cicero in his entirety, yet Cicero doesn't exist in his entirety, as we made plain enough earlier; he is hardly half there in fact, whether we think of vocabulary, idiom, rhythms, or corpus of writings.

Nosoponus Where does he exist in his entirety then?

Bulephorus Nowhere except in himself. But if you want to express the whole Cicero you cannot express yourself, and if you do not express yourself your speech will be a lying mirror. It will be just as ridiculous as painting your face and pretending to be Petronius[446] instead of Nosoponus.

Nosoponus You talk in riddles.

Bulephorus I'll put it more bluntly. Torturing oneself to reproduce Cicero in his entirety by your sort of method is to behave like a fool. It's impossible, even if it were any use; and it wouldn't be any use if it were possible. The only way Cicero can be reproduced in his entirety is if we try not to copy those virtues of his exactly, but to produce something equally good after the pattern set by him, or, if we can, something even better. It may well be that the most Ciceronian person is the one least like Cicero, the person, that is, who expresses himself in the best and most appropriate way, even though he does so in a manner very different from Cicero's – which would hardly be surprising, considering that everything has been completely altered. We can compare the situation in which someone who in his youth sat for Apelles[447] has his portrait painted again in his old age. He will now be quite altered, and if the second artist wants to paint him exactly as Apelles painted him, that very fact will make this artist different from Apelles.

Hypologus Now you're producing a riddle fit for the Sphinx,[448] if a person is to be unlike someone else at the very point where he is like him.

Bulephorus Wouldn't we have the same situation if someone sang at a funeral the way Hermogenes[449] used to sing songs for a wedding or made a speech in the high court of the Areopagus[450] using the sort of movements Roscius[451] would use on the stage? However, we may legitimately endeavour to be just like Cicero in one thing. We may pursue the palm of eloquence along the same paths by which Cicero attained it.

Nosoponus And what were they?

Bulephorus He didn't sentence himself to imitate one person only, did he? No, he found in every great orator[452] something that lent itself particularly to imitation. And here Demosthenes was his chief, but not his sole model; and even Demosthenes he did not consider a model to be imitated in his entirety – he picked out what appealed to him. Nor did he follow him passively, but rejected certain features by the exercise of deliberate choice, and corrected others. And even where he judged him good, he still challenged him and endeavoured to improve on the original. Secondly, he filled the store-chambers of his mind to bursting by studying the authorities on every subject, by reading up every topic old and new; he made himself thoroughly familiar with the history of leading Roman families,[453] with his country's rites, institutions, laws, decrees, and resolutions; not only was he an eager dweller in the inner chambers of the philosophers, but he frequently withdrew to the secret haunts of the Muses; from some experts[454] he learnt the art of delivery, from others the art of gesture. Now anyone who copies Cicero in the detail of all this, doing exactly what he did, will finish up quite unlike Marcus Tullius, but the person who does something equivalent or similar to what Cicero did, will in fact turn out someone to whom we can give the title 'Ciceronian.'

Nosoponus Do please be a little more explicit.

Bulephorus I mean the person who studies Christian philosophy with as much application as Cicero did pagan philosophy; who drinks in the psalms and prophets with as much enthusiasm as he did the poets; who works as hard and as long to understand the commands of the apostles, the rites of the church, the origins, progress, and decline of the Christian world as he laboured to grasp the rights and laws governing the provinces, municipalities, and allied states associated with the city of Rome; who, finally, adapts all he has learnt by such studies to suit his present situation. He will have some right to claim the title of Ciceronian.

Nosoponus The only effect all that will have, it seems to me, is to make us speak in a Christian way, not a Ciceronian one.

Bulephorus But surely you won't consider anybody a Ciceronian if he doesn't speak in a way that fits his subject, and doesn't understand what he's talking about?

Nosoponus Of course not.

Bulephorus But this is what does result from the endeavours of our present day would-be Ciceronians. The purpose of our inquiry is to prevent it happening to us. There is nothing to stop a person speaking in a manner that is both Christian and Ciceronian, if you allow a person to be Ciceronian when he speaks clearly, richly, forcefully, and appropriately, in keeping with the nature of his subject and with the circumstances of the times and of the persons involved. Some people have indeed suggested[455] that the ability to speak well is not a question of skill but of judgment. Cicero himself neatly defines eloquence in his *Partitiones*[456] as 'sense expressing itself with fluency,' nor is there any doubt that this is the type of eloquence that he himself practised. But good God! how far short of this definition those people fall who endeavour to speak in Ciceronian fashion on subjects which are totally and in every respect alien from Cicero, which moreover they neither understand nor care for. This idea that everything that diverges from Cicero is a disgusting example of bad Latin is a pernicious hallucination which we must banish from our minds if we are to win among Christians the reputation that Cicero won among his contemporaries. 'Good sense is of writing well the source and starting point,' as that most acute of critics[457] said. So what then is the proper source of an eloquence worthy of Cicero? An understanding richly supplied with a thorough knowledge of all kinds of subjects, especially the ones you have decided to talk about, an understanding prepared by theory, by much practical experience in writing and speaking, and by long thinking on the subject; and, the fountain-head of the whole activity, a heart that genuinely loves what it proclaims and genuinely hates what it attacks. Combined with these there must be capacity for judgment, common sense, and discernment, which as gifts of nature cannot be part of any instruction in the art. I ask you, from what source will those people acquire all this, who read nothing but Cicero, who desire no author but Cicero to 'thumb by night and thumb by day'?[458]

Nosoponus All the same, that was a neat observation about people who have been out in the sun for some time going brown, and those who have sat for any length of time in a perfumer's shop carrying the scent of the place away with them when they go.[459]

Bulephorus I find that a very good comparison. All they carry away is a colouring of the skin and a faint aroma that soon vanishes. Anyone who is satisfied with that kind of achievement may sit as much as he likes among Cicero's perfume jars and rose beds or bask in his sunshine. I would prefer to take internally any fine aromatic substances that are going and get them into my system, so that I don't just scatter a whiff of perfume over the people near me, but am myself thoroughly heated and invigorated, and then, whenever the occasion demands, a voice will issue forth which can be recognized as the product of a sound, well-nourished personality. A speech that holds the hearer's attention, that moves him, that sweeps him away on some tide of emotion, is born out of the depths of the speaker's person, not out of his skin. I don't mean to suggest that the material available in Cicero is either unremarkable or in any way unsatisfactory, but that he alone will not prove an adequate source for a rich treatment of any and every subject. In short, we must learn how to imitate Cicero from Cicero himself. Let us imitate him as he imitated others. If he settled down to reading a single author,[460] if he submitted himself to one single guide and mentor, if he thought concern for words more important than concern for matter, if he never wrote except at bedtime, if he tortured himself for a whole month over one letter, if he thought anything eloquent that did not fit with his subject, then let us do the same in order that we may become Ciceronians. But if this is all very different from what Cicero did, let us instead follow his real practice: let us make sure our minds are thoroughly equipped with the necessary knowledge; let us first take care of what to say[461] and only then of how to say it, and let us fit words to matter, not the other way round; and while we are speaking let us never lose sight of what is appropriate to the subject. A speech comes alive only if it rises from the heart, not if it floats on the lips. Let us be acquainted with the theory of our art, for it has much to contribute to invention, arrangement, treatment of arguments, and the avoidance of whatever is irrelevant or indeed damaging to our case. If a genuine case has to be argued, let us give first place to sound judgment, though even in fictitious cases handled for practice, it is a good thing if what is said sticks to the realms of probability.[462]

Cicero[463] wrote that the mind of Laelius breathed in Laelius' written word; but it is stupid to try deliberately to write in another man's humour and endeavour to have Marcus Tullius' mind breathing in what you write. All that you have devoured in a long course of varied reading must be thoroughly digested and by the action of thought incorporated into your deepest mental processes, not your memory or word-list. Then your mind, fattened on fodder of all kinds, will generate out of its own resources not a speech redolent of this or that flower or leaf or herb, but one redolent of your personality, your sensitivities, your feelings, and the reader will hail not snippets abstracted from Cicero, but the manifestation of a mind packed with every kind of knowledge.

Cicero had read every one of his predecessors, and he had decided after careful thought where each of them merited approval or criticism; yet you cannot recognize any one of them specifically in Cicero, only the force of a mind invigorated by all that they had to say. If the example of your idol does not convince you, let us look at the examples offered us by nature. Bees don't collect the material for making honey from just one bush, do they? No, they flit in their wonderful busy way round every type of flower, herb, and bush, often going far afield for the stuff to store in their hive. And what they bring is not honey to begin with. They turn it into a liquid in their mouths and inner parts, and then reproduce it, transmuted into their own substance; in it one recognizes not the taste or smell of any flower or shrub the bee has sipped, but a creation of the bee itself, compounded from all the contributory elements.[464] Similarly, goats don't feed always on the same kind of leaf in order to produce the milk peculiar to their species, but find nourishment in every kind of greenery, and what they produce is not the juice of plants but the milk into which they have transformed them.

Nosoponus Yes, but all the same it matters where the bee collects the honey-juice, or what leaves the goats eat. Yew makes the honey poisonous,[465] and the milk tastes different according to whether the goat has fed on oak or willow leaves.

Bulephorus I quite agree. But let's take a look at craftsmen. Do people who are hoping to become famous as sculptors or artists confine themselves to emulating one single skilled hand? As they seek to become masters of their craft, don't they rather pick out the separate features that appeal to them in the various masters, and imitate them with the intention of improving on them if they can? If an architect sets out to create a splendid mansion, does he derive all the details from one single building? Of course he doesn't – he uses his judgment to select successful features from several buildings. He will not acquire much of a reputation if the observer recognizes that this or that building has been copied in its entirety. Yet it would be more tolerable to follow a model slavishly in a building than in a speech. So what reason have we for confining ourselves so scrupulously to Cicero alone?

People go wrong twice over when they not only tie themselves to a single lesson book but also, coming quite unprepared by any rhetorical theory, read no one but Cicero, and do no more than read him. What is the use of fixing your eyes on Cicero unless you bring eyes that are trained? How will it help me to sit looking all day at pictures by Apelles and Zeuxis[466] if I know nothing about painting? But suppose you have studied oratorical theory, and suppose some skilled practitioner then takes a number of speeches in which Cicero's expertise is particularly displayed, and points out to you[467] the tone, the basis or ground, the nicely devised propositions,[468] the order in which these are presented, the way they are distributed under heads, discussed, amplified, and rounded off, the way the introduction contains the germ of all that is to come later, the way the individual sections are linked together, the exercise of judgment and the ability to make the right decision, which can be observed but not taught by rules; suppose he points out to you the orator's wise handling of the case, his reasons for dealing with each topic in the place he has chosen, his reasons for omitting some things and postponing others, his methods in manipulating the two types of emotion,[469] and finally points out the clarity, grandeur, and richness of his style, then you will perceive wonders in Cicero that our inveterate spectator never perceives. No one who does not understand an art can imitate it, and no one can understand it unless he practises it. A work of art does sometimes give considerable pleasure to those who know nothing of art, but how little does such a man really see?

Nosoponus And where better to go for your art than to Cicero?

Bulephorus Yes indeed. No one was a more felicitous exponent[470] of it, no one was a more finished practitioner. But Quintilian's teaching was more detailed and covered a wider range – he doesn't just expound general principles but starts with the rudiments and sets out all the successive stages, the theory of rhetoric, its application, and the development of proficiency, including quite a lot of material that Cicero either omitted[471] or merely touched on in passing, for example, the whole problem of arousing emotion, the different types of aphorisms and their employment, the methods of amplification, the invention of propositions, their enumeration, and their treatment, the way the basis or ground of a case may be altered and how these bases may conflict, and the practice of reading, imitating, and composing. But while one should not be ignorant of theory, it is no use growing old over it. If we follow it too anxiously it makes us speak worse, when it was invented to make us speak well. Our skilful expositor will teach much more than a textbook. Quite a number of people, both Greek and Latin users, have tried to do without theory,[472] but, in my opinion, were not particularly successful. So we must be careful, my dear Nosoponus, not to do what they do, and after a quick sip of theory, believe we can turn into Ciceronians simply by industriously reading Cicero. If such people acquire anything of Cicero, it is nothing but a veneer, a reflection, a faint aura of him.

Nosoponus I quite agree that there are many people like that, Bulephorus, and I have never approved of their way of doing things.

Bulephorus These warnings are not intended for you – this song is sung for Hypologus and myself. And now, my dear friend, let us look without prejudice at this question: first of all whether it is proper, and secondly whether it is worth while, to pay so dearly in effort and lost sleep for the honour of the title 'Ciceronian.'

Nosoponus Nothing is more honourable, and what is honourable must be right and proper.

Bulephorus Let's look into this 'right and proper' concept first. You agree, I think, that Cicero's style would not have met with approval in the time of Cato the Censor,[473] as it was too elaborate and fancy to suit the standards of that age. Life was sober and frugal; so was speech. Why, even in Cicero's own time there were men who still breathed that primitive austerity, men like Cato of Utica, Brutus, and Asinius Pollio,[474] who wished for something sterner, less theatrical, more manly in Cicero's oratory; and that at a time when eloquence was at the height of its development, dominating the popular assembly, the chamber of the senate, the lawcourts, where indeed the jury expected[475] and even demanded of the advocates[476] an embellished style designed to please. Surely you don't think that something that was considered rather unmasculine in Cicero could be thought right and proper for Christians, whose philosophy of life is directed rather to good living than to stylish and elegant speaking, whose behaviour should be totally dissociated from anything that borders on artificiality and theatrical pleasure?

But suppose we allow it to be right, do you think the results justify the effort? The whole purpose of oratory is to persuade, but in this, how much more cogent Phocion was than Demosthenes,[477] Aristides than Themistocles,[478] how much more effective Cato than Cicero,[479] who on several occasions made things worse for the accused by speaking on their behalf, and helped to acquit them by appearing for the prosecution.[480] I am not interested at the moment in the fact that his oratory was magnificent indeed. It is a finer thing to be a Phidias[481] than to be a secretary or a cook, even though the work of these people is more essential to the country than Phidias' statues. The art of the painter and the sculptor came into existence for the purpose of delighting the eyes, and once it has done that it has fulfilled its function. But eloquence which does nothing but delight is not eloquence, for eloquence came into existence for quite a different purpose; and if it does not fulfil that purpose, it should not be considered a proper activity for a good man.

Yet even if we allow that Cicero's eloquence served some purpose in its time, what use is there for it today? In the lawcourts? But the business there is all conducted by means of clauses and sections and legal terminology, by procurators and advocates who are anything but Ciceronian, before adjudicators who would think Cicero a barbarian. There is not much more use for it in the council-chamber, where individuals put forward their views to a small group, and that's done in French or German. In any case, most business nowadays is carried out by privy council, attended by at most three men, usually of no great education; every one else is merely informed of their decisions. Even if Latin were the language in which administration was carried out today, who would put up with Cicero orating[482] his way through those speeches he delivered against Verres,[483] Catiline,[484] Clodius,[485] Vatinius?[486] What senate would have time and patience enough to endure the speeches he made against Antony,[487] even allowing for the fact that he delivered these at a time when his style was showing signs of age and had become less abundant and exuberant?

So how are we going to use this Ciceronian eloquence which costs so much effort to acquire? For addressing the public? The public doesn't understand the language of Cicero, and no matters of state are discussed with the public. As for sermons, this style of oratory is quite unsuitable. So what use will there be for it, except on diplomatic missions, which are conducted in Latin, especially at Rome, but from tradition rather than from conviction, and for ceremony rather than for any useful purpose? Practically nothing of a serious nature is dealt with on such occasions: the whole speech is taken up with the praises of the person to whom you are sent, and with protestations of good will on the part of the person by whom you are sent, and with a lot of platitudes. In short, the whole thing is of such a nature that it's an achievement if you avoid the appearance of flattery, when flattery itself is inevitable. The customary reply to this speech is even more tiresome: it's often heavily boring because the speaker goes on at such length; on many an occasion it's also embarrassing to the man who is being praised so immoderately, and risky as well as embarrassing to the speaker, for he gets into a sweat as he recites what he has learnt by heart, he gets stuck, and he loses the thread of what he is saying, either because he's forgotten it or because he's nervous. What appreciation should be accorded such a speech, when the performer has usually learnt it off after some professional rhetorician has worked it up? Our orator deserves no credit except for stamina in recitation. So nothing is done here except for the formal exchanges; the serious business is dealt with in private, through letters and conversations in French.

Well then, on what stage shall our Ciceronian seek to perform? Shall he write Ciceronian letters? But to whom? To scholars. Scholars are few and far between, and they care nothing for Ciceronian diction, so long as the text is wholesome, sensible, free from grammatical error, and learned. To whom then shall he write? To four Italians,[488] who have lately begun to proclaim themselves Ciceronians – though, as I have already shown, nothing is less like Cicero; they hardly possess even a faint reflexion of Cicero. Now if this achievement, such as it is, did not cost much, if it fell into our laps without effort, if it did not interfere with things of greater usefulness, then it would perhaps be something not to be rejected. As it is, you must ask yourself whether it is right to pay the price of so many long hours of work, so much hard effort, not without danger to your health, for the glory of being admitted by four silly young Italians into the catalogue of Ciceronians.

Nosoponus Don't you approve of the desire to speak well?

Bulephorus Marcus Tullius does not insist[489] that the philosopher be eloquent. Now can you think of any pagan philosopher so noble that you would consider him superior to any Christian?

Hypologus No indeed, the whole of Greek philosophy is evanescent and nugatory compared with the philosophy of Christ.

Bulephorus How then can we have the effrontery to insist that a Christian employ Ciceronian eloquence, which cannot be imitated in any case, and which the pagans considered hardly fitting for a man of serious disposition? A man who speaks differently from Cicero does not necessarily speak badly. And a man who speaks in a manner inappropriate to his subject certainly does not speak well. This cannot be said too often.[490] Besides, armour is useless if it is good only for display, and so is not even ready to hand when action calls. Sometimes pressing circumstances require us to write twenty letters in the same day. What shall my Ciceronian do then? In any case, how rare is the correspondent who would be charmed by a Ciceronian turn of phrase.

What of the fact that Cicero himself employs various styles? He appears in one guise when he is expounding philosophy in a quiet, easy-going, conversational style, in another when conducting a case, in another in his letters, where his language is for the most part unpolished and spontaneous. This is as a letter should be, for it supplies the place of an actual conversation between friends. It is surely preposterous to devote the same care to writing a personal letter as Cicero devoted to preparing his defence of Milo. Shall we expend a month's toil on a shortish letter that deals with something not particularly important? Not even Marcus Tullius would have been prepared to pay the price for the eloquence he displays in his forensic oratory if it had cost as many sleepless nights as one letter costs us, in spite of the fact that there were in his time so many opportunities in the state for employing eloquence, in spite of the fact that the pursuit of eloquence flourished at the public and private level, and that proficiency in it was much easier to acquire.

The student who tortured himself for days searching for a good opening phrase was rightly twitted[491] for trying to speak better than he could. There is in Cicero a happy facility which is the gift of nature, an inborn lucidity of expression. If nature has denied us this, why do we torment ourselves to no avail? Even crazier are the people who, in times that are quite different, when the whole scene of human activity has been changed, when there is hardly any use anywhere for Ciceronian oratory, wear themselves away to nothing in their consuming desire to be thought Ciceronians, and nothing but Ciceronians.

Nosoponus You're putting up a splendid case, to be sure, but I can't get free of this hankering of mine – it's got too deep a hold on my mind.

Bulephorus I am not trying to deflect you from a desire to emulate Cicero, provided it's kept within bounds, provided you emulate Cicero where he is best, provided you emulate rather than slavishly follow, provided you strive to be as good as your model rather than indistinguishable from him, provided you don't fight against your own natural bent, provided you don't seek to have your speech so fitted to Cicero that it doesn't fit your subject. Above all, you must avoid trying too hard, which is always disastrous, and never more so than in speaking. Finally, you must not feel that if you fail in your objective your life is ruined, and that existence as a non-Ciceronian is pointless, since there are thousands of educated men without this title who have won distinction during their lives and lasting reputation after their deaths.

Nosoponus Well, that's how I do feel right now.

Bulephorus I too felt like that once, but I recovered from the disease.

Nosoponus How did you manage it?

Bulephorus I sent for a doctor.

Nosoponus Please tell me who.

Bulephorus An eloquent and effective one.

Nosoponus But who was it?

Bulephorus Aesculapius[492] and Hippocrates[493] couldn't compare with him.

Nosoponus You're keeping me on tenterhooks.

Bulephorus There's not a doctor more readily available or kinder or more trustworthy: and he doesn't treat the liver or stomach, he heals a man in his inmost being.

Nosoponus If you grudge telling me his name, at least let me know the medicine.

Bulephorus You shall know the name and the medicine: it was Dr Word and he treated me with a course of reasonable words.[494]

Hypologus Naturally: 'The word has power to heal the sickness of the soul.'[495]

Bulephorus That's how I returned to life from that sickness, Nosoponus. Now if you will take over the role I've been playing up to now, I'll take the part of Dr Word.

Nosoponus Very well, if that's what you want.

Bulephorus When I was in the grip of a violent attack of the disease, the doctor began by saying, as I now say to you: Poor fellow, you are suffering from a nasty bout of false shame[496] caused by the fact that you can't take the insult you share with thousands of other men.

Nosoponus What insult do you mean?

Bulephorus The one of being refused the name of Ciceronian.

Nosoponus I must confess, that's what's giving me the pain.

Bulephorus But, for love of the Muses, tell me this – whom will you offer me as a Ciceronian apart from Cicero himself? Let's start with the early orators. In the extremely long catalogue which Cicero put together in the *Brutus*,[497] there are hardly two whom he honours with the title of orator, so it is even less likely they could be considered Ciceronians. Then take Julius Caesar.[498] He can't be called Ciceronian, because he lived at the same time as Cicero, and because he had chosen an entirely different style of speaking. His sole intention was to express himself in correct and appropriate Latin.[499] But what a tiny part of Cicero that represents. In any case, it's no very great achievement[500] for an orator to speak good Latin, though it's inexcusable if he can't. What's more, we have nothing of Caesar's except a few letters and his *Commentaries* on his own campaigns – though scholars are deeply divided on the question of the authorship[501] of these. At all events, there is no speech of his extant, and it was in oratory that Cicero was supreme. I could say the same of Caelius,[502] Plancus,[503] and Decius Brutus;[504] we have a fair number of letters written by them and preserved by the indefatigable Tiro;[505] rather fewer from Pompey, Cornelius Balbus, Lentulus, Cassius, Dolabella, Trebonius, Vatinius, Sulpicius, Aulus Caecina, Bithynicus,[506] Marcus Brutus, Pollio, Caesar,[507] and some miscellaneous other people, all of whom were contemporary with Cicero, so that one might just as well call Cicero a Caelian as Caelius a Ciceronian.[508] In these letters the only point of similarity is a lucid, straightforward, correct employment of the Latin language. But you do not find in this the whole Cicero you set up as your model. And what comment shall I make on Sallust,[509] who belonged to the same age as Cicero but is totally different from Cicero in style?

Nosoponus Just say nothing at all about those shaggy unkempt Ancients, writing when neither life nor eloquence had taken on any polish, nor about those people who ran their course together with Cicero. Bring on those who followed Cicero.

Bulephorus All right then. I don't suppose you consider Seneca[510] Ciceronian?

Nosoponus Anything but, especially in prose. For the tragedies[511] recognized by scholars don't look the sort of thing Seneca could have written.

Bulephorus What about Valerius Maximus?[512]

Nosoponus He resembles Cicero as much as a mule does a man. You would hardly think this writer came from Italy or lived when he apparently did, his whole style of expression is so eccentric. You would say he was some African[513] or other, with a style more mannered than you would ever find in poetry.

Bulephorus Suetonius[514] then?

Nosoponus He is quite a bit further removed from Cicero than Seneca is. Neither in vocabulary nor sentence structure nor lucidity nor use of figures nor in taste does he remind one of Cicero.

Bulephorus Do you consider Livy[515] worthy of this honour?

Nosoponus In the first place, he's a historical writer, secondly he's undisciplined; besides, several people said[516] his Latin smacked of his home town of Padua, meaning that he didn't write in a completely Roman fashion.

Bulephorus After that I don't dare to offer Tacitus.[517]

Nosoponus Nor would it be any use.

Bulephorus Perhaps you will admit Quintilian[518] to your list.

Nosoponus He made a point of being different even from Cicero. I wish his *Declamationes* were extant. The *Declamationes* we have[519] show very little of Cicero.

Bulephorus I've got someone you can't disapprove of – Quintus Curtius.[520]

Nosoponus He's a historical writer.

Bulephorus True, but there are quite a lot of speeches in his history.

Nosoponus He is more straightforward than the rest, but, as the proverb goes,[521] not a patch on Parmeno's pig.[522] Many of his usages differ from Cicero's.

Bulephorus If you will not have him, you will not, I imagine, have Aelius Spartianus, Julius Capitolinus, Aelius Lampridius, Vulcatius Gallicanus, Trebellius Pollio, Flavius Vopiscus,[523] and Aurelius Victor?[524]

Nosoponus Far from thinking them worthy of the name of Ciceronian, I can find hardly anything to approve in them, apart from a straightforward account of events. They don't do much to keep the wells of Latin undefiled!

Bulephorus Well, there's Aemilius Probus[525] for you.

Nosoponus He's so good natured, with his praise of the people whose lives he writes, that you would do better to call him an encomiast rather than a historical writer.

Bulephorus Perhaps you will have Ammianus Marcellinus.[526]

Nosoponus His expression is difficult, and his arrangement of words constantly suggests he's writing poetry, as for example in *ut captivos redderet nostros* 'our captives to restore.' I would sooner acknowledge Velleius Paterculus,[527] though I won't dignify him either with this honour.

Bulephorus You will acknowledge even less, I imagine, those who wrote epitomes[528] – Florus,[529] Eutropius,[530] and Solinus.[531]

Nosoponus I will acknowledge them if any scholar acknowledges them on the specific count of being Ciceronian. They certainly have something of the authors they are imitating.

Bulephorus But I must turn back in my course – we have forgotten the two Plinys.[532] I know you will not allow the elder to be mentioned here, perhaps you will admit the younger.

Nosoponus No indeed – strict guardians of standards in this matter absolutely forbid the young to touch his letters, for fear they will turn out Plinians, not Ciceronians.

Bulephorus But he was rather successful in the speech he wrote[533] in praise of Trajan.

Nosoponus Most successful, but he does not show us Cicero.

Bulephorus I deliberately pass over the poets, as I can easily guess what you are likely to say, even if I suggest the most famous and most gifted of all: Virgil, Horace, Ovid, Lucan, and Martial.[534]

Nosoponus Horace has no trace of Cicero; there is some similarity in Virgil, but not very marked; Ovid could be thought the Cicero of poets; Lucan has been described as more like an orator[535] than a poet, but he's one quite foreign to Cicero's type; Martial comes very close to Ovid's happy knack and we could allow him a little Ciceronian praise if he had not written prose epistles to preface a number of his books – good Lord, what unciceronian ones they are!

Bulephorus Suppose I bring forward Lucretius?[536]

Nosoponus You might just as well bring forward Ennius and Lucilius.[537]

Bulephorus Scholars admire Aulus Gellius'[538] brilliant phraseology.

Nosoponus Neither his content nor his diction will suit – the diction's affected, and almost too exuberant with its wealth of vocabulary, while the subject matter is in very short supply.

Bulephorus Macrobius[539] then?

Nosoponus Now you offer me Aesop's silly crow.[540] He's put together his patchwork out of bits filched from others, so he doesn't speak with his own voice; and if ever he does, you may well believe it's some poor Greek stammering in Latin.[541] Like that bit out of the second book of his commentary on the *Somnium Scipionis*:[542] *Et hoc esse volunt quod Homerus, divinarum omnium inventionum fons et origo, sub Poetici nube figmenti, verum sapientibus intelligi dedit* 'and this they claim to be that which Homer, of all divine discoveries the fount and source, beneath the cloak of a poetic fiction gave as truth to the wise for their understanding.'

Bulephorus Some see clever writing in Symmachus'[543] letters.

Nosoponus Let them, if their ambition is to be forced and tiresome.

Bulephorus I say, we've left out Apuleius.[544]

Nosoponus I'll compare him with Cicero when one takes it into one's head to compare a jackdaw with a nightingale.

Bulephorus I'll concede that as far as *The Golden Ass* and the *Florida* go, but in the *Apology* he approaches Cicero's standard.

Nosoponus Certainly he's not so far off, but he's still an enormous way behind. But you've also forgotten Martianus Capella,[545] if you want to propose writers like that.

Bulephorus Suppose we move on to those who were half-Christian. What do you think of Boethius?[546]

Nosoponus A fine philosopher, as a poet not the worst, but from Cicero's style far removed.

Bulephorus Ausonius?[547]

Nosoponus I concede him talent and learning. His writings, like his life, smack of the affectations and extravagance of the court. Far from being a Ciceronian he gives the impression of deliberately aiming at a style different from Cicero's. So it would be an insult, not an honour, to give him the title of Ciceronian, like calling a German someone who really was a German but who wanted to be thought a Frenchman.

Bulephorus Not to take you round all the byways, let's go to the Christians, if you like, to see if we can find one who deserves to be called Ciceronian. Among them you will, I imagine, give your approval to Lactantius,[548] who was said to flow[549] with the 'lactic' stream of Ciceronian eloquence.

Nosoponus So he was, but by one who was himself not a Ciceronian.[550]

Bulephorus But you can't deny that Lactantius did aspire to Ciceronian eloquence. That's made clear by the preface to the third book of his *Divinae institutiones*, where he is about to defend the truth of the philosophy of Christ, and prays for eloquence, if not actually Ciceronian, at least very like Cicero's.

Nosoponus His attempt was relatively successful, though not absolutely so.

Bulephorus How do you make that out?

Nosoponus Because at the beginning of his introduction[551] to that work he writes: *Alioqui nihil inter Deum hominemque distaret, si consilia et dispositiones illius maiestatis aeternae[552] cogitatio assequeretur humana*, 'otherwise there would be no difference between God and man if human thought could attain to the counsels and dispositons of that eternal majesty.' Where did Cicero ever use *dispositiones* in the sense of *decreta* 'decrees'?

Bulephorus So it was his very attempt to be like Cicero that made him unlike Cicero – it is indeed characteristic of Cicero to reinforce a single idea by using two words meaning the same or nearly the same thing, hence Lactantius' phrase *consilia et dispositiones*. For all you know, he may have aimed at hiatus between vowels in different words in order to be Ciceronian, as in *consilia et* and *cogitatio assequeretur*. Perhaps he deliberately sought a Ciceronian arrangement of words too, so as to produce a scazon[553] at the end of the sentence unit like Cicero's *balneatore* and *archipirata*. Lactantius frequently employs cadences of this sort in this very same preface, like *inhaerere* in the very first period, and *instruere possimus*, and a bit further on *apud Graecos*, and then *luce orationis ornata*, and then 'to do it again and again'[554] *honesta suspecta*, followed by *honorasti*, and shortly after *nominis tradas*, and again *ut sequerentur hortarer*, and a bit later again *reliquerunt*. He certainly copies a Ciceronian trick in often finishing with a double trochee,[555] as in *contulerunt, convocamus, sopiamus, inchoamus*, and once he has the closing cadence *quaesisse videatur*.[556] All this shows that he really endeavoured to write like Cicero. Yet one would be justified rather in excluding Lactantius from the title of 'Follower of Tully' on the grounds that he did not bring to the defence of the Christian philosophy the learning, the force, or the sensitivity which Marcus Tullius brought to the civil cases he defended. Of all the rest whom shall I cite first, or last? Cyprian?[557]

Nosoponus He wrote more like a Christian than a Ciceronian.[558]

Bulephorus Hilary?[559]

Nosoponus Goodness me, nothing like. His expression is difficult and obscure, and he strides about in his Gallic buskins, as the great man says,[560] trailing along a great string of words[561] which have no place in pure Ciceronian style.

Bulephorus Sulpicius,[562] I imagine, will seem worthy of the honour.

Nosoponus He is to be sure gentler and pleasanter and clearer and simpler than Hilary, but his style reveals him as Gallic.[563] He is certainly a man of piety, but is lacking in force and weight, and his manner of writing is florid rather than vigorous.

Bulephorus You will admit Tertullian[564] then?

Nosoponus You must be joking. He deliberately and of set purpose obscured good sentiments with bad words, and was more extreme even than Apuleius.[565]

Bulephorus Surely you will not reject the eloquent and learned Jerome.

Nosoponus I salute him as a man pre-eminent in knowledge and eloquence, but not as a follower of Tully – that flogging he received[566] turned him against the imitation of Cicero.

Bulephorus Well then, Augustine.

Nosoponus He has one Ciceronian characteristic – he does go round his subject with an enormous drawn-out period, but he hasn't much else, apart from this, and he doesn't reproduce[567] Cicero's ease of utterance or his mastery of treatment.

Bulephorus Paulinus?[568]

Nosoponus He has hardly a faint reflection of Cicero, being not particularly successful in what he says or how he says it.

Bulephorus Well then, Ambrose.[569]

Nosoponus You may see in him a Roman orator, but not a Ciceronian one. He delights in clever allusions and triumphant concluding remarks and talks entirely in aphorisms. With his long and short sentence units and his balanced number of syllables, he is rhythmical and melodious, which produces a style peculiar to himself and inimitable, but totally different from Cicero's.

Bulephorus At least recognize the Roman Gregory,[570] the first of the popes to bear that name.

Nosoponus I recognise a man of spirituality, who speaks his mind. In this he comes nearer to Cicero than Ambrose did, but his style is turbid,[571] and dominated by Isocratean canons[572] of arrangement, a feature quite foreign to Cicero – but that is what he was taught at school.

Bulephorus Leo the Tuscan[573] then, the first pope of Rome to bear that name. Everyone admires his eloquence.

Nosoponus His style is, I agree, nicely rhythmical and very clear, and expresses sound ideas, but it has no resemblance to Cicero.

Bulephorus Suppose I go to Burgundy and bring you Bernard?[574]

Nosoponus I recognize in him a good man, which is part of being an orator,[575] a man of inherent refinement with a natural charm of style, but so far from being a Ciceronian that you would hardly suspect from his writings that he had ever read Cicero.

Bulephorus Now you've rejected him, I wouldn't dare offer you Bede,[576] Remigius,[577] Claudius,[578] Hesychius,[579] Anselm,[580] or Isidore.[581]

Nosoponus Stop naming me persons who are just choppers and mutilators[582] of their adopted tongue; they spoil what they take from others; when they produce what is their own they can hardly speak at all. In them eloquence was very sick indeed.

Bulephorus I'm afraid you will say it was dead if I name those who came later. So I won't suggest Alexander of Hales,[583] Peter of Ghent,[584] and countless other writers of the same kidney;[585] but I will propose the two leaders of the troop, Bonaventure[586] and Thomas.[587]

Nosoponus Bonaventure has words in abundance, but they're of any and every sort; and Thomas is a complete Aristotelian, quite impassive in his writing, concerned only to inform the reader.

Bulephorus True enough in his *Quaestiones*. But when he takes the role of orator or poet, he has quite a strong suggestion of Cicero.

Nosoponus Poems[588] indeed! It seems to me that he reveals the least command of language precisely when he makes an attempt at fluency and fine writing, as he does when handling the subject of the Eucharist. But that's enough of those scholastic theologians. You will look in vain for any eloquence from them, let alone Ciceronian eloquence. Bring out some others, if you have any.

Bulephorus Very well, we will turn to another type of writer nearer to our own time.[589] Eloquence was to all appearances quite dead and buried for several generations, and didn't come to life again until quite recently among the Italians. With us it was even later. The leader in the rebirth of eloquence in Italy was, it seems, Francesco Petrarch,[590] a great and celebrated figure in his own time, but now hardly read at all. He had an ardent mind, a vast knowledge, and a not inconsiderable power of expression.

Nosoponus I quite agree. But there are places where one misses in him a real understanding of the Latin language, and his whole style suggests the lack of polish of an earlier age. Anyway, who could call him a Ciceronian, when he never even attempted to be one?

Bulephorus There is no point then in bringing in Biondo[591] and Boccaccio,[592] as they were his inferiors both in expressive force and in accurate employment of the Roman tongue. You will not listen even to Giovanni Tortelli.[593]

Nosoponus Not on these hustings at any rate.

Bulephorus He was followed by a great crop of learned persons who were all consciously vying with each other in imitation of Cicero. Is there any one of that number to whom you will grant the honour of this title? Francesco Filelfo[594] perhaps?

Nosoponus I would do so if he pleased the learned world as much as he pleased himself. Indeed, he strove earnestly to model himself on Cicero, but with no great success. He is nowhere less like Cicero than in the very place where he should have been most like him, I mean in his speeches. In his letters he offers a fair adumbration of Cicero. I am not trying to be disparaging – I acknowledge these as men who should be remembered forever by posterity, men who did great service to learning. But to be a Ciceronian is something not within the reach of ordinary mortals.

Bulephorus Leonardo of Arezzo[595] seems a second Cicero to me.

Nosoponus In ease of expression and in clarity he comes close enough to Cicero, but he is deficient in muscle and other oratorical virtues. There are times when he fails to preserve a pure Latin idiom, in spite of the fact that he was a man of learning as well as honour.

Bulephorus I know you won't agree to Guarino[596] or Lapo[597] or Acciaiuoli,[598] or to Antonio Beccaria,[599] Francesco Barbato,[600] Antonio Pasini[601] of Todi, or Leonardo Giustiniani,[602] or Achille Bocchi[603] (and there are others whose names I don't recall at the moment), the reason being that the only literary work most of them are known for is translations from the Greek, and in translation there is no credit for invention of material, which is a major part of eloquence.[604]

Nosoponus I despise none of them, but none of them will I honour with the title of Ciceronian.

Bulephorus Well, then, I will offer you Poggio[605] the Florentine, a man of lively eloquence.

Nosoponus He had a fair amount of natural ability, but needed more technique and knowledge – the Latin that poured out of him was at times disgustingly incorrect,[606] if we believe Lorenzo Valla.[607]

Bulephorus Very well, let's put Valla in his place.

Nosoponus He comes closer to Quintilian's care and attention to detail than to Cicero's unstudied ease, though he is more finished and has fewer faults than the rest.

Bulephorus I deliberately pass over the names of many whom your discriminating ear will undoubtedly reject; I mention only the most outstanding. You will certainly admit Ermolao Barbaro,[608] if anyone, to the honour of the title.

Nosoponus Now you have produced a truly great and inspired figure, but one whose style was very different from Cicero's, being more studied even than Quintilian's and Pliny's; and his interest in philosophy did nothing to improve it.

Bulephorus What about Giovanni Pico,[609] count of Mirandola?

Nosoponus There we have an absolutely superhuman genius, an intellect capable of everything, but his style too was marred by his interest in languages and philosophy and even theology.[610]

Bulephorus You are familiar with his relative Gianfrancesco Pico della Mirandola?[611]

Nosoponus He won't do by a long chalk, as they say. He's too much of a philosopher and a theologian, though otherwise a great man. But how can you justify naming him among Ciceronians? – when discussing imitation with Pietro Bembo,[612] he condemned the Cicero-imitators.

Bulephorus You've certainly given him very high praise, if indeed anyone can be too much of a theologian.

Nosoponus He can, in the running for this prize.[613]

Bulephorus Ah good, I've found one, I think, that you won't reject – Angelo Poliziano.[614] I daren't offer Marsilio Ficino.[615]

Nosoponus I quite agree that Angelo was endowed with angelic gifts;[616] a phenomenon, whatever kind of writing he turned his mind to, but there's no connection with Ciceronian style; he is to be admired for quite different virtues.

Bulephorus If I introduce into this troop Codro Urceo, George of Trebizond, Theodorus Gaza, Janus Lascaris, Georgio Merula, Marcus Musurus and Marullus,[617] I can more or less guess what you will say. You will disqualify the whole tribe of Greeks with whom your pet Cicero is so unpopular. However, I wouldn't like anger, hatred, or love to have a vote in this election.

Nosoponus Nor shall they have. As Lascaris[618] is still alive, we must not say too much about him. By his gracious manner he bears witness to the nobility of his birth.[619] He's a man of penetrating judgment, showing considerable incisiveness in his *Epigrams*. He might have been numbered among the candidates for the title of Ciceronian if his frequent involvement in diplomatic missions and the business of kings had not called him away from literary studies. As for Codro,[620] he could employ the Latin language with some skill, and was not without taste, but, being in agreement with Epicurus,[621] he was indifferent to this fame we are discussing, since he considered it something out of the ordinary run of things and not to be acquired cheaply. I acknowledge George of Trebizond[622] as a man of exceptional learning who did great service to literary studies, and Theodorus Gaza[623] as even more accomplished than he was. The former seems to have sought consciously to reproduce the idiom of Cicero; Gaza preferred to copy Aristotle. No one has been more successful than he in translating from Greek into Latin or from Latin into Greek. When he writes something original, two things grate on the fastidious reader: his passion for philosophy, in which he was totally absorbed, and that essential Greekness of speech which stays with Greeks when they speak Latin and which they hardly ever unlearn.

Bulephorus What is to prevent a Greek acquiring a perfect command of the Roman tongue, if Britons and Frisians can do so? Especially since the Greek language shows the greatest affinity to Latin in vocabulary and in turns of phrase?

Nosoponus I leave others to judge what success Britons and Frisians[624] have had. It seems to me that affinity of language is an obstacle to purity of usage. An Irishman is more likely to speak in pure Roman idiom than a Frenchman or a Spaniard. Just as a Frenchman will find it easier to speak good German than good Italian or Spanish. But to proceed with our list of candidates: I know Georgio Merula[625] came from Alexandria, but I don't know whether he was a Greek; his translations from Greek were impressive and elegant, such that he could be compared with many of the Ancients. As for Marullus,[626] I have read a few things of his, which would be tolerable if they displayed less paganism. I knew Marcus Musurus[627] personally, a man remarkably erudite in every discipline, but in his poetry unnatural and somewhat obscure; apart from one or two prefaces he left nothing in prose, as far as I know. I was surprised that a Greek knew so much Latin. He too was drawn away from the Muses by events, for he was summoned to Rome[628] by favour of Pope Leo, and had just become archbishop[629] when he died prematurely.

Bulephorus You will accept Pomponio Leto[630] then?

Nosoponus He contented himself with correct employment of the Latin language, and aimed at nothing beyond that.

Bulephorus Sacchi[631] then?

Nosoponus He would have been effective in writing history if he had found happier subject-matter. In his *De optimo cive* and his *Panegyricus* he makes some approach to reproducing Cicero, but he is still so far off that the literary world would not vote him the title of Ciceronian; though apart from that he was learned, eloquent, and if I am not mistaken,[632] a good man.

Bulephorus What about Filippo Beroaldo the Elder?[633] I can see, you are shaking your head, I knew it would be so.

Nosoponus No, I am nodding in agreement if you are commending me a man who has done noble service to literary studies; but if you are proposing that he should be inscribed on the list of Ciceronians, then I do refuse. I am more likely to accept Filippo Beroaldo the Younger,[634] though he actually wrote very little.

Bulephorus There would be little point in my listing Giorgio Valla,[635] Cristoforo Landino,[636] Mancinelli,[637] Pietro Marso,[638] Battista Pio,[639] Cornelio Vitelli,[640] the two Niccolòs, Leoniceno[641] and Leonico,[642] Bartolomeo Scala,[643] Paolo Cortesi,[644] Pietro Crinito[645] and Jacopo Antiquario.[646]

Nosoponus What a hotchpotch of a list that is, with all kinds of different people in it! You may ignore the likes of Mancinelli and Vitelli and Marso when eloquence is in question, and Battista Pio attempted a peculiar style of his own. Scala considered himself Cicero-like, but Poliziano didn't even consider him to have written Latin, in fact he didn't even give him credit for writing sense. I shall say something about Paolo Cortesi later.[647] Pietro Crinito is far from the Ciceronian stamp, though I salute the man's erudition. Leoniceno was a medical man, not a literary one. Leonico has always lingered with devotion in the shrines of philosophy, especially Platonic philosophy; he set out to compose Platonic and Ciceronian dialogues, and he displays just as much eloquence as can be rightly expected of such a philosopher nowadays. I don't think he himself would wish to be called Ciceronian. He's still alive, a man whose recondite learning is matched by integrity of character.

Bulephorus What of Domizio Calderini?[648]

Nosoponus There were great hopes of him, if the luxurious habits of Rome followed by premature death had not cut short the career of study which he had begun so well as a young man.

Bulephorus Scipione Fortiguerra[649] next.

Nosoponus I recognize in him a man unostentatiously learned in both Greek and Latin literature, but from what he wrote it does not appear that he strove after eloquence of the Ciceronian type.

Bulephorus You will not, I imagine, reject Girolamo Donato,[650] the Venetian noble.

Nosoponus His letters, which are practically the only thing of his we have, make it clear that he could have achieved anything if he had been prepared to turn his mind to it, but affairs of state distracted the man from the peace and quiet of literary studies.

Bulephorus Do you acknowledge Antonio Sabellico?[651]

Nosoponus I acknowledge a man with a natural gift of eloquence and not devoid of art either, one who at times displays considerable expertise as a public speaker. He was quite distinguished in history, but only in the sort that requires his style of writing.

Bulephorus So far we have been talking mostly about the dead, but we must look to the living, as the proverb[652] says. Though possibly you will hesitate to say freely what you think about people who are still alive.

Nosoponus Not at all, since I'm hardly prepared to admit that this glory has fallen to the lot of any mortal man as yet.

Bulephorus You know Paolo Emilio?[653]

Nosoponus Yes, I salute his recondite learning, his industry, the holiness of his life, and his complete reliability as a historian. Ciceronian eloquence he neither sought nor displays.

Bulephorus I propose Giovanni Battista Egnazio.[654]

Nosoponus You have named a man who displays uprightness and integrity as well as erudition and eloquence, but the experts refuse to vote him the honour of the title 'Follower of Tully.' He preferred to speak in a learned style rather than a Ciceronian one, and he has achieved his aim.

Bulephorus How about Paolo Bombace?[655]

Nosoponus Personally I admire Paolo Bombace as a man with a heart of gold; hardly anyone has ever been more of a true friend. But he had to watch his health and consequently didn't let himself write much. Before long, being a man of some honour and principle, he was disgusted by the shabby, contemptible bickerings of the people who wanted to replace him[656] – he held the public chair of Greek at Bologna – so he turned to civic administration: eventually he was summoned to Rome and chose to make money rather than grow old in the service of learning.

Bulephorus Perhaps you will be more sympathetic to the younger men. What do you think of Andrea Alciati?[657]

Nosoponus I will tell you what scholars think, who know the man better than I do. They are prepared to apply to this man in both its parts the compliment that Cicero[658] divided between Quintus Scaevola and Lucius Crassus, calling Crassus the speaker with most knowledge of the law, and Scaevola the lawyer with most ability as a speaker. Alciati showed what his powers of eloquence were in the preface to his Tacitus – in the *Notes* he was concerned with giving information, not with oratorical display.

Bulephorus From among the Italians we haven't, I think, omitted all that many who deserve mention. Wait a moment, I've just remembered Girolamo Aleandro,[659] the man who was recently made archbishop of Brindisi[660] by favour of Clement VII. Perhaps we shouldn't have passed him over in our review.

Nosoponus What he could achieve in this line is not at all clear from his writings. His published works are very few in number, and don't show him making any attempt to establish himself as a Ciceronian. In any case, for a long time now civil administration and wartime diplomacy have otherwise engaged a man finely equipped with linguistic skills who is quite wasted on such profane concerns.

Bulephorus In my opinion Alberto Pio, Prince of Carpi,[661] comes closer to Cicero's style of expression than Aleandro does. As yet he hasn't published anything, as far as I know.[662] Oh, there is one book I've seen, though it might be better to call it a very long letter,[663] written in response to Erasmus – but it's said by some to be a known fact that the work was shaped by another's hand.[664]

Nosoponus The author does certainly come close, whoever he is, in so far as anyone can who has involved himself since youth with theology and philosophy.[665]

Bulephorus You see how many writers of repute I have named, Nosoponus, and you won't allow a single one of them to have the glorious title of 'Ciceronian.' Perhaps some escape my memory. You suggest some, Hypologus, if you know any.

Hypologus There are the two Celios, Ricchieri[666] and Calcagnini.[667] Maybe you omitted them deliberately.

Bulephorus No, it was certainly not deliberate.

Nosoponus Ricchieri was a man of piety and wide reading, but certainly not one to be admitted to a contest of eloquence. The other is his superior in learning as well as eloquence; his Latin is correct and stylish, but has a flavour of scholastic philosophy about it, which has so far prevented him not from being numbered among the eloquent, but from being numbered among the Ciceronians.

Bulephorus There are one or two that I am passing over deliberately, as our discussion will bring us back[668] to them at a more suitable moment. In the mean time, if you agree, let us take a short trip to France, a country where learning has long been in a flourishing state, though I propose to name only outstanding figures who have acquired a reputation as writers through books published in the last few years. It's not so long since Robert Gaguin[669] was held in great repute, but he was appreciated more for his spoken than his written Latin.

Nosoponus Among his contemporaries to be sure, but now he would hardly be admitted among speakers of Latin.

Bulephorus Is there any point in my mentioning the two brothers Fernand?[670]

Nosoponus I won't have them.

Bulephorus Or Gui Jouvenneaux?[671]

Nosoponus Even less.

Bulephorus Josse Bade?[672]

Nosoponus I would allow him to compete for this glorious title sooner than

Guillaume Budé.[673] On the whole, Bade's endeavours have met with considerable success, though they would have met with more if domestic worries[674] and his commitment to making money[675] hadn't interfered with the quiet detachment that accords with literary studies, which any candidate in this competition must be able to enjoy. That's the situation, however much Budé's exceptional and manifold gifts of intellect compel our admiration.[676]

Bulephorus Jacques Lefèvre[677] is thought very distinguished.

Nosoponus A pious and learned man, but he preferred to express himself as a theologian rather than a Tullian.

Bulephorus Perhaps you will accept Jean de Pins.[678]

Nosoponus He could have been numbered among our contestants if the bustle of his involvements and his high ecclesiastical office had not forcibly cut him off from his studies. At one time he certainly showed great promise when he celebrated the rites of the Muses at Bologna. Now I hear he has been made bishop, but I don't know what this has done for his writing. Maybe it has done more for his scholarship than his status.[679]

Bulephorus You acknowledge Nicolas Bérault?[680]

Nosoponus I acknowledge a man not unlike de Pins in the unlaboured fluency of his style, but he never really exerted his full strength in this direction. He was more successful in speaking than in the written word. I have an idea of what his possibilities are, but he's rather too ready to avoid anything demanding an effort.

Bulephorus I would have no hesitation in putting forward François Deloynes[681] if he had been able to demonstrate in an oration or a book the qualities he revealed in his unpremeditated letters to friends. These qualities were quite remarkable in a man who lived in an age not particularly propitious, who wasted practically his whole life on authors like Accorso, Bartolo, and Baldo.[682] In his old age he happily took on a new lease of life in studies of a more cultured kind. Death recently removed him from this earth – a death timely enough for him, for he died an old man, but premature for the studies which this excellent person was, as it emerged, born to advance and adorn. We still have with us Lazare de Baïf.[683] He has earned great renown for his one treatise, and that not a long one, on ancient dress, and has given us reason to hope great things of him, if he continues to run as he has begun in the race of literary studies. Though being primarily concerned to give information, he prefers, it seems, to be clear-cut and Attic rather than Ciceronian.

Another and by no means contemptible pair have just come to mind – you are familiar with Claudius Cantiuncula of Metz and Cornelis de Schepper?

Nosoponus I know them both personally. Cantiuncula[684] is a delightful person, so naturally he can sing[685] the sweetest songs on any subject – I mean in prose, I don't know how effective he is as a poet – and he's moving swiftly and with some success towards the ideal established by Cicero. He has pretty well attained Cicero's fluency, clarity, richness, and charm. But for some time he's been prancing about the stage, engaged on diplomatic missions for rulers, when the business we're talking of requires complete peace of mind. Yet even so he improves on himself every day, as if he had all the Muses with him as his travelling companions as he flits over land and sea. He is remarkable for having reconciled with eloquence a knowledge of the law and an understanding of philosophy. As for de Schepper,[686] apart from being well versed in every intellectual discipline, he shows equal facility in composing prose and verse, though he too goes in for these energetic roles in life.[687]

Bulephorus What is your opinion of du Ruel?[688]

Nosoponus The one I should have of a man expert in medical knowledge, and completely reliable as a translator from Greek. He preferred this kind of fame to a reputation as a follower of Tully.

Bulephorus Where shall I put Petrus Mosellanus[689] of Trèves? Shall I count him as German or French?

Nosoponus It doesn't matter which, as far as our present business goes.

Bulephorus Do you recognize him as a Ciceronian?

Nosoponus I admire his equal competence in both Latin and Greek, his generous character completely free from meanness, his tireless industry, his bright, lively, lucid style. Nothing was to be considered beyond his capabilities, if a premature death had not, to the great grief of all scholars and with no small detriment to literary studies, removed from our midst a young man who had only recently entered the lists.[690]

Bulephorus Let us now change course, if you agree, and move from France to England, fruitful nurse of gifted minds. Oh, I almost left out Germain de Brie.[691] You must know him. He's equally at home writing in Greek or Latin, poetry or prose, or translating Greek into Latin. Will you not receive even him among your followers of Marcus Tullius?

Nosoponus He has not yet completed the course. He has achieved richness and clarity, but in quite a number of points he is unlike Cicero. Even so he justifies our having high hopes of him, if he maintains his present devotion and enthusiasm. In the mean time we are glad to cheer one who is running well.

Bulephorus Now then, let's go to Britain. That land contains many aspirants after Tullian diction, but I shall name only persons who have sought fame by publication. If I offer William Grocyn,[692] you will reply that there is nothing of his in print except for one little letter,[693] polished though it is and accomplished, and the Latin good. He preferred to write nothing rather than see nothing, for he suffered from bad eyesight. He was by nature suited to the craft of the letter, as his taste was for laconic brevity and accurate employment of language. You could call him an Attic writer in this genre, and he had no ambitions in any other. Cicero's abundant style he could not bear, if ever he found himself reading any work of his. And he didn't favour the laconic only in the written word – he spoke laconically as well.[694] So I will not put forward any claims on his behalf. But I have no hesitation in proposing Thomas Linacre.[695]

Nosoponus I know him – an extremely learned man, but his attitude towards Cicero was such that even if either style had been equally in his grasp, he would have chosen to resemble Quintilian rather than Cicero – he was no better disposed towards Cicero than the general run of Greeks. He never tries for sophisticated ease, he abstains from emotional effect more religiously than any Attic stylist, and he likes conciseness and precision, being primarily concerned to instruct his reader. His aim was to walk in the steps of Aristotle and Quintilian. Praise him as much as you will, I've no objection, but he can't be called a follower of Cicero, as his intention was to be unlike Cicero.

Bulephorus Richard Pace[696] is still with us.

Nosoponus Now he could have been counted among the candidates for Ciceronian eloquence, if he had not been so fond of dashing things down without preparatory thought. Besides, when he was still a young man in the middle of his studies popes and kings began to employ him, and that more or less swamped him with worldly concerns.

Bulephorus I'll leave England, but only after proposing Thomas More.[697]

Nosoponus Indeed a man blessed by nature with great abilities, a mind that could have achieved anything if it had been free to devote itself entirely to literary studies. But when he was a boy, hardly the faintest whiff of the higher culture had penetrated to England. And later on, his parents' authority obliged him to study the law[698] of that nation, than which law nothing could be less cultural; after that he was occupied as a lawyer, and then appointed to public office;[699] he hardly had a glance to spare for the cultivation of eloquence, even in his leisure hours. Finally he was induced to move to court, and being now immersed in the floods of royal and state business[700] is more able to love learning than to pursue it. In any case, the style he favoured has more affinity with Isocratean patternings and dialectical exactitude than with Cicero's smooth, flowing eloquence, though in sophisticated polish he is no whit inferior to Cicero. As he spent a considerable time in his younger days on writing poetry,[701] you can spot the poet even in his prose writing.

Bulephorus Let's leave England then, as I don't want to nominate William Latimer[702] or Reginald Pole.[703] Latimer is a man of piety who has preferred to master theology rather than Ciceronian eloquence, and the other, though a great admirer of Cicero and quite a successful imitator, has so far not been prepared to publish anything with his name on it. His personal letters demonstrate his powers, but I will not make public things which he hasn't yet himself allowed out into the light. That island contains innumerable other potential candidates, young men of great promise, but at the moment we are acting the critic, not the prophet. It's no wonder that young people blossom forth in a country where the king himself[704] not only encourages the naturally talented by rewarding them, but sets an example that should spur on even the dullest. His two little books[705] testify both to his encouragement of piety and to his own talent and eloquence.

Nosoponus I certainly admired those books enormously. They were not unciceronian, except in so far as the subject-matter and the royal dignity apparently require their own special style.

Bulephorus So all that remains is to sail off to Holland?

Nosoponus I think to Scotland first.

Bulephorus I wouldn't object, if I knew of anyone[706] there whom I thought you would accept. I would rather we went to Denmark, which has given us Saxo Grammaticus.[707] He's the author of a splendid and impressive history of his own people.

Nosoponus I approve of his lively and intense mind, his style, which is never careless or inattentive, his impressive range of expression, his close-packed pungent remarks, the dazzling variety of his figures of speech, such that I am quite unable to stop wondering how a man from Denmark managed at that period to achieve such powers of eloquence. All the same, there is hardly a Ciceronian feature in him.

Bulephorus Off to Holland then.

Nosoponus No, Zeeland first, in case you miss anyone.

Bulephorus That region too produces some able intellects, but most of them are ruined by intemperance. To be sure, I can offer you Adriaan Cornelissen[708] of Barland from there – in his writings you can recognize the lucidity and ease characteristic of Cicero's style.

Nosoponus Yes, he approximates in this area, but he does not reflect Cicero in his entirety.

Bulephorus It's an easy passage from Zeeland to Holland, which is a prolific enough mother of good minds, but no respect is shown for eloquence there, and it's difficult for the inborn abilities to develop in such an atmosphere of self-indulgence. I'll offer you Erasmus of Rotterdam from there, if you will let me.

Nosoponus You undertook to talk about writers. Him I don't even count as a writer, let alone put him among the Ciceronians.

Bulephorus What's that I hear? I always thought he could be rated among our most prolific writers.[709]

Nosoponus So he can, if to be a prolific writer is to cover lots of paper with ink. The sort of writing we're talking about is one thing; just writing is quite another. Otherwise people who copy out books for a living will be called 'writers,' when the correct term is rather 'scribes.' Writing, for us, is what bearing a crop is to land; reading is to us what fertilizing is to land; thinking and correcting are the equivalent of harrowing, digging and trenching, pruning, pulling up the tares,[710] and all the other operations without which the seeds won't shoot or won't flourish once they've started growing.

Bulephorus Well then, how about Erasmus?

Nosoponus He throws everything off in a hurry;[711] none of his works come to birth, they are all abortive; occasionally he does write a real book, but he does it 'balanced on one foot';[712] and he hasn't sufficient mental discipline to reread what he has written even once; nor does he do anything but write, when one should only take pen in hand after reading for a long time, and even then not very often. Furthermore, he doesn't even set out to write in Ciceronian style, being quite prepared to use words invented by theologians, and sometimes even words of very low origins.

Bulephorus Willem Hermans[713] showed more discrimination.

Nosoponus He favoured the Attic style, as his letters show, and was a sound poet, but another example of that criminal habit of self-indulgence that corrupts and destroys so many intellects of promise.

Bulephorus Do you know Gillis van Delft?[714]

Nosoponus Yes, a man of wide-ranging knowledge, and not a bad versifier if he had added vigour to his facility.

Bulephorus It's not long since Maarten van Dorp[715] died.

Nosoponus A gifted mind able to turn to anything, and a not unattractive personality, but he preferred to follow others' judgments[716] rather than his own. In the end theology alienated him from the Muses.

Bulephorus What do you think of Jacob Teyng?[717]

Nosoponus A man who generated high hopes, but one who is far from being Ciceronian.

Bulephorus Let's move on to Frisia if you're ready. That country really does produce what they call minds of the brightest and best, but Comus[718] doesn't mix well with the Muses. I'll say nothing of the Langens and Canters,[719] since it's enough to cite Rodolphus Agricola[720] to represent the rest.

Nosoponus I acknowledge in him a man of superhuman mentality, of deep learning, with a style far from commonplace, solid, vigorous, polished, controlled, but he has a touch of Quintilian in expression and of Isocrates in word arrangement, though he rises to greater heights than either of them, and is also more expansive and lucid than Quintilian is. He achieved what he aimed at, and I have no doubt that he could have produced a likeness to Cicero if he had bent his enthusiasms in that direction. Yet there were obstacles to bar his way to the highest glory, such as the unpropitious setting of a country and an age in which hardly any respect was shown for politer literature, together with the rather intemperate habits of the whole nation. If he had stayed in Italy, he could have been one of the greatest, but he preferred Germany.

Bulephorus There is Haio Herman[721] of the same nation.

Nosoponus I see in him a young man of almost divine ability, though we have no example of his writing available except for a few letters – but nothing could be purer, sounder, more pleasing than they are. He may possibly manage to win the title if he displays industry to match his natural gifts.[722]

Bulephorus I don't think we should leave out Westphalia, which has given us Alexander Hegius.[723]

Nosoponus There you name a man of erudition, of integrity, of eloquence, but one who despised fame and therefore did not labour to produce anything great.

Bulephorus Westphalia gave us Hermann von dem Busche[724] too.

Nosoponus He has a happy knack in composing verses; in his prose he displays great powers of mind, wide reading, keen judgment, a fair amount of vigour, but his phrasing is more like Quintilian's than Cicero's.

Bulephorus You are not acquainted, I think, with Conradus Goclenius?[725]

Nosoponus Now do you mean the man in Brabant who's been such an ornament for years to Busleyden's College – the Collegium Trilingue[726] as it's also called? In fact he's an ornament to the whole university, fine centre of learning that it is.

Bulephorus That's the very man I mean.

Nosoponus I know him very well indeed.

Bulephorus Now are you aware of any deficiency that prevents his being considered a Ciceronian?

Nosoponus In my opinion an intellect like that could do anything it seriously wanted to do, but he prefers to generate fat rather than writings.

Hypologus I know one thing in which he's very different from Cicero.

Bulephorus And what's that?

Hypologus We're told that Cicero[727] had a very long thin neck. Goclenius has a good fat one, and it's so far from being long that his chin is practically on his chest.

Bulephorus We're talking about styles, not necks. But to move on from

Westphalia, Saxony has young men of great promise, who lead us to expect something more than ordinary from them, including Christoph von Carlowitz.[728] He's distinguished by his noble ancestry, but even more so by his disciplined learning and character. But I won't weary you with a list of people whose powers are still maturing, are, so to speak, 'still in green leaf.'[729] I will move on to other Germans, the most important of whom was Reuchlin.[730]

Nosoponus A great man, but his style was redolent of his age, which was still rather rough and unpolished. The same is true of Jakob Wimpfeling[731] and his contemporaries, whose labours none the less brought great benefit to learning in Germany. Wimpfeling is experiencing[732] a new lease of life, so to speak, in his nephew Jakob Spiegel.[733]

Bulephorus Well then, you accept Reuchlin's pupil Philippus Melanchthon?[734]

Nosoponus A mind like that would have met with every success, if it had been totally committed to literary studies. But the truth is Melanchthon was not really interested in fame of this sort. He was content with a happy ease of expression that came naturally to him and so didn't bring much to the business of writing in the way of art or pains; and even if he had desired such fame, his style would possibly not have proved forceful enough. He gives the impression of being a born extempore speaker, and now, being intent on other pursuits,[735] he seems largely to have abandoned any interest in fine writing.

Bulephorus The next one for you is Ulrich von Hutten.[736]

Nosoponus He shows quite considerable brilliance and range of expression in his prose, and was even more successful in bringing off verse, but on the whole, came nowhere near the ideal set by Cicero.

Bulephorus We should have mentioned Willibald[737] before this – he was the first to foster a concern for style in Germany, and made eloquence honorable by his noble character and exalted rank.

Nosoponus He certainly pursues our goal, but he doesn't reach it.[738] It is not lack of ability that prevents him, but the combination of administrative duties and poor health[739] – though he certainly more than anyone deserves the best. His impromptu style is so good that it's obvious what he could do if he really exerted his powers.[740]

Bulephorus The whole of Germany has high praise for Ulrich Zasius.[741]

Nosoponus Not so high as a man of his ability merits. As well as having a thorough knowledge of the law, which is his profession, he has at his command the ability to write or speak extempore with an unlaboured fluency. His words, like his sentiments, are sound and well considered, yet his speech seems to flow from some never-failing spring – it never fades, halts, or falters. Even in his writings there's a youthful alacrity and vitality, so that you would never think you were reading an old man. Yet he's more like Poliziano than Cicero.[742]

Bulephorus Well then,[743] instead of Willibald I offer you Bruno Amerbach[744] of Basel, the most generous-souled man that nature ever formed.

Nosoponus As far as one can tell from just a taste, he would have been great if a premature death had not snatched him away from his studies while still in his youth.

Bulephorus Will you have Henricus Glareanus,[745] the Swiss?

Nosoponus He chose to spend his whole life on philosophy and mathematical disciplines, and didn't try to achieve a Ciceronian style, which isn't really suited to mathematical exactitude.

Bulephorus There is just one more, and if you will not have him we will move on to Hungary.

Nosoponus Who's that?

Bulephorus Ursinus Velius.[746]

Nosoponus A successful writer of verses and quite a good prose writer too; he has plenty of imagination and taste. He's said to be writing an account of the campaigns[747] of Ferdinand, king of Hungary and Bohemia, and once that's appeared, we shall be able to say something more definite.

Bulephorus I am sure his powers of eloquence will do justice both to the distinction of his prince and the greatness of his subject. Mention of him has brought us to Hungary where he now lives, and I know no one else there except for Jacobus Piso.[748] He was an eager aspirant after Tullian diction, but first the court, then misfortune, and recently death have snatched him from us.

Nosoponus Yes, I heard that, and I was sorry.[749]

Bulephorus Poland has some whom you cannot despise, but I will mention only those who have provided a sample of their abilities in published works. Chief among them is Andreas Critius,[750] bishop of Plock, who keeps his abilities all in ready money,[751] as it was once put; he's a successful poet and is even more successful in prose; when writing extempore he demonstrates fluency backed by scholarship, a style that delights by never-failing liveliness.

Nosoponus I have sampled just a few of his writings, which give me great cause for hope – or would do so, if participation in diplomatic missions and involvement in administration of state and church were not forcing him out of the quiet seclusion in which literature thrives.

Bulephorus As for Spain, it's only a short time since it began to bloom again and recover[752] its former intellectual glory, and it doesn't have all that number of learned and eloquent men whose writings have brought them to the world's notice. One it does have is Elio Antonio de Nebrija.[753] He's erudite and widely read, but he's one whose name you will not allow in the catalogue of Tullians.

Nosoponus You are right there.

Bulephorus Nor even López,[754] nor Sancho,[755] I imagine.

Nosoponus Sancho is a theologian and didn't want this sort of fame. The other is much less successful in panegyric than in vituperation. Neither the one nor the other is a Ciceronian. Ginès[756] shows more promise.

Bulephorus I shall be surprised if you bar Juan Luis Vives[757] from the honourable title.

Nosoponus Personally I find in him no lack of ability, learning, or powers of memory; he has at his command an abundant supply of ideas and means of expression, and though his style grated just a little when he was beginning, his eloquence is getting riper every day. If neither life nor enthusiasm desert him, we have good cause to hope that he will eventually be numbered among the Ciceronians. There are some people whose attempts at writing go the way of Mandrabulus,[758] as the proverb has it. Vives improves on himself daily. He has a talent that can be turned to anything, and for that reason is uniquely adapted to the skill of declamation. Still, there are a few of Cicero's virtues that he has not yet brought to perfection, notably the aesthetically pleasing quality of his idiom and its flexibility.[759]

Bulephorus I know of several literary men from Portugal as well, whose intellectual gifts have been demonstrated to the world in published works, but I know none of them personally except for one Caiado[760] – he wrote neat epigrams and easy unlaboured prose, but there was too much clever persiflage in his talk.[761]

See how many countries we have traversed, Nosoponus, looking for one Ciceronian, and we haven't found a single person yet on whom you would deign to bestow this title, which you desire so passionately and so painfully for yourself. How many writers from the days of ancient Rome have we named, how many from the centuries that followed, how many whose memory was handed on to us by the previous generation, how many from our own time. Among them there are a few whom a fastidious critic might well reject, but how many there are who have by their learning and eloquence adorned, glorified, and ennobled their own age, their own country, the church, and literature, and even so we have not as yet found any Ciceronian. The only thing left to do is to go to the Islands of the Blest and look for someone there to give the title to. People waste little emotion on misfortunes they share with nearly everyone else. The Spaniard is not unhappy because he has not got fair hair, nor the Indian because he is dusky, the Ethiopian because he is black and flat-nosed; so why should you make yourself miserable and be unable to accept meekly the reproach of not being a Ciceronian? I don't know whether not being a Ciceronian is a bad thing, but if it is, won't you bear without distress a disadvantage you share with so many men of great distinction?

Nosoponus All very well, but this glorious title has been achieved by Christophe de Longueil,[762] and he was a man born in Brabant and educated in France. To him alone of men born north of the Alps do the Italians concede the prize; all the rest they disqualify as uncultured boors.

Bulephorus To be sure, Longueil won high praise, but he paid dearly for it. For long he suffered and toiled, and finally died in mid-course with the struggle unfinished, to the great detriment of literary studies; and to those he would have contributed much if he had not bent his whole mind and all his powers of intellect to satisfying his passion for an empty title. Even so, he used not to restrict himself to Cicero alone – he had ranged through authors of every kind and had mastered every liberal discipline as well as jurisprudence; nor was he content with imitating Cicero's superficial features – he showed himself discriminating and resourceful in developing material, skilful and effective in handling arguments, displaying those impressive natural gifts of his everywhere. So there is no reason why those apes of Cicero should cast up Longueil at us. Other gifts made him great, even if he had not been a Ciceronian, and this very pursuit of a vain title all but withered the fruit of his studies, and cut short his life. Even so, Longueil fell far short of Cicero, in that he lacked material on which to employ that marvellous eloquence, whereas Cicero was able to apply it to real matters of serious import.[763] Longueil wrote *Letters*,[764] extremely elegant ones, I admit, and finished in a most satisfying way, but many of them are on very trivial topics, even more of them on artificial ones, like a good many of the Younger Pliny's[765] *Letters*. What is more, I don't think such compositions should be counted as letters. What have Seneca's *Letters* in common with letters, except for the title? But in Cicero's *Letters* nothing is far-fetched and extraneous. Either he writes down the comments[766] on serious and important matters which he would make in person if circumstances allowed, or he chats about personal affairs and intellectual interests with his absent friends just as people do when they are together. What's more, Cicero did not publish his own *Letters*, and seems to have written some of them without his usual care for style. That is why a good many of those collected by Tiro, Cicero's freedman, have disappeared. Presumably they would not have perished if scholars had considered them worthy of immortality. So my first point is that we do not find in most of Longueil's *Letters* either the simplicity and charm of natural speech, or a feeling of reality. Second, since neither Longueil's fortunes nor his interests were the same as Cicero's, it follows that his imitation of Cicero is on occasion out of place and irksome.

For example, Marcus Tullius, a senator and a man of consular rank, writes to men of similar standing about the manoeuvrings of military commanders in provinces and about the preparedness of the armed forces; he points out danger; he prophesies the outcome. When Longueil imitates Cicero and writes in similar vein to his learned friends living their quiet peaceful lives, professing his concern over major political issues, doesn't the unnaturalness of it repel the reader? What is more, hidden away in his study, he sometimes commits to writing quite groundless rumours such as circulate in common talk, rumours not fit to be mentioned even in the casual conversation of a man of intelligence.

But, you will say, in the two speeches he left, supposedly delivered[767] in the Capitol, he presented us with Cicero. Now I must confess that I read these speeches with great admiration as well as great pleasure. They gave me an even more exalted estimate of his abilities than I had already; he quite exceeded my expectations, in spite of the fact that I had formed a very sanguine opinion of him before this. Here he has deployed, it seems to me, all the potential of his own native genius together with everything he had absorbed from Cicero's speeches. Yet what a tiny portion of Cicero we find in these speeches of Longueil's, speeches worked on for so many years, so often put back on the anvil,[768] so often submitted to the censure of critics – and that lack is not Longueil's fault, but the fault of the times he lived in.[769] Cicero always spoke in a manner absolutely befitting his subject, Longueil hardly could do so, since today Rome does not have the conscript fathers or the senate, or the authorization of the people, or voting by tribes, or the regular Roman magistrates, or the laws, electoral assemblies, the ancient forms of procedure for legal action, provinces, townships of municipal status, allies, citizens;[770] in short, Rome is not Rome. It has nothing but ruins and rubble, the scars and signs of the disasters that befell long ago. Take away the pontiff, the cardinals, the bishops, the curia and its officials, the emissaries of princes, of churches, colleges, and abbacies, take away the swill of men who make a living from the trafficking of the place, or who gravitate there looking for freedom or hoping to make their fortune, and what will Rome be? It may well be said that the kingdom of the pontiffs, handed on from Christ, is more majestic than that of senate and Roman people ever was, even maybe than that of Octavius Caesar.[771] I do not mind, so long as you admit that the kind of kingdom is quite different. This is why the same form of speech will not do for both, if we believe that to be Ciceronian is to make what one says appropriate to the subject being treated.

But our splendid young man tempered his speech to suit the sympathies of those who still dream of ancient Rome, 'mistress of the world, the race that wears the toga,'[772] just as the Jews haven't yet stopped dreaming of their Moses and the temple at Jerusalem. Furthermore, Christophe was young, and great not by reason of office held or deeds done or on any other count than that of intellectual ability, and though I personally think this finer than if he had exercised political power, such a personality bears no resemblance to Cicero.

Now take the subject-matter of the speeches. Longueil had become involved in a dispute with some young Italian, who had, I believe, been put up to the idea of coming forward as rescuer of Ciceronian eloquence from the 'barbarians.' Now from what I hear there is at Rome a sort of club of people[773] with more culture than religion; they have a reputation as literary figures, and are generally held in great esteem. These persons with time on their hands fanned the flames of this conflict, sides were taken, and feeling ran high – that city will hunt for amusement anywhere and everywhere. Longueil's side was at a disadvantage because of Luther, on whose account anything from the German area, not to say everyone from north of the Alps, was in bad odour at Rome. Moreover, Christophe, though by nationality a barbarian – for those characters still use this sort of word, as if the whole scene of events had not been completely altered – anyway, Christophe, on the suggestion of a number of more generous persons,[774] had, in recognition of his admirably pure style, been made an honorary citizen of Rome. In times gone by this gift was of practical use as well as bringing honour to the recipient. But nowadays[775] what does it mean to be a citizen of Rome? Considerably less than being a citizen of Basel,[776] if you are prepared to disregard words without substance, and value the solid and real. It was this honour that inspired the resentment directed against the 'barbarian'[777] on the part of the rival claimant to eloquence and his supporters. Eventually it was arranged to give this leisured group the pleasure of having Longueil plead his case in the Capitol[778] – this is what they call a not particularly splendid hall where boys act plays in order to exercise their wits – and a cheeky youth was put up to the job of reciting a speech of accusation[779] written by somebody else which he had learnt by heart. The main points of the accusation were as follows: first, Christophe de Longueil, years before as a boy in an exhibition speech in praise of France,[780] where he was then living, had dared to compare it in some points with Italy; second, in the course of it he had said three words in praise of Erasmus and Budé, a barbarian praising fellow barbarians;[781] third, he was said to have been suborned by these and despatched to Italy to carry away all the best books to the barbarians, so that they could dispute with the Italians the first place in the world of scholarship; finally, being a barbarian and of undistinguished parentage, he was quite unworthy of the honour of bearing the name of Roman citizen. So there you have a splendid subject for flexing the muscles of your Ciceronian eloquence.

But Longueil played his part in this farce with dead seriousness, deploying an absolutely amazing arsenal of words, with a great display of ingenuity, extreme forcefulness, and at times with considerable wit, parodying the age of Cicero in exactly the same way as the author of the *Batrachomyomachia*[782] does Homer's *Iliad*, when he applies to frogs and mice and silly unimportant things the splendid words and deeds of gods, goddesses, and heroes. So Longueil piles up the peril to his life,[783] the armed contingents of soldiers, the gang of gladiators, whose violence has interfered with the authority of the highest estate of the realm and with the freedom to act according to law. He conjures up a vision of the Rome of old, mistress of the world, and of its leader and protector, Romulus, with his Quirites;[784] he sees before his mind's eye the conscript fathers[785] and the august house that was absolute master of kingdoms, the people distributed into their classes and tribes,[786] justice administered by the praetors,[787] the tribunes' right of veto;[788] he dreams up a world where the city on its seven hills has provinces, colonies, municipalities, allies;[789] he has a decree of the senate read out, he has laws cited. I'm surprised he didn't remember the water-clocks, nine of which were, I think, the usual allowance for a speech for the defence. In one place he is stirring up those famous 'passions,'[790] he is calling on those ancient chiefs of the Roman state, rousing them from their tombs,[791] and what not. The whole thing is extremely amusing.

Now I am prepared to see some point in a piece of fun like this, if such themes are used in schools of rhetoric to give students practice, even though Quintilian[792] rightly urges that the counterfeit practice speech should approach as nearly as possible to a real court case. (He evidently disapproved of teachers taking their themes for declamation from the tales of poets, which are not real or even likely.) Such preparatory exercise speeches can produce worthwhile results in students when a genuine historical situation is used, as the sentiments and the wording have to be made consistent with the historical setting. But it remains true that a student will be better prepared for tackling genuine cases if he handles problems with some relevance to contemporary conditions: for example, whether it is to the advantage of a state if its princes marry off their daughters or sisters to husbands in far distant territories; whether it advances Christian piety to have the leaders of the church burdened with temporal sovereignty; whether a young man is better advised to acquire knowledge of the world by reading or by travel and practical experience; whether it is good for a child designated or born to bear rule to spend much time on literature and liberal disciplines.

But to go back to Longueil's subject-matter. It was neither a subject taken from the past that could be consistent with the period depicted if treated with creative imagination, nor yet a subject that of its own nature fitted the period and characters presented. So how could Longueil possibly reproduce in his entirety the Cicero who spoke without inhibition before the senate and people of Rome, in a setting in which Antony's weapons really had been beaten off and fear of death removed?[793] Yet in treating this topic, this exceptional young man performed with such ability, with such nimbleness of mind, that I know of no one today, even among the Italians – may I be forgiven for saying so[794] – whom I consider able to perform a similar feat. So I am certainly not trying to disparage Longueil's glory. I cannot help admiring intellects of that calibre, even if they are ill-disposed towards me.[795] My purpose in saying all this has been simply to help our young people in their studies, to prevent them from torturing themselves through misplaced scrupulosity in their pursuit of Cicero's likeness, and from being distracted by their concentration on this from more useful and more necessary studies. So now you have the facts of the matter, and the speeches are available[796] to prove me wrong if I am not telling the truth.[797]

So now I would like you to reckon up whether it is worth while for minds so richly endowed by nature to expend so many years and so much toil on such exhibition pieces, not to speak of still being at them when they die. What benefits Longueil would have bestowed on the Christian religion, or on learning, or on his country, if he had applied to matters of importance the long hours of mental effort he devoted to those stage-performance speeches!
Nosoponus Really, I feel quite sorry for Longueil, and can hardly make any reply.
Bulephorus Beside these, he tells us he wrote five speeches in praise of Rome.[798] What a splendid expenditure of effort! He would have put it to much better use if he had employed his oratorical skills on a few speeches intended to inspire that city and those of its inhabitants in particular who profess good letters with reverence for Christ and a love of holy living. You understand what I am saying, Nosoponus, or rather what I am leaving unsaid.[799] But on whom was all this effort bestowed? The senate? The senate, if there is such a thing at Rome, doesn't understand Latin. The people? The people, far from appreciating the idiom of Cicero, speak a barbarous tongue.[800] But that's enough of these display pieces. He has a real and significant subject to deal with in his speech against Martin Luther.[801] But how could he be a follower of Marcus Tullius here, where he was discussing subjects of which Marcus Tullius had absolutely no idea? A

speech cannot be in the Tullian tradition, that is, be of the finest sort, if it does not accord with the times or the people or the subject it is concerned with. His passages of vituperation are quite in the Tullian vein, but when he eventually comes to listing the main heads of Luther's errors, he becomes obscure and barely intelligible to Luther's supporters. But this was just the point where the subject required the greatest clarity on the part of the speaker, if he wanted to be Ciceronian. This introductory speech makes it easy enough to deduce how he would have handled the subject when it came to refuting Luther's dogmas and substantiating his own position, as he sedulously avoids employing the words proper to our faith. Together with many other words which I discussed earlier,[802] he never, for example, uses *fides* 'faith,' but substitutes for it *persuasio* 'persuasion.' Once or twice, however, he does use the name 'Christian,' by an oversight I imagine, as that term is nowhere to be found in the works of Marcus Tullius Cicero. Though even here he said much that was very effective, and went wrong for no other reason than his excessive anxiety to be Ciceronian, preferring his speech to conform to Cicero rather than to his case.

Nosoponus All the same, some Italians do applaud these speeches to an incredible extent.

Bulephorus True, 'those they praise, but they read the other things.'[803] How many more people thumb the *Colloquia*,[804] the light-hearted nonsense of the Dutch word-spinner,[805] than the writings of Longueil, however carefully worked over, however polished, however Ciceronian, however κεκροτημένα, to use a convenient Greek word?[806] What is the reason? Simply this – in the former, the subject itself is interesting and holds the reader's attention regardless of the language in which it is treated, but the speeches are stage performances devoid of life, and the reader nods off and snores. A work that serves some purpose makes even modest stylistic competence satisfying, whereas something that offers pleasure and nothing else cannot content its readers for long, especially if they study literature not merely in order to express themselves in a civilized manner, but in order to live better lives. In short, those who fired[807] that young man to pursue the glory of Ciceronianism did not do well either by him or by literary studies. But we have probably gone on far too long about Longueil.

Nosoponus You've passed over Jacopo Sadoleto[808] and Pietro Bembo[809] intentionally I presume.

Bulephorus Intentionally indeed – I didn't wish to include in with the crowd men of such distinction, whose like one meets but rarely nowadays. There is nothing of Bembo's available,[810] as far as I know, except for a number of letters, in which I admire the clear, sound style, an Attic style, I could call it. I also admire in them the integrity, civilized attitudes and remarkable generosity of spirit which shine back at us through the words. In my opinion, it was the friendship of such men that was Longueil's greatest good fortune and distinction. As for Sadoleto, he is pretty well Bembo's equal[811] in general, but in his stylish commentary on Psalm 50 he is not so keen on being thought a Ciceronian as to forget his own position as bishop of Carpentras[812] or to ignore the requirements of his subject. In fact he is prepared to use ecclesiastical Latin words even in his letters. Well then, did he not employ a Ciceronian style when speaking? He did not. Or rather, he did – because he spoke as Cicero probably would speak on such subjects if he were alive now, that is, in a Christian manner on Christian topics. I can bear this kind of Ciceronian – men endowed with the finest intellects, thoroughly accomplished in every branch of learning, gifted with discrimination and powers of judgment, who, whether they set up Cicero alone as their oratorical ideal, or a few outstanding exemplars, or all scholarly writers, cannot help speaking in the best possible way.[813]

Nosoponus The learned world thought highly of Battista Casali.[814]

Bulephorus The speech *De lege agraria*,[815] which he published just before his death, shows clearly that he made great efforts to catch the main characteristics of Cicero's idiom, and to this extent he more or less achieved what he wanted: he has plenty of brightness, an elegant vocabulary, and pleasing word-arrangements. Still, there is a vast amount missing, if you compare him with Cicero.

Nosoponus At any rate, everyone is quite unanimous in praising Pontano;[816] the learned all vote him the prize for Ciceronian diction.

Bulephorus I am not so unperceptive or so ungenerous that I don't acknowledge Pontano as a great man with many exceptional gifts of mind. I too am carried away on that flowing tide of speech, my ears are entranced by the delightful music of his sweet-sounding words, and such is the dignity and majesty of his utterance that a kind of radiance seems to envelop me.

Nosoponus So what is to prevent your acknowledging him as a Ciceronian?

Bulephorus In my opinion, it would make no difference to his reputation for good or ill. I have sampled a few of his works. He treats non-Christian material, general topics,[817] such as courage, obedience, and glory, which are easy to handle in a showy way and easily generate a string of aphorisms, and he treats them in such a way that it's difficult to tell whether he was a Christian or not. His treatise *De principe*[818] is written in the same tone and style. Apart from these things, I don't recall reading anything of his, except for a few dialogues[819] after the style of Lucian. But I shall acknowledge as Ciceronian only a man who treats things that belong to us and to our lives with a Ciceronian sureness of touch. In epigram he would have been thought of more highly if he had avoided obscenity; even in his *Dialogues* he is too ready to admit it. In his *Meteora* and *Urania*[820] he chose material which lends itself to fine writing, and he did indeed treat a good subject well; I don't look for Christian style in works of such a kind. Elsewhere I do at times feel a lack of appropriateness and harmony of subject and expression, and of those barbs[821] which Marcus Tullius leaves in the mind even after the book has been laid aside. Certainly Pontano will not be Ciceronian under the terms of the law which you prescribed for us, as I could point out in his books hundreds of words which occur nowhere in Cicero. As a final point, you can see how rarely Pontano, who is incontrovertibly to be accounted one of the foremost of literary figures, is actually found in the hands of readers.

Nosoponus To follow Pontano we have Sannazaro.[822] He wrote a splendid poem about the virgin birth of Christ, which was wildly applauded by Roman audiences.

Bulephorus That's abundantly attested in the briefs (as they call them nowadays) of Leo and Clement[823] – and in the preface added by Cardinal Egidio,[824] not to mention others. The approval he met with was fully justified. At any rate, I myself have read both his works with great pleasure – he's also the author of the *Piscatory Eclogues*. Who would not idolize such ability in a young nobleman? He is to be preferred to Pontano on the grounds that he didn't scorn to treat a religious topic, and didn't treat it perfunctorily or unattractively. But, in my opinion at any rate, he would have won more acclaim if he had treated his religious subject in a rather more religious manner. Baptista Mantuanus[825] didn't go so far wrong[826] on this point, though he shows more resourcefulness in general when treating this kind of subject. But in Sannazaro's case, what was the point of all those invocations of the Muses and Phoebus? And what do we make of it when he depicts his Virgin meditating especially on the sibylline oracles,[827] when he inappropriately brings in Proteus[828] prophesying about Christ, and fills everything with nymphs, hamadryads, and nereids?[829] How strange to Christian ears sounds this verse, addressed, if I'm not mistaken, to the Virgin Mother:[830] *Tuque adeo spes fida hominum, spes fida deorum* 'Thou alone true hope of men, true hope of gods.' I am sure he wrote *deorum* 'gods' instead of *divorum*[831] 'saints,' because *deorum* fitted the metre. Amidst all his virtues, I find it rather a pity that his frequent employment of elision makes his phrasing jerky. In short, if you produce this poem as a sample of a young man practising the art of writing poetry, I shall greet it with acclaim, but if as a poem written by a man of mature years as the expression of religious feeling, I shall find infinitely preferable the one hymn of Prudentius on the birth of Jesus[832] to Sannazaro's three whole books. I certainly don't see this poem as capable of laying low with its sling-stone the Goliath[833] that threatens the church, or soothing with its harp the madness of Saul, which is what the prefaces say in its praise.[834] Yet I don't know which is more reprehensible – for a Christian to treat non-Christian subjects in a non-Christian way, concealing the fact that he is a Christian, or to treat Christian subjects in a pagan way. The mysteries of Christ should be handled not only with learning but with religious feeling. It is not enough to regale the mind of the reader with some trivial, temporary delight; one must arouse emotions worthy of God, and that can only happen if you have an intimate grasp of the subject you are treating. You will set no one on fire if you are cold yourself, nor will you inflame your reader with love of things heavenly if you care for them little or not at all. If those ornaments of style, those seductive figures of speech with which we first entice the supercilious reader and then hold him are ready to hand, either offering themselves freely without great searchings on our part or not costing us much effort, I see no reason for rejecting[835] them, provided first things come first. What a strange thing if we were to find a devotional topic odious simply because it was treated in a devotional manner. But how can it be treated devotionally if you never take your eyes off your Virgils and Horaces and Ovids? Unless of course you approve of the efforts of those people who have collected snippets of verses from here, there, and everywhere in the Homeric or Virgilian corpus, and strung them together into a patchwork poem[836] on the life of Christ. A very toilsome way of writing, but did such productions ever force the tiniest tear from anybody's eye? stir anyone to love God? or reclaim anyone from a life of sin? But it's not all that much different when people trick out a Christian subject with words, phrases, figures of speech, and rhythms put together out of Cicero. What credit does that chanter of other men's poems deserve? Only that he has conscientiously busied himself with his Homer or his Virgil. What reward does this sort of Ciceronian get? He is applauded for busying himself industriously with the writings of Marcus Tullius, but only by those who have busied themselves in the same way and can recognize the source of each picking. The thing does, I admit, offer a certain pleasure, but one very few people appreciate, and even they have soon had enough of it; and it is a pleasure with nothing to offer apart from itself. Writing of this sort is totally devoid of that feature without which, according to Quintilian,[837] eloquence cannot impress, and that lies in the power to stir the emotions. And yet we see ourselves all the while as Virgils and Ciceros.

Tell me this, Nosoponus. If someone were to break up a mosaic[838] with a fine representation of the rape of Ganymede,[839] and try to rearrange the same stones to depict Gabriel bringing the celestial message to the maiden of Nazareth, wouldn't the resulting work be stiff and unsatisfactory, not because the materials were bad, but because they did not fit the requirements of the subject?

Nosoponus But poets can point to a tradition going back to ancient times.

Bulephorus Horace[840] has some lines that are relevant here: 'That does not permit the fierce / To mingle with the tame, serpents to pair with birds, / Or tigers mate with lambs.' In my opinion the Muses, Apollo, and all the other gods of poetry have less in common with the mysteries of Christian devotion than serpents with birds or tigers with lambs, especially when the subject is a serious one. If a writer incidentally throws in a dash of the old stories with humorous intention, one can accept such a practice, rather than approve it. All Christian speech should have the savour of Christ, without whom nothing is pleasing or impressive, useful or creditable, stylish or eloquent or learned. Of course, schoolboys may participate in games by way of preparation for serious things later on, but can anyone really endure those pagan training exercises when the subject is real, serious, and, what is more important, spiritual?

Nosoponus What do you advise me to do then? Throw Cicero away?

Bulephorus No, no. Any young candidate for eloquence must always have Cicero in his pocket – and in his heart.[841] But we must certainly throw away the captious fault-finding attitude displayed by certain persons who are always rejecting works, in every other respect learned and well expressed, and decreeing them not fit to read simply because they were not worked up with an eye to the imitation of Cicero. In the first place, the Ciceronian idiom does not suit every cast of mind, so that the attempt to imitate it is bound to fail; second, if you do not have the natural gifts which will enable you to reproduce that inimitable flair for the perfect expression, what is more stupid than torturing yourself over the unattainable? Besides, the Tullian idiom does not suit every topic or person to be treated, and even if it did, it is better to let some things go than pay too dear for them. If his eloquence had cost Marcus Tullius as much as ours does us, he would, I am sure, have neglected the finer points of oratory to some extent. It costs too much when the price is such an outlay in years, health, and life itself. It costs too much when to achieve it we neglect areas of learning which are far more essential to us. It costs too much when the price is our devotion to God.

If we learn how to speak effectively in order to delight a leisured audience, is it worth toiling such long hours merely to achieve good theatre? If our aim is to persuade people to honourable conduct, remember that Phocion the Athenian was a more effective speaker than Demosthenes. Cato of Utica won his point more often than Marcus Tullius.[842] Or perhaps our purpose is to write books that people will constantly be thumbing. Well, even if a style just like Cicero's could be ours for the asking, we would still need to apply our rhetorical expertise to achieving a variety of style that would save the reader from being sickened by sameness. Variety is of such importance in life that it is not a good thing to use even the best all the time. Variety is the spice of life; that's what the Greek proverb[843] says, and it's true whatever you are talking about. The main reason why Homer and Horace are so highly thought of is that their impressive variety of subject and style prevent their readers getting bored. Nature shaped us for variety, giving each man his own characteristics, so that it would be difficult to find two people sharing the same abilities or passions. There is nothing more fastidious and difficult to please than individual taste, and we have to devour such a huge quantity of books in our pursuit of learning; so who could endure being constantly engaged in reading, if all the writers employed the same style and a similar idiom? It is better therefore in the case of books, as in a banquet, to have some things of a lower standard, rather than have everything absolutely identical. What kind of a host would he be who invited a crowd of guests, hardly two of whom agree in questions of palate, and served up all the dishes seasoned in the same way, even if the individual dishes were delicacies fit for Apicius?[844] As it is, different people are taken by different styles, so nothing fails to find a reader. Not to reiterate that your ambition conflicts with nature herself, who intended speech to be the mirror of the mind. Minds differ far more than voices and physical features do, and the mirror will lie unless it reflects the true born image of the mind. The very thing which the reader enjoys is getting to know the writer's feelings, character, disposition, and type of mind from the way he writes, just as he would by living on familiar terms with him for several years. This is why different people display such different attitudes towards the various writers, according to whether the moving spirit proves congenial or antipathetic, attracts or repels, just as a person's physical appearance pleases some and gives offence to others. I'll illustrate this from my own experience. When I was young I adored all the poets, but as soon as I became better acquainted with Horace, the others by comparison began to stink in my nostrils, though marvellous enough in absolute terms. What do you think was the reason, if not a certain secret affinity of spirit sensed through the silent letters? This genuine, true born reality cannot breathe through the utterances of those who express nothing but Cicero.

Besides, decent men, even if not particularly blessed with fine features, don't wish to wear a mask in order to make themselves look handsome, and wouldn't even agree to be painted with features other than those nature gave them. It's dishonest to impose on others by disguising oneself, and the idea of a lying mirror or a portrait that represents a man not as he is but as he would like to be is quite ludicrous. And it would be an even more shocking deception, if I, Bulephorus, set out to be taken for Nosoponus or anybody else. So men of letters are surely right to ridicule those presumptuous fellows who send packing authors characterized by learning and eloquence, authors worthy of an immortal name, and more or less banish them from their libraries, simply because they preferred, in their writing, to express themselves rather than Cicero. It is after all a form of imposture not to express yourself but to perform a kind of conjuring trick and appear as somebody else. I do in fact doubt whether we would find many people who would want to change their whole physical appearance for somebody else's, even if God gave them the chance,[845] and I think there would be even fewer who would exchange their whole mind and character for another's. For one thing, nobody wants to be different from what he is; for another, nature has seen to it that each of us is endowed with a mixture of characteristics which ensures that even if there is some fault in our make-up it is balanced by accompanying virtues. Speech reveals the features of the mind much as a mirror reflects the face, and to change the natural image into something different is surely the same as appearing in public wearing a mask.

Nosoponus Mind your speech doesn't jump the barrier,[846] as they say. It seems to me to have been so carried away as to condemn the whole idea of imitation – yet instruction, imitation, and experience are the three chief components of the art of speaking[847] – unless of course those who imitate Cicero put on someone else's face, while those who imitate any other writer keep their own!

Bulephorus I welcome imitation with open arms – but imitation which assists nature and does not violate it, which turns its gifts in the right direction and does not destroy them. I approve of imitation – but imitation of a model that is in accord with, or at least not contrary to, your own native genius, so that you do not embark on a hopeless enterprise, like the giants fighting against the gods.[848] Again, I approve of imitation – but imitation not enslaved to one set of rules, from the guidelines of which it dare not depart, but imitation which gathers from all authors, or at least from the most outstanding,[849] the thing which is the chief virtue of each and which suits your own cast of mind; imitation which does not immediately incorporate into its own speech any nice little feature it comes across, but transmits it to the mind for inward digestion, so that becoming part of your own system, it gives the impression not of something begged from someone else, but of something that springs from your own mental processes, something that exudes the characteristics and force of your own mind and personality. Your reader will see it not as a piece of decoration filched from Cicero, but a child sprung from your own brain, the living image of its father, like Pallas from the brain of Jove.[850] Your speech will not be a patchwork or a mosaic, but a lifelike portrait of the person you really are, a river welling out from your inmost being.

Above all, you must make sure you thoroughly understand the matter you undertake to treat. That will supply you with a flood of things to say, with genuine unassumed emotions. That will make your speech live, breathe, move, influence, carry away; it will make it express you wholly.

Now we mustn't assume that any and every feature dependent on imitation is necessarily spurious and fraudulent. A certain amount of care for one's personal appearance is no shame to a man[851] and also improves the natural looks, for example, washing, controlling the features and, above all, concern for good health. If you should take it into your head to try to make your face look like someone who doesn't resemble you at all, you will waste your time. But if you observe someone not all that unlike yourself making his face hideous with a gaping guffaw of extravagant laughter, or spoiling his looks by frowning, wrinkling his brow, turning up his nose, drawing back his lips, rolling his eyes, and similar behaviour, you can improve your own appearance by avoiding such tricks, and you will not then be borrowing another's face, but getting your own under control. Again, you will see people whose looks are not improved by hair that's uncombed or far too long, so you may well take the opportunity of putting your own to rights. On the other hand, if you observe how attractive a person is made by an unassuming cheerfulness of expression, modesty of eye, a set of the whole face that expresses integrity, with no sign of ill temper or arrogance, frivolity or indiscipline, it will be no cheap deception to model your face on the pattern of his. For you yourself can ensure that your mind corresponds to the face.[852]

But physical beauty comes in many forms, so you mustn't automatically assume that where a person differs from somebody you admire he must necessarily be inferior. As I said before, it is possible for people to be very different and yet absolutely equal. By the same token, there is no reason why someone who doesn't look at all like Cicero shouldn't actually be more attractive than someone who resembles him closely.

Now let's put aside our personal enthusiasms for a while, and give an opinion based on reason, not feeling. If your Peitho[853] gave you the option of being Quintilian[854] or the writer of the *Rhetorica ad Herennium*,[855] rather than yourself, which would you choose?

Nosoponus Personally, I would rather be Quintilian.

Bulephorus In spite of the fact that the other is so much more like Cicero? Would you rather be Sallust[856] or Quintus Curtius?[857]

Nosoponus Sallust.

Bulephorus But Quintus Curtius comes closer to Cicero. Would you rather be Leonardo of Arezzo[858] or Lorenzo Valla?[859]

Nosoponus I would prefer to be Valla.

Bulephorus Yet Leonardo is nearer to Cicero. Would you choose to be Ermolao Barbaro[860] or Cristophoro Landino?[861]

Nosoponus Barbaro.

Bulephorus Yet the other one is much closer to Cicero. Would you rather be Poliziano[862] or Paolo Cortesi?[863]

Nosoponus Poliziano.

Bulephorus Yet Cortesi thinks he should be considered a Ciceronian. Now would you rather be Tertullian[864] – apart from the heresy – or Bede?[865]

Nosoponus Tertullian.

Bulephorus But Bede has more of a Ciceronian idiom. Would you rather be Jerome[866] or Lactantius?[867]

Nosoponus Jerome.

Bulephorus But the other quite apes Cicero. So you see that coming closer to Cicero does not make a speaker automatically better, nor does diverging make him automatically worse. Furthermore, speakers may vary very much among themselves, and yet all be Atticists.[868] In the same way, speakers may all be classed as Ciceronians, even if their styles are very different, if they are equals in oratorical ability. So who can endure those persons of little knowledge when they superciliously reject anything that doesn't bear the mark of the Tullian idiom, which they measure merely in scraps of words, characteristic phrases, and particular rhythms? No one is going to pursue the Tullian idiom in any convincing manner unless he is equipped for the task by wide reading, familiarity with many disciplines, and general knowledge, not to mention native ability and powers of judgment, which I spoke of earlier. Yet I will endure that stupid bit of arrogance in a young person; I will put up with it in scholars if they have many outstanding qualities to compensate for this blotch on their characters. But who can put up with men of advanced years who have no other ambition than to be Ciceronian, who erase men more learned and more eloquent than themselves from the list of writers on the grounds that they have dared at some points to move outside Cicero's prescribed boundaries? At the same time, they themselves are so unciceronian that they are constantly left high and dry without any support from grammar.[869]

There are some whose names I will not mention, who perhaps 'have it in their prayers'[870] to become famous even for this sort of thing. I will mention Bartolomeo Scala, who found Ermolao and Poliziano unciceronian[871] but considered himself Ciceronian, however much he conceals the fact. I find Poliziano's wildest fancies preferable to what Scala laboriously worked out in all seriousness. Paolo Cortesi makes no secret of his ambitions in this direction either, but, good Lord, his letter[872] diverges far more from the Ciceronian image than the letter from Poliziano which he is answering. Where Cortesi seems to me to be most unlike Cicero is in the fact that practically everything he says misses the point. He conducts his case as if Poliziano is seeking to discourage imitation of Cicero, as if he doesn't want a writer to take any author at all as his model, when what Poliziano does do is censure those who come without any reading in good authors, without any knowledge, without any experience, and merely set about reproducing Cicero's outward features – persons whom for this reason he calls Cicero's apes. He censures those who beg words piecemeal from Cicero, who are always stepping in somebody else's footprints,[873] who produce nothing of their own, who do nothing but imitate, and imitate nothing but bits and pieces of words. He says he cannot bear people who advertise themselves under Cicero's placard when the last thing they are is Ciceronian, and who have no hesitation in pronouncing on men of eminence. His advice to his friend is to spend a long time reading Cicero as a first choice, but not just Cicero, to read all the many other outstanding authors as well, and when he has 'worn the pages out, knows them by heart, has inwardly digested them,'[874] then, if ever he takes pen in hand, to put aside that carping anxious concern for imitating Cicero and Cicero only, never letting his eyes stray from the figure of Cicero, for the reason that this very anxiety makes one less likely to reach the goal one is aiming for. Is this deterring people from imitating Cicero? Is this teaching that no one should be imitated at all? The man who comes equipped, fattened up, so to speak, with his wide reading, who recalls, as he starts to write, the best features of each of the authors he has read – is he not imitating someone, even if he is not tied down to his models, even if he is not in bondage to them, but consults his own feelings and the subject on which he proposes to speak? But Cortesi does say he has no love for Cicero's apes: 'I would have a writer, my dear Poliziano, resemble Cicero not as an ape does a man, but as a son does a father' – saying exactly the same as Poliziano had said. He pursues this point at great length, and then, as if forgetting himself, confesses that he would rather be Cicero's ape than other people's son. If 'other people' includes Sallust, Livy, Quintilian, Seneca, who wouldn't rather resemble these writers as a son does a father, than resemble Marcus Tullius as an ape does a man? Then he has a great deal to say against those who stuff themselves with authors of all kinds without digesting what they read. Their style, he says, is coarse, broken, uneven. But what has this to do with Poliziano's letter? If he agrees with him, why does he reply as if he disagrees? If he disagrees, he should have refuted Poliziano's points. It is a particularly Ciceronian characteristic to recognize what is in dispute and where one is in agreement with one's adversary, to identify the real point at issue in the case, and not to say anything that has no bearing on it. The letter Cortesi produced with all his care was prolix[875] rather than Ciceronian, and Poliziano, treating it as irrelevant, made no reply. But Poliziano, who was called unciceronian, offers a much better representation of Cicero, and in a shorter letter at that, because his opinions are shrewd, while his language is appropriate, stylish, and expressive – though I am well aware that Poliziano's abilities received only grudging recognition from Italian men of letters, why I do not know.[876] I am not saying all this in order to scoff at Cortesi, as it's no shame to come second to the almost inimitable Poliziano, but in order to show students by an actual example what imitating Cicero really means.

Hypologus You're taking us by such a roundabout twisty route, Bulephorus, that I feel my name is Hyponosus,[877] not Hypologus. Why don't you say quite plainly what you think about Cicero and about the idea of imitating him?

Nosoponus That's what I'd like, too. Your conduct of the case has almost got me to the point of deciding to follow your advice.

Bulephorus All that remains to do, I think, is to draw together and sum up our rather disconnected discussion.

Nosoponus What do you really think of Marcus Tullius?

Bulephorus I consider him the supreme master of the art of speaking and, for a pagan, a good man. If he had studied the philosophy of Christ, he would, I think, have been numbered with those who are now honoured as saints for their blameless and spiritual lives. Technique and experience contributed much to his oratory, of course; but far the greatest part he owed to natural endowment, which no one has it in his power to give himself. In my opinion there is no single Latin author who should be more read and esteemed[878] by schoolboys and students who are being educated to the glories of eloquence – though I would support the reading of the Latin poets[879] before starting on Cicero, in so far as this form of literature is more suited to those of tender years.

Nor would I have anyone called to the serious[880] imitation of Cicero unless he has first grasped the principles of rhetoric. Next I wish him to have someone available who can draw his attention to the speaker's technique, as painters take some famous picture and point out to their pupils its technical felicities and failures. Again, it is my wish that Marcus Tullius should occupy the first and foremost place in the scheme of study, but that there should be others as well; and my view is that he should not be blindly followed, but taken as a pattern and even challenged. Anyone who merely follows treads in someone else's footsteps and obeys rules. It's a true saying that one cannot walk properly if one is always placing one's foot in someone else's footprints,[881] and no one will ever learn to swim if he hasn't the courage to throw away his float.[882] The true imitator tries not so much to say identical things as similar things, sometimes not even similar things but equivalent things. The challenger endeavours to speak even better if he can. No artist has ever been so perfect that one cannot discover something in his work that could be bettered.

Furthermore I would not have this imitation carried out anxiously and meticulously, as this very thing prevents us achieving what we are after. Nor do I think our passion for Cicero should turn us against all other writers: I think we should first read all the best writers and extract from the best the best that each has to offer – it isn't necessary to imitate anyone in every feature. We shouldn't scorn even writers like Aristotle,[883] Theophrastus,[884] and Pliny,[885] who don't help to improve our style, to be sure, but do supply us with material.

Then I wouldn't have anyone so dedicated to the imitation of Cicero that he abandons his own essential nature and expends health and life in the pursuit of something he will never achieve because his native genius is against it[886] or which will cost him far too dear[887] if he does eventually achieve it. Nor would I have this as a man's only activity: pursuing the renown of a Ciceronian style should not mean that you neglect the essential disciplines of a liberal education.

You must avoid like the plague men who are always declaring that it is a sin to use a word which doesn't occur in the works of Cicero. Now that common usage is no longer the arbiter in determining what is correct in Latin, we have every right to employ any word found in a good author when need for it arises, and if it seems rather strained or far gone in obsolescence because few writers use it, we shall bring it out into the light and smoothe the way to its acceptance by employing it frequently in appropriate contexts. What harm is there in this, considering that the ancients borrowed from Greek whenever the Latin term was either missing or less expressive? So why should we abstain from using words, when occasion demands, which we have found in respectable authors?

We should shun with equal determination those persons who are always loudly proclaiming that anything that fails to conform to Cicero's pattern in vocabulary, phraseology, and rhythm should be rejected as quite unfit to be read; for it is possible, with different stylistic virtues, to be, if not like Cicero, at least comparable to him. Let us have nothing to do with this fault-picking censoriousness. Rather let us, in reading our authors, display in all seriousness the attitude of mind which Ovid[888] jestingly tells us he found himself displaying in his various affairs with girls. He found a tall girl attractive because of her heroic stature, a short one attractive because she was easy to handle; youthful bloom commended a young one, experience one who was a bit older, the naivety of an uneducated girl was delightful, in an educated one the attraction was wit, in a fairskinned girl he adored the loveliness of her colouring, in a dusky one he imagined I know not what lurking charm. If we show the same generosity of spirit and extract from each writer whatever deserves commendation, we shall disdain none of them, but channel off something from each to give a flavour to our own speech.

Above all we must be on our guard lest an age as yet innocent and unformed be led astray by the outward show of the title 'Ciceronian' and turn out not Ciceronian but pagan. This kind of plague is not yet extinct but constantly threatens to break out afresh – under one showy front lurk the old heresies, under another Judaism, under another paganism.[889] A good many years ago for example, those factions of Platonists and Aristotelians sprang up among the Italians. Away with these labels which mark opposed attitudes; let us rather inculcate ideas that encourage and nourish mutual benevolence in study, in religion, in the whole of life. Where sacred things are concerned, one must right at the start absorb convictions that are truly worthy of a Christian. If that happens, we shall find nothing that offers more scope than the heavenly philosophy, nothing more delightful than the name of Jesus Christ, nothing more pleasing than the words used by the luminaries of the church to deal with matters of the faith. Nor will pleasure be taken in any speech that does not fit the speaker's personality and accord with his subject; and a person who treats matters of the faith in the phrases of unbelievers and contaminates his Christian subject-matter with pagan follies will be thought a positive monstrosity. Even if a certain leniency is here accorded to youth, those of more advanced years are not to assume the same prerogative.

Anyone who can be Ciceronian only by being unchristian is not even Ciceronian. He does not speak in a manner befitting his subject, he has no intimate understanding of what he is talking about, he has no genuine feelings roused by what he is discussing. Finally, he doesn't elaborate and embellish themes provided by the faith he professes, as Cicero embellished topics provided by his own day and age.[890] This is the purpose of studying the basic disciplines, of studying philosophy, of studying eloquence, to know Christ, to celebrate the glory of Christ. This is the goal of all learning and all eloquence.

Another thing to remember is that we must imitate the most distinctive thing that Cicero offers us, and that lies not in mere words nor in the outer layer of verbal expression but in substance and sentiments, in intellectual ability, in right judgment. What is the good of a son being like his father in physical feature if he is unlike him in mind and character?

Finally, if we never have the happiness of being voted Ciceronians by that clique, we must bear with equanimity something we have in common with all those distinguished men whose names we have listed. It is foolish to pursue something you cannot achieve.[891] It is self-indulgent to make yourself miserable over something which so many outstanding writers have endured without a qualm. It shows no sense of what is fitting to aspire to things that are not suited to us. It shows lack of judgment to adopt a style that conflicts with what the situation demands. It is madness to pay so dearly in effort and lost sleep for something which is hardly ever going to be of use.

This is the kind of medicine that doctor used to cure me of my sickness, and if you are prepared to swallow it down, I have every hope, Nosoponus, that the fever will leave you, and you too, Hypologus.

Hypologus Oh, I got better long ago.

Nosoponus And I'm nearly cured, except that I've had the disease so long I'm still conscious of a few remaining symptoms.

Bulephorus Those will gradually fade away, and if necessary, we will fetch in Dr Word again.

Notes

Works cited frequently in these volumes are referred to in the notes in abbreviated form only. A list of the abbreviations and full bibliographical information are given in Works Frequently Cited (pages 606–8). In these volumes references to the correspondence are to the English translation of the letters in CWE, where these have already been published, or to the Latin edition of Allen. Since Allen's numbering of the letters has been adopted in CWE, letters are cited by epistle number and, where applicable, line number (for example Ep 66; Ep 373:5–6). In references to letters not yet published in CWE 'Allen' will be inserted before the letter and line numbers (for example, Allen Ep 1814:23).

References to the works translated in these volumes refer to page numbers.

Introduction

ix

1 *Oeuvres complètes*, completed by I. Silver and R. Lebègue 18 vols, (Paris 1914–67)

2 Those of 1500, 1508, 1515, 1517–18, and 1533; see Phillips xi–xii.

3 Those lettered A to H by Clarence Miller in the introduction to his critical edition in ASD IV-3 40–64, where forty-one early editions are discussed

4 On the much controverted date of Erasmus' birth, see A.C.F. Koch The Year of Erasmus' Birth and other Contributions to *the Chronology of His Life* (Utrecht 1969) and the note on it by Margaret Mann Phillips in *Erasmus in English* 6 (1973) 14–15.

x

5 See ASD I-1 vii–x and CWE 23 xiii–xv. According to Allen the letter to Johann von Botzheim was published by Froben in April 1523 and again, in a much expanded version, in September 1524. See Allen I 1 introduction. The 1523–4 catalogue is translated in CWE 24 694–7; the 1530 catalogue, from Ep 2283 to Hector Boece, is translated ibidem 697–702.

6 See, for instance, R. Pfeiffer, 'Die Wandlungen der "Antibarbari"' in *Gedenkschrift zum 400 Todestage des Erasmus von Rotterdam* (Basel 1936) 50–68, reprinted in his *Ausgewählte Schriften* (Munich 1960) 188–207.

7 See the discussion of the sentence 'Quid autem aliud est Christi Philosophia quam ipse *renascentiam* vocat quam instauratio bene conditae naturae' in A.H.T. Levi *Pagan Virtue and the Humanism of the Northern Renaissance* (London: The Society for Renaissance Studies 1974) 12–15.

xi

8 See Levi *Pagan Virtue and the Humanism of the Northern Renaissance* (above, n7).
9 The *Panegyricus*, the *Institutio principis christiani* (ASD IV-1) and the *Querela pacis* (ASD IV-2) were edited by Otto Herding, the *Praise of Folly* (ASD IV-3) by Clarence Miller, and the *Ciceronianus* (ASD I-2) by the late Pierre Mesnard.
10 Erasmus used the titles *Querela* and *Querimonia pacis* indiscriminately. See Otto Herding's introduction to his edition in ASD IV-2 7.

xii

11 On Erasmus' catalogues of his works, see above, n5.

xiii

12 The printer may have been Jamat Métayer of Tours. I quote from the edition of Charles Labitte (Paris 1874) 272: '(1) Un poeme de mesdisance, pour reprendre les vices publics ou particuliers de quelqu'un, comme celles de Lucilius, Horace, Juvenal et Perse. (2) Toute sorte d'escrits, remplis de diverses choses et de entrelardez, comme entremets de langues de boeufs salees. (3) Le nom vient des Grecs, qui introduisoyent sur les eschafauts, aux festes publiques, des hommes desguisez en Satyres qu'on feignoit estre demy-dieux lascifs et folastres par les forests ... [qui] nuds et barbouillez, avoyent pris une liberté d'attaquer et brocarder tout le monde impunement. On leur faisoit anciennement dire leurs vers injurieux tout seuls, sans autre sujet que pour railler et mesdire d'un chascun: puis on les mesla avec les comediens, qui les introduisirent parmy leurs actes pour faire rire le peuple: à la fin les Romains plus graves et plus serieux les chasserent du tout hors des theastres.'
13 Gilbert Highet in the *Oxford Classical Dictionary*, sv *satire*
14 For an account of exactly how the confusion and conflation of meanings occurred, together with the etymological mistakes on which they were based, see J.W. Jolliffe *Satyre: Satura: ΣΑΤΥΠΟΣ, A Study in Confusion* Bibliothèque d'Humanisme et de Renaissance (Geneva 1956) 84–95. The printer of the *Menippé* may well have drawn on Robert Estienne's entry 'Satyra' in the 1531 *Thesaurus latinae linguae*, quoted by Jolliffe, who mentions the general sixteenth-century view that the Latin satirists were working from Greek models, in spite of statements to the contrary by Horace and Quintilian. It was Lambin (in the 1561 edition of Horace) and Casaubon (in the 1605 *Libri duo de Satyrica Graecorum Poesi, et Romanorum Satira*) who rightly questioned the general view.

xiv

15 See also Otto Herding's introduction to the text in ASD IV-1 3–21 and, building on it, Tracy *Politics* 17–21.
16 Cf Ep 447:384–9.

xv

17 The possibly self-destructive aggressive traits in Thomas More's personality are controversial. The best guide to the public life is J.A. Guy *The Public Career of Sir Thomas More* (Brighton: 1980). See also, however, the aggressively anti-Lutheran polemic and, for instance, Frank E. Manuel's article 'Thomas More – Reconsideration' *The New Republic* (24 June 1978) 37–41, which fully acknowledges the 'hidden violence in More'; Richard Marius *Thomas More* (New York 1984).

xvi

18 See Sears Jayne *John Colet and Marsilio Ficino* (Oxford 1963); Ep 108:86–7; E.E. Reynolds *Thomas More and Erasmus* (London 1965).

19 Thomism in the sixteenth century was regarded as a humanistic alternative to Scotism. See R.G. Villoslada *La universidad de Paris durante los estudios de Francisco de Vitoria* O.P. (1507–22), Analecta Gregoriana (Rome 1938) and J.-P. Massaut, 'Erasme et Saint Thomas' in *Colloquia Erasmiana Turonensia* ed J.-C. Margolin (Paris and Toronto 1972) 2 vols II 581–611.

xvii

20 See A. Godin, 'De Vitrier à Origène; recherches sur la patristique érasmienne,' in *Colloquium Erasmianum* (Mons 1968) 47–57.

xviii

21 *Querela pacis* 56–7

xix

22 *Adagia* I ix 12 (LB II 338A)

xxi

23 The reference is to 1 Cor 1:18ff.

24 In the tripartite structure of the *Folly* (Erasmus himself called it the *Moria*), see Clarence Miller in ASD IV-3 18, and the sources there quoted.

xxii

25 On the Neoplatonist spirituality of ectasy contained in the final pages of the *Folly*, see M.A. Screech *Ecstasy and the Praise of Folly* (London 1980).

xxiii

26 See J.-P. Massaut *Josse Clichtove, l'humanisme et la réforme du clergé* 2 vols (Paris 1968).

27 *Erasmus in English* 11 (1982) 19–26

xxvi

28 The metaphor of 'rebirth' was becoming commonplace in the early sixteenth century. Jesus himself according to St John (in the Vulgate translation) said 'Nisi quis renatus fuerit ex aqua ex Spiritu sancto' (John 3.5) and Peter (1 Peter 1.23) talks of the 'renati non ex semine corruptibile.' The difficulty lies in the precise form 'renascentia' which, while an obvious feminine abstract in *t*,

is unusual Latin. Professor Graeme Clarke of the Humanities Research
Centre of the Australian National University has drawn my attention to the
usage of the term 'nascentia' in Vitruvius 9.6.2: 'Qui ... non ex nascentia
sed ex conceptione ...'

29 See A.H.T. Levi 'Erasmus, the Early Jesuits and the Classics' in *Classical Influ-
ences on European Culture AD 1500–1700* ed R.R. Bolgar (Cambridge 1976)
and St Thomas More *Selected Letters* ed E.F. Rogers (Yale 1961) 124.

30 Felix Gilbert, in *The Pope, His Banker, and Venice* (Cambridge, Mass. and London 1980), argues that there was a much stronger case for the intervention
of Julius II in the war of the League of Cambrai than Erasmus allows for, and
contrasts Erasmus' strident comments on the behaviour of Julius II with the
contemporary view of Titian (Tiziano Vecellio, c 1487–1576) that the pope
necessarily 'proposes the ordering of the Christian world according to the
prescriptions of the Church whose head, the Pope, is ruler of the Res Publica
Christiana.'

xxvii

31 See J.A. Fernandez 'Erasmus on the Just War' *Journal of the History of Ideas* 34
(1973) 209–26.

32 For the political background to the *Querela*, see Otto Herding's introduction in
ASD IV-2 and Tracy *Politics*.

xxix

33 The influence of Pico over Erasmus is a recent discovery. For the evidence see
I. Pusino 'Der Einfluss Picos auf Erasmus' *Zeitschrift für Kirchengeschichte* 46
(1927) 75–96; R. Marcel, '*L'Enchiridion militis christiani, sa genèse et sa doctrine, son succès et ses vicissitudes,*' in *Colloquia Erasmiana Turonensia* II
613–46; A.H.T. Levi, *Pagan Virtue and the Humanism of the Northern Renaissance*
(above, n7); and D.P. Walker, 'Origène en France,' from *Courants religieux
et humanisme à la fin du xve au début du xvie siècle* (Paris 1959) 101–19.

PANEGYRIC FOR ARCHDUKE PHILIP OF AUSTRIA/
PANEGYRICUS AD PHILIPPUM AUSTRIAE DUCEM

Introductory note

2

1 In notes on the Spanish background I am grateful for expert help given me by
Dr R.W. Truman of Christ Church, Oxford.

4

2 Translations by B. Radice in *Pliny: Letters and Panegyricus* Loeb Classical Library 1969

3 See B. Radice 'Pliny and the Panegyricus' *Greece and Rome* 15.2 (1968) 166–72.

4 Listed in the *Oxford Classical Dictionary* 2nd ed (1970) sv Panegyric, Latin; text
edited by R.A.B. Mynors (Oxford Classical Texts 1964)

5

5 See Bainton *Erasmus of Christendom* 146ff.

Dedicatory letter

6

1 Nicolas Ruistre] Ruistre (c 1442–1509) served four successive dukes of Burgundy as secretary and councillor. He was chancellor of the University of
Louvain from 1487 and bishop of Arras from 1501. Cf Ep 177 introduction.
2 gives greeting] This preface to the *Panegyricus* is Ep 179 (February 1504).
3 One Philip to another] Philip the Good (1396–1467), Charles the Bold (1433–
77), Maximilian, (1459–1519), and Philip the Handsome (1478–1506)
4 by his very brow] Cf Cicero *Ad Atticum* 14.136.1; *Adagia* I viii 48.
5 lack of ability] Horace *Odes* 1.6.12

7

6 on tiptoe] *Adagia* IV iii 66
7 the fourth ... flattery] Gorgias 463 B–C

Panegyric for Archduke Philip of Austria

8

1 Marcus Tullius truly said] Cicero *Pro Sulla* 31
2 son of Croesus] Herodotus 1.85; Aulus Gellius 5.9.1 and 5; Valerius Maximus
1.8 ext 4
3 Echedes] Echeclous in Gellius, Echecles in Valerius Maximus

10

4 Hesperus] the evening star
5 Joanna] Joanna the Mad, (1479–1555), second daughter of Ferdinand II of
Aragon (v of Castile) and Isabella the Catholic, queen of Castile. She married Philip in 1496 and was the mother of Charles v. The death of her only
brother John without an heir and then the deaths of her elder sister Isabella,
queen of Portugal, and of the latter's infant son unexpectedly left Joanna
the heiress of the Spanish kingdoms. Despite her already apparent mental
instability, she was declared successor to the crown of Castile in her mother's
will of 1504. Philip's death in 1506 pushed her into open insanity. She was
effectively replaced as ruler and withdrew in 1509, with her husband's corpse,
to Tordesillas, where she lived on for forty-six years, still as queen of
Castile.
6 a graceful throng] Virgil *Aeneid* 1.498ff

11

7 fourth of November] The day Philip left Brussels in 1501
8 Homer] *Iliad* 22.60, *Odyssey* 15.348. Ferdinand and Isabella were born in 1452
and 1451.
9 father-in-law] Ferdinand II of Aragon

12

10 The poet] Virgil *Eclogues* 10.69
11 love ... anxious fear] Ovid *Heroides* 1.12
12 King Louis] Louis XII, king of France 1498–1515
13 eager for your arrival] These words soon acquired ironic force, when by Isabella's will (1504), Ferdinand, after thirty years as king of Castile, was excluded from the title and succession which went to their daughter Joanna and her husband.
14 Your sister] Margaret of Austria (1480–1530) was married as a child to Charles VIII of France and in 1497 to John, heir to Aragon and Castile, who died the same year. In 1501 she married Philibert II, duke of Savoy, who died in 1504. When the archduke Philip died in 1506, her father Maximilian made her the guardian of Philip's six children, and from 1518 regent of the Netherlands.
15 Scipio] P. Cornelius Scipio Africanus Major crossed to Africa in 204 BC and was given his title after his defeat of Hannibal in the battle of Zama the following year.
16 Paulus Aemilius] L. Aemilius Paulus Macedonicus ended the third Macedonian war by defeating king Perseus at the battle of Pydna in 168 BC.
17 Alexander Severus] Roman emperor 222–35. His departure from Rome for the Rhine is described in Hist Aug *Alexander Severus* 59.

13

18 Terence's] *Adelphi* 30ff, where Micio describes both kinds of fear
19 Virgil] *Aeneid* 4.573

14

20 one nail ... another] Cicero *Tusculanae disputationes* 4.35.75; *Adagia* I ii 4
21 comic poet] Terence *Adelphi* 3
22 Better ... back of his head] Cato *Res rustica* 4.1; Pliny *Naturalis historia* 18.6.31; cf *Querela pacis* 313, *Adagia* I ii 19.
23 three children] Eleonora, Charles, and Ysabeau
24 little Aeneas] Cf Virgil *Aeneid* 4.328.
25 the poet] Martial 10.78.8

15

26 Greek bard's] Homer *Odyssey* 1.282ff, 2.216ff
27 prince's health] Philip was ill with measles at the end of April 1502 at Balaguer on his way to Toledo (cf 25 below) and again with intermittent fever in Savoy in the spring of 1503 on his way home.
28 practice] Ie the Roman *devotio*, whereby a Roman general vowed himself to death and the enemy's army with him
29 false rumour] Suetonius *Claudius* 12.3

16

30 Keep safe ... with you] Cf Horace *Satires* 2.5.110 and *Epistles* 1.6.67.
31 Willem Hermans] Erasmus' friend and contemporary at school at Deventer, at this time a monk at Steyn. Cf Ep 33 introduction.

32 length] Literally *lustrum*, the five-year interval between the Roman censors' ritual purification
33 the year ... custody] Horace *Epistles* 1.1.21
34 Callipedes] A comic actor famous for his impersonation of a runner while staying in the same spot. The implication is that of 'slow coach.' *Adagia* I vi 43
35 Tiberius Caesar] Suetonius *Tiberius* 38.1

17
36 a husband] Don John of Aragon and Castile; cf n14.
37 a wife] Joanna; cf n5.
38 life] Philip was born in Bruges on 22 July 1478.
39 native soil ... forgetful of itself] Ovid *Ex Ponto* 1.3.35ff
40 legends say] Cf Hesiod *Theogony* 477ff. Jupiter's mother, Rhea, hid the child in a cave on the island of Crete to protect him from Kronos.
41 Circe and Calypso] Cf *Odyssey* 10.467ff and 5.81ff.
42 Homer] Eg *Iliad* 8.539 and *Odyssey* 5.136
43 Cosa] The modern Ansedonia, but Suetonius (*Vespasian* 2.1) names the village Phalacrine as Vespasian's place of birth.

18
44 Curtian Lake] A pond in the Roman forum so named to commemorate the ritual self-sacrifice of M. Curtius
45 Augustus] Cf Suetonius *Augustus* 57.1.

19
46 Cecrops ... triumphs] A conventional list apart from Cecrops, the mythical first king of Athens, sometimes said to be either the son of Hephaestus or of the earth
47 old man] Terence *Adelphi* 73

20
48 three days] In 167 BC, bringing to an end the Macedonian wars. Cf Plutarch *Aemilius Paulus* 32.
49 one day] In 201 BC. Cf Livy 30.45.
50 three-day period] To celebrate the subjection of Dalmatia, the victory of Actium, and the conquest of Egypt; cf Suetonius *Augustus* 22.

21
51 on that day] Louis XII met Philip at St Quentin on 16 November 1501.
52 received you] On 25 November
53 senate] References in this passage to 'senate' and 'council' are apparently both to the *bureau de l'hôtel de ville*, which received the archduke and his duchess on 16 November 1501 on their entry into Paris. See *Registres des délibérations du Bureau de la ville de Paris* ... I ed François Bonnardot (Paris: Imprimerie nationale 1883).
54 Amphictyons] The administrative council for the cult of Apollo at Delphi

22

55 university] The rector of the university at this time was Michel Gaudaire, from 10 October to 15 December.

56 grandfather and great-grandfather] Charles the Bold and Philip the Good

57 armed conflict] Philip's visit to France was a triumph for his francophile advisers, notably his chancellor, François de Busleyden; cf n149. The dukes of Burgundy and the emperor Maximilian were repeatedly at war with France over the frontier between France and the Netherlands until the peace of Senlis (1493). Both Maximilian and Ferdinand were members of the Holy League signed at Venice in 1495 in response to the French invasion of Italy the previous year. Shortly after the signing of the League, Ferdinand sent an expedition under Gonzalo de Cordoba (the 'Gran Capitán') against the French forces occupying the Kingdom of Naples.

58 Blois] Philip stayed there from 7 to 17 December.

23

59 queen of France] Louis xii had married Anne, duchess of Brittany and widow of Charles viii, in 1498.

60 Tours] Philip left for Poitiers on 20 December.

61 king of Navarre] John d'Albret (d 1516)

62 father] Alan the Great, who received Philip's sister Margaret in 1499

63 three days] From 22 January 1502

24

64 grandson] Ferdinand was born on 10 March 1503.

25

65 as the poet says] Cf Virgil *Georgics* 1.434.

66 function] Cf *Institutio principis christiani* 207.

67 We are leaning ... falling wall] Hist Aug *Hadrian* 23.14

68 Balaguer] See n27.

69 in adversity] *Adagia* iii v 4

70 touchstone] Pliny *Naturalis historia* 33.8.24; *Adagia* i v 87

26

71 your wife's parents ... concerned] Such reluctance as they showed to see Philip leave Spain can be explained, at least in part, by the breach with France in 1502 following the partition of the kingdom of Naples and their wish to keep him away from further dealings with Louis xii. Philip entered France on 28 February 1503, leaving Joanna at Alcalá.

72 France and Spain] Apparently the treaty of Lyons (April 1503). Already in the month before he left Spain (ie, in January 1503) Philip was claiming to the French to have authority to negotiate for peace on behalf of Ferdinand. Taking up an earlier proposal of the French, Philip proposed, and it was agreed by the treaty, that the rights of both Louis xii and Ferdinand to Naples should eventually be ceded to Philip's son, the future Charles v, and that the latter should marry Louis' daughter Claude. The whole affair gained valuable time for the Spaniards. In the month the treaty was signed, Gonzalo de Cordoba

decisively defeated the French army at Cerignola and occupied the city of
Naples shortly afterwards. By a treaty of 1504, the French recognized the
Spaniards as lawful possessors of the kingdom of Naples.
73 Marcus Antonius] Plutarch *Antony* 26

27
74 sister's husband] Philibert II 'the Handsome' (ruled 1497–1504). Philip arrived
in Savoy on his visit to his sister Margaret on 11 April 1503.
75 precious jewel] Pearl (*margarita*)
76 father] The emperor Maximilian

28
77 Cádiz] On the Spanish coast, where Hercules was traditionally worshipped
78 Alexander the Great] Cf Plutarch *Moralia* 181D: 'I do not feel that my deeds …
are to be weighed against one word of Heracles' – a cryptic reference, since
Heracles was not noted for his words.

29
79 angry deities] Cf *Odyssey* 10.73ff.
80 wretched] Eg *Odyssey* 5.436, 17.501
81 Osiris, Bacchus, Theseus, and Aeneas] Osiris is identified with Bacchus by
Herodotus 2.144. As vegetation gods they travelled back and forth between the earth and the underworld. Theseus was famous for his Attic and
Cretan adventures; Aeneas led the Trojan exodus and resettlement in Italy.
82 Herodotus] 1.29ff; after instituting a reform programme, the Athenian statesman went into voluntary exile and travelled to Egypt, Cyprus, and Lydia.
83 Homer] *Odyssey* 1.3
84 Afranius] A Roman comic dramatist of the 2nd century BC whose work survives only in fragments. The words are quoted in Aulus Gellius 13.8.3.

30
85 four hands … ears] Zenobius 1.54 (FHG 627 11C)
86 Sophocles] *Locrian Ajax* fragment 14. Cf Plato *Republic* 8.568A and *Adagia* III v
97.
87 those who hurry] Horace *Epistles* 1.11.27
88 Pythagoras, Plato, Apollonius] Pythagoras of Samos emigrated to Italy; Plato
travelled extensively and on several occasions visited Sicily; Apollonius,
the neo-Pythagorean philosopher of Tyana and miracle worker of the first
century AD, travelled as far as India.
89 Alexander … Caesar] Alexander overthrew the Persian empire, subjugated
Egypt, and led an expedition into India; Caesar, after pacifying Asia Minor
and Egypt, subjugated Gaul, invaded Britain, and established the Rhine as
the frontier against the German tribes.
90 warm breezes] Cf *Moria* 86; Horace *Odes* 1.4.1, 3.7.3, 4.5.6.

31
91 violent war] A reference to the fighting over Naples and Philip's attempt to
arrange a treaty between Ferdinand and Louis XII. See n57 and n72.

92 proverb] *Adagia* I v 62. Quoted in Aulus Gellius 2.22.24

93 fickle chariot] Cf Horace *Epistles* 2.1.177.

94 Hadrian] Roman emperor (76–138 AD). His tour of the provinces kept him away from Italy for seven years. Erasmus over-simplifies Hadrian's motives to allow a favourable comparison with Philip. The emperor's journey was undertaken, not only from personal curiosity, but for the sake of military reorganization and economic and political stability.

95 Spartianus] Hist Aug *Hadrian* 17.8

32

96 despised ... kings] Hist Aug *Hadrian* 13, but with emphasis on the fact that most kings were glad to accept his friendship

97 Nestor] Renowned councillor; he participated in the Trojan war when he was already of advanced age.

98 Marius] Marius (157–86 BC) fought campaigns in Africa, Italy, and in the east; he was embroiled in a power struggle with Sulla to his dying day.

99 Homer] *Iliad* 3.64ff

100 Cicero] *Pro lege Manilia* 10.28, where he lists knowledge of military science, courage, authority, and good fortune

33

101 a man's character ... fortune] Cf Cornelius Nepos *Atticus* 25.1.6 and *Adagia* II iv 30.

102 Homer] Erasmus may have in mind *Odyssey* 1.32ff.

103 Plautus] *Poenulus* 1270

104 Libanius] Erasmus had already edited three declamations of the Greek sophist Libanius; see the dedicatory letter to Nicolas Ruistre (Ep 177, 17 November 1503).

105 imperial ancestry] Ie the house of Hapsburg, going back to the election of Rudolf I in 1273

106 grandfather ... and great-grandfather] Charles the Bold (1433–77) and Philip the Good of Burgundy (1396–1467)

107 rustic poem] Calpurnius Siculus, a poet living in Nero's time, 7.83ff

34

108 Penelope ... Niobe] Penelope remained faithful to her husband during his long absence; Claudia, a Vestal virgin, was renowned for her filial devotion; Cornelia, the daughter of Scipio Africanus, was descended from a line of distinguished Roman statesmen. This is a conventional list except for Lampito, or Lampido, the wife of King Archidamus of Sparta and mother of Agis (cf Plato *Alcibiades* 1.124A, Plutarch *Agesilaus* 1).

109 four times] To Eleonora, Charles, Ysabeau, and Ferdinand

110 Horace] *Odes* 4.4.29, 31

111 grandfather] Frederick III, king of the Romans 1440, emperor 1452–93

112 additional lands] A reference to the successive voyages of Columbus to the new world, beginning in 1492

35

113 Timotheus] Athenian general who died in 354 BC; his luck was proverbial (cf *Adagia* I v 82).

114 Sulla] Roman dictator whose belief in his luck earned him the name *Felix* 'Lucky'; cf n131.

115 Tuditanus] Cf Cicero *Philippics* 3.16. Nothing is known about Tuditanus apart from this incident. Valerius Maximus (7.8.1) refers to him as a notorious madman.

116 snake charmers] For the Psilli of north Africa see Pliny *Naturalis historia* 7.12ff and 28.30ff; Suetonius *Augustus* 17.4.

117 one of the philosophers] Chilon, according to Plutarch *Moralia* 86c

118 darling of the world] Suetonius *Titus* 1

36

119 King Henry] Philip and Henry VII met on 9 June 1500 in the church of St Peter outside Calais, on English territory. Henry's main interest was to consolidate the treaty of May 1499 for the export of wool from England to the Netherlands.

120 since his accession] Fifteen years earlier

121 Syracuse] During his absence his brother-in-law, Dion, seized power in Syracuse.

122 by white horses] As a symbol of triumph; cf Horace *Satires* 1.7.8.

37

123 Gyges] King of Lydia; Herodotus 1.8–12

124 Psophidius] The poor man of Arcadia who was content with his small property; cf Valerius Maximus 7.1.2.

125 Tellus] The Athenian, who (Solon tells Croesus) was the happiest of men; Herodotus 1.30.4

126 Cleobis and Biton] The brothers of Argos, said by Solon to be next happiest; Herodotus 1.31

127 Polycrates] Tyrant of Samos; Herodotus 3.40ff

128 Timotheus] Cf n113; Cornelius Nepos 13.3.5.

129 Metellus] L. Caecilius Metellus was blinded in 241 BC when saving the sacred image of Pallas from a fire in the temple of Vesta.

130 his grandson's] Q. Caecilius Metellus Macedonicus (consul in 143 BC) was the political rival of Scipio Aemilianus, but it was his descendant Metellus Nepos who was challenged by Cato Uticensis in the election for the tribunate in 63 BC.

131 Felix] Cf n114.

132 elected consul] Livy 28.38

133 Greek proverb] *Adagia* I v 82; cf *Moria* 141.

38

134 conjugal fidelity] In fact Philip's infidelities are believed to have contributed to his wife's mental breakdown; cf M. Prawdin *The Mad Queen of Spain* (London 1938) ch. 8.

39

135 you illustrate] Cf *Institutio principis christiani* 212. According to Ammianus
Marcellinus 17.4 a bee symbolizes a king because he needs both honey and
a sting.

136 Pliny] *Naturalis historia* 2.18

137 Maecenas] Cf Seneca *Epistulae morales* 114.4.

40

138 Vespasian] Suetonius *Vespasian* 15.16

139 Titus] Suetonius *Titus* 6

140 Lucius Cinna] Cf Seneca *De clementia* 1.9.2ff. The conspirator was Gnaeus
Cornelius Cinna, if the story is historical; Lucius was the name of his father
and grandfather.

141 Hadrian] Hist Aug *Hadrian* 5.5; 24.8

142 Antiochus] King of Syria 137–128 BC; cf Plutarch *Moralia* 184D.

143 Demetrius of Phalerum] Philosopher, orator, governor of Athens 317–307 BC,
and later librarian of Alexandria; cf Plutarch *Moralia* 189D.

41

144 Alexander Severus] Hist Aug *Alexander Severus* 18.1

145 parasites] Latin *Gnathonum*, ie, men like Gnatho in Terence's *Eunuchus*

146 smoke-sellers] Hist Aug *Alexander Severus* 36.3; cf *Adagia* I iii 41.

147 careful ... love] The play on words in *diligentior ... deligendis ... diligas* is lost
in translation.

148 Lampridius] Hist Aug *Alexander Severus* 65.4

149 François de Busleyden] Philip's tutor and later his chancellor, who accompanied him to Spain and died at Toledo on 23 August 1502. Cf n57 and Ep
180:200ff.

42

150 Nestor] Counselling Agamemnon in the Trojan war, eg Homer *Iliad* 9.179ff

151 Parmenio] General to both Philip II of Macedon and Alexander the Great; cf
Plutarch *Alexander* passim.

152 Leonidas] A relative of Alexander's mother and supervisor of his studies; cf
Plutarch *Alexander* 5.

153 Octavius] C. Octavius, later Augustus. For his efforts to enlist Cicero as
adviser, see Cicero *Ad Atticum* 16.8 and 9.

154 Phoenix] Achilles' tutor, cf Homer *Iliad* 9.485ff.

155 Zopyrus] Herodotus 3.153ff; Babylon was captured on his advice.

156 ten Nestors] *Iliad* 2.371ff

157 Darius wanted] Herodotus 4.143, but with reference to Megabazos; it was
Zopyrus who mutilated himself to enter Babylon as a spy. Cf Plutarch
Moralia 173A.

158 Polycrates] Herodotus 3.42

159 Paulus Aemilius] Plutarch *Aemilius Paulus* 35

160 Africanus] Ie Scipio Africanus Major; Livy 45.40.7

43

161 Homeric Pallas] In Homer's *Iliad* 1.207 Pallas stops Achilles from drawing a sword on Agamemnon.
162 Nero] Suetonius *Nero* 37.3
163 Julia] Hist Aug *Antonius Caracalla* 10.29
164 Ulysses] *Odyssey* 12.173ff, though in fact Odysseus is tied to the mast and only his men have their ears stopped
165 Aeneas] *Aeneid* 5.862ff
166 King Antigonus] Plutarch *Moralia* 182C

44

167 Antiochus III] Plutarch *Moralia* 183F
168 shepherd of the people] *Iliad* passim; cf *Institutio principis christiani* 229.
169 guardian] *Republic* passim; cf *Institutio principis christiani* 273.
170 devourer of his people] *Iliad* 1.231; cf *Institutio principis christiani* 229.

45

171 Vespasian and Nero] Suetonius *Vespasian* 16.2; *Nero* 32.4

46

172 Otho] Suetonius *Otho* 12.2
173 astrologers] Tracy *Politics* 19 suggests that Erasmus wrote this passage in deference to Philip's beliefs. He himself considered astrologers charlatans.
174 Heliogabalus] Roman emperor 218–22 AD
175 Trajan and Severus] Roman emperors ruling 98–117A and 193–211 AD respectively

47

176 Cato the Censor] Plutarch *Cato the Elder* 24
177 Octavius Caesar] Suetonius *Augustus* 71.1
178 Titus] Suetonius *Titus* 7.1
179 Vespasian] Suetonius *Vespasianus* 16.1
180 Momus] The Greek personification of fault-finding; cf *Moria* 94 and *Adagia* I v 74 (*Momo satisfacere*).
181 Hector] Cicero *Ad familiares* 5.12.7

49

182 Agesilaus] Spartan king (444–360 BC); cf Xenophon *Agesilaus* 11.5.
183 play the stork] Cf Aristophanes *Birds* 1355–7; Plato *Alcibiades* I 135E; Aristotle *Historia animalium* 9.13.2. The stork was a symbol of *pietas*; cf *Querela pacis* n7.
184 conspiracies] Suetonius *Augustus* 19.1
185 a woman's advice] Livia's advice to Augustus; cf Seneca *De clementia* 1.9.6
186 Alexander the Great] Plutarch *Alexander* 9.6
187 Phocion's] Plutarch *Phocion* 1–2; Valerius Maximus 3.8 *ext* 2
188 Scipio's] Valerius Maximus 4.1.6; 10
189 Cato's] Plutarch *Cato the Elder* 6; Cornelius Nepos *Cato* 2.4

51

190 Severus] Hist Aug *Alexander Severus* 18.7

191 C. Fabricius] C. Fabricius Luscinus, famous for his incorruptibility; Aulus Gellius 4.8.6; Cicero *De oratore* 2.268

192 Carians] Proverbial for treachery: Cicero *Pro Flacco* 65; *Adagia* I vi 14. Cf *Querela pacis* 318.

193 Antalcidas] Athenian general (fl fourth century BC); cf Plutarch *Moralia* 192C, referring to rivers of Athens and Sparta.

52

194 Milo] Milo of Croton, whose fame as an athlete was legendary; cf Valerius Maximus 9.12.9 *ext*

195 Alexander] Plutarch *Moralia* 341E

196 Julius Caesar] Plutarch *Julius Caesar* 39.8, referring to his near defeat by Pompey's forces at Dyrrhachium on the coast of Thessaly

53

197 Symplegades] The legendary Clashing Rocks between which the Argonauts had to pass to enter the Hellespont

198 Syrtes] The dangerous shallows off the north coast of Africa

199 time of peace] This passage on the evils of war is to be compared with *Adagia* IV i 1 (*Dulce bellum inexpertis*) and *Querela pacis* 316–17.

200 As Cicero says] *Pro Milone* 4.11; Lucan *Pharsalia* 1.277; cf Ep 288:55.

201 Marius] C. Marius Victorinus, the fourth-century grammarian and commentator on Cicero

54

202 Homer] Eg *Iliad* 2.698

203 the most eloquent of poets] Virgil *Eclogues* 9.27; the two cities are 65 km apart.

204 vices of war] Erasmus may have in mind Lucan 2.251ff.

55

205 justest of wars] Cf *Querela pacis* 311.

206 Lernean swamp] Cf *Adagia* I 3 27; *Moria* n310.

207 just and mindful] Virgil *Aeneid* 4.521

56

208 Julius Caesar] Cf Cicero *Pro Marcello* 8.25.

209 Augustus] Suetonius *Augustus* 28.1

210 Lucius Cinna] Cf n140.

211 golden hook] Cf *Adagia* II 2 60.

212 Otho] Roman emperor for three months in 69 AD; cf Suetonius *Otho* 10.4.

213 members of the same body] Romans 12:5; Ephesians 4:4; Ep 288:39–40; *Querela pacis* n93

214 Plato] *Republic* 547C, 548A

215 Aristotle] *Politics* 1271b

57

216 Cyanean rocks] Ie the Symplegades, the Clashing Rocks at the entrance to the Hellespont

217 King Agesilaus] Plutarch *Moralia* 190F, cf n182.

58

218 Alexander the Great] Plutarch *Alexander* 21

219 Julius Caesar] Suetonius *Julius* 14.1

220 Scipio] Livy 26.50, where the chieftain is named Allucius. Cf Valerius Maximus 4.3.1.

221 Avidius Cassius] Hist Aug *Avidius Cassius* 9.5ff

222 Numa] Roman king (715–673 BC); he was renowned for cultural and religious institutions rather than military exploits.

223 temple of Janus ... closed] Plutarch *Numa* 20. The closing signified peace.

224 Titus Manlius] In 235 BC. His correct name is Aulus Manlius.

225 twice] In 29 and 25 BC. Suetonius (*Augustus* 22) says that they were closed three times.

226 gates of war] Ie, of the temple of Janus; see note 223.

59

227 Hercules ... Brennus] Another conventional list, the Latin names all in the plural. Brennus refers either to the Gallic king who according to tradition captured Rome in 390 BC or to the invader of Macedonia and Greece in 279 BC.

228 after the nations ... in war] The Roman general Scipio Africanus and his brother Scipio Asiaticus were named after their respective military successes at the turn of the third century BC; Germanicus, the adopted son of the emperor Tiberius, was given this name for his services in the German provinces; Britannicus, son of the emperor Claudius, was named after his father's conquest; 'Dacicus' was the title given to the emperor Trajan after his triumph over the Dacians in 102 AD; 'Geticus' was suggested as a title for the emperor Caracalla, to commemorate his exploits in the region.

60

229 Tullus] Tullus Hostilius was the third king of Rome. He and his predecessor Romulus were warlike men; the second king, Numa, was more concerned with religious institutions. See n222.

230 Archbishop of Besançon] Cf 41 and n149.

231 two illnesses] Cf 15 and n27.

61

232 Sardanapalus] The Assyrian king who became legendary for his luxury and effeminacy

233 physical strength ... mental vigour] Cicero *De oratore* 3.9.36, quoting Isocrates

62

234 unhardened clay] Horace *Epistles* 1.2.69ff, referring to unglazed clay, and Quintilian 1.1.5

63

235 paternal grandfather] Frederick III, king of the Romans from 1440, emperor 1452–93
236 maternal great-grandfather] Philip the Good of Burgundy, 1419–67
237 maternal grandfather] Charles the Bold of Burgundy, 1433–77
238 *Cratylus*] 395ff
239 ancestor Philip] Philip the Bold of Burgundy, 1363–1404

64

240 'the Great'] More generally known as 'the Good'
241 lilies ... eagle ... lion] The lilies must refer to France, perhaps because of Philip's vassal's obligations to Louis XII; the eagle symbolizes the Holy Roman Empire; the lion features in the coat of arms of Burgundy.
242 rust] Horace *Satires* 2.1.43
243 Homer] Not in Homer but in Simonides, quoted by Plato in *Laws* 7.818B. Cf *Adagia* II iii 41.
244 Greek proverb] Plato *Lysias* 205D; cf *Adagia* I vii 55.

65

245 whole of Spain] The conquest of the Moorish kingdom of Granada by Ferdinand and Isabella was completed at the start of 1492. The crowns of Aragon and Castile were already united by the marriage of Ferdinand and Isabella in 1469.
246 bonds ... of adamant] *Adagia* I vii 43; *Querela pacis* 320 and n173.
247 Homer's words] Eg *Iliad* 17.514; *Odyssey* 1.267

66

248 snow-white pearl] An elaboration of the 'white pebble' for marking a happy day, according to Roman custom
249 sedition] This looks like a reference to the events of 1488, when Maximilian entered the Low Countries at the head of German troops as the declared enemy of France. The Flemish had the support of Charles VIII, and from 2 February to 16 May 1488 Maximilian was held prisoner in Bruges. Philip meanwhile had been moved to Malines in the care of Flemish nobles; Ghent was in revolt under Jan Coppenhole. Maximilian eventually withdrew his army in February 1489. See H. Pirenne *Histoire de la Belgique* (Brussels 1907) III 41ff.
250 only a boy] Philip had been titular ruler (by the peace of Arras) of Flanders and Burgundy since his mother's death in 1482. As count of Flanders in January 1483 at the age of four and a half he was admitted to be the figurehead of the government set up by the Flemish estates under the domination of Ghent.

67

251 Homer] *Iliad* 2.489–90
252 Cicero] *Ad Atticum* 1.14.3 and 2.1.1, with reference to Isocrates
253 Mercury] As the patron of literature, especially rhetoric
254 tragic poet] Seneca *Phaedra* 607

68

255 Timanthes] A painter of the late fifth century BC, a native of Cythnus and
resident in Sicyon; Pliny *Naturalis historia* 35.73; Cicero *Orator* 22.74; Quintilian 2.13.13

256 Cologne] Philip left Maximilian at Innsbruck on 6 October 1503 and reached
Cologne on the twenty-seventh.

69

257 Not a single person ...] This purple passage (to bottom of page) is closely
modelled on ch 22 of the younger Pliny's *Panegyricus* addressed to the
emperor Trajan.

70

258 winter weather] It was early January.

71

259 applause and acclamation] Compare the long acclamations of the emperors by
the senate quoted in the Hist Aug.

72

260 sardonic] Cf *Adagia* III v 1 (*Risus sardonius*).

261 Homer's phrase] *Iliad* 6.484

262 the same poet says] *Odyssey* 16.215

263 Homer describes] *Odyssey* 19.471–2

75

264 saints] Literally, 'gods.' Erasmus' characteristic fusion of Christian and classical terms defies translation.

265 lord of Maigny] Thomas de Plaine, Sieur de Maigny (d 1507), was chancellor
of Burgundy from 1496; cf Ep 76.

266 bishop of Arras] Nicolas Ruistre; see n1.

PRAISE OF FOLLY / *MORIAE ENCOMIUM*

Introductory note

78

1 All editions before 1540 and some later editions are listed in C.H. Miller's
introduction to *Moriae encomium* ASD IV-3 40–64. Cf also 24ff.

2 Cf ASD IV-3 36–8.

3 Epp 304, 337, 347; Erasmus' reply to Dorp is also translated in Erasmus *Praise
of Folly* trans B. Radice (Harmondsworth: Penguin 1971) 211–52.

4 Rogers Ep 15. For further attacks on *Moria* and Erasmus' replies see ASD IV-3
26ff.

5 See J. Austin Gavin and Thomas M. Walsh '*The Praise of Folly* in Context: The
Commentary of Gerardus Listrius' *Renaissance Quarterly* 21 (1971) 193ff. A
good deal of the commentary is quoted or summarized in translation in the
notes to ASD IV-3.

6 Ep 641:5–6. Erasmus defends himself in a letter to Martin Bucer (Allen Ep 2615:171–80) against the accusation that he wrote the notes himself.

7 See B. Radice 'Holbein's Marginal Illustrations to the *Praise of Folly*' *Erasmus in English* 7 (1975) 9–17.

8 Letter to Marten van Dorp, Allen Ep 337:86–94

9 See F.H. Reusch ed *Die Indices Librorum Prohibitorum des Sechzehnten Jahrhunderts* (Tübingen 1886) 85.

10 A full account of Italian Catholic hostility to Erasmus is given by Marcella and Paul Grendler 'The Survival of Erasmus in Italy' *Erasmus in English* 8 (1976) 2–22.

11 See B. Corrigan 'Croce and Erasmus: The *Colloquies* and the *Moria* in Italy' *Erasmus in English* 7 (1975) 22 and F. Vander Haeghen ed *Bibliotheca Erasmiana* (Ghent 1893; repr Nieuwkoop 1961) 123.

79

12 Reusch 220

13 *Ibidem* 403

14 For a full account see ASD IV-3 28–9.

15 J.-C. Margolin *Erasme par lui-même* (Paris 1965) 5. See also his three bibliographies of scholarly work on Erasmus between 1936 and 1970 (Paris 1963, Paris 1969, Paris and Toronto 1977).

16 ASD IV-3 39, 60, 66

80

17 The essentials of this are accessible in the commentary on his own translation (New Haven 1979).

18 See Rosalie L. Colie, 'Problems of Paradoxes,' in *Twentieth-Century Interpretations of the 'Praise of Folly'* (Englewood Cliffs, NJ 1969) 92–7.

19 Allen Ep 337:126–42

20 M.A. Screech 'L'Eloge de la Folie et les études bibliques d'Erasme' *Réforme et humanisme: Actes du IVe colloque du Centre d'Histoire de la Réforme et du Protestantisme* (Montpellier 1975, 94)

21 Richard Sylvester 'The Problem of Unity in *The Praise of Folly*' *English Literary Renaissance* 6.2 (1976) 125–39

22 The chapter divisions were introduced by A.-C. Meusnier de Querlon in 1765 and are retained as a convenient form of reference in many subsequent editions, though not in ASD.

Prefatory letter

83

1 to his friend Thomas More] This prefatory letter is Ep 222. For its date see n25 below.

2 Athene] *Odyssey* 21.1

3 Democritus] Greek atomic philosopher (c 460–c 370 BC), later known as 'the laughing philosopher,' perpetually amused by the follies of mankind

4 with all men] Suetonius *Tiberius* 42 and *Adagia* I iii 86; usually translated as 'a

man for all seasons' following the translation of Richard Whittinton, who applied the phrase to More in his *Vulgaria* of 1520

5 memento] Catullus 12.13

6 defend it] As he did in his long letter to Maarten van Dorp of 1515 (Rogers Ep 15)

7 and fun] Added in *1514*

8 Homer ... Nut] Added in *1514*. *The Battle of Frogs and Mice* is in fact a parody of Homer of the fourth century BC. *The Gnat* and *The Garlic Salad* are from the apocryphal *Appendix Vergiliana; The Nut* is also apocryphal.

9 Polycrates] A rhetorician of the fourth century BC, the author of several encomia, some of which were criticized by Isocrates, who wrote a reply to his encomium of the mythical Egyptian tyrant Busiris.

10 and ... Isocrates] Added in *1514*

11 Glauco] Plato *Republic* 2.358E

12 Favorinus] Savant and favourite of the Emperor Hadrian; none of his work survives.

13 Thersites and] Added in *1514*. Thersites was the ugliest man in the Trojan War.

14 Synesius] A fifth-century bishop, author of a satire on the sophists in praise of baldness; this was sometimes included in early editions of the *Moria*.

15 and the parasite] The following words to 'St Jerome' were added in *1514*.

16 Apotheosis] Seneca's *Apocolocyntosis* or 'pumpkinification' of Claudius

17 Gryllus] Circe's pig in Plutarch's *Bruta animalia ratione uti* (985Dff), who argues with Odysseus that his life was preferable to man's

18 an ass] Lucian's *Lucius the Ass* and Apuleius' *The Golden Ass* probably both derive from the same source.

84

19 St Jerome] *Commentaries on Isaiah*, prologue

20 If they want] Added in *1514*

21 stick] A childish amusement; Horace *Satires* 2.3.248

22 goat's wool] Proverbial for quibbling; Horace *Epistles* 1.18.15; *Adagia* I iii 53

23 self-love] *Adagia* I iii 92

24 daily bread] Aristophanes *Clouds* 648

85

25 1508] This year first appears in Froben's edition of 1522 and is impossible: Erasmus was in Italy until 1509. 'From the country' may refer to England where *Moria* was professedly written, or to somewhere outside Paris where Erasmus was revising the *Adagia* for the edition published in 1511.

Praise of Folly

86

26 frowns] Terence *Adelphi* 839; *Adagia* I viii 48

27 nepenthe] The herb mixed with wine to drive away cares; *Odyssey* 4.220

28 Trophonius' cave] The oracle was consulted by descending a pot-hole and

being carried along an underground river; it took time to recover from the experience. Cf *Adagia* I vii 77.

29 mild west breezes] Horace *Odes* 1.4.1, 3.7.2, 4.5.6. Cf *Panegyricus* 30.

30 garb] The fool's cap and bells shown in the first and last of Holbein's marginal illustrations

31 Midas] given ass's ears for preferring the sound of Pan's pipes to Apollo's lyre; Ovid *Metamorphoses* 11.153ff; *Adagia* I iii 67

32 damaging title] Ie in the eyes of Folly, who perversely suggests that the Ancients preferred the professional teachers of 'wisdom' (the Greek sophists)

87

33 infinity doubled] *Adagia* I ii 63: literally 'through two octaves'

34 crow ... plumage] Phaedrus *Fables* 1.3; Horace *Epistles* 1.3.19

35 Ethiopian] *Adagia* I iv 50

36 elephant ... gnat] *Adagia* I ix 69

37 lamp-oil] *Adagia* I iv 62

38 and Phalaris] Added in 1514. Phalaris, tyrant of Acragas in Sicily, was said to have roasted his victims in a bronze bull; his encomium was written by Lucian.

39 tongue] *Adagia* I v 73; 'ill-timed' (ἀκαιρίμαν) was added in 1522.

40 good things] *Odyssey* 8.325

41 look on my face] Cicero *Ad Atticum* 14.13.13; *Adagia* IV ix 17

42 apes in purple] *Adagia* I vii 10

88

43 asses in lion-skins] *Adagia* I iii 66

44 Thales] Early scientist and one of of the Seven Sages of Greece: *Adagia* III vii 26

45 foolish-wise] Lucian *Alexander* 40; *De copia* I 11 (CWE 24 317–18)

46 horse leeches] Perhaps a misunderstanding of Pliny *Naturalis historia* 11.40, or Prov 30:15, allegorically interpreted

47 'So much for that'] Plato *Symposium* 22C; Aristophanes *Pluto* 8

48 Chaos] Origin of the world in Hesiod *Theogony* 116

49 Orcus, Saturn] Italian gods identified with Hades and Kronos

50 Japetus] One of the Titans and father of Atlas; *Iliad* 8.457 and Hesiod *Theogony* 507

51 Plutus] Greek god of wealth in Hesiod *Theogony* 969–74 and subject of a comedy by Aristophanes; here given the title usually given to Zeus

52 chosen ... gods] The twelve or twenty 'select' Olympian gods discussed by St Augustine in *City of God* 7.2

53 fare very badly] Lucian (*De sacrificiis* 9) remarks that the gods would go hungry without the food and drink from sacrifices.

54 go hang himself] Juvenal 10.53

55 It is ... father] Modelled on a Homeric formula

56 stern Athene] Sprang fully armed from the head of Zeus; cf n429.

89

57 Freshness] *Neotes*. Erasmus appears to have invented this nymph.

58 blacksmith] Hephaestus or Vulcan, son of Jupiter and Juno

59 Homer] *Hymn* 33.5. Erasmus quotes the phrase in Greek.
60 Aristophanes] *Plutus* 266–7
61 one foot in the grave] Plautus *Miles gloriosus* 627
62 hot-blooded] Horace *Odes* 3.14.27
63 Delos] birthplace of Apollo and Artemis; Ovid *Metamorphoses* 6.333
64 waves] Like Aphrodite
65 hollow caves] As Thetis and the Nereids were in *Odyssey* 4.403
66 unsown, untilled] *Odyssey* 9.109; applied to the Golden Age by Horace in
   Epodes 16.42–4
67 asphodel] The poor man's vegetable in Hesiod *Works and Days* 41
68 moly] The magic herb in *Odyssey* 10.305 or the soporific named by Pliny in
   Naturalis historia 21.105; all the plants listed are useful for scents, oils, and
   soporifics.
69 panacea] Cures all ills in Pliny *Naturalis historia* 25.11
70 gardens of Adonis] Pots of short-lived herbs and flowers displayed for the
   spring festival of Adonis; *Adagia* I i 4
71 she-goat nurse] Amalthea, who reared the infant Zeus when his mother had
   hidden him on Crete to save him from being swallowed by his father
   Kronos; Ovid *Fasti* 5.115
72 Drunkenness ... Ignorance] names invented by Erasmus
73 Philautia] *Adagia* I iii 92
74 Misoponia] Only in Lucian *Astrologia* 2
75 Tryphe] Aristophanes *Ecclesiazusae* 973
76 Negretos Hypnos] *Odyssey* 13.79
77 helping mortals] Pliny *Naturalis historia* 2.18

90
78 Alpha] Martial 2.57 and 5.26; *Adagia* II iv 18
79 mighty-fathered] *Iliad* 5.747
80 cloud-gathering] *Iliad* 1.160 and 470
81 father ... men] Homer *Iliad* 22.167; Virgil *Aeneid* 1.65
82 makes ... tremble] Virgil *Aeneid* 9.106
83 triple-forked] Ovid *Metamorphoses* 2.848
84 Titanic visage] Lucian *Icaromenippus* 23 and elsewhere
85 make a child] Euripides *Heracleidae* 524; Lucian *Dialogus deorum* 22.1. In Erasmus' text the expression appears in Greek font.
86 beard] *Adagia* I ii 95, quoting Lucian *Eunuchus* 9 and and Horace *Satires* 2.3.35
87 quarternion] The first four whole numbers on which Pythagoras based his
   cosmology
88 offer his neck] Juvenal 6.43
89 Lucretius] His *De rerum natura* starts with an invocation to Venus.
90 in their purple] Horace *Odes* 1.35.12

91
91 Sophocles] *Ajax* 554; *Adagia* II x 81
92 frowns] Horace *Epistles* 2.2.128
93 painful age] *Iliad* 8.103
94 itself] Seneca *Oedipus* 594

95 second childhood] Lucian *Saturnalia* 9; *Adagia* I v 36
96 drunk ... forgetfulness] Virgil *Aeneid* 6.715

92
97 'I hate ... his years.'] *Adagia* IV i 100
98 Plautus] *Mercator* 304; the three letters are *amo* 'I love.'
99 honey] *Iliad* 1.249
100 better] *Iliad* 1.223
101 lily-sweet] *Iliad* 3.152
102 'For thus ... like'] *Odyssey* 17.218; *Adagia* I ii 22
103 tree] Eg Daphne; Ovid *Metamorphoses* 1.532-67
104 bird] Ceyx and Alcyone; Ovid *Metamorphoses* 11.410-78
105 grasshopper] Tithonus; Servius' commentary on Virgil's *Georgics* 3.328 and
     Aeneid 4.585
106 snake] Cadmus and Harmonia; Ovid *Metamorphoses* 4.571-603

93
107 plump ... glossy] Horace on himself as a pig from Epicurus' herd in *Epistles*
     1.4.15-16
108 Acarnanian porkers] Ie delicious, tender; *Adagia* II iii 59
109 special boast] Dutch proverbs say of Brabanters and Dutchmen that the older
     they are the stupider they become; a reminder that Erasmus was himself a
     Dutchman. Cf *Adagia* IV vi 35.
110 Medea] Restored the youth of Jason's father Aeson; Ovid *Metamorphoses*
     7.262ff
111 Circe] Made Odysseus' men younger when restored to human shape; *Odyssey*
     10.229ff
112 Aurora] Prolonged the life of Tithonus (who was her lover, not her grandfa-
     ther; his son Memnon had no daughter), but did not give him eternal youth
     and changed him into a grasshopper; Homer *Hymn* 5 218
113 Phaon ... Sappho] Ovid *Heroides* 15; Lucian *Dialogus mortuorum* 9.2
114 'more ... Morychus'] *Adagia* II ix 1; the name is derived from the Greek μορύσ-
     σειν 'to smear.'
115 Old Comedy] Eg by Aristophanes in *Frogs*
116 born from a thigh] Bacchus' mother Semele was destroyed when Jupiter ap-
     peared to her in full glory, but the baby was sewn into his thigh until ready
     to be born; Ovid *Metamorphoses* 3.310-15
117 crooked-counselled] Homeric epithet of Kronos; eg *Iliad* 2.205

94
118 alarms] *Adagia* I viii 63
119 fixed grim stare] Sophocles *Ajax* 452
120 sound sense] In *Adagia* I viii 38 Erasmus quotes the Greek phrase from Aris-
     tophanes *Plutus* 37 and Euripides *Andromache* 448.
121 'golden Aphrodite'] Eg *Odyssey* 8.337; described as 'laughter-loving' in *Odys-*
     sey 8.362
122 Flora] Her spring festival (*Floralia*) was notorious for its licence; Ovid *Fasti*
     331-54

123 Endymion] Diana's human lover, visited in his perpetual sleep; Cicero *Tuscul-anae Disputationes* 1.38

124 Momus] Fault-finding personified; cf *Adagia* I v 74.

125 Até] Blind infatuation; thrown down from heaven in *Iliad* 19.91ff; *Adagia* vii 13

126 Kolakia] See above 89.

127 'living an easy life'] *Iliad* 6.138; *Odyssey* 4.805

128 Priapus] Fertility and garden god; made of fig-wood in Horace *Satires* 1.8; *Adagia* I vii 85

129 Mercury] Hermes in the Homeric hymn (4) on his tricks and thefts; cf Horace *Odes* 1.10.

130 Vulcan] Hephaestus, who plays the buffoon in *Iliad* 1.584ff and 18.397

131 *cordax ... ballet*] The *cordax* was an obscene dance in Old Comedy; the Greek word translated *ratatan* is found only in Aristophanes *Plutus* 290; the bare-foot ballet comes from Lucian's *De saltatione* 12.

132 Atellan farces] Noted for obscenity; Ovid *Fasti* 5.101 and Tacitus *Annals* 4.14

133 Harpocrates] Horus, the Egyptian god of silence; *Adagia* IV i 52

134 Corycaean god] Ie eavesdropping. The cave on Parnassus symbolizes unsuc-cessful attempts at concealment; *Adagia* I ii 44

95

135 mother Nature] Cicero *De natura deorum* 1.8

136 passions] Cicero *Tusculanae disputationes* 3.19 and 4.12; cf Plato *Timaeus* 69D.

137 reason's solitary power] The Platonic division of the faculties, eg in *Phaedrus* 246ff

138 hoarse] Latin *ad ravim*; Plautus *Aulularia* 336 and *Adagia* IV i 70

139 Nature] Or possibly Jupiter is meant

140 by her folly] Aulus Gellius 15.25.2

141 Plato's apparent doubt] *Timaeus* 76E and 90E

142 enters an ox] Quoted in *Adagia* I iv 62 and I i 42

143 Minerva] *Adagia* I i 42

144 ape ... in purple] *Adagia* I vii 10 and 11

96

145 drawing lots ... king] To preside over the festivities; Horace *Odes* 1.4.18

146 myrtle branch] Passed round by the singer to the guest whom he wished to sing next; *Adagia* II vi 21

147 Friendship ... everything.] Cicero *De amicitia* 4.17; *Adagia* II ii 75

148 air, fire, and water] *Adagia* II ii 75

149 blessings] Cicero *De finibus* 1.20.65

150 poop and prow] Cicero *Ad familiares* 16.24.1; *Adagia* I i 8

151 Crocodile's Syllogism] The crocodile promises a woman to return her child if she guesses correctly what he will do with it. If she says he will return it he will eat it to prove her wrong; if she says he will not she will be wrong unless he eats it. Quintilian 1.10.5

152 Heap] Go on adding one to a pile until it is agreed you have a heap; then remove one, and is it that which makes the heap? The conundrum is credit-ed to Chrysippus; Cicero *De divinatione* 2.4.11; Lucian *Symposium* 23; Horace *Epistles* 2.1.44–5; Persius *Satires* 6.80

153 Horns] What you have not lost you still have, but what if you have not lost a cuckold's horns? Aulus Gellius 18.2.9; Lucian *Symposium* 23; Quintilian 1.10.5

97

154 common sense] Latin *pinguis Minerva*; *Adagia* I i 37, quoting Columella *De re rustica* 12.1

155 winking ... faults] Much of this passage is taken from Horace *Satires* 1.3.

156 like to like] *Adagia* I ii 22

157 eagle ... snake] Horace *Satires* 1.3.27; quoted in *Adagia* I ix 96. The snake is the symbol of Asclepius, god of healing, whose centre of worship was Epidaurus.

158 packs ... backs] Persius *Satires* 4.24; Phaedrus *Fables* 4.10; *Adagia* I vii 90

159 Argus-eyed] Argus, set to watch over Io when she became a heifer, had a hundred eyes; Ovid *Metamorphoses* 1.625

160 εὐήθεια] Plato *Republic* 3.400E

161 ugliness looks like beauty] Theocritus 6.18–19; *Adagia* I ii 15

162 old man ... woman] *Adagia* I ii 62 (*Cascus cascam ducit*); an archaic or dialect term for *vetus*

98

163 kisses ... wife] Juvenal 6.276

164 stepmother] Quintilian 12.1.2; *Adagia* II ii 95

165 decay] Latin *putidas*, a word coined by Erasmus

166 decorum] Cicero *De oratore* 1.29.132; *De officiis* 1.4.14; Quintilian 11.3.177; *Adagia* IV v 2

167 Nireus] The handsomest of the Greeks after Achilles, according to Homer *Iliad* 2.671, while Thersites was the ugliest; the comparison is drawn in Ovid *Ex Ponto* 4.13.15–16. Nestor and Sappho's lover Phaon represent age and youth.

99

168 pig ... Minerva] *Adagia* I i 40

169 willing ... you are] Martial 10.47.12

170 men of Megara] Proverbial for people of no importance; *Adagia* II i 79

171 mail-clad ranks] Horace *Odes* 4.14.29–30

172 blare ... harsh note] Virgil *Aeneid* 8.2

173 Demosthenes] Fled from the battle of Chaeronea, according to Plutarch's *Life* 20; *Adagia* II ii 97

174 Archilochus' advice] To throw away his shield and get another; Archilochus fragment 5 (West)

175 scum of the earth] For the sentiment cf *Querela pacis* 316.

176 Delphic oracle] Plato *Apology* 20D; Diogenes Laertius 2.37

177 laughter] This is not recorded of Socrates, who was efficient as an official; Plato *Apology* 32A–D

100

178 midge's humming] Aristophanes *Clouds* 146 and 157

179 half a sentence] Diogenes Laertius 2.41

180 seen a wolf] *Adagia* III viii 56 and IV v 50; cf Aulus Gellius 8.9.

181 Isocrates] Cicero *De oratore* 2.3.10. ASD IV-3 98 punctuates differently.

182 agitation] Cicero *Pro Roscio Amerino* 4.9; *Pro Milone* 1.1

183 Quintilian] 11.1.44; 12.5.4

184 'Happy ... philosophers!'] *Republic* 5.475D; cf Ep 393:22 and *Institutio principis christiani* 214.

185 two Catos] Cato the Censor (234–149 BC), and Cato of Utica (95–46 BC), who failed to save the Roman republic against Caesar

186 Gracchi brothers] Roman social reformers of the second century BC, praised by Plutarch (*Lives* 19) but later condemned as demagogues (Tacitus *Annals* 3.27)

187 so much of philosopher] As author of his *Meditations*

188 such a son] Commodus, emperor 180–92

189 degenerate son] Cf Pliny *Naturalis historia* 14.147

190 someone] Seneca *Epistulae morales* 104.27

191 So it's ... were fools] Added in *1514*

192 the ass ... lyre] *Adagia* I iv 35

101

193 camel] *Adagia* II vii 66; Erasmus' use of the dancing camel here and elsewhere is discussed by Richard Sylvester 'The Problem of Unity in *The Praise of Folly*' *English Literary Renaissance* 6.2 (1976) 125–9.

194 like Cato the Wise] Martial *Epigrams* 1 preface

195 wolf] *Adagia* III viii 56

196 Timon] The misanthrope of Athens, subject of a dialogue by Lucian translated by Erasmus and More

197 wild men ... oak trees] Statius *Thebaid* 4.340

198 Amphion and Orpheus] Amphion built the walls of Thebes with his music and Orpheus moved trees and animals; Horace *Ars poetica* 391–9, with a rather different allegorical interpretation of the myths.

199 fable] Told to the Roman mob by Menenius Agrippa to teach the need for co-operation between the different classes of society; Livy 2.32

200 a fox and a hedgehog] Attributed to Aesop by Aristotle in *Rhetoric* 1393b22 and Plutarch in *Moralia* 790D. The fox tells the hedgehog not to remove his parasites lest they are replaced by hungrier ones, so the Athenians are advised not to get rid of their current magistrates.

201 white hind] Said by Sertorius to give him divine guidance; Plutarch *Sertorius* 11 and 20

202 Spartan] The lawgiver Lycurgus, who showed the difference between a trained and an untrained dog in Plutarch *De liberis educandis* 4

203 horse's tail] Best pulled out by removing the hairs one by one; Plutarch *Sertorius* 16

204 Minos and Numa] Minos retired every nine years to be inspired by Zeus (an ancient interpretation of *Odyssey* 19.178) and Numa told the Romans he was advised by the nymph Egeria; Livy 1.19.5

205 house of Decius] Three members were legendary heroes of Rome; Cicero *De finibus* 2.19.61 and Livy 8.6 and 9

206 Curtius] Marcus (not Quintus) Curtius rode his horse into a chasm in the

forum when an oracle said that the sacrifice of Rome's greatest strength
would preserve the republic; Livy 7.6; Augustine *City of God* 5.18

207 cast in bronze] Horace *Satires* 2.3.183
208 surnames] Names to commemorate victories, such as Africanus or Asiaticus

102

209 Democritus] See n3.
210 fire and water] *Adagia* IV iii 94
211 the honour of] Added in *1516*
212 'even the fool ... event'] *Iliad* 17.32; *Adagia* I i 30–1
213 Alcibiades] Plato *Symposium* 215A. These small boxes or statuettes of Silenus
    had a grotesque face and opened to show a god inside. As a symbol of
    things not being what they seem, see *Adagia* III iii 1.
214 at first sight] *Adagia* I ix 88

103

215 bluntly] Latin *pinguiore Minerva*; *Adagia* I i 37
216 Dama] A slave in Horace *Satires* 2.5.18 and 2.7.54
217 dropped from heaven] Quoted in *Adagia* I viii 86
218 god and master] Used of Domitian; Suetonius *Domitian* 13
219 eye ... chance] *Adagia* I i 92 (*uti foro*); quoting Terence *Phormio* 79
220 'Drink or depart'] Cato *Disticha* 2.2.3; *Adagia* I x 47

104

221 and I'm ... of life] Added in *1514*
222 truer than truth] *Adagia* IV ix 2
223 Helicon] Virgil *Aeneid* 7.641
224 citadel of bliss] Augustine *City of God* 12.21
225 diseases] Seneca *Epistulae morales* 75.8–14
226 good deeds] Cf Aristotle *Ethica Nicomachea* 2.2.7.
227 Seneca] *Epistulae morales* 71.27; 85.2–12
228 Republic] Lucian said in his *Vera historia* (2.17) that Plato was the only person
    fit to live there.
229 Ideas] The Platonic εἴδη or Forms
230 gardens of Tantalus] Proverbial for what did not exist; *Adagia* II i 46
231 'than if ... fixed'] Virgil *Aeneid* 6.471
232 Lynceus] The sharp-eyed Argonaut; Horace *Epistles* 1.1.28 and *Adagia* II i 54
233 precisely] Latin *ad amussim*; *Adagia* I v 90, referring to a carpenter's ruler
234 king and free] Horace *Satires* 1.3.124–5 and *Epistles* 1.1.106–8

105

235 pleasant to his wife] Horace *Epistles* 2.2.133
236 concern] Terence *Heautontimorumenos* 77
237 poets say] Eg Homer in *Iliad* 8.51
238 sand] Counting sands in *Adagia* I iv 44
239 maidens of Miletus] According to Aulus Gellius (15.10.1) they developed an
    urge to commit suicide and were only cured by an emergency ruling that
    their bodies should be displayed naked at their funerals.

240 Diogenes ... Brutus] Diogenes Laertius (6.76) quotes the tradition that the Cynic killed himself but says (4.14) that Xenocrates died by a fall. Cato of Utica, Cassius, and Brutus all committed suicide after defeat in battle.

241 Chiron] When wounded by Hercules the centaur preferred death to immortality; Lucian *Dialogus mortuorum* 26

242 Prometheus] In one legend made men out of clay; Lucian *Prometheus* 2.11–13

243 Aristophanes] *Plutus* 266–7

244 drybones] Terence *Adelphi* 587

106

245 Greeks say] Aristophanes *Plutus* 1024; *Adagia* I ix 9

246 Phaon] Cf above n167.

247 pubic hairs] Martial 10.90

248 withered breasts] Horace *Epodes* 8.7–8

249 failing desire] Horace *Odes* 4.13.5

250 sweet fantasy] *Adagia* II x 9

251 proverbial beam] *Adagia* I x 21

252 clap yourself] Horace *Satires* I i 66

253 verbal wizards] Plato *Phaedrus* 266E; *Adagia* II iii 62

107

254 Thoth] The Egyptian god said to have invented letters and numbers

255 king in Plato] Thamus, king of Egyptian Thebes; Plato *Phaedrus* 274C–D

256 'demons'] Plato *Cratylus* 398B; the derivation from *daimones* 'gifted' is unlikely.

257 good laws] Macrobius *Saturnalia* 3.17.10; *Adagia* I x 61

258 Chaldaeans] The soothsayers of the ancient world

259 the doctor ... many men] *Iliad* 11.514

260 as it ... so many] Added in *1514*

261 flattery] Plato *Gorgias* 463A

262 just as rhetoric is] Added in *1514*

108

263 Bees ... instincts] Bees lack sexual instinct in Virgil *Georgics* 4.198–9

264 broken-winded] Horace *Epistles* 1.1.9

265 bites the dust] *Iliad* 22.17; Virgil *Aeneid* 11.418

266 famous cock] In Lucian's *Gallus* (*The Dream* or *The Cock*) it had once been Pythagoras.

267 sponge] Thought to be an animal in Pliny *Naturalis historia* 9.69 and Plutarch *De sollertia animalium* 980B–C

268 Gryllus ... hazards] Added in *1514*. Cf n17.

269 long-suffering] In Erasmus' text the word appears in Greek font (μοχθηρός), but Homer does not in fact use this epithet.

109

270 like the giants] Cicero *De senectute* 2.5; *Adagia* III x 93

271 can't even sin] Theologians considered the young and the mad to be morally incapable of sin.

272 delicate ear] Persius 1.107; *Adagia* II ix 53

110

273 truth ... wine and children] *Symposium* 217E, thus interpreted by Marsilio Ficino whom Erasmus has followed; *Adagia* I vii 17

274 Euripides] *Bacchae* 369

275 two tongues] *Andromache* 451 and *Rhesus* 394 (the latter not now ascribed to Euripides)

276 black into white] Juvenal 3.30

277 blowing hot and cold] Aesop *Fables* 35 (Perry); *Adagia* I viii 30

278 no one to tell them the truth] Cf *Panegyricus* 9.

279 prematurely ... senile] *Odyssey* 19.360; *Adagia* III x 62

280 picture of a wise man] A caricature of Erasmus himself?

111

281 wandering in your mind] Horace *Satires* 2.3.221; Seneca *Epistulae morales* 94.17

282 off the track] Terence *Eunuchus* 245; *Adagia* I i 48

283 Socrates shows] Really Pausanias in *Symposium* 180D

284 Horace] *Odes* 3.4.5

285 Plato] *Phaedrus* 244A-245A, where Socrates distinguishes between poetic, Bacchic, prophetic, and erotic frenzy

286 the sybil ... insane] Virgil *Aeneid* 6.135

287 vengeful furies] Virgil *Aeneid* 4.473

288 quite different] Cf Cicero *Tusculanae disputationes* 3.4.9–3.5.11

289 Cicero] *Ad Atticum* 3.13.2, a letter written soon after Cicero went into exile, though he does not really express such a wish

290 Horace's Argive] In *Epistles* 2.2.132ff; Erasmus' text differed from ours in making 'broken' agree with the bottle, not the seal (*laesae*, not *laeso*), but he probably took it as a transferred epithet, as here translated.

112

291 hellebore] Believed to be a cure for insanity; Horace *Satires* 2.3.82 and *Adagia* I viii 51

292 donkey for a mule] Theognis 996; *Adagia* III i 55

293 borderline case] Socrates' view in Xenophon *Memorabilia* 3.9.6–7

294 Croesus] Proverbial for riches; *Adagia* I vi 74

295 wise ... his life] Pliny *Naturalis historia* 7.41; *Adagia* II iv 29

113

296 changing ... to round] Horace *Epistles* 1.1.100

297 fifth element] The 'philosopher's stone'; Erasmus consistently attacks alchemy. Cf the colloquies *Alcumistica* and πτωχολογία (Thompson *Colloquies* 238ff and 248ff).

298 'The intent ... great design.'] Propertius 2.10.6; *Adagia* II viii 55, ascribing it to Tibullus

299 their ship] The following words to 'Malea' were added in 1514.

300 Malea] The south-east promontory of Laconia, notorious for shipwrecks; cf *Adagia* II iv 46. There is a pun on *alea* 'dice.'

301 gout] Horace *Satires* 2.7.14–18

302 my kidney] Latin *nostrae farinae* 'my flour'; Persius *Satires* 5.115 and *Adagia* III v 44

114

303 Christopher] Legend made him gigantically tall; Polyphemus is the Cyclops of the *Odyssey*.

304 Barbara] Gave protection against lightning and explosions and was the patron saint of gunners

305 Erasmus] The patron saint of sailors against storms at sea (St Elmo); he is not associated with riches elsewhere, and Erasmus is probably joking.

306 second Hippolytus] A third-century martyred saint, said to have been dragged to his death by horses, like Hippolytus son of Theseus in Greek legend

307 another Hercules] Associated with St George for killing the hydra as George killed the dragon

308 pardons] Indulgences, consistently attacked by Erasmus, as are superstitious practices connected with the cult of saints; see also Allen Epp 2205:76–84 and 2285:86–114.

309 next to Christ] Cf Matt 20:21.

310 Lernean morass] Hercules killed the hydra in the swamp of Lerna; *Adagia* I iii 27

311 St Bernard] The devil told him he must recite seven special verses from the Psalms daily in order to gain salvation, but refused to reveal them. The saint retorted that it did not matter, as he recited the whole psalter every day.

115

312 poison] A story taken from Ausonius *Epigrams* 19.3

313 Had I ... of folly] Adapted from Virgil *Aeneid* 6.625–7

314 precise instructions] Seneca *De brevitate vitae* 22 and Horace *Ars poetica* 431

116

315 Aeneas ... Brutus ... Arcturus] The first two recall Juvenal 8.181–2, and Arcturus might refer to the star mentioned by Cicero in *De natura deorum* 2.42.110, but more probably Erasmus is thinking of Geoffrey of Monmouth's *History of the Kings of Britain*, where Brutus, grandson of Aeneas, is Brut, eponymous founder of Britain, and Arcturus is King Arthur, from whom the Tudor monarchs liked to think they were descended; Henry VIII's elder brother, who died young, was named Arthur.

316 everywhere] Added in *1514*

317 Nireus] See n167.

318 ass ... lyre] *Adagia* I iv 35

319 pecks his hen] Juvenal 3.90–1

320 Hermogenes] The famous singer mentioned in Horace *Satires* 1.3.29

321 rich man] Calvisius Sabinus in Seneca *Epistulae morales* 27.5

322 their like] Literally 'lettuce-like lips' (*similes labra lactucae*) an obscure saying quoted in Jerome *Letters* 7.8 and discussed in *Adagia* I x 71

117

323 Venetians] Possibly Erasmus alluded to their theory that they descended from the Trojans. See P. Labalme *Bernardo Giustiniani: A Venetian of the Quattrocento* (Rome 1968) 262.

324 tooth and nail] Latin *mordicus*: *Adagia* I iv 22

325 magic arts] Eg Henry Cornelius Agrippa and Georg Faust
326 Philautia ... Kolakia] The Greek words for self-love and flattery; see 94.
327 Horace] *Epistles* 1.18.6
328 form of praise] Listrius notes that Erasmus did this successfully in his
    Panegyricus.
329 mules] *Adagia* I vii 96

118

330 Flattery ... eloquence] Plato *Gorgias* 463A
331 nothing ... for certain] The point of view of the Sceptics, taught in the Acade-
    my in the third and second centuries BC; Cicero *De oratore* 3.18.67
332 sturgeon] Evidently a delicacy then as now; Martial 13.91
333 Apelles or Zeuxis] The two most famous painters of Greece
334 of my name] Someone called Morus, according to Listrius. Thomas More mar-
    ried his first wife in 1505, but there is no real evidence for this story nor is
    there proof that it applied to him.

119

335 Plato's cave] The image of men as cave-dwellers who can see only the shad-
    ows of reality is developed in *Republic* 7. Cf 150.
336 Mycillus in Lucian] In *Gallus* 1 he complains that he cannot escape from pover-
    ty even in dreams because the cock wake him up.
337 no benefit ... company] Seneca *Epistulae morales* 6.4
338 racing ... triumph] Literally 'with four white horses'; Plautus *Asinaria* 279;
    Horace *Satires* 1.7.8; discussed in *Adagia* I iv 21
339 rich hopes] Horace *Epistles* 1.15.19
340 owe ... to Hercules] Latin *dextro Hercule*; Persius *Satires* 2.11 and *Adagia* I i 73
341 Saturn's son] Jupiter
342 underworld Jupiters] *Vejoves*, plural of 'anti-Jove,' an Etruscan deity identified
    with Jupiter by Ovid in *Fasti* 3.429ff
343 confound ... earth] *Adagia* I iii 81; Eris, goddess of discord and mother of Até,
    produced the golden apple which led to the judgement of Paris and the
    Trojan war because she was not invited to the wedding of Peleus and Thetis.

120

344 in a manner] Ie by imitation
345 Diana] Shipwrecked foreigners were sacrificed to her at her temple at Tauris;
    Ovid *Ex Ponto* 3.2.53 and *Tristia* 4.4.63
346 Rhodes] Because of its cloudless sky; Pliny *Naturalis historia* 2.62
347 Tarentum] Horace *Odes* 1.28.29
348 Lampsacus] On the Hellespont, birthplace of Priapus; Virgil *Georgics* 4.111

121

349 Democritus] See n3.
350 lean over to watch] An idea taken from Lucian's *Icaromenippus* (translated by
    Erasmus in 1522)
351 poet's] Added in *1514*
352 step-mother's tomb] Proverbial for feigned grief; *Adagia* I ix 10
353 to his belly] Horace *Epistles* 1.15.32

354 at home] Added in *1514*

355 childless old men] Horace *Satires* 2.5.23

356 rich old women] Juvenal 1.39

357 communism of property] A reference to the Pythagorean maxim 'Among friends all things are held in common'; *Adagia* I i 1

122

358 St James's shrine] The popular pilgrimage shrine at Compostella; cf *Peregrinatio religionis ergo* (Thompson *Colloquies* 287–8).

359 Menippus] The Cynic satirist who is the hero of *Icaromenippus,* ch 15 of which is imitated here

360 golden bough] As a magical wand of office; Virgil *Aeneid* 6.137 and *Adagia* I i 97

361 Greek epigram] *Anthologia Palatina* 9.173, in which five words of ill omen are extracted from the first five lines of the *Iliad*

362 thinking-shop] Like that of Socrates in Aristophanes *Clouds* 94

363 ass of Cumae] Aesop's ass in the lion's skin; *Adagia* I vii 12 and I iii 66

364 Phalaris] See n38.

365 Dionysius] Tyrant of Syracuse who according to tradition became a schoolmaster after he was deposed; *Adagia* II viii 93

366 most of them] Added in *1532*

367 Palaemon ... Donatus] Roman grammarians of the first and fourth centuries AD; Donatus taught St Jerome and his grammar was a standard textbook in the Middle Ages.

123

368 the spirit of Virgil ... in themselves] As Ennius dreamed that Homer's spirit was in him; Persius *Satires* 6.10–11; Horace *Epistles* 2.1.50–3.

369 back-scratching] *Adagia* I vii 96

370 The whole world] The following passage to 'will be wasted' in the next paragraph was added in *1516.*

371 jack-of-all-trades] Possibly a dig at Thomas Linacre, who became Henry VIII's physician in 1510 and was nearly sixty when this passage was added in 1516

372 eight parts of speech] A common subject of grammar books. Erasmus himself wrote a tractate *De constructione octo partium orationis* (London 1513).

373 Aldus ... more than five] The great humanist printer of Venice, who up to this date had published his own Latin grammar in 1493, 1501, 1508, and 1514, and three Greek grammars (Lascaris in 1494, Gaza and Apollonius in 1495). His own was published posthumously in 1515.

374 kings of Persia] Horace *Odes* 3.9.4

375 free race] The proverb is quoted by Lucian *Pro imaginibus* 18; cf Horace *Ars poetica* 9–10 and *Adagia* III i 48.

376 immortality] Eg Horace *Odes* 4.8.28–9

124

377 *Art of Rhetoric*] The treatise *Ad Herennium* was once attributed to Cicero, but its authenticity had been challenged since the fifteenth century; the reference to folly is in 1.6.10.

378 Quintilian] Famous as a writer on oratory rather than as an orator himself; *Institutio oratoria* 6.3 deals with laughter.

379 *Iliad*] *Adagia* IV v 51

380 Persius or Laelius] Named as examples of the learned and not-so-learned in Cicero *De oratore* 2.6.25

381 nine years] As advised by Horace in *Ars poetica* 388

382 sleep ... all things] *Odyssey* 7.289; Moschus *Idyll* 2.3

383 'That's him'] Said of Demosthenes in Cicero *Tusculanae disputationes* 5.103; cf Pliny *Epistles* 9.23.3 and Persius *Satires* 1.28

384 three names] A mark of good family in Rome; Juvenal 5.127

125

385 Stelenus] Probably a mistake for Sthenelus, companion of Diomedes in *Iliad* 2.564. Telemachus is Odysseus' son, Laertes his father.

386 Polycrates] See n9.

387 Thrasymachus] The fifth-century sophist who takes part in Plato's *Republic*

388 Alcaeus ... Callimachus] Greek lyric poets, mentioned together in Horace *Epistles* 2.2.99

389 'The hesitant mob ... views'] Virgil *Aeneid* 2.39

390 Sisyphus] A never-ending task, as was his punishment in Hades; *Odyssey* 11.593ff

391 opinion on opinion and] Added in *1514*

392 copper pots] The famous oracle of Dodona spoke through the rustling of oak leaves or the clanging of copper pots or gongs; *Adagia* I i 7

393 goat's wool] See n22.

394 Stentor] The Greek at Troy whose voice equalled that of fifty men; *Iliad* 5.785, Juvenal 13.112, and *Adagia* II iii 37

395 fleeting shadows] *Odyssey* 10.495

126

396 ditch or stone] Horace *Satires* 2.3.59

397 quiddities, ecceities] Added in *1512*. These are terms used by the scholastics in their disputes about the nature of universals. The quiddity is the principle which determines a thing's species; the ecceity is the term used by Scotus to define what makes a thing this individual member of a species rather than another member.

398 Lynceus] See n232.

399 touchy lot] Latin *genus irritablile*, the phrase used by Horace of poets in *Epistles* 2.2.102

400 Camarina ... noxious plant] Camarina, the swamp which was drained against Apollo's orders, with the result that the city was sacked by its enemies; proverbial for being the cause of one's own disasters; *Adagia* I i 64. The noxious plant, bean trefoil, an emetic in Aristophanes *Lysistrata* 68; *Adagia* I i 65

401 schoolmen's definitions] Added in *1514*

402 bolt holes] Lucian *Eunuchus* 10

403 Vulcan's net] Where he trapped his wife Venus with her lover Mars; *Odyssey* 8.270ff

404 double axe from Tenedos] Proverbial for cutting through ambiguities and arguments; *Adagia* I ix 29

405 threadbare] All these questions are in Peter Lombard's *Sentences* and were discussed by many commentators. For full annotation on points concerning scholasticism and theology see ASD IV-3 146ff.

127

406 if he had consecrated] Added in *1516*

407 What was ... resurrection] Folly implies that the scholastic theologians were more interested in debating abstract subtleties than questions of moral and religious significance.

408 There are] The following passage to 'even squalid' on page 129 was added in *1514*.

409 crumb and stitch] Cicero *Pro Quinctio* 15.49

410 realists, nominalists] Those who believed that the universal idea existed outside individuals, and those who thought it only a logical category

411 Thomists, Albertists, Ockhamists, and Scotists] Followers of Thomas Aquinas, Albertus Magnus, William of Ockham, and Duns Scotus

412 'Faith ... not seen'] Heb 11:1

128

413 mother of Jesus ... immaculate] The dogma had long been controversial and was not accepted by the Paris theologians until 1496.

414 Peter ... the keys] Matt 16:19

415 formal ... indelible marks] The four types of cause are Aristotelian; the sacraments of baptism, confirmation, and ordination were held to be indelible because they could not be repeated.

416 'God is ... in truth'] John 4:24

417 the apostles] Added in *1516*

418 condemned questions ... 'battle of words'] 1 Tim 1:4, 6:4,20; 2 Tim 2:16, 23; Titus 3:9

419 Chrysippean subtleties] Those of the philosopher of the third century BC who elaborated and set down the Stoic tenets

420 Chrysostom, Basil] St John Chrysostom and St Basil, bishop of Caesarea, were Fathers of the Greek church; Erasmus edited their works as well as those of St Jerome.

129

421 *quodlibet*] A subject chosen from a free range of theological problems, originally for public disputation, then as a written exercise

422 or heretic] Added in *1515*

423 reweaving Penelope's web] An endless task, as she unwove at night what she wove by day, to defer deciding between her suitors; *Odyssey* 2.104–5 and *Adagia* I iv 42

424 Atlas ... shoulders] Virgil *Aeneid* 4.247; Ovid *Metamorphoses* 4.656ff

130

425 greatest of Aristotelians] Ἀριστοτελικώτατος, a coinage of Erasmus', and a genuine tribute, though Aquinas knew no Greek

426 correct] The argument is technical, referring to the elaborations of speculative grammar; see further ASD IV-3 156ff. Of the second pair of phrases, *ollae*

fervere and *ollam fervere*, one is a historic infinitive and the other an infinitive of reported speech.

427 They also ... all this] Added in *1514*
428 the most extensive ... of all] Ie the empyrean
429 help him ... Athene] Vulcan split Jupiter's head with his axe to enable him to give birth to Athene fully armed.
430 fillets] Probably a reference to the doctoral padded cap or bonnet, such as Erasmus is generally shown wearing in his portraits
431 tetragram] The four hebrew consonants in the name of Jahweh or Jehovah
432 solitaries] The word 'monk' is derived from the Greek *monos* 'alone' or 'solitary.'

131

433 and ... boat] Added in *1514*
434 or ... colour] Added in *1514*
435 Cilician goat's hair ... Milesian wool] Coarse and very fine wool: Virgil *Georgics* 3.306 and Horace *Epistles* 1.17.30
436 They ... other] Added in *1514*
437 Cordeliers ... Bullists] Cordeliers and Friars Minor are Franciscans in general; Colettines, Minims, and Bullists are branches of the Franciscan order.
438 and they ... Bullists] Added in *1514*
439 Bernardines] Cistercians, so called after St Bernard of Clairvaux
440 Brigittines] Founded by St Bridget of Sweden. 'The Brigittines ... Jacobins' was added in *1514*.
441 Augustinians] The order of friars founded in 1256 to which Erasmus belonged
442 Williamites] Founded in the twelfth century by St William of Maleval
443 Jacobins] Dominicans, originally so called in France because their house in Paris was in the Rue Saint-Jacques
444 Most ... help from me] Text to 132 (... help from me.) added in *1514*
445 his own rule] John 15:12

132

446 sponge] Eg St Simeon Stylites and his followers, the pillar ascetics
447 petty prayers] Latin *preculae*; the word can also mean 'rosary beads.'
448 faith and charity] Matthew 25:35–40; the words 'faith and' were added in *1532*.
449 I do not ... own deeds] Cf Luke 18:9–14.
450 Abraxasians] A Gnostic sect who believed in 365 heavens, a number they calculated by adding up the numerical equivalents of the Greek letters in the word *abraxas*.
451 mendicants] The friars, who were not cloistered and lived by begging; they were especially active in preaching and hearing confessions.
452 hornets' nest] *Adagia* I i 60
453 Cerberus] Virgil *Aeneid* 6.420

133

454 or if] Text to 134 (... in such a way.) added in *1514*
455 Bel] Daniel 14

456 Horace] *Satires* 2.7.21

457 blinder than a mole] *Adagia* I iii 55

458 Jesus ... sins of the world] John 1:29. Clarence Miller (ASD IV-3 164) explains this passage on the symbolism in the name Jesus with refrence to J. Chomarat 'L'Eloge de la folie et ses traducteurs français au xxe siècle' *Bulletin de l'Association Guillaume Budé* 2 (June 1972) 179–80.

459 Niobe] Turned to stone by grief at the loss of her children; Ovid *Metamorphoses* 6.302ff; *Adagia* III iii 33

460 Priapus] Horace *Satires* 1.8.44–50. Watching the rites of the witches Canidia and Sagana, Priapus burst his buttocks.

134

461 an introduction ... a bad one] Cicero *De inventione* 1.15.20, 17.23, and 18.26; Quintilian 4.1.42

462 'Now ... taking him?'] Virgil *Eclogues* 3.19

463 has never ... heaven] Ie is irrelevant; Lucian *Alexander* 54; *Adagia* V v 44

464 Cherubic Doctors] Added in 1532; the great scholastics were given such honorific titles, by which they were known to later generations.

465 *Mirror of History ... Deeds of the Romans*] The *Speculum historiale* of Vincent of Beauvais and the *Gesta Romanorum*, both of the thirteenth century, were popular sources of moral anecdote.

466 allegorically ... anagogically] The three adverbs were added in 1522. Medieval commentators on the Scriptures gave each text four interpretations; a literal meaning, an allegorical meaning which drew out the religious lesson, a tropological (moral) meaning, and an anagogical (mystical) meaning

467 chimaera] The composite beast of fable, here recalling the opening words of Horace's *Ars poetica*

468 emotions ... exclamations] Cicero *De oratore* 3.60.224; Quintilian 11.3.44–5

469 hellebore] See n291.

470 laughter] See n377 and n378.

135

471 ass ... lyre] *Adagia* I iv 35

472 a Paul or an Antony] More probably the Apostle and St Antony of Padua, both famed for their preaching, than the fourth-century Desert Fathers

473 disgraceful] Added in 1514

474 hair's breadth] Literally 'finger's breadth'; *Adagia* I v 6

136

475 lap of the gods] Horace *Odes* 1.9.9

476 insignia] Erasmus has a similar symbolic passage in *Institutio principis christiani* 215; the choice of sceptre, crown, and mantle here recalls Matthew 27:28–9.

477 For the most part] Added in 1522

478 to shed ... shame] Latin *faciem perfricuere*: Quintilian 11.3.160; *Adagia* I viii 47

137

479 Phaeacians] In *Odyssey* 6.8 the Phaeacians are noted for luxurious living.

480 suitors] Said to be idle layabouts in Horace *Epistles* 1.2.28

481 which Echo ... than I can] Added in *1514*; because she has the last word?
482 of the ladies] Added in *1514*
483 the noblemen] Added in *1514*
484 on the meaning] The symbolic meanings here and in the next paragraph were traditional.
485 careless look-out] *Iliad* 10.515; in Erasmus' text the words appear in Greek font; ἀλαοσκοπίη puns on the word *episkopos* 'bishop' in its literal sense of 'overseer.'
486 spiritual riches] Corinthians 1:2

138
487 'Supreme Holiness'] In the *Enchiridion* (LB V 49B) Erasmus emphasizes that ecclesiastical titles should denote function, not status or power; cf *Institutio principis christiani* 248.
488 salt] Matthew 5:13
489 sea of profiteering] Latin *mare bonorum*; *Adagia* I iii 29
490 something more suggestive] Listrius sees here a reference to the reputed pederasty of Julius II.
491 lights of the world] From the original version of the vespers hymn for the feast of St Peter and St Paul

139
492 For them ... ignominious end] Cf *Julius exclusus* 171.
493 Paul] Romans 16:8
494 mere nod] *Adagia* IV ix 39
495 Gospel] Matthew 19:27
496 fire and sword] *Adagia* IV viii 11
497 befits wild beasts] Cf *Querela pacis* 306.
498 Furies] Virgil *Aeneid* 7.323ff
499 old men] Julius II was over sixty when he became pope in 1503 and started his ten-year campaign to extend papal territories; cf *Julius exclusus* 196.
500 upside down] *Adagia* I iii 85

140
501 German bishops] The prince-bishops, some of whom were also imperial electors, whose feudal secular powers could be more important to them than their religious duties, eg Johann II Markgraf von Baden, elector and bishop of Trier (*Neue Deutsche Biographie* x 539–40) and the three fighting prince-bishops of Würzburg listed in NDB x 544–6 (Information given to the translator by Clarence H. Miller)
502 their rights to] Added in *1514*
503 any] Added in *1514*
504 'regulars'] Ie the canons regular

141
505 princes] Replaced 'pontiffs' in *1514*
506 Nemesis] The personification of avenging justice, though it is not she but Fortuna who bestows advantages

507 Timotheus] Athenian general of the fourth century BC; he was called Eutyches 'lucky'; *Adagia* I v 82

508 'The creel ... sleeps'] *Adagia* I v 82; *Panegyricus* 37

509 'The owl ... wing'] A reference to the luck of Athens: the owl was sacred to Athene; *Adagia* I i 76

510 born on the fourth] Ie the fourth month, like Hercules, and so destined to trials in life; *Adagia* I i 77

511 Sejanus's nag] It brought misfortune to its owners; Aulus Gellius 3.9.6 and *Adagia* I x 97

512 gold of Toulouse] Whoever touched it died in agony; Aulus Gellius 3.9.7 and *Adagia* I x 98

513 notebooks] His collection of proverbs, first published as *Collectanea* in Paris in 1500, then in an enlarged edition as *Adagiorum chiliades* in Venice in 1508.

514 'the die's cast'] *Adagia* I iv 32, recalling Caesar's words on crossing the Rubicon; Suetonius *Caesar* 32

515 pleasing princes] Horace *Epistles* 1.17.35

142

516 nothing to the point] Aristophanes *Ecclesiazusae* 751; *Adagia* I v 45

517 'To play ... wisdom.'] From the spurious *Disticha* of Cato (2.18.2), a late classical or early medieval compilation of sentences used as a school-book in the Middle Ages and Renaissance

518 porker] Horace's description of himself in *Epistles* 1.4.15–16

519 'Mix folly ... in season'] Horace *Odes* 4.12.27–8

520 'to seem ... short-tempered'] Horace *Epistles* 2.2.126–8

521 childish] The epithet 'childish' (the word appears in Greek font: νήπιος) is in fact applied to Telemachus only in its strict sense, when he is a baby (*Odyssey* 11.449), though Homer uses it in both *Iliad* and *Odyssey* in its extended sense to denote foolish, childish behaviour of adults.

522 passions] Horace *Epistles* 1.2.8

523 Cicero's famous tribute] *Ad familiares* 9.22.4

524 Sorbonne] The seat of the Paris faculty of theology where Duns Scotus, the 'Doctor Subtilis,' had lectured

525 to the devil] Literally 'crows' (*ad corvos*); *Adagia* II i 96

526 desks] Horace *Satires* 1.1.120

527 Greek words] From no 68 in the anonymous collection of *Priapeia*; see also Horace *Satires* 1.8.

528 Lucian] *Gallus* 2

529 Ecclesiastes] 1:15

143

530 Jeremiah] 10:14, 10:7 and 12; 9:23

531 and in making ... Ecclesiastes] Added in *1514*

532 he cries] Eccles 1:2; 12:8

533 in which ... fools] Added in *1514*

534 Ecclesiasticus] 27:11. Added in *1514*

535 Gospel] Matt 19:17

536 Proverbs] 15:21

537 He who ... grievance] Eccles 1.18
538 Surely too] Text to 'with all?' (on page 144) added in *1514*
539 preacher] Eccles 7.4
540 And I gave ... folly] Eccles 1:17
541 evangelist's teaching] Matthew 19:30; Mark 10:31; Luke 13:30
542 chapter 44] Either a misprint in the text of 1514 or a mistake; the correct refer-
    ence is Sir 41:15.
543 development ... argument] Quintilian 5.11.3
544 Aristotle] The phrase is quoted in *Rhetoric* 1.6.23 (1363a7) without a verb, and
    is interpreted by Erasmus here and in *Adagia* II i 65 as meaning that no care
    is taken of cheap possessions. Later editors supply 'is broken,' meaning that
    the labour of carrying the full pot home is wasted.

144

545 Ecclesiasticus] Sir 20:33, 41:15
546 Ecclesiastes] 10:3
547 great king] Ie Solomon, in Prov 30.2
548 Paul] 2 Cor 11:23
549 in his ... Corinthians] Added in *1514*
550 But at this point] The following passage to 'back to Paul' (147) was added in
    1514.
551 Greek pedants] The Latin diminutive (*Graeculi*) is contemptuous, with a pun
    on *graculi* 'jackdaws'; *Adagia* I vii 22
552 crows' eyes] Explained in *Adagia* I iii 75 as destroying the work of superiors or
    'stealing the laurels'
553 three tongues] The humanists insisted that a knowledge of Greek, Latin, and
    Hebrew was essential for theological study, and Erasmus supported the
    trilingual foundation at Louvain.

145

554 renowned theologian] Nicholas of Lyra (d 1349), the well-known biblical com-
    mentator to whom Erasmus often slyly refers in the saying of the ass
    playing the lyre (*Adagia* I iv 35). The expanded translation attempts to convey
    the double meaning of *gloriosus*.
555 five tongues] Greek, Latin, Hebrew, Chaldean, Dalmatian
556 'to the unknown god'] Acts 17:23, discussed by Jerome in his commentary on
    Titus 1:12
557 words of Luke] 22.35–6
558 fire with water] *Adagia* IV iii 94

146

559 in royal style] *Adagia* II viii 86
560 sparrows and lilies] Matthew 5:4–5 and 11, 10:29, 6:28
561 ordered ... bought] Luke 22:35–6
562 sheathed] John 18:11
563 another] Possibly Jordan of Quedlinburg, the Augustinian hermit and mystic
    who died in 1370 or 1380; Listrius identifies him only as 'Jordanus.'

564 Habakkuk's words] 3.7. Jordanus misinterpreted the word *pellium* 'tent' (made of skins) as 'human skin.'

565 Paul] Titus 3:10. In his commentary on this verse Erasmus says he heard of this incident from Colet, who was present when it happened. See further ASD IV-3 187.

147

566 lawyer from Tenedos] *Adagia* IV i 7 (*Tenedius patronus*), referring to a shrewd or persevering lawyer

567 thou shalt ... live] Exodus 22:18

568 hotfoot] Literally 'roughshod' (*pedibus peronatis*), a phrase only in Persius *Satires* 5.102

569 Chrysippus and Didymus] The Stoic philosopher reputed to have written over 700 works and the grammarian of the first century BC who was credited with nearly 4,000, none of which survives (Diogenes Laertius 7.7 and Seneca *Epistulae morales* 88.37)

570 blockhead] Literally 'figwood,' meaning 'useless'; Theocritus 10.45 and *Adagia* I vii 85

571 Paul] 2 Cor 11:19

572 'Receive ... as a fool'] 2 Cor 11:16

573 'I do not ... foolish'] 2 Cor 11:17

574 'We are ... Christ's sake'] 1 Cor 4:10

575 And again ... authority] Added in *1514*

576 as a ... benefit] Added in *1514*

577 'Whoever ... truly wise'] 1 Cor 3:18

578 And according ... fools] Added in *1514*; Luke 24:25

579 that godlike] Added in *1514*

580 'God's foolishness ... men'] 1 Cor 1:25

581 Origen] The Greek Father of the church whom Erasmus so much admired; see his *Homilies on Jeremiah* (PL 25 630–2), translated by St Jerome.

582 'The doctrine ... perishing] 1 Cor 1:18

583 Psalms] 69:5 (Vulgate 68:6). But as Listrius notes, Christ was thought to be speaking not for himself but as the mouthpiece of sinful Christians.

584 But there ... foolishness] Added in *1514*

585 Brutus and Cassius] Described as pale and thin by Plutarch *Caesar* 62

586 Nero] Tacitus *Annals* 15.62ff

587 Dionysius] The tyrant of Syracuse who dismissed Plato from his court

588 Paul] 1 Cor 1:27 and 1:21

589 prophet] Isaiah 29:14, quoted in 1 Cor 1:19

148

590 children] Matt 11:25; Luke 10:21

591 (The Greek ... wise.)] Added in *1514*

592 relevant passages] Matthew 23:13–15 and 23–7; Luke 11:42–3

593 What else ... wise?] Added in *1514*

594 donkey] Matthew 21:2

595 dove] Matthew 3:16

596 not of ... hawk] Added in *1514*
597 young mules] Only mentioned five times according to ASD IV-3 189
598 his sheep] John 10:1–27; Matthew 25:32–3
599 sheeplike character] *Historia animalium* 9.3.1 (610b22); *Adagia* III i 95
600 John ... Apocalypse] John 1:29 and 36; Revelations 5–7
601 wisdom of the Father] 1 Cor 1:18 and 24
602 folly of mankind] Replaced 'our folly' in *1516*
603 man's form] Phil 2:7
604 made sin] 2 Cor 5:21
605 folly of the cross] 1 Cor 1:21
606 children] Matt 18:3; Mark 10:15; Luke 18:17
607 lilies] Matt 6:28; Luke 12:27
608 mustard-seed] Matt 13:31; Mark 4:31; Luke 13:19
609 sparrows] Matt 10:29; Luke 12:6
610 how ... governors] Matt 10:18; Mark 13:9–11; Luke 21:12–14
611 not to seek ... seasons] Acts 1:7
612 forbade ... knowledge] Gen 2:17
613 Paul] 1 Cor 8:1
614 St Bernard] In his fourth sermon on the Ascension (PL 183 310–12)

149
615 Numbers] 12:11
616 Saul] 1 Sam 26:21
617 David] 2 Sam 24:10
618 'Father forgive ... they do'] Luke 23:34
619 Paul] 1 Tim 1:13
620 psalmist] Ps 24.7 (Vulgate), 25:7 (RSV)
621 proper place] Perhaps at 147 where Ps 69:5 is quoted; see n583 above.
622 Then perhaps ... folly] Added in *1514*
623 in some form] Added in *1522*
624 apostles ... new wine] Acts 2:13
625 Festus ... mad] Acts 26:24

150
626 donned the lion-skin] Ie taken on too big a task; *Adagia* I iii 66
627 Platonists] Ie the Neoplatonists, especially Plotinus and those of the later
   Florentine Academy
628 bound down] Plato *Gorgias* 493A
629 as they truly are] Ie not as shadows in the cave; see 119 n335 and next
   paragraph.
630 Plato defines] *Phaedo* 80E
631 inspired] As Socrates says in Plato *Apology* 39C
632 myth in Plato] *Republic* 7.514A–17A
633 last to the soul] The division into three goods is Platonic and is repeated by
   Aristotle, eg *Laws* 743E and *Ethica Nicomachea* 1098b12.

151
634 having ... possess] Cf 1 Cor 7:29–30.

635 drank oil ... wine] Said in the *Golden Legend* to have happened to St Bernard when meditating on the Scriptures

636 lust ... envy] All the seven deadly sins except avarice

637 intermediate affections] See *Enchiridion* LB V 19A–20B where Erasmus refers to Origen's commentary on St Paul; the division into body, soul, and spirit is stated in 1 Thess 5:23. Erasmus follows Plotinus in ascribing the passions to the body rather than the soul, but distinguished between the grosser and the more refined passions which have something of the soul in them.

638 country] *Patriae* replaced *patris* in *1532*.

639 they say] Added in *1516*

152

640 the pious] Added in *1516*

641 Plato] *Phaedrus* 245B

642 For anyone ... object of his love] P.O. Kristeller 'Erasmus from an Italian Perspective' *Renaissance Quarterly* 23 (1970) 11 notes that this echoes Ficino's commentary on the *Symposium* of Plato.

643 prophet] Isa 64:4, quoted in 1 Cor 2:9

644 the part of Folly] A deliberate allusion to Luke 10:42, the 'best part' chosen by Mary, which Christ said should not be taken from her despite Martha's pleas. Some later texts read *Mariae* for *Moriae*.

153

645 sound without sense] Virgil *Aeneid* 10.640

646 in the body or outside it] 2 Cor 12:2

647 overshot the mark] Lucian *Gallus* 6; Plato *Cratylus* 413A

648 Greek proverb] Adapted from Aulus Gellius 2.6.9; see *Adagia* I vi 1. Both refer to 'a gardener' (*olitor*) not a foolish man.

649 old saying] Martial 1.27.7; *Adagia* I vii 1

650 Clap your hands] *Plaudite*: the conventional ending of Roman comedy

651 The End] Greek τέλος, replacing the ending of the earlier editions *Finis Moriae in gratiam Mori*

JULIUS EXCLUDED FROM HEAVEN: A DIALOGUE /
DIALOGUS JULIUS EXCLUSUS E COELIS

Introductory note

156

1 See the reviews of the question in *Opuscula* 41–8, Pascal 7–14 (by J.K. Sowards) and McConica 451–3 and 467–71.

2 *Opuscula* 41–2 and 55–7

3 See the list of editions in *Opuscula* 55–62.

4 Ep 961:47

5 See L. Geiger 'Studien zur Geschichte des französischen Humanismus' *Vierteljahrschrift für Kultur und Literatur der Renaissance* 1 (1886) 2–48 and

G. Tournoy-Thoen 'Deux épîtres inédites de Fausto Andrelini et l'auteur du *Julius exclusus*' *Humanistica Lovaniensia* 18 (1969) 43–75

6 Pastor VI 437–8n, Hauser 609–11, Stange, especially 92ff, and most recently G. Gebhardt *Die Stellung des Erasmus von Rotterdam zur Römischen Kirche* (Marburg 1966) 377–95

7 *Opuscula* 55 item 2; N. van der Blom has argued, rather unconvincingly, that the initials represent a pseudonym of Erasmus: 'F.A.F. Poeta Regius, l'auteur du *Julius exclusus*' *Moreana* 29 (March 1971) 5–11.

8 Tournoy-Thoen (see above n5) 50

9 Bainton 'Erasmus and Luther' 19

10 *Opuscula* 59 item 13

11 See Oulmont 235 (based on a confusion of editions), Hauser 607 (retracting his earlier support for Hutten's authorship), and E. Böcking ed *Ulrici Hutteni equitis Germani opera* (Leipzig 1859–70) IV 422 (attributing the dialogue to Andrelini, though publishing it among Hutten's works).

12 P. Paschini 'L'autore del dialogo satirico contro Giulio II' *Atti dell'Accademia degli Arcadi* 13–14 (Rome 1937) 85–98

13 Ep 961:46; see Bainton 'Erasmus and Luther' 25.

14 References in *Opuscula* 42n

15 Ep 532:27–8

16 Ep 961:53

17 For example Epp 622, 636, 785, 908

18 Erasmus *was* present during the printing of one edition: see C. Reedijk 'Erasme, Thierry Martens et le *Julius exclusus*' in J. Coppens ed *Scrinium Erasmianum* (Leiden 1969) 2 vols II 368–9.

19 Epp 961 and 967

157

20 Rogers Ep 83 p 188–9

21 Cf Erasmus' comparison of Julius and Leo in Ep 335.

22 See Pineau *Erasme et la papauté* 1–10

23 H.C. Porter ed and D.F.S. Thomson trans *Erasmus and Cambridge: The Cambridge Letters of Erasmus* (Toronto 1963) 62–5 and J.K. Sowards 'Erasmus and the "Other" Pope Julius' *Wichita State University Bulletin* 48.1 (February 1972; University Studies 90)

24 Allen II 418–20, based on Ep 502:10; see also Ep 431.

25 Latin text of the epigram in Pineau 'Erasme est-il l'auteur du *Julius*?' *Revue de littérature comparée* 5 (1925) 385–7, *Opuscula* 35–7, Reedijk *Poems* 391–3; English translation in Pascal 18–19, J.K. Sowards 'Erasmus and the Making of the *Julius Exclusus*' *Wichita State University Bulletin* 40.3 (August 1964; University Studies 60), and Tracy *Politics* 27–8

26 Reedijk *Poems* 391–3n; cf Hauser 613–14.

27 C. Reedijk 'Een Schimpdicht van Erasmus op Julius II' *Opstellen door Vrienden en Collegas Aangeboden aan Dr F.K.H. Kossmann* (The Hague 1958) 186–207

28 See 138–9 above.

29 For example Epp 245 and 262

158

30 J.K. Sowards 'The Two Lost Years of Erasmus: Summary, Review and Speculation' *Studies in the Renaissance* 9 (1962) 185–6

31 Particularly from Andrea Ammonio, who had connections in Rome and with the della Rovere family: see Epp 236, 239, 243, 247, and also 251 and 257.

32 See Pastor VI 235–46. The Borgia affair is not mentioned in Erasmus' extant correspondence.

33 Stange 84–116 (on France) and 132–99 (on conciliarism); see also Stange's review of the article by Paschini (above, n12) in *Zeitschrift für systematische Theologie* 18 (1941) 535–88; for qualified support of Stange see A. Renaudet *Erasme et l'Italie* (Geneva 1954) 112 and Tracy *Growth of a Mind* 137 and n (see also Tracy *Politics* 144–5 n55).

34 See for example Oulmont 235, Stange 116–31, and Pascal 25–8 (introduction by Sowards).

35 Epp 622:16–18 and 636:16–20, echoed by More in *To a Monk* (Rogers Ep 83)

36 Stange 92–116

37 Ep 240:36; see also J. Hutton 'Erasmus and France: The Propaganda for Peace' *Studies in the Renaissance* 8 (1962) 103–27.

159

38 For detailed accounts of this French propaganda, see Lemaire de Belges V lxiv ff, Oulmont 215–37, and P. Spaak *Jean Lemaire de Belges: sa vie, son œuvre et ses meilleures pages* (Paris 1926) 83ff.

39 Cf J.K. Sowards 'Erasmus in England 1509–14' *University of Wichita Bulletin* 37.2 (May 1962; University Studies 51) 10–12.

40 Renaudet in *Erasme et l'Italie* (above, n33) 112 considers that Erasmus could not possibly have written these eulogies; he suspects therefore that the *Julius* emanated from the entourage of one of the dissident cardinals. Certainly Andrelini had written a long eulogy of d'Amboise, translated by Jehan d'Ivry as *Les faictz et gestes de ... monsieur le legat* (Paris: G. Eustace 1508; British Library C 34 h 9), but this in no way resembles the passage in the *Julius*.

41 *Opuscula* 99n

42 McConica 460

43 Ibidem 454–60

160

44 See McConica 461 and M. O'Rourke Boyle 'Weavers, Farmers, Tailors, Travellers, Masons, Prostitutes, Pimps, Turks, Little Women, and Other Theologians' *Erasmus in English* 3 (1971) 1–7.

45 See Porter (above, n23) 38–61.

46 Pineau *Erasme et la papauté* 19–24, E.V. Telle 'Le *De copia verborum* d'Erasme et le *Julius exclusus e coelis*' *Revue de littérature comparée* 22 (1948) 444–6, Bainton 'Erasmus and Luther' 20–1, Ferguson in the notes to his edition in *Opuscula* and Sowards in his notes to Pascal's translation. Most of these parallels are referred to in the notes to the text below.

47 Pineau 'Erasme est-il l'auteur du *Julius*?' (above, n25) 394

48 Stange 49–54; see also Ep 967:188–96 where Erasmus defends himself on similar lines.
49 Cf D.F.S. Thomson 'The Latinity of Erasmus' in *Erasmus* 123–4.
50 See 164–5 below.
51 Cf McConica 471 and Tracy *Growth of a Mind* 137.
52 The fullest account is still that of Rodocanachi, which reads at times like a commentary on *Julius exclusus* – testimony to the basic factual accuracy of the dialogue, whatever its satirical distortions.

161
53 See 197 and n209 below.
54 Bainton *Erasmus of Christendom* 285–9
55 *Adagia* III i 1; see Phillips 281.
56 Creighton IV 164–5 and Pastor VI 230–1 and 437
57 *Il Principe* ed L.A. Burd (Oxford 1891) 250–2 (ch 11)
58 See 177 and n90; the rehabilitations of Julius in Creighton IV 165–9, Gregorovius VIII 116–19, and Pastor VI 438–54 also lay stress on this point.
59 Quoted by Creighton IV 166
60 On this journey see Epp 200–13, Bainton *Erasmus of Christendom* 99–115, *Opuscula* 38–41, Sowards 'Erasmus and the Making of the *Julius exclusus*' (above n25), 8–9 and especially P. de Nolhac *Erasme en Italie* (Paris 1888).
61 Nolhac (above, n60) 82; there is no documentary evidence to support this.
62 The works are lost: see the catalogue of his works in Allen I 37.

162
63 Phillips 105
64 'To the Christian Nobility of the German Nation' *Luther's Works* (Philadelphia 1955–   ) XLIV especially 155–6
65 See *Opuscula* 42 and 53.
66 Ibidem 55–9
67 Pascal 33–4
68 Cf the Sorbonne's censure of a work entitled 'Paradis du Pape Jule' in *Catalogus librorum qui hactenus a Facultate Theologiae Parisiensi ... censura digni visi sunt* (Antwerpiae: in aedibus Joan. Steelsii 1545) sig D, 4r (British Library C 107 a 3).
69 Epp 961 and 967
70 Cf Pineau *Erasme et la papauté* 29–51.

163
71 Ibidem 45–7 and McConica 458–62
72 In *Opuscula* 338–61; Erasmus certainly had a hand in this work and passionately endorsed it.
73 McConica 462–7; see also W.J. Bouwsma's intervention (ibidem 477) on possible medieval precedents.
74 Cf Thompson *Under Pretext of Praise* 98.
75 *Opuscula* 53
76 Paraphrased by Pastor VI 469–70

77 See J.J. Beard 'Letters from the Elysian Fields: A Group of Poems for Louis xıı'
   Bibliothèque d'Humanisme et Renaissance 31 (1969) 27–38.
78 Cf Sowards in Pascal 27–8.

164
79 See Marcia L. Colish 'Seneca's *Apocolocyntosis* as a Possible Source for Erasmus' *Julius exclusus*' *Renaissance Quarterly* 29 (1976) 361–8. The work was
   first printed at Rome in 1513; it was included in the 'Erasmian' edition of
   Seneca (1515) with notes by Beatus Rhenanus.
80 These are the works on which G. Thompson bases *Under Pretext of Praise*, her
   study of Erasmus' satirical fiction; on Lucian's influence, see especially
   C.R. Thompson *The Translations of Lucian by Erasmus and St Thomas More* (Ithaca 1940).
81 These are most closely imitated in the colloquy *Charon*; it is interesting that
   this, like much of the *Julius*, is an indictment of war, and that one speaker is
   a 'Genius' called Alastor.
82 Cf R.P. Adams *The Better Part of Valor: More, Erasmus, Colet and Vives on
   Humanism, War and Peace, 1496–1535* (Seattle 1962) 73.

165
83 Cf W. Kaiser *Praisers of Folly* (Cambridge, Mass 1963) 35–50.
84 Thompson *Under Pretext of Praise* 87–103
85 Ibidem 99
86 See for example *Institutio principis christiani* 245–53 and *Moria*, especially 135–
   6.

166
87 Cf McConica 454.
88 J.A. Froude *Life and Letters of Erasmus* (London 1900) 156
89 Paris 1512, reprinted in d'Héricault and Montaiglon eds *Oeuvres complètes de
   Pierre Gringore* (Paris 1858) I 198–286; see also Oulmont 271–97.
90 As at the Gymnasium Erasmianum in Rotterdam in 1969 and in a BBC
   television documentary on Erasmus shown on Good Friday 1974. A perfor-
   mance of the complete work by undergraduates at University College Oxford
   in 1960 was received, according to the director, in puzzled silence.
91 Future references are to the line numbers of the Latin text in *Opuscula*.

167
92 Cf D.F.S. Thomson 'The Latinity of Erasmus' in *Erasmus* 124–32.
93 From Plautus and Terence: *actutum* (11), *approbe* (12), *gannire* (139), *astutia*
   (211), *sedulo* (224), *inhiare* (341), *graecissare* (366), *probe* (380), *Apage* (384),
   deierare (422), *tantillum* (496), *techna* (561), *furcifer* (616), *deglubere* (928), *nugari*
   (988), *obtundere* (990), and phrases like *rem acu tetigit* (44), *callere sensum*
   (96), *obturare os* (310), *bona verba* (337), *pro delectamento* (366), *discedere minus*
   (528); from later Latin: *crepare* (78), *conspurcere* (81), *marcidus* (85), *larvalis*
   (232), *comatulus* (249), *stabularius* (490), *inculpatus* (596), *catastrophe* (631), *idol-
   um* (711), *nugamenta* (840), *medela* (950), *phreneticum* (964), *byssus* (1031). It
   will be noticed that most of these are found in the early part of the dialogue.

94 Such as: *naviculator* (150), *muliercula* (164), *pauperculus* (305)
95 Such as: *verissime, modestissime, invictissime* (243–6)
96 Cf D.F.S. Thomson 'The Latinity of Erasmus' in *Erasmus* 115.
97 See *Opuscula* 55 and 63.
98 Pascal 33–5; the French translation of A. Bonneau (1877) has been republished, with a new introduction and notes, by J.-C. Margolin in *Guerre et paix dans la pensée d'Erasme* (Paris 1973) 48–103.

Julius Excluded from Heaven: A Dialogue

168
1 Genius] In pre-Christian Rome, the guardian spirit of a man or of a place; as used here, the term obviously has satirical pagan associations. See also n23 below.
2 knowledge] See Luke 11:52 and especially Matt 16:19, the *locus classicus* for the matter of Petrine authority and the papal claims; for these theories and the controversy surrounding them, see M.M. Winter *Saint Peter and the Popes* (Baltimore and London 1960) 7–11 and 17–18, Pineau *Erasme et la papauté* 34n, and H. von Campenhausen 'Die Schlüsselgewalt der Kirche' *Evangelische Theologie* 4 (1937) 143–69. Some of Julius' contemporaries dubbed him *armiger* 'bearer of arms' rather than *claviger* 'bearer of keys' and it was rumoured that he had flung the keys of St Peter into the Tiber, wishing to wield only the (temporal) sword of Paul: see Gregorovius VIII 66 and 71n, and Rodocanachi 103.
3 wrecker of cities] Latin *urbium eversor*; the phrase recurs in a denunciation of tyranny in the adage *Sileni Alcibiadis* (III iii 1; see Phillips 276).
4 oak] The crest of the della Rovere family, derived from the Latin form of the name, *Roboreus* 'oaken'
5 triple crown] The papal tiara: see Rodocanachi 82–3 on the sumptuous headgear made for Julius.
6 robe ... jewels] Cf Pastor VI 282 on the cope worn by Julius at Bologna (where Erasmus saw him).
7 tyrant] Cf Lemaire de Belges III 259, writing in 1511 of the richness of the papal tiara, bejewelled like that of an oriental prince.

169
8 Simon ... Christ] Acts 8:18–24
9 Pestis Maxima] 'Supreme Plague'
10 hit ... head] Cf *Adagia* II iv 93
11 Pontifex Maximus] 'Supreme Pontiff'
12 Trismegistus] A pun on this Graeco-Latin form of the name and style of the Egyptian deity Thoth, 'the Thrice-Great'
13 Optimus] Probably another pun, based on the conventional designation of Jupiter, 'Optimus Maximus'. In the *Ciceronianus* Erasmus describes a speech at Rome in which the orator compared Julius to 'Jupiter Optimus Maximus' with his triple thunderbolt; see 384 and also Allen Ep 1805:85–6.
14 'saint'] There follows a series of puns on the word *sanctus*, meaning both

'holy' and 'saint'; Julius compares 'Saint' Peter's title unfavourably with the traditional papal title 'his Holiness.'

15 'cock-and-bulls'] A pun on the literal meaning of *bulla*, a bubble: the seal on these documents was normally a 'bubble' of lead.

16 drunk] A charge also made in Erasmus' epigram on Julius and by many other contemporaries: see Pastor VI 268 and Rodocanachi 81 and n4.

17 First of all ... armour] This description corresponds with contemporary satirical portraits of Julius: see Pastor VI 360–1 and Rodocanachi facing 96.

170

18 Your whole body ... drink] In fact, Julius displayed remarkable physical vigour throughout his reign, despite suffering from gout; see Pastor VI 212–14 and Rodocanachi 7–8.

19 life] Perhaps inspired by Terence *Phormio* 268, where the slave Geta plays much the same role as Genius here

20 pagan Julius] A comparison also made in the epigram and in Epp 205:42–3 and 262:3, but one which Julius might have accepted, since his flatterers and fellow-countrymen also compared him with Julius Caesar and other Roman emperors: see Gregorovius VIII 53 and 110, Rodocanachi 177, Creighton IV 165, and Pastor VI 212.

21 *Ma di si!*] The force of these syllables is clear enough, but there are several possible interpretations: Italian: 'Ma di si' (But [come on!] say yes); Greek 'Mὰ Δί si' (Yes, by Zeus), cf Rabelais *Le Quart Livre* ed R. Marichal (Geneva 1947) 276 ('Briefve declaration' ch 15); Latin (contracted): 'Mater Dei, si' (Mother of God, yes). Perhaps the expression became proverbial: it reappears in an anti-papal context in the *Satyre Menippée de la vertu du Catholicon d'Espagne* (1594) 58 (BL G15471).

22 stick] Julius quite often lashed out with his staff; see G. Vasari *The Lives of the Painters, Sculptors and Architects* trans A.B. Hinds (London 1963) IV 122 and 130 and Rodocanachi 7.

23 evil genius] A reference to the contemporary theory that a man was born with two genii, good and evil: see *Adagia* I i 72 and D.T. Starnes 'The Figure Genius in the Renaissance' *Studies in the Renaissance* 11 (1964) 234–44.

24 hurl ... excommunication] The expression here, *torquere fulmen*, is usually associated with Jupiter (*Aeneid* 4.208 for example); cf n13 above. Julius frequently used the spiritual weapons of excommunication and interdict against his political opponents, as the dialogue reveals.

25 consecrate] A reference to the consecration of the host during the celebration of the mass

171

26 old-fashioned] Perhaps a reference to the long-standing controversy over why miracles were apparently much more frequent in the early church than in more recent times; the debate went back at least to the time of Origen; see M.F. Wiles 'Miracles in the Early Church,' in C.F.D. Moule ed *Miracles* (London 1965) 221–2.

27 I'll explain ... vigils] Cf the very similar passage in the *Moria* (138) on the neglect by high ecclesiastics of their pastoral and spiritual duties.

28 Ligurian] The della Rovere family came from Savona, and Julius was born at Albizzola near the town (Rodocanachi 3n).

29 wage] See *Adagia* III iv 86. Bandello (*Novelle* I 31) recorded Julius' own boast that, as a boy, he had taken onions to market in Genoa in a small boat. He was always interested in nautical affairs and enjoyed sailing (Rodocanachi 143).

30 by my mother] A mistake: Julius' father Raffaelle della Rovere was brother to Sixtus IV, while his mother was a Greek named Theodora Manerola; see the genealogical table in Creighton III 100. On Sixtus' nepotism, see Gregorovius VII 246–8.

31 epilepsy] There is no evidence for this assertion, which probably arises from the comparison with Julius Caesar; cf *Opuscula* 72:160n.

32 pox] There is little evidence for this, although Julius' master of ceremonies Paris de Grassis suspected that his master had the disease (Rodocanachi 71n). In any case, Erasmus often uses syphilis as a symbolic symptom of corruption in high places, for example in the colloquies *Militis et Carthusiani* and *Ementita nobilitas*.

33 exile] On Julius' 'alliance' with the invading Charles VIII and subsequent flight to France, see Creighton III 177–8 and Pastor V 424–5.

172

34 you, scared ... at once] Matt 26:69–72, Mark 14:66–70, Luke 22:56–7, and John 18:17

35 king ... lords] 1 Tim 6:15, Rev 17:14 and 19:16; there appears to be no record of this blasphemous prophecy, and it may be included simply to substantiate the charge of indulgence in sorcery and fortune-telling made against Julius later in the dialogue.

36 money] Julius' election in 1503 was procured by the most open corruption: see Creighton IV 60 and Pastor VI 209n.

37 Crassus] Cf *Adagia* I vi 74a. Crassus was a Roman statesman and general (d 53 BC) who accumulated an immense fortune from his political manoeuvrings.

38 I have managed ... pope] Many historians and some contemporaries agree with Julius' estimate of himself, at least in the sphere of secular politics and in the establishment of the papal states: see Creighton IV 166–8, Pastor VI 216–19, Rodocanachi page i, L. Ranke *History of the Popes* trans E. Foster (London 1868) I 40, and the work of Brosch.

39 Thraso] The type of the braggart soldier, from the character in Terence's *Eunuchus*; the comparison is all the more apt since, like Julius, Thraso is most susceptible to flattery, proud of his ingenuity, and seeks to be feared rather than loved.

40 I interpreted ... something to resign] That is, Julius only awarded benefices to those who already held an office, which had to be abandoned and could then be sold; see Rodocanachi 32–4 for details of this practice and the income derived from it.

41 the new currency ... Italy] Julius reformed the debased papal currency in 1507–8: see Rodocanachi 93. Pastor (VI 227) comments that 'both trade and the revenue were immensely benefited by these operations.'

42 Venetians in battle] At Agnadello, 14 May 1509
43 one nail ... another] *Adagia* I ii 4

173
44 Spaniards] See Pastor VI 430–1; Julius' reliance on Spanish aid in expelling the French resulted, unhappily for him, in an increase of Spanish influence in Italy.
45 beard] Most cardinals of the time wore beards, but it was unusual for a pope: see Rodocanachi 84 and 125–6. It must have caused a stir, as twenty years later Rabelais recalls Julius' 'grande et bougrisque barbe' (*Pantagruel* xxx; on Rabelais and the dialogue, see C.R. Thompson in *Philological Quarterly* 22 (1943) 80–2). The explanation here is not supported by Pastor VI 339 and n, nor by Rodocanachi 125–6, who thinks that Julius had made a vow not to shave until the French should have been expelled.
46 Ravenna] 11 April 1512; although technically a French victory, this bloody battle seriously weakened Louis XII's army and cost the life of his brilliant commander Gaston de Foix. Threats to the rear from Swiss and Venetian forces caused the French to withdraw behind the Alps. See C. Oman *A History of the Art of War in the Sixteenth Century* (London 1937) 130–52.
47 Another time ... own] In August 1511; see Rodocanachi 137–9 and Pastor VI 368–72. Erasmus in Cambridge heard a false report of Julius' death in September; see Ep 228:21.
48 treaty ... Cambrai] Concluded on 10 December 1508
49 five million ducats] The true figure was probably about one tenth of this: see Brosch 273.
50 doctor] Probably one Samuel Zarfati; see Pastor VI 370n. For Julius' physicians and treatment, see ibidem 432–3, Rodocanachi 9, 117, and 137–9, and Ep 240:40n.
51 put ... touches] Literally, 'to put on the colophon': cf *Adagia* II iii 45.
52 at least the money ... expired] Julius ordered that his treasure should pass only to his successor, not to the conclave as a whole, and that it should be used only for a war against the Turks (Rodocanachi 34).
53 not even I ... father was] A baseless charge, repeated twice more (175, cf n69 below), but one which might have been made against Julius' uncle and patron Sixtus IV; see Creighton III 56–7.
54 no learning ... never acquired] An exaggeration, but one which suggests where Julius' real interests lay, in the patronage of art rather than learning. For example, he endowed fine new buildings for the university at Rome, but was niggardly with the teachers (Rodocanachi 87–8); a bungled effort to pose as a patron of poetry is amusingly described by Paris de Grassis (Creighton IV 274–5 and Rodocanachi 172–3). Julius commanded that a sword rather than a book be placed in the hand of his statue by Michelangelo; see Vasari (above, n22) IV 123.
55 It seems ... soft] Genius' remark is puzzling: it somewhat resembles asides found in Aristophanes when something obscene appears, and may perhaps be intended to suggest sadistic sexual behaviour towards Julius' boy favourites.

174

56 youths ... pleasure] Allegations of Julius' homosexuality (also made in the epigram) are dismissed by Pastor VI 320n; see also Creighton IV 130.

57 under our agreement ... before] The custom of granting plenary indulgences to papal soldiers was by no means original with Julius; Erasmus also condemned the practice in the colloquy *Charon* and in the *Querela pacis* (320). Julius offered such indulgences in particular to anyone slaying the Bentivogli of Bologna (Creighton IV 89). A variant in two early editions specifically uses the word *indulgentiae*: see *Opuscula* 78:255 variant.

58 clothed ... stranger] An adaptation of Matt 25:35–6

59 those who prophesied ... shut out] See Matt 7:22–3.

60 *two* swords] Although founded on Scripture (Luke 22:38), the doctrine of the temporal sword of the papacy is the product of medieval exegesis: see Pastor VI 450–1 and *Opuscula* 79:276n. Erasmus attacked the doctrine in the adage *Dulce bellum inexpertis* (IV i 1; Phillips 336) and in the *Moria* (see 146).

61 sword of the spirit] Eph 6:17

62 Malchus ... sword] John 18:10. This incident, as developed by Peter here, figures frequently in Erasmus' anti-war writing: see passages in *Querela pacis* (303) and the adage *Dulce bellum inexpertis* (IV i 1; Phillips 336). On its less rigorous interpretation by medieval exegetes, see A. Vanderpol *La guerre devant le Christianisme* (Paris 1911) 15. Note that Julius has enough Scripture to attack Peter on his weak points (cf 172).

175

63 I consider it ... walls] On Julius' affection for his native province, see Pastor VI 211n and Creighton IV 92. For illustrations of Julius' arms and inscriptions, see Rodocanachi facing pages 32, 164, 168, 172, and R. Weiss 'The Medals of Julius II (1503–1513)' *Journal of the Warburg and Courtauld Institutes* 28 (1965) 163–82. The word translated 'coins' would also refer to commemorative medals, of which Julius had many struck.

64 heavenly Jerusalem] A sermon on this subject, and its earthly embodiment the church, was delivered by Tommaso de Vio at the second session of Julius' Lateran Council (Pastor VI 410–11 and Creighton IV 149–50).

65 name ... hallowed] Matt 6:9, Luke 11:2

66 'nephew ... sister'] Cf n30 above. In 1512 Julius presented to the Swiss a banner bearing the inscription: 'Pope Julius II, nephew of Sixtus IV, of Savona' (Pastor VI 418).

67 Franciscans] Sixtus IV rose to be General of his order (Pastor IV 205–7).

68 his successors ... them] Cf a passage in the 1518 preface to the *Enchiridion* (Allen Ep 858:499–528) where Erasmus castigates contemporary monasticism in the names of Augustine, Benedict, and Francis.

69 I'm his son] There seems to be no basis for this charge, but Ferguson (*Opuscula* 81:311n) offers a convincing explanation based on a confusion with two other 'nephews' (the usual euphemism) of Sixtus; cf Brosch 4.

70 I renewed ... death] The bull was originally dated 14 January 1505 and was renewed on Julius' orders, as he lay dying, at the fifth session of the Lateran Council (Creighton IV 72–3 and 163, Pastor VI 434–5 and 440).

176

71 Bologna] On this episode, see Creighton IV 86–92, Pastor VI 259–89, and Rodocanachi 64–75.

72 A pretty thought!] *Bona verba*, meaning 'words of good omen' in Ovid and Tibullus, but used ironically by Terence (*Andria* 204) and by Erasmus here (also 179, 187, and 191 below) and in the adage *Sileni Alcibiadis* (III iii 1; Phillips 284); in each case, the speaker pretends to be shocked by the plain speaking of his opponent.

73 Bentivoglio] Giovanni II Bentivoglio (1443–1509) duke of Bologna 1462–1506. Erasmus selects him (with Ovid and the children of Israel) as an example of a hopeful exile in *Adagia* III i 92. His family returned to Bologna in May 1511 but was expelled once more in June 1512 (Creighton IV 128–9 and 152).

74 the city ... building] Confirmed by Rodocanachi 69

75 agreement] Bologna had been a possession of the papacy, but in 1447 Pope Nicolas V had recognized its virtual independence, which was confirmed by Pius II in 1458 and by Julius himself on his accession; documents in A. Theiner ed *Codex diplomaticus dominii temporalis S. Sedis* (Rome 1862) III 371, 405–6 and 515–16

76 attached to him] This is a matter of dispute; see the contrasting views of Pastor VI 261 and Rodocanachi 69. On the expression, see *Adagia* I iv 22.

77 others] Julius had acquired the aid or acquiescence of France and most of Bologna's neighbours before setting out for the city; it was the approach of French troops which finally decided the flight of the Bentivogli (Pastor VI 263–5, 274–5, and 279–80).

78 monuments] See *Opuscula* 84:356n for contemporary accounts; the most famous 'monument' was the huge bronze statue of Julius commissioned from Michelangelo and destroyed when the city fell in 1511: see Vasari (above, n22) IV 122–3.

79 triumph] Accounts in Pastor VI 281–3 and Rodocanachi 75. Erasmus was in Bologna at the time of this triumph, 11 November 1506 (Epp 203 and 205).

80 Octavius and Scipio] See below, nn184–5

81 'Thy kingdom come'] Matt 6:10 and Luke 11:2

82 Venetians] On Julius' relations with Venice, see F. Seneca *Venezia e papa Giulio II* (Padua 1962) and G.B. Picotti *La politica italiana sotto il pontificato di Giulio II* (Pisa 1949); see also Creighton IV 98–115, Pastor VI 232–58 and 297–320, and Rodocanachi 94–102.

177

83 talking Greek] The word used is *graecissare*, probably with a double meaning: in the classical language it meant 'to imitate the Greeks' and is thus in this context a reference to the Greek Orthodox 'schism,' which refused to recognize the papal supremacy and the Petrine succession; in later Latin it came to mean 'to speak Greek,' in the sense of withholding information by whispering in an unknown tongue. In addition, in Erasmus' time, a knowledge of Greek brought with it suspicion of heterodoxy.

84 joke] On Venetian libels and sarcasms, see *Opuscula* 53 and the examples in Pastor VI 306 and 309.

85 they were handing ... dispensations] For details of Venice's offences, see Pastor VI 301.

86 Christ] Matt 19:27, Mark 10:28, and Luke 18:28; cf passages in the adage *Sileni Alcibiadis* (III iii 1; Phillips 289) and the *Moria* (139).

87 towns] Particularly Faenza and Rimini (Pastor VI 247 and Rodocanachi 24–6)

88 duke of Ferrara] On this episode, see Pastor VI 327–62, Rodocanachi 106–23 and 165–8, and Chambers 81–93. Alfonso d'Este ruled Ferrara from 1505 until his death in 1534; in 1501, under pressure, he had married Alexander VI's daughter Lucrezia Borgia (Pastor VI 107–10).

89 taxes] Possibly a reference to Ferrarese inroads on the papal salt monopoly; see Pastor VI 328.

90 relative] Julius' nephew Francesco Maria della Rovere (1490–1538), duke of Urbino in 1508 and one of Julius' favourites; see Creighton IV 124–5 and 164 and Rodocanachi 13–14. It is noteworthy that even here Julius is not accused seriously of nepotism, the besetting sin of a number of his predecessors. See Pastor VI 218–22 for a defence of Julius in this sphere (somewhat qualified by Rodocanachi 10–16).

91 cardinal of Pavia] Francesco Alidosi, murdered in the streets of Ravenna in 1511; he had been Julius' legate in Bologna, where he had incurred the hatred of Francesco Maria, the army commander. It is generally accepted that far from ordering the murder, Julius was deeply grieved by it: Alidosi had been one of his closest associates (so close that a homosexual relationship was rumoured; see Creighton IV 130n). On the murder, see Creighton IV 129–30, Pastor VI 350–1, and Rodocanachi 131–3.

92 my daughter's husband ... lot] Giangiordano Orsini of Bracciano, married in 1506 to Felice, Julius' daughter by a woman called Lucrezia (Rodocanachi 11–12). The sense here is that Orsini, Julius' closest male dependent, was the obvious candidate for the duchy of Urbino, but had neither the necessary ambition nor the qualities required by Julius.

178

93 condition] An election-capitulation including this point had been accepted by Julius' short-lived predecessor Pius III, and Julius was compelled to accept it too; see Pastor VI 211, but also Rodocanachi 5–8, who found that Julius actually signed only the first few articles.

94 'Let piety ... else'] The epigram is attributed to Julius Caesar by Cicero and quoted by Suetonius *Julius* 1.30.5; it is also mentioned in Erasmus' epigram on Julius.

95 next move] On the Council of Pisa and Julius' reply, see Brosch 224–50, Creighton IV 131–51, Pastor VI 334–94 and 405–15, Rodocanachi 135ff, and A. Renaudet *Le concile gallican de Pise-Milan: documents florentins (1510–1512)* (Paris 1922); as the acts of the council are lost, the diplomatic documents collected by Renaudet are of particular value.

96 Nine cardinals] Carvajal, Francesco Borgia, Briçonnet, de Prie, and Sanseverino were the principal 'deserters,' but the council was also proclaimed in the name of Philip of Luxembourg, Adriano Corneto, Carlo del Carretto (who all protested that they were not involved: cf 181), and Ippolito d'Este (whose support was half-hearted); see Pastor VI 334, 353, and 363–4.

97 on the authority ... France] The alleged powers of the emperor and the French
   king depended on the decree *Frequens* of the Council of Constance; see
   Pastor VI 352 and B. Tierney *Foundations of the Conciliar Theory* (Cambridge
   1955) 78–9 and 224.

98 seamless coat ... one piece] Matt 27:35, Mark 15:24, Luke 23:34, and John
   19:23–4; interpreted by Erasmus as symbolic of the *spiritual* unity of the
   Church in his *Paraphrases* on Luke 23:34 (LB VII 462F–3A) and in the colloquy
   Puerpera

99 Cercopes] *Adagia* II vii 35; the Cercopes, renowned for their cunning, were
   changed into monkeys by Jupiter.

100 Morychus] *Adagia* II ix 1; Morychus was the Sicilian nickname for Bacchus,
    treated as a figure of fun.

101 more ignorant ... log] Latin *indoctior stipite*, an adage not found in the *Adagia*
    but in Terence *Heautontimorumenos* 877

102 Lerna] Cf *Adagia* I iii 27; the hydra killed by Hercules inhabited the swamp of
    Lerna.

103 stands ... earth] Cf a passage in the *Apologia contra Stunicam* (LB IX 361C–E) in
    which Erasmus opposes such papal pretensions.

104 a kind ... men] A reference to the formula *quasi Deus in terris* often applied to
    popes by their flatterers and even on official documents; see for instance
    Pastor VI 429 and note and Lemaire de Belges III 260 (quoting Augustine's
    disapproval of such claims).

179

105 Civil laws ... death] On the power of the people to depose bad rulers, compare
    passages in the adages *Dulce bellum inexpertis* and *Sileni Alcibiadis* (IV i 1
    and III iii 1; Phillips 341 and 280). See also Peter's solution 180.

106 council ... synod] Latin *concilium ... conciliabulum*; I have translated the latter,
    a pejorative diminutive, by 'synod,' since the Pisan assembly had its origin
    in a synod of the Gallican church at Tours in 1510.

107 monstrous creature] Another reference to the hydra of Lerna; cf 178 and n102
    above. Pineau (*Erasme et la papauté* 42) suggests that this list of crimes was
    inspired by the life of Alexander VI rather than that of Julius.

180

108 heresy] Possibly an ancient tradition of the Church, reflected in (or based on)
    Gratian *Decretum* I xl 6 (PL 187 214–15); the principle was much discussed
    during the great schism: see B. Tierney *Foundations of the Conciliar Theory*
    (Cambridge 1955) 8–9, 58–67, 248–50 and Pineau *Erasme et la papauté* 41–5.

109 recant] Literally 'a palinode is easy'; cf *Adagia* I ix 59.

110 a rising ... world] Erasmus does not disapprove of tyrannicide in a number of
    passages, for example in the *Institutio* (231) and in the adage *Scarabeus
    aquilam quaerit* (III vii 1; Phillips 243–4).

181

111 decision] See Acts 15:6–29.

112 some people ... James] A belief based on James' authority in Jerusalem and
    some pseudo-Clementine writings, and widely held by Protestants; see

M.M. Winter *Saint Peter and the Popes* (Baltimore and London 1960) 30–4 and 76–8. Compare Tommaso de Vio's defence of Peter's primacy among the apostles, in attacks on the Pisan council (Pastor VI 385).

113 the emperor ... go into] Maximilian finally withdrew his support from the Pisan council fairly late in its existence, but had had doubts much earlier (Pastor VI 375–84).
114 I proclaimed ... Rome] On 18 July 1511
115 cardinals] Eight new cardinals were created on 10 March 1511 (Pastor VI 343–4).

182

116 I reverted ... schooled for it] In fact the Lateran Council was postponed until 3 May 1512 because of the dangerous state of northern Italy (Pastor VI 406 and Hefele VIII 300). Erasmus had been hoping to accompany the English delegate Fisher to the original council (Epp 252 and 255), and his disappointment, apart from any satirical intention, may explain the distortion here.
117 letter] Summarized in Pastor VI 361–2
118 cardinal of Rouen] Georges d'Amboise (1460–May 1510), archbishop of Rouen and chief minister of Louis XII. His opposition to Julius arose both from Gallican feeling and from frustrated ambition; see Creighton IV 89–92 and Pastor VI 191–5.
119 cardinal of Santa Croce] Like d'Amboise, Bernardino Lopez de Carvajal (1455–1523), leader of the Spanish cardinals, had aspired to the papacy in 1503, and defeat by Julius rankled; see Pastor VI 387. Both these prelates seem to have been hard-headed ecclesiastical politicians like Julius himself, with few policies for reform, although d'Amboise did succeed in reforming certain French monasteries; see A. Renaudet *Préréforme et humanisme à Paris* (Paris 1916) 327ff.
120 a lot of things] Cf the letters to Henry VIII in Creighton IV 289–91.
121 I had sworn ... reign] Cf n93.
122 He kept saying ... special case] For the appeals of the Pisan council to Julius, see Creighton IV 142 and 148, and Rodocanachi 145.

183

123 to cure the ills of the church] All accounts of the Pisan council agree that the piety and reforming zeal of the participants lagged far behind their hatred of Julius: see summaries of the deliberations in Creighton IV 139–43 and Pastor VI 390–4.
124 dénouement] Cf *Adagia* I ii 36.
125 tooth and nail] *Adagia* I iv 15, literally 'with feet and hands'

184

126 one nail ... another] *Adagia* I ii 4
127 Holy Spirit] The Lateran Council opened on 3 May, the Feast of the Invention of the Holy Cross; the mass of the Holy Spirit was sung by Cardinal Riario (Pastor VI 406–7).

128 praise for me] An oration was delivered by Egidio Antonini of Viterbo after the mass had been sung (Pastor vi 407–8 and Hefele viii 343–8); a speech better described as 'full of praise for' Julius was that of Cristoforo Marcello at the fourth session on 10 December: see Pastor vi 429.

129 I turned ... against France] France was laid under interdict at the third session (3 December), the schismatic council having fled to Lyon (Pastor vi 422–3).

130 transferring ... Lyon] The great fair of Lyon was transferred to Geneva: see O. Raynaldus *Annales ecclesiastici* (Bar-le-Duc and Paris 1864–83) xxx 602 (anno 1512 item 97).

131 regions of France] Brittany, united to the French crown only by recent marriage, was exempted; the duchess Anne was the friend and ally of Julius. See Rodocanachi 173 and 63.

132 The first session ... among them] Allowing for the satirical contrast with the fictional account of the Pisan council, this passage fairly sums up the achievements of the Lateran Council during Julius' lifetime; it should be said that the cumbrous procedure followed was typical of such gatherings: see Hefele viii 349–57 and 364–72.

133 I've won] Perhaps a quotation of Julius' exultant cry to Paris de Grassis on hearing of the French retreat, quoted in Pastor vi 417

134 three cardinals] Carvajal, Briçonnet, and Sanseverino; the first two had been deposed and excommunicated on 24 October 1511 (Pastor vi 374).

135 the eventual outcome ... decide] In fact the schismatic council was utterly discredited and almost disbanded at the time of Julius' death (Pastor vi 415); the schism came to an end soon afterwards with the reconciliation of Louis xii and Leo x.

185

136 Camarina moved] Cf *Adagia* i i 64; the reference is to a marsh which, when drained to prevent plague, afforded easy access to invaders, and the proverb is the equivalent of 'out of the frying-pan, into the fire.'

137 campaigns] Since Charles viii's expedition to Naples in 1494; but the wars of Italy continued until 1559.

138 the English king ... as yet] On these 'mountains of gold' see Ep 266, where Erasmus deplores their employment for war. See also *Adagia* i ix 15, for the use of the term to mean 'false hopes.'

139 'Most Christian'] According to French propaganda the title was awarded to Pepin the Short in the eighth century in recognition of his gift of territory in Italy to the papacy – the origin of the temporal power and problems of the popes; see Lemaire de Belges ii 466–7 and iii 243. In 1512 Julius planned to transfer the ancient title (*and* the kingdom) to Henry viii (Chambers 38–9).

140 horse's mouth] *Adagia* i vii 90, literally 'from the tripod' (of the Delphic oracle)

141 wolf ... lambs] See *Adagia* iv vii 91; the proverb refers to treacherous friendship.

142 Genoese] Julius, a native of Genoese territory, had been incensed when in 1507 the French crushed, with great severity, a popular rising in Genoa against the French governor (Creighton iv 92); in 1512, after Ravenna, the Genoese again cast off the French yoke (Pastor vi 415).

186

143 What's ... muttering] The Latin could also mean 'Why are you silent?'

144 calling ... barbarian] This was indeed a popular habit (see *Moria* 117, and the pasquinades cited in Chambers 123), and one particularly associated with Julius: see Creighton IV 164n, Pastor VI 416, Oulmont 215 and 221–6, and especially Rodocanachi 102–5.

145 no respecter of persons] Cf Matt 22:16 and Luke 20:21, a phrase frequently repeated by Paul, for example in Eph 6:9.

146 Ethiopians] Julius sent preachers to India, Ethiopa, and the Congo, and also took great interest in missions to the new world: see Pastor VI 440–1 and, on the general ecumenical question at the time, F.M. Rogers *The Quest for Eastern Christians* (Minneapolis 1962).

147 Greeks] A reference to the failure of the attempt at reconciliation with the orthodox church at the Council of Florence in 1439; see D.J. Geanakoplos *Byzantine East and Latin West* (Oxford 1966) 84–111. The most important article of the bull *Laetentur coeli* concerned with this affirms the primacy of the Roman see; cf Denzinger *Enchiridion symbolorum* (Barcelona 1955) 253, article 694.

148 Is it ... all men] An almost literal quotation of 1 Cor 9:11; the irony is that there Paul is defending his materially 'unproductive' work as an apostle.

149 even if ... lives] Terence's Thraso (cf n39 above) was renowned for snoring day and night: *Eunuchus* 1079.

150 we give ... prices] The usual charges levelled at Julius and several predecessors: see Pastor VI 224–5.

151 move ... earth] Literally 'to mix heaven and earth'; cf the examples in *Adagia* I iii 81.

187

152 Germans] The Germans were traditionally portrayed as drunkards as, for instance, in the colloquy *Diversoria* (Thompson *Colloquies* 147).

188

153 whatever ... all] Probably a reference to Luke 12:3

154 As to their lives ... feet] The movement of this passage clearly recalls Folly's attack on princes and popes in the *Moria* (138–9). See also the attacks on honorific titles in the adage *Sileni Alcibiadis* (Phillips 276); the titles listed here include those of the king of Spain ('Catholic'), of the doge and senate of Venice ('Most Serene'), and of the emperor ('August').

155 swords] On various papal gifts, see Chambers 31, Pastor VI 264, 342n, and 413, and Rodocanachi 62, 106, and 143. On their origin and significance, see J. Kreps 'La Rose d'Or' *Questions liturgiques et paroissiales* 11 (Louvain 1926) 71–104 and R. Dowling 'The Gifts of a Pontiff' *Dublin Review* 114 (1894) 61–75 (mentioning the gift of a golden oak-branch from Sixtus IV to Siena cathedral).

156 boys] Anne de Bretagne sent two noble youths to Julius' court; insinuations of pederasty were not far behind. See E. Böcking ed *Ulrici Hutteni equitis Germani opera* (Leipzig 1859–70) IV 448n.

157 we scratch ... mules] *Adagia* I vii 96

189

158 time being] The first agreement between Louis XII, Maximilian, and Julius was concluded at Blois in 1504, but nothing came of it; a more enduring alliance was made at Cambrai on 10 December 1508, although Julius did not adhere to it until the following March (Pastor VI 257 and 298–300, Rodocanachi 62 and 97–9).

159 cities ... occupying] The ostensible purpose of the League of Cambrai was to arrange a crusade, but in the secret articles Brescia, Bergamo, Cremona, Chiara d'Adda, and all Milanese fiefs were promised to France, and Friuli, Padua, Roveredo, Treviso, Verona, and Vicenza to the emperor (Pastor VI 299).

160 out of hand] On the prosperous situation of France after the battle of Agnadello, see Pastor VI 318.

161 king of Spain] Ferdinand of Spain entered on a Holy League with the pope and Venice on 5 October 1511 (Pastor VI 367–73).

162 Venetians] In fact, Julius had acquired the support of Venice before that of Ferdinand; the republic, exhausted by war and fearful of French domination, had accepted humiliating terms on 15 February 1510. See Creighton IV 108–10 and F. Seneca *Venezia e papa Giulio II* (Padua 1962) 138–47.

163 emperor] At Julius' instigation, Maximilian made a truce with Venice in 1512, and took little part in subsequent campaigns (Creighton IV 151).

164 Scots] Henry VIII joined the Holy League on 17 November 1511 (Chambers 37–9); the traditional Franco-Scottish alliance, which had flourished during the Hundred Years War, was still very much alive, as the campaigns of 1513 show. See C. Oman *A History of the Art of War in the Sixteenth Century* (London 1937) 285–321.

165 the most strait-laced of kings] When the parsimonious but peace-loving Henry VII died in 1509, the wildest hopes were entertained of his successor, hopes both of liberality towards the arts (see Epp 215 and 333) and, as here, of success on the battlefield.

166 related ... Spain] By his marriage with Catherine of Aragon

190

167 Hungary] Ladislas II had been invited to join the League of Cambrai, the bait being the recovery from Venice of some territory on the Adriatic (Pastor VI 299).

168 Portugal] King Emmanuel seems to have played no part in Italian politics at this time.

169 duke of Burgundy] Archduke Charles, the future Charles V

170 at that time ... France] Since 1505 Ferdinand had been fighting the Moors of the Barbary Coast; in 1511 his army there was transferred to Europe at Julius' request (Pastor VI 367).

171 Padua] Recaptured by Venice from Maximilian's lieutenant on 17 July 1509 (Creighton IV 106–7).

172 Gelderlanders] Karel van Egmond, duke of Gelderland, waged intermittent war against the house of Hapsburg for over thirty years as an ally of the French; see the article in *Biographie nationale de Belgique* and Tracy *Politics* 71–107.

173 the life of ... early kings] References to St Thomas Becket and such statutes as the Constitutions of Clarendon 1164, the Statute of Provisors 1351, and the Statutes of Praemunire 1352 and 1365; see M. McKisack *The Oxford History of England: The Fourteenth Century* (Oxford 1959) 272ff.

174 task] In fact Henry's attack on Guyenne in 1512 was a fiasco; see J.J. Scarisbrick *Henry VIII* (London 1968) 28–31.

175 no previous pope ... Turks] For the vain efforts of various popes to unite Christendom against the infidel, see Hefele VII 1298ff (Pius II), VIII 185–91 (Alexander VI), and VIII 347–353 (Julius' own Lateran Council). Julius' remark here reflects Erasmus' particular horror of war between so-called Christians; see for instance *Querela pacis* (315) and the adage *Dulce bellum inexpertis* (IV i 1; Phillips 344). For his rather ambiguous view of the justice of a 'crusade,' see the *De bello turcico* (LB V 345–68).

191

176 But if ... the head of the church] These two speeches represent the conflicting 'evangelical' and 'sacerdotal' views of the Church; the conflict is most simply stated in the adage *Dulce bellum inexpertis* (IV i 1; Phillips 344). See *Opuscula* 115:977n for other references; this is one of the most convincing internal proofs that Erasmus wrote the dialogue.

177 But Christ ... head] Eph 1:22 and 5:23, and Col 1:18

192

178 Constantine] The spurious nature of the donation of Constantine had been fully exposed by Lorenzo Valla in 1440; see C.B. Coleman *Constantine the Great and Christianity* (New York 1914). Many attributed the troubles of the papacy to this legendary gift of temporal power, for instance Lemaire de Belges III 252 and V lxvi (on Petrarch's similar opinion).

179 decretals] Gratian *Decretum* I xcvi 13–14 (*PL* 187 460)

180 Nothing but ... father] Valla's refutation was based on historical and philological evidence; Julius' reasoning is simpler and characteristic.

193

181 shadow of a great name] See the introductory note 166–7. In 1507 Maximilian planned to have Julius formally crown him at Rome, but he was unable to cross hostile Venetian territory and had to content himself with the title of Roman emperor elect, which Julius confirmed in February 1508.

182 my triumphs] On some of these triumphs, see Pastor VI 286–8 and 417–18, and Rodocanachi 79–80 and 167.

183 coins] This certainly happened at Julius' entry into Bologna, for which coins were specially minted (Pastor VI 283 and n).

184 the Scipios, the Aemilii] Two families who distinguished themselves in the wars of the Roman republic. The greatest was Scipio Africanus (236–184/3 BC), conqueror of Carthage; his contemporary Aemilius Paulus conquered Macedonia. The families were united when Scipio's son adopted Aemilius', who became another famous general, and was known as Aemilianus Africanus Minor.

185 Augusti] 'Augustus' was a title bestowed on almost all early Roman emperors, following the precedent of the first, Octavius Caesar. Imperial triumphs at Rome were notorious for their extravagance.

186 if you'd seen ... with me] This detailed description was probably 'inspired' by Julius' triumph at Bologna, which Erasmus saw; cf Bainton 'Erasmus and Luther' 20–1 on a similar passage in the *Paraphrase* on Mark 11 (LB VII 243C–F).

187 General Braggart] A reference to Plautus' *Miles gloriosus*, the epitome of the swaggering stage-soldier; I have promoted him to convey the superlative adjective in the Latin.

194

188 keys of the kingdom] Matt 16:19

189 sheep to feed] John 21:15–17

190 sealed ... approval] Matt 16:15–18

191 healed ... body] Acts 5:15

192 freed ... devils] See Luke 9:1.

193 restored ... life] Acts 9:36–41

194 Sapphira ... power] Acts 5:1–10

195 What had your triumphs ... world] Acts 5 and Julius' triumphs are also contrasted in the *Apologia contra Stunicam* (LB IX 361A–B).

196 cross] Tradition has it that St Peter was martyred on an inverted cross in Rome under Nero; for his imprisonment, see Acts 12.

197 Christ commanded ... blessed] Matt 5:11–12

198 Paul] 2 Cor 11:23–30

195

199 any man ... in him] A reminiscence of 2 Cor 6:10

196

200 greater plague ... world] Lemaire de Belges demonstrated in two short works of 1511–12, *Histoire de Sophy* and *Saufconduit*, that Muslim princes were indeed less detrimental to Christendom than Julius (Lemaire de Belges III 199–229).

201 Aristotle] *Politics* 7.1 (1323a25–6); cf a passage in the adage *Sileni Alcibiadis* (III iii 1; Phillips 278).

202 seventy] The date of Julius' birth is uncertain, but 1441–3 is the likely period (Rodocanachi 3n).

203 mix fire with water] *Adagia* IV iii 94

204 take ... no notice of us] According to Rodocanachi 83, Julius' use of lavish display was calculated to avoid this.

205 fear us] Cf *Adagia* II ix 62, the proverb particularly applied to tyrants: 'let them hate us, so long as they fear us.'

206 riches ... vices] A pun involving *divitiis* 'wealth' and *vitiis* 'sin'

197

207 they roared ... vein] Such an oration is lampooned in the *Ciceronianus* 384.

208 salt ... savour] Matt 5:13, Mark 9:50, Luke 14:34

NOTES TO PAGES 197–201

209 architect] On Julius as a builder see Pastor vi 455–502, Rodocanachi 40–7, 54–7, and 147–52, and J. Klaczko *Rome and the Renaissance: The Pontificate of Julius II* (London and New York 1903) 10–46 and 117–41. Folly had suggested that over-scrupulous monks should have a new heaven built for them (132).

210 cast ... mould] Cf *Adagia* iii v 44.

211 waving his stick] Cf 170 above; this cross-reference helps to suggest that Julius departs as little penitent as he had arrived.

THE EDUCATION OF A CHRISTIAN PRINCE / *INSTITUTIO PRINCIPIS CHRISTIANI*

Introductory Note

200

1 One copy bears the date 1515, but this is clearly a printing error; see A. Vincent 'Les premières éditions de l'*Institutio principis christiani* d'Erasme' *Mélanges offerts à M. Marcel Godet* (Neuchâtel 1937) 91–6.

2 See Epp 334:178–80 and 337:95–6. In the letter to Botzheim, however, Erasmus twice asserts that he did not write it until after he had been appointed councillor to Prince Charles (probably in January 1516): see Allen I 19 and 44.

3 Ep 272

4 See Epp 370:15–20 and 392. It is possible that Erasmus presented a copy of the *Institutio* to Charles in person: see Ep 414:13n.

5 Exceptions are his recipe for diverting resentment from the prince (257) and his advocacy of the occasional 'benign deception' (260).

6 Many of Erasmus' allusions to classical writers have been noted by our predecessors, L.K. Born, O. Herding in ASD iv-1 (1974), and M. Isnardi Parente, to whom we are particularly grateful for copies of her book and related articles. We have noted most of these allusions, but have omitted those which merely represent vague analogies of thought rather than clear reminiscences. There is no evidence that Erasmus made any use of medieval writings on the subject, which are discussed by Born 99–128.

201

7 See for instance the quotations from Homer (242), from 'Diogenes' (245), and from Seneca (265).

8 See Phillips 96–121.

9 All these are translated in Phillips 213–353; we have pointed out many parallels in our notes, but the overall resemblance is so close that to indicate them all would be tedious. Similarly, we have indicated some parallels in the *Moria*, where the passage 135–6 is, again, virtually an *Institutio* in miniature, in the *Panegyricus*, and also a few of the many in the *Querela pacis*; in the last case, the source of the analogies may well be the same adages rather than the *Institutio*.

10 It is very likely that much of this practical wisdom was derived from Erasmus' own experience of conditions in the Low Countries, and it may often be seen as scarcely veiled criticism of the policies there of Prince Charles' grand-

father Maximilian. This aspect of Erasmus' political thought has been greatly clarified by Tracy *Politics*.

11 The work has been shared between us as follows: the translation of chs 1–4 is
primarily the work of NMC; the translation of chs 5–11 and the annotation is
primarily that of MJH.

12 See ASD IV-1 112–18 on the editions (listed on page 132) and the variants. We
have noted, and usually incorporated, all significant variants found in the
1518 text, although in fact they are not very numerous.

13 Cf ibidem 129.

202

14 P. Ellwood Corbett trans *Erasmus' 'Institutio Principis Christiani'* Peace Classics
(London 1921 and 1939)

15 ASD IV-1 133–219

Dedicatory letter

203

1 The dedicatory letter is Ep 393.

2 Xenophon] *Oeconomicus* 21.12

3 Shunamite] 1 Kings 1:2–3

4 Proverbs] Prov 8:16

5 her] Wisd 7:11

6 Homer's mind] *Odyssey* 10.302–6

7 Plutarch] *Moralia* 778D

8 Alexander] Plutarch *Moralia* 782A; *Alexander* 14

204

9 Philip] He died on 25 September 1506; cf Ep 205:11

10 servant] A reference to his appointment as councillor; cf Ep 370:18n.

11 Isocrates' work] The *De institutione principis ad Nicoclem regem*, which formed
an introduction to the *Institutio* in Froben's edition.

12 aphorisms] Cf Ep 523.

13 recently invested] Charles was invested with the government of the Netherlands on 5 January 1515.

1 / The birth and upbringing of a Christian prince

206

1 ancestry] Erasmus uses the term *maiorum imagines*, which denoted originally
the portraits or wax figures of famous ancestors placed in the atrium of a
Roman house, but which was often used metaphorically; see Suetonius *Vespasian* 1 and Sallust *Jugurtha* 4.5.

2 barbarians] Aristotle *Politics* 4.3.7 (1290b5) and Herodotus 3.20, both of whom
mention the Ethiopians; cf also Plato *Laws* 4.715C. Montaigne, in 'Des can-
nibales' (*Essais* I xxxi) attributed similar political naivety to the contemporary
Brazilian Indians.

3 ship] The simile of the helmsman and the ship of state occurs frequently in Plato, for example in *Gorgias* 512B and *Republic* 1.341C–D (where it is combined with another favourite simile of both Plato and Erasmus, that of the doctor), and especially in *Republic* 6.488–9; see also Aristotle *Politics* 3.2.1 (1276b23).

4 feelings] Cf Plato *Republic* 1.342E, another comparison with seamanship.

5 Aristotle] *Politics* 3.9.5–7 (1285a33–1285b4)

6 our own times] In the adage *Aut fatuum aut regem nasci oportere* (I iii 1; Phillips 220), Erasmus makes it clear that he would prefer an elective monarchy; here, addressing a hereditary prince, he is more circumspect. At the time, the emperor and the king of Poland were still, in theory, freely elected.

7 from the very cradle] *Adagia* I vii 53

8 mature] An allusion to the Stoic doctrine of the *semina virtutum*; see for example Cicero *De finibus* 5.7.18 and Quintilian 2.20.6.

208

9 For this task] On the choice of the prince's tutor, cf *Panegyricus* 62: it is possible that, when writing the *Panegyricus*, Erasmus was himself a candidate; see Tracy 18–19. For Erasmus' general views on schooling and schoolmasters see M.L. Clarke 'The Educational Writings of Erasmus' *Erasmus in English* 8 (1976) 23–31 and J.K. Sowards' introduction to CWE 25–6 xvii–xxi.

10 Seneca] *De brevitate vitae* 15.2, cited from memory; see also, for this whole passage, Seneca *Epistulae morales* 52 'On Choosing our Teachers.'

11 decency] Cf Plutarch *Moralia* 3F–4A (*De liberis educandis* 6), on the selection of suitable slaves to be the companions of the young masters.

12 flatterers] Cf Seneca *De ira* 2.21.8 and Plutarch *Moralia* 12D–13C (*De liberis educandis* 17); this is the subject of ch 2 of the *Institutio*.

209

13 cradle] Cf above 206 and n7.

14 a birthright is enough] A frequent complaint of Socrates and his disciples: cf Plato *Protagoras* 319–20 and Xenophon *Memorabilia* 4.2.6.

15 benefices] There is a suggestion here that the tutor should be an ecclesiastic, but it is interesting that Erasmus gave unqualified approval to only one contemporary school, Colet's St Paul's, which had a married headmaster and lay governors; see *De pronuntiatione* CWE 26 379.

210

16 carved on rings] Advice also given in *De ratione studii* (CWE 24 671)

17 Seneca] *Epistulae morales* 94.17, alluding to the use in the ancient world of hellebore to cure madness

211

18 soil] This and the previous simile of the trainer of wild animals are taken from Plutarch *Moralia* 2E–F (*De liberis educandis* 4).

19 public fountain] The simile is found in Plutarch *Moralia* 778D.

20 coinage] The majority of coinage offences carried the death penalty at this time, many being categorized as high treason; this was the case in English

law until as late as 1832. See L. Radzinowicz *A History of English Criminal Law* I (London 1948) 600–1 and 652–4.

21 older] Plato *Republic* 2.377A
22 Aesop's fable] For these fables, see A. Hausrath ed *Corpus fabularum Aesopicarum* (Leipzig 1956–67) 155, 176 and 3 respectively; the last, the eagle and the beetle, inspired the important adage of 1515 *Scarabeus aquilam quaerit* (III vii 1; Phillips 229–63), on which Erasmus drew extensively for the *Institutio*.

212

23 Phaethon] Son of Helios, he tried to drive his father's solar chariot; when the horses bolted, Zeus slew him to avoid universal conflagration. See Ovid *Metamorphoses* 2.1–332.
24 Cyclops] The one-eyed giant Polyphemus; see Homer *Odyssey* 9.
25 bees and ants] See Pliny *Naturalis historia* 11.5–23 and 36 respectively; these similes were commonplaces of political treatises.
26 king] Cf Pliny *Naturalis historia* 11.16–17; see also Virgil *Georgics* 4 and Seneca *De clementia* 1.19.3, a passage paraphrased below 225–6. Confusion over the sex of the bees' ruler was not resolved until the end of the sixteenth century; cf Rev Charles Butler *The Feminine Monarchy* (1609).
27 realm] Cf below 256.
28 Plato's cave] *Republic* 7.514–18, a celebrated image illustrating the difference between the real and ideal worlds; the prisoners in the cave mistook for reality the shadows of men and objects cast by a fire.
29 good or bad] Cf Isocrates *Ad Nicoclem* 50.

213

30 wax masks] See above 206 n1.
31 happiness] These Stoic commonplaces may be derived from Seneca *Epistulae morales* 93.2–5.
32 and immutable] The words are in Greek, probably a reminiscence of Aristotle *Politics* 2.5.12 (1269a8); in the Basel *Opera* of 1540 the word 'laws' also appears in Greek which, as L.K. Born notes (149 n34), conforms more closely to Erasmus' usual practice with Greek in the *Institutio*, where it is used parenthetically rather than integrated grammatically.

214

33 thesis of Plato's] *Republic* 5.473C–D and 6.499B–C
34 dregs of the people] Cf the attack on Median rulers in Xenophon *Cyropaedia* 1.6.8.

215

35 integrity] A number of ancient writers list the basic moral qualities required in the good prince, for example Xenophon *Agesilaus* 10.1 and Aristotle *Politics* 1.5.3–5 (1259b23–1260a4). The individual virtues here are discussed at length by Aristotle *Nicomachean Ethics* 6.5 (1140a24–b11) on wisdom, 4.3 (1123b1–1125a17) on magnanimity, and 3.10–12 (1117b23–1119b18) on restraint.
36 wealth] Cf Seneca *Epistulae morales* 44.3–5, on true nobility as the product of philosophy rather than of high birth.

37 distraction] Erasmus' emblematology here appears to be original; cf *Moria* 136.

38 actor] For the commonplace simile of the stage king, cf *Moria* 103.

39 father to the state] Another commonplace; see for example Xenophon *Cyropaedia* 8.1.1, Aristotle *Politics* 1.5.2 (1259b1–2), Cicero *Republic* 2.26.47 and Seneca *De clementia* 1.14.2 (on the title 'Father of His Country' given to Roman emperors).

40 allegiance] Cf the discussion of different forms of monarchy in Aristotle *Politics* 3.9 (1284b35–1285b19).

216

41 pagan] A theme developed by St Augustine *De civitate Dei* 5.18, with examples of the noblest deeds of the pagan Romans. Erasmus had originally written 'gentile,' but replaced this by 'pagan' (*ethnicus*) in the 1518 Basel edition, perhaps to strengthen the contrast.

42 Julius] Perhaps a reference to Pope Julius II as well as to Julius Caesar; cf the comparison between them in *Julius exclusus*.

43 institutions] A constant theme of Erasmus' evangelism; cf *Moria* 131.

217

44 Turks] As Louis XII of France and the Venetians had done in 1502; see C. de la Roncière *Histoire de la marine française* III (Paris 1906) 46–56.

45 Francis] Cf *Moria* 130–1 and the colloquy Ἰχθυοφαγία (Thompson *Colloquies* 356).

46 acknowledge you] Cf Matt 10:38 and Luke 14:27.

218

47 misfortune] Cf the Greek aphorism 'wisdom is acquired by suffering' quoted in Hesiod *Works and Days* 218, Aeschylus *Agamemnon* 177 and Plato *Symposium* 222B.

48 Africanus] Valerius Maximus 7.2.2, the source for Erasmus' *Apophthegmata* 5 Scipio Maior 14 (LB IV 258B); the great Roman general Scipio Africanus made this remark about those who failed to make adequate military preparations for a campaign.

49 older men] Cf Cicero *De officiis* 1.34.122.

50 hide] Cf Xenophon *Cyropaedia* 8.7.23.

219

51 prince do] Cf Isocrates *Ad Nicoclem* 31.

52 its prince] Cf Cicero *Laws* 3.14.31, referring to the early history of Rome under monarchy.

53 Plutarch] *Moralia* 780E (*Ad principem ineruditum* 3)

220

54 Nero ... Heliogabalus] The three Roman Emperors perhaps most often vilified by posterity, Nero (ruled 54–68), Gaius Caligula (37–41) and Heliogabalus (218–222)

55 St Denis] This appears to be a slightly inaccurate reference to Pseudo-Dionysius the Areopagite *De ecclesiastica hierarchia*; the three hierarchies are

the celestial, the ecclesiastical, and the legal, referring to the Mosaic law: see 5.2 (PG 3 501–4); in another passage (3.3; PG 3 429) the writer compares the position of the bishop in his hierarchy to that of God, but there is no comparison with that of the prince.

56 sheet-anchor] Cf *Adagia* I i 24: *Sacram ancoram solvere*; the sheet-anchor was called the 'sacred anchor' in Latin.

221

57 at fault] The whole paragraph closely imitates Plutarch *Moralia* 780E–F (*Ad principem ineruditum* 3).

58 should be] A reworking of another passage from the same essay, *Moralia* 782D–E

59 desires] Cf Plato *Laws* 1.635D.

60 masters] A theme developed by St Augustine *De civitate Dei* 4.3 and 19.15

61 pagans] A marginal note in the original editions refers to the self-sacrifice of the legendary Codrus of Athens (eleventh century BC) described by Lycurgus *In Leocratem* 84–7 and by St Augustine *De civitate Dei* 18.19, and of the emperor Otho (AD 69) described by Suetonius *Otho* 10–11.

222

62 Plato] *Republic* 1.347C and 7.520D–521B

63 master] Perhaps inspired by Aristotle's account of tyrannical Persian fathers who treated their sons like slaves: *Nicomachean Ethics* 8.10.4 (1160b24–33); on the comparison between a prince and a father, see above 215 n39.

64 Phalaris] Tyrant of Agrigentum in the sixth century BC, who roasted his enemies inside a brazen bull: cf *Adagia* I x 86.

65 Dionysius] The tyrant of Syracuse, renowned for his extravagance and the subterfuges he used to fill his coffers; cf below 265.

66 Seneca] *De clementia* 1.12.1

67 Aristotle] *Politics* 3.5.1 (1279a33) and 4.8.3 (1295a18–24)

223

68 Mezentius] King of Caere in Etruria, who appears as a bloodthirsty tyrant in Virgil *Aeneid* 7–10

69 'Lord'] Suetonius *Domitian* 13; Erasmus habitually refers to him as 'Domitius' rather than 'Domitianus,' but no doubt the Roman emperor is meant.

70 On the other side] These contrasting portraits are in part inspired by Seneca *De clementia* 1.13, but that of the tyrant in particular bears a close resemblance to that in the adage *Scarabeus aquilam quaerit* (III vii 1; Phillips 233–40).

224

71 Claudius] The bloody tastes of the Emperor Claudius are described by Suetonius *Claudius* 34; his reputation for tyranny also owes something to the writings of Seneca, tutor to his successor Nero.

72 Busiris] Tyrant of Egypt who habitually sacrificed strangers and was himself killed by Hercules

73 Pentheus] The tyrannical king of Thebes in Euripides' *Bacchae*; see also Horace *Epistles* 1.16.73–9 and Ovid *Metamorphoses* 3.513–733.

74 Midas] The famous king of Phrygia, generally presented as a fool rather than a
   tyrant by the Ancients; cf Ep 105:48–51. But in *Adagia* I iii 67 Midas' 'long
   ears' are interpreted as a symbol of his tyrannical use of informers and spies;
   he was given donkey's ears by Bacchus whom, like Pentheus, he had
   offended.
75 improves him] These concise contrasts echo passages in Aristotle *Politics* 5.8.6
   (1311a5–8) and Xenophon *Hiero* 2.7ff.
76 many hands and many eyes] Xenophon *Cyropaedia* 8.2.10
77 feared] Cf below 243 n175.

225
78 own people] Plato *Republic* 8.566E–567A
79 Aristotle has expounded them] *Politics* 5.9.8 (1314a15–25)
80 saying] *Adagia* I x 45: *E diametro opposita*, quoted here in Greek
81 Aristotle ... a pagan] On Erasmus' distrust of Aristotle as a model for theologians at this time, see Phillips 264, 273–4 and 331–2, all passages from the
   Adagia of 1515.
82 Seneca] A close paraphrase of a passage in *De clementia* 1.19.3

226
83 eagle] Cf the adage *Scarabeus aquilam quaerit* (III vii 1; Phillips 245–6), for the
   lion and the eagle; the latter was of course the imperial emblem.
84 words] 1 Sam 8:11–18. In his interpretation of these scriptural passages on the
   tyrant Erasmus clings to an ethical definition of tyranny which was being
   supplanted by a more strictly juridical definition, given shape particularly by
   Jean Bodin: see M. Isnardi Parente 'Erasmo, Bodin e i due paradigmi clas-
   sici del buon principe e del tiranno, letti nella tradizione biblica' in J.-C. Margolin ed *Acta Conventus Neo-Latini Turonensis* (Paris 1980) 1001–9.
85 'tyrant'] Probably a reference to the republican Romans' hatred of the title: see
   for example Cicero *Republic* 2.30.52.

227
86 Deuteronomy] 17:16–20
87 Ezekiel] 22:27
88 Plato] *Republic* 3.416A–B
89 lion] *Ibidem* 9.588–590
90 ends] *Ibidem* 1.345C–D
91 Paul] 2 Tim 4:17
92 Solomon] The quotations are from Prov 28:15, 29:2 and 28:28.
93 Isaiah] 3:4

228
94 among you] Matt 20:25–6
95 rule] A theme discussed by St Augustine *De civitate Dei* 5.12
96 Seneca] *De beneficiis* 2.18.6
97 Aristotle tells us] *Politics* 5.7.19 (1310a9–11)

229

98 father of the country] Cf above 215 n39.

99 detested] For further contemporary condemnation by Erasmus of tyrants, see the adages *Aut fatuum aut regem nasci oportere* (I iii 1; Phillips 219–25) and *Sileni Alcibiadis* (III iii 1; Phillips 276–80 and 284), as well as *Scarabeus aquilam quaerit*, already cited.

100 as Aristotle rightly put it] *Politics* 1.2.8 (1254a27)

101 'father of gods and men'] Homer *Iliad* 15.47, quoted in Greek and translated. See also Aristotle *Nicomachean Ethics* 8.10.4 (1160b27), where this passage in Homer is used to illustrate the paternal nature of the ideal king.

102 'Father'] Matt 6:9, Luke 11:2

103 in Homer] *Iliad* 1.231, quoted in Greek; a favourite phrase, used in the same context in the *Panegyricus* 44 (together with the next Homeric tag here) and in the adage *Scarabeus aquilam quaerit* (Phillips 234)

104 this same Homer] *Iliad* 1.263, quoted in Greek and translated

105 Julius Pollux] A rhetorician under the emperor Commodus (161–92 AD). The two quotations are from his *Onomasticon* 1.40–2; in each case, Erasmus first quotes the Greek text.

230

106 immovable] The word which this translates was inadvertently omitted from Erasmus' Greek text.

107 always … balance] This clause was added to the Latin text in 1518, although no addition was made to the Greek text; presumably it represents Erasmus' second thoughts on the translation of the Greek, and should have replaced 'favouring justice,' which has been kept in erroneously. The corresponding Greek phrase is indeed obscure, and modern scholarship has emended it to give the meaning 'more scrupulous in regard to justice than the scale of the balance.'

108 pagan teacher] The *Onomasticon* of Julius Pollux is in fact a rhetorical handbook which includes the thesaurus of terms utilized here; Erasmus presents it as a moral tract, which was not its author's intention.

109 Plato's phrase] See Xenophon *Memorabilia* 1.2.5, quoting Socrates.

110 Homer said] *Iliad* 1.231

111 Augustus] Seneca *De clementia* 1.9.5

231

112 He … many] An adaptation of a line from the early poet Laberius quoted in Seneca *De ira* 2.11.3

113 law] Erasmus had debated the question of tyrannicide with More and had published his declamation in 1506 with the *Luciani opuscula*; see Ep 191.

114 divine] See Aristotle *Politics* 3.9.7 (1285b5) and Cicero *De officiis* 2.12.41–2.

115 image of God] Plutarch *Moralia* 780E, a theme developed in the adage *Aut fatuum aut regem nasci oportere* (I iii 1; Phillips 219)

116 the best] Cf Plato *Republic* 9.576D and Aristotle *Politics* 4.2.2 (1289a39–b5).

117 democracy] A theme discussed by Aristotle *Politics* 4.1ff (1288b10ff). The 'mixed state' was a subject of much controversy in the sixteenth century, with

the rise of monarchical absolutism; cf Isnardi Parente 31–2. In Erasmus' homeland, for example, the traditional checks imposed on the prince by the Estates General were being eroded at this time; see Tracy *Politics* 19, 35, and 133 n24.

118 Aristotle] *Politics* 4.2.2 (1289a40)

232

119 proverb] *Adagia* II iii 61, based on Aristotle *Politics* 1.2.22 (1255b30)
120 will see] Cf Plato *Republic* 6.484c.
121 Xenophon] *Oeconomicus* 21.12
122 received it] Cf below 281 n12.

233

123 philosophers] Aristotle *Politics* 1.2.10–11 (1254b3–10) and Seneca *De clementia* 1.3.5; this favourite commonplace was developed in Christian terms by St Augustine *De civitate Dei* 9.9 and 19.21.
124 heart] This simile is probably of late medieval origin; the Ancients preferred the simile of the intellect (cf Isnardi Parente 90 n90).
125 spirits] The Galenical tradition of physiology, dominant in Erasmus' time, held that the heart, blood, and lungs between them produced or mediated three kinds of 'spirit': vital, animal, and natural. The lungs transform air into vital spirit, and the arterial blood carries this to the brain where it, or some of it, is converted into animal or 'cerebral' spirit to permeate the nervous system. The liver converts food-substances from the intestines into venous blood, and endows it with natural spirit, which enables growth and nutrition. See O. Temkin *Galenism* (Ithaca, NY and London 1973) ch 4.
126 last vestiges of life] Cf Hippocrates *De morbis* 4.40.2 and Aristotle *De partibus animalium* 3.667a33–4

234

127 'Magnificent'] Possibly a reference to Lorenzo de' Medici, 'Il Magnifico,' although earlier Erasmus had praised him as a patron of the arts (Ep 145:91–5), and at this time had high hopes of his son, now Pope Leo X. Erasmus frequently denounced the extravagant titles behind which princes hid their worthlessness, for example below 248, in the *Adagia* (Phillips 223 and 234), in the *Moria* 136 and in *Julius exclusus* 188.
128 Augustus] Suetonius *Augustus* 53
129 proverb] *Adagia* II iii 31, a quotation from Seneca *Epistulae morales* 47.5 or Macrobius *Saturnalia* 1.11.13
130 laws of the pagans] Cf the *Digest* of Justinian 1.1.4.
131 Paul] Philem 10–16
132 one Lord] Based on Matt 23:10
133 no need of it] The autonomy of soul and body is a commonplace of Platonic thought; cf for example, *Phaedo* 65–6.
134 Circe's art] The story of how the sorceress Circe turned Odysseus' companions into animals is told in Homer *Odyssey* 10.

235

135 free will] This is of course one of the central doctrines over which Erasmus
was to take issue with Luther in the *De libero arbitrio* and the *Hyperaspistes*.

136 Paul] Rom 13:1–8

137 among yourselves] These words are not in the Greek text of Erasmus' New
Testament, but in his commentary on Rom 13:8 (LB VI 636C–D) Erasmus
suggests this as a possible interpretation of the passage, which would otherwise mean 'have no debts to anyone at all'; the latter was Ambrose's interpretation, which Erasmus ultimately accepted in his New Testament note –
but it would not help his argument here.

138 it is on record ... didrachma] See Matt 17:24–7.

139 Gospel] Matt 22:16–22

236

140 respect] A play on *impetrat* 'acquires' and *imperat* 'commands'

141 Aristotle says] *Politics* 1.2.23 (1255b31–4)

237

142 Aristotle put forward the idea] *Politics* 1.2.20 (1255b11–12)

143 under the hammer] *Adagia* III i 67, literally 'bought at the stone,' an expression
found in Cicero *In Pisonem* 15.35; it is a reference to the stone or stone
elevation on which the praetor stood at slave sales, as Erasmus explains in
Adagia II x 77.

144 Croesus] Herodotus 1.88

145 monarch ... world] Cf below 285 n16.

146 Olympic contest] Cf Plato *Laws* 7.807C–E and 8.840 for the simile of the athlete
in training.

238

147 what is excellent ... difficult] A proverb quoted frequently by Plato, for example in the *Republic* 4.435C and 6.497D, and in the *Cratylus* 384B; also found
in Plutarch *Moralia* 6C. Cf *Adagia* II i 12.

148 proverb] *Adagia* I iii 1 (translated in Phillips 213–25), found in Seneca *Apocolocyntosis* 1.1; this was one of the adages much expanded in the 1515 edition;
see introductory note 201 above.

149 Plato looks for] *Republic* 6.503C–D and 8.547–8

150 Nero's nature] Cf Ep 272:28–30.

151 Plato wanted] *Republic* 7.539A–B

152 less secure] Cf Erasmus' translation of Galen's essay 'On the Best Kind of
Teaching' (LB I 1057D): some teachers had taken the dialecticism of the
Academy to an extreme where it issued in an absurd and crippling suspension
of judgement, even, for example, about the existence of the sun.

239

153 Homer] *Iliad* 2.24–5, quoted below 279

154 Virgil's similar picture] *Aeneid* 1.305

155 on holiday] This theme is developed further in ch 10.

240

156 deceptions] Cf Seneca *De ira* 2.13.2, a famous passage contrasting the ease of
virtue with the difficulty of vice.

157 Solomon] 1 Kings 3:5–12

158 Midas] Cf above 224 n74. For this famous story, see Ovid *Metamorphoses*
11.85–193: Bacchus granted Midas one wish; the king chose to wish that
everything he touched should turn to gold.

241

159 sceptre] Plutarch *Moralia* 354F and 371E (*De Iside et Osiride*); cf *Adagia* II i 1
(Phillips 175).

160 hippopotamus] On the development of this emblem, see M.W.M. Pope *The
Story of Decipherment* (London 1975) 27. In Horapollo's *Hieroglyphica* (first
published 1505) 1.55 the bird on the sceptre held by the Egyptian gods is a
hoopoe, but by the sixteenth century it had become a stork, the emblem of
filial piety (e.g. in Alciati's *Emblemata*); the contrast between the bird and the
parricidal hippopotamus was made by Horapollo 1.56 and Plutarch *Moralia*
962E. The sceptre usually depicted only a hippopotamus claw rather than the
whole beast.

161 Plutarch] Translated from *Moralia* 355A, except that there the eyes are closed
rather than missing altogether. The same example, together with that of the
sceptre and the eye, appears in the adage *Scarabeus aquilam quaerit* (III vii 1;
Phillips 251–2).

162 insignia] Cf above 215.

242

163 statue] Cf Plutarch *Moralia* 780A (*Ad principem ineruditum* 2); Plutarch points
out that at least a statue, filled with clay, stone, and lead, will remain
'upright,' unlike an uneducated ruler.

164 no heart] Perhaps a reminiscence of Cicero *Tusculanae disputationes* 1.9.18–19,
an account of the materialist philosophers who held that the heart was the
seat of the intelligence or even of the soul; Cicero points out that the adjec-
tives *excors* and *vecors*, literally 'without a heart,' had come to mean 'sense-
less, feeble-minded.'

165 Homer] Cf *Iliad* 1.343 and 3.109, quoted in Greek and probably from memory,
since Erasmus uses a different word for 'look.'

166 physician] A favourite simile of both Plato (*Gorgias* 521–2 and *Politicus* 293–6)
and Aristotle (*Politics* 3.11.5:1287a32–1287b5), which recurs frequently in
the *Institutio*; see in particular 266–7, a passage on the usefulness of the doctor's art, which is closer to Plato's application of the simile than the passage
here, which stresses the moral qualities of the good doctor in the manner of
Aristotle. Indeed, Erasmus might have echoed Galen's opinion that the
theoretical and ethical aspects of the doctor's art require him to be also something of a philosopher; a proper moral philosophy distinguishes the true
doctor from the potential poisoner alluded to in this passage and below 254;
see Erasmus' translation of Galen's essay 'That the Best Doctor Should Also
Be a Philosopher' in LB I 1063A–B and 1064A.

243

167 But ... prince] This sentence was added in the Basel edition of 1518, no doubt to underline the aptness of the comparison.

168 Aristotle] *Politics* 3.11.12 (1288a15–19), and cf 1.5.7 (1260a15).

169 Nereus] An old sea god, father of the fifty beautiful sea-nymphs, the Nereids, enumerated in Homer *Iliad* 18.38–49 and Hesiod *Theogony* 240–64

170 Milo] The great athlete of Crotona, six times victor in the Olympic wrestling; see Pausanias *Description of Greece* 6.14.5–8.

171 Maximinus] Roman emperor AD 235–8, originally a Thracian peasant, who was taken into the Roman army by Septimius Severus on account of his physical prowess; he was supposed to have been eight feet six inches tall: see Hist Aug *Maximini duo* 6.8.

172 Tantalus] Renowned for wealth and avarice, and for his punishment in the underworld; cf *Adagia* I vi 22 and Horace *Satires* 1.1.68ff.

173 what is right] Cf Plato *Laws* 6.762E and Cicero *Laws* 3.2.5, although both suggest that the ruler should previously have obeyed a master as well as 'what is right.'

174 'I desire ... reason'] Juvenal *Satires* 6.223; the remark is made there by a tyrannical wife ordering the execution of an innocent slave; perhaps this accounts for the association of women with tyrants at the end of the paragraph.

175 'Let them ... fear me'] *Adagia* II ix 62; the original source of the slogan is given by Cicero in *De officiis* 1.28.97 as the *Atreus* of Accius, now lost; it was also quoted by Seneca *De clementia* 1.12.4 and 2.2.2 and *De ira* 1.20.4; indeed, as Erasmus says in the *Adagia*, almost every ancient writer seized on it.

176 own people] Cf Gal 6:10.

244

177 call you] Cf Xenophon *Cyropaedia* 1.6.22.

178 Seneca] Cf *De clementia* 1.12.1, although Seneca mentions only Dionysius there. On Dionysius and Phalaris, see above 222; Polycrates was tyrant of Samos in the sixth century BC: see Herodotus 3.39ff for his misdeeds.

179 Plato] *Republic* 2.380B–C; the phrase 'in his laws' does not necessarily refer to the *Laws*, as Isnardi Parente (104 n122) has pointed out on the evidence of *Adagia* I i 1 (LB II 14B).

180 representation of God] Cf above 231 and n115.

181 and foolishness] Added in the Basel edition of 1518

2 / The prince must avoid flatterers

245

1 flatterers] There are a number of borrowings in this chapter from Plutarch's essay 'How to Distinguish a Friend from a Flatterer' (*Quomodo adulator ab amico internoscatur* in *Moralia* 48E–74E), the most comprehensive classical treatment of the subject, which Erasmus himself translated into Latin and republished with the first edition of the *Institutio*. But the theme of the powerful flatterer, whom both Plutarch and Erasmus regard as infinitely more dan-

gerous than the mere sycophant, was also a commonplace of contemporary political thought: cf *Moria* 117–18.

2 Diogenes] Plutarch *Moralia* 61C, where the remark is attributed to Bias, as it is in Erasmus' *Apophthegmata* 7 Bias 4 (LB IV 324F). Erasmus was obviously quoting from memory, and confused with this a similar remark of Diogenes about the 'detractor' rather than the tyrant in *Apophthegmata* 3 Diogenes 109 (LB IV 182E).

246

3 laws of the Ancients] By the Twelve Tables of Rome a thief who came by night or who used a weapon might be killed out of hand. Later, the penalty for theft was scourging and restitution of the stolen property twofold or fourfold according to the nature of the charge; see the *Digest* of Justinian 47.2.50.

4 a seller of empty promises] Literally 'a seller of smoke,' hence the peculiarly appropriate punishment; the term was used of members of the imperial household who accepted bribes in return for false promises of advancement. The practice is described in Hist Aug *Antoninus Pius* 6.1–5, and the example here in ibidem *Severus Alexander* 36.2–3, quoted in *Adagia* I iii 41: *Fumos vendere*.

247

5 Anyone ... mind] Added in the Basel edition of 1518

6 Carneades] Plutarch *Moralia* 58F, the source for Erasmus' *Apophthegmata* 7 Carneades 32 (LB IV 337F)

7 positive example] As Erasmus felt he had done in the *Panegyricus*: see Ep 180:42–68.

8 sheet-anchor] *Adagia* I i 24; cf above 220 n56.

9 Astrologers] On the dangers of astrology, cf *Panegyricus* 65; for Erasmus' general view of the science, see 282 n15 below.

248

10 Plutarch] *Moralia* 48E–74E, specifically here 60–1

11 Folly ... self-love] Cf *Moria* 89.

12 Plato] *Laws* 5.731D–732B

13 Apelles] See Plutarch *Alexander* 4.2; Apelles of Colophon, court painter to Philip of Macedon and his son, was the most famous artist of antiquity.

14 Octavius] Suetonius (*Augustus* 70) describes a banquet at which the emperor Augustus (Octavius) was dressed as Apollo; he always made the god an object of special honour.

15 'colossus' statues] See for example Suetonius *Nero* 31 (a statue 120 feet high) and *Vespasian* 23 (who preferred to have the money).

16 Alexander] Cf Plutarch *Alexander* 42.2; for the full story see below 280.

17 Darius] Cf Plutarch *Moralia* 173A; Erasmus tells the story himself in Ep 272: 13–20 and in *Adagia* II x 64: Darius, given a large pomegranate, expressed the wish that for every seed in it he could have another man like his trusted counsellor Zopyrus.

18 Scipio] The great Roman general Scipio Africanus captured New Carthage

(Cartagena) in Spain in 209 BC; on hearing that a beautiful captive was
betrothed to an honourable youth, he commanded that she be released and
that her ransom, collected by her relatives, be handed over to the couple as
a wedding gift; see Livy 26.50 and Valerius Maximus 4.3.1.

19 honorary titles] On this subject, see above 234 n127.

20 'his Holiness'] Cf *Julius exclusus* 169.

249

21 Alexander Severus] Hist Aug *Alexander Severus* 18.1

22 'Father of His Country'] A title given to Julius Caesar and offered to a number
of Roman emperors, some of whom refused it because of the odium which
Caesar had brought upon himself; see for example Suetonius *Julius* 76, *Tiberius*
26, and *Nero* 8.

23 'Invincible'] A title given to Maximilian by Erasmus himself in the address of
Ep 393, the dedicatory epistle to the *Institutio*

24 'Serene'] *Serenissimus*, again a title of the Roman emperors; see *Codex Justini-
anus* 5.4.23.

250

25 allow everything] Nonetheless, in ch 6 Erasmus advises that the prince should
obey the laws. There is probably also an allusion here to the famous maxim
of Ulpian; see below 264 n4.

26 Demetrius Phalereus] Plutarch *Moralia* 189D, the source of Erasmus' *Apophthegmata* 5 Demetrius 34 (LB IV 250B); Demetrius was governor of Athens
under the Macedonians 317–307 BC.

27 pagan] Compare Erasmus' warning against Isocrates in the epistle to Charles,
203 above.

28 transformed into conduct] An echo of a famous dictum of Ovid (*Heroides*
15.83), *Abeunt studia in mores* 'studies are transformed into conduct/
character,' quoted for example by Francis Bacon *Essays* 50 'Of Studies'

29 Achilles ... Caesar] Cf the adage *Aut fatuum aut regem nasci oportere* (I iii 1;
Phillips 214–16) on the many pernicious examples to be found in ancient
history and mythology.

30 Arthur and Lancelot] The Arthurian romances had been among the earliest
best-sellers after the invention of printing in the editions produced, for
example, by Caxton in England and Verard and Le Noir in Paris. Erasmus has
in mind here the whole chivalrous ethos of the Burgundian court: Prince
Charles had been introduced to these romances by his tutor (from 1509)
Chièvres; previously Adrian of Utrecht had attempted to instruct his royal
pupil in some of the classical works recommended here by Erasmus. On all
this, see Tracy *Politics* 59–69.

31 four senses] Erasmus added 'of the theologians' in the Basel edition of 1518,
perhaps to make it clearer that he was referring to the techniques of medieval exegesis, the interpretation of Scripture on the four levels, literal, allegorical, tropological, and anagogical: cf *Moria* 134. See also the adage *Sileni
Alcibiadis* (III iii 1; Phillips 275–6).

251

32 *Republic*] A partial text was rediscovered in 1820; in Erasmus' time the work was known only by quotations from it by other writers.

33 Julius] Perhaps a deliberate ambiguity, suggesting both Julius Caesar and Pope Julius II: cf above 216 n42.

34 Seneca] On the general equation between tyrants and bandits see *De beneficiis* 2.18.6; for examples of the 'rage' of the Persian tyrants Xerxes, Cyrus, and Darius, see for instance *De ira* 3.16–17 and 3.21.1.

35 Phalaris] The collection of letters attributed to the tyrant of Agrigentum (cf above 222 n64) was published very frequently from 1470 onwards, usually in the Latin translation by Aretino; it was not until 1697 that it was definitely shown to be spurious by Richard Bentley.

36 Perillus] He had constructed the brazen bull in which men condemned by Phalaris were to be roasted alive; he was himself its first victim.

37 Alexander] The first reference is to Alexander's honourable treatment of Darius' mother, wife, and two unmarried daughters, whom he had captured; see Plutarch *Alexander* 21.1–3. To judge by Erasmus' subsequent allusion to the woman's 'spirit,' the second reference is to the conduct of Timocleia (ibidem 12.1–3); Plutarch, however, does not attribute her release to the fact that she was married: she had killed a Macedonian soldier who attacked her, but showed no fear when brought before Alexander for judgment, and was released by her admiring captor.

252

38 *De copia*] Published in 1512; on the use of *exempla*, see CWE 24 608–10. Erasmus uses here the rhetorical term *amplificatio* 'expansion,' the way in which style may elevate the subject.

39 clemency] On Caesar's reputation for clemency, see Suetonius *Julius* 75–6; Erasmus' view that it was simulated, also found in the *Panegyricus* 40, probably derived from his unusual hostility to Caesar; see Tracy *Politics* 142–3 n37.

40 Vespasian's tax] Cf *Adagia* III vii 13, based on the story in Suetonius *Vespasian* 23; the quotation is from Juvenal *Satires* 14.204–5. Urine was used by fullers in their trade.

41 Nero] Suetonius *Nero* 32, the source for Erasmus' *Apophthegmata* 6 Nero 4 (LB IV 276A)

42 Aristides] An Athenian soldier and statesman of the fifth century BC, whose name was a byword for honesty; see Plutarch *Aristides*.

43 Epaminondas] Theban soldier and statesman of the fourth century BC renowned for the nobility of his character; see Plutarch's *Life*, as excerpted by Pausanius *Description of Greece* 9.13–15.

44 Octavius] The emperor Augustus

45 Trajan] Roman emperor AD 98–117

46 Antoninus Pius] Roman emperor AD 137–61; the texts, except LB, read 'Antonius.'

47 Alexander Mammeas] Better known as Alexander Severus, Roman emperor AD 222–35

48 Hebrews] See below 286 n25.

253

49 Philip] Plutarch *Moralia* 178C–D, the source for Erasmus' *Apophthegmata* 4 Philip 18 (LB IV 194B)

3 / The arts of peace

1 ancient writers] In fact, few earlier writers made war the subject of separate study; cf Tracy *Politics* 3.

254

2 received] Cf below 281.

3 own lives] Cf above 221 n61.

4 magic rings] Cf the allusion to a ring of this kind in the adage *Scarabeus aquilam quaerit* (III vii 1; Phillips 253). *Dactyliomantia*, divination by rings, was a common practice; Agrippa von Nettesheim gives numerous recipes for the manufacture of such rings in his *De occulta philosophia* (1529) bk I ch 47.

5 'potion'] Erasmus uses the Graecism '*philtron*,' which suggests specifically a love-potion, and is thus particularly apt in this context.

6 loyal] Cf Cicero *De officiis* 2.15.53, quoting a letter from Philip of Macedon to his son on this subject.

255

7 the wife] Erasmus was to develop these principles in the *Institutio christiani matrimonii* of 1526; see in particular LB V 671ff.

8 far away] See below, ch 8.

9 mixed marriage] See below, ch 9.

256

10 Mithridates] Aulus Gellius 17.17.2 and Valerius Maximus 8.7 ext 16

11 Alexander] Plutarch *Alexander* 45 and 47

12 Alcibiades] Plutarch *Alcibiades* 23; an Athenian, he adopted the customs of the Spartans. In both these cases, Plutarch records suspicions that the policy was a mere ruse.

13 Philip] Philip of Burgundy, Prince Charles' father, had died prematurely in Spain in 1506; see Ep 205, the *Panegyricus*, and Tracy *Politics* 12–13. On 'tours far afield' cf below 261 n6.

14 Gelderlanders] Karel van Egmond, duke of Gelderland, had waged intermittent war against the house of Hapsburg since 1492, and Erasmus regarded this war in his native land as a particularly painful example of 'civil war' between Christians: see Tracy *Politics* 71–107 (ch 4 'The Mystery of Our War with Guelders').

15 king bee] See above 212 n26.

16 Aristotle's *Politics*] 5.8.8 (1311a25)

17 protection] Cf Isocrates *Ad Nicoclem* 21.

257

18 Aristotle's advice] *Politics* 5.9.16 (1315a8–9)

258

19 innovation] On the dangers of sudden change, a commonplace of ancient
political thought as well as of Erasmus', see for example Aristotle *Politics*
2.5.13 (1269a14–18) and Plato *Laws* 7.797–8; see also below 269.
20 Peripatetic terms] Aristotle *Nicomachean Ethics* 1.8.2 (1098b13–15) and *Politics*
7.1.2 (1323a25–7); see also Plato *Laws* 3.697B and the ironic use of this
division in *Julius exclusus* 196. 'External goods' meant wealth, power, and
glory.

259

21 Xenophon] *Cyropaedia* 1.2.2–8, on the educational system of the Persians
22 of their own accord] A principle frequently enunciated by Socrates; see for
example Plato *Republic* 4.425D and *Laws* 5.731C and 9.860D; cf also Plutarch
Moralia 446E, where, however, it is applied only to philosophers.
23 Plato has written] *Laws* 6.766A
24 Plato has forcibly remarked] *Republic* 6.493B

260

25 benign deception] Cf Plato *Republic* 3.414B–C on 'opportune falsehoods' and
'noble lies'; for examples, see ibidem 415C and *Laws* 2.664A and 6.769E.

4 / Revenue and taxation

1 Revenue and taxation] For the background to this chapter in the context of
contemporary economic and fiscal policy, see A. Renaudet 'Erasme écono-
miste' in *Mélanges offerts à M. Abel Lefranc* (Paris 1936) 130–41 and the useful
notes and references in ASD IV-1 190–3. For examples of the exceptionally
heavy taxation levied in the Low Countries during this period to finance the
various wars, see Tracy *Politics* 37–8 and 77–8.
2 Fabius Maximus] The celebrated adversary of Hannibal; on his scorn for glory,
compare the quotation from Ennius in Cicero *De senectute* 4.10: 'He valued
safety more than the mob's applause,' that is, his unpopular delaying tactics
exhausted Hannibal and saved Rome.
3 Antoninus Pius] Roman emperor AD 137–61; see for example Hist Aug *Marcus
Antoninus* 12.9, on his refusal to take an unmerited share in his brother's
glory.
4 officialdom] Much of this advice was probably directed at Prince Charles'
grandfather Maximilian: cf Tracy *Politics* 58. For a story of speculation under his rule, see the colloquy *Convivium fabulosum* (Thompson *Colloquies* 264).
5 proverb] *Adagia* I v 67, literally 'the rope breaks under too much strain'

261

6 foreign tours] Possibly an allusion to the grant of a huge subsidy by the
Estates General of the Netherlands to Prince Charles for his projected
Spanish voyage in February 1516; see Tracy *Politics* 82. See also the adage

Spartam nactus es, hanc orna (II v 1; Phillips 303–4) on his father Philip's
unlucky voyages to England and Spain; cf above 256.

7 Plato] *Republic* 4.421D; stated in more general terms, as here, by Aristotle
Politics 4.9.4–5 (1295b7–8)

262

8 corn ... clothes] Compare the more detailed denunciation of such taxes on
essentials in the adage *A mortuo tributum exigere* (I ix 12; Phillips 227).

9 'assizes'] The Latin word is *asisiae*; although primarily used of juridical assemblies, it also designated various kinds of tax assessment (cf Old French
assise) or even taxation itself; see J.F. Niermeyer *Mediae latinitatis lexicon minus*
(Leiden 1976). Erasmus is presumably using it to translate the Dutch word
for excise taxes, *accijnzen*; cf Tracy *Politics* 58.

10 import duties] On Erasmus and the customs, see below 270 and n37.

11 monopolies] For a still stronger condemnation of monopolies, see the adage *A
mortuo tributum exigere* (I ix 12; Phillips 226).

12 proverb] A maxim quoted in Cicero *Paradoxa Stoicorum* 6.3.49

13 Charles] For Erasmus' low opinion of Charles the Bold, duke of Burgundy and
great-grandfather of Prince Charles, see the adage *Spartam nactus es, hanc
orna* (II v 1; Phillips 303). Charles died in battle in 1477, leaving no male heir,
and this led to a prolonged struggle for the inheritance between France and
the house of Austria, with all the attendant social disorders to which Erasmus
refers. For information on the state of the coinage in the Low Countries up
to this time, see the appendices by John H. Munro in CWE 1 (especially 312)
and 2 (especially 309–13).

5 / Generosity in the prince

263

1 help someone] According to Suetonius *Titus* 8.1, the Roman emperor Titus
remarked at the end of a day in which he had helped no one: 'Friends, I
have wasted a day.'

2 poets] For examples of gods taking human form and rewarding those who
welcomed them, see the stories of Baucis and Philemon in Ovid *Metamorphoses* 8.611–724, of Hyrieus in Ovid *Fasti* 5.493–544, and of Falernus in Silius
Italicus *Punica* 7.166–211.

3 withheld] This passage probably refers to the relatively new practice of billet-
ing mercenary soldiers on citizens; cf Tracy *Politics* 58.

4 followers] For the idea that the prince is judged by the activities of his followers, cf Isocrates *Ad Nicoclem* 2.

264

5 Plato] *Laws* 5.729E

6 *Xenios*] 'Hospitable,' and thus 'protector of the rights of hospitality'; cf Homer
Odyssey 9.270–1 and the passage in Plato cited in the previous note.

6 / Enacting or amending laws

1 obeys the laws] Cf Plato *Laws* 4.715C; this was also a principle of canon law; see Gratian *Decretum* Pars prima dist 9 c 2 (PL 187 49). In the *Panegyricus* (43) Erasmus expounds this traditional medieval constitutionalism as an antidote to those flatterers who tell the prince that he is above the law; cf Tracy *Politics* 19.

2 embodiment of the law] Cf Aristotle *Politics* 3.8.2 (1284a11–14), Cicero *Laws* 3.1.2, and Plutarch *Moralia* 780C–E; on this commonplace of Ancient political theory, see G.J.D. Aalders in *Palingenesia* 4 (Wiesbaden 1969) 315ff.

3 small number] Cf Isocrates *Panegyricus* 78 and *Areopagiticus* 7.40–1.

4 decided] A reference to the famous maxim of Ulpian, 'What the prince has decided, that is the law,' incorporated in the *Digest* of Justinian 1.4.1; cf *Panegyricus* 43.

5 Plato too requires] *Republic* 4.425C–E

265

6 Dionysius] Possibly a reminiscence of the spurious bk 2 of Aristotle's *Oeconomica* (2.2.20, 1349a14–1350a6) which gives a list of the tyrant Dionysius' stratagems for making money; but the particular device mentioned here is not found in any classical author.

7 Epitades] Epitadeus, a Spartan magistrate accused of hastening the decline of Sparta in this way by Plutarch in *Agis and Cleomenes* 5.2

8 punishments] See Plato *Laws* 4.722–3 on the desirability of brevity and the general tendency to use compulsion rather than persuasion.

9 Seneca] *Epistulae morales* 94.38; in fact, Seneca is quoting Posidonius's disapproval of Plato's opinion: Seneca himself clearly agrees with Plato on this point.

10 Plato does not allow] *Laws* 1.634D–E

11 Antoninus Pius] Hist Aug *Antoninus Pius* 12.3

12 Xenophon] *Oeconomicus* 13.6–10

13 Ancients] On the principle, see Cicero *De oratore* 1.58.247; on the practice, see for example Aristotle *Politics* 2.5.4 (1268a8–9) on the maintenance of war orphans and rewards for information, at Athens and elsewhere.

266

14 was entitled to a reward] This phrase was added in the Basel edition of 1518; the sentence was previously an anacoluthon.

15 Plato rightly warns] *Laws* 9.862E

16 unturned] *Adagia* I iv 30

17 cut ... part] A reminiscence of Ovid *Metamorphoses* 1.190–1, part of a speech made by Jupiter to justify his intention to destroy impious mankind

267

18 Plato thinks] *Laws* 11.936C

19 is in good health and] Added in the Basel edition of 1518

20 beg] On the contemporary attitude to beggars and Erasmus' views on the

able-bodied poor, see the colloquy Πτωχολογία in Thompson *Colloquies* 248–54, especially the introduction.

21 Marseille] Valerius Maximus 2.6.7; strolling players were also excluded.

22 monasteries] On the idleness of monks, a favourite target of contemporary satire, cf *Moria* 131–2. Erasmus' experience of the colleges of the University of Paris doubtless inspired the following remark; both institutions are fiercely criticized in the colloquy 'Ιχθυοφαγία; Thompson *Colloquies* 312–57

23 tax farmers] Cf above 262.

24 usurers] Erasmus considered usurers a degree less harmful than monopolists but in the adage *A mortuo tributum exigere* (i ix 12; Phillips 225–6) he pointed out that, historically, usury had always been frowned on.

25 agents and retainers] This development should be compared with a similar passage in More's *Utopia* bk 1: *Complete Works* E. Surtz and J.H. Hexter eds (New Haven and London 1965) iv 62–4.

268

26 government of the state] Cf Aristotle *Politics* 2.6.2 (1269a34–6) and Plutarch *Solon* 22.

27 proverb] *Adagia* i vii 33

28 sumptuary laws] On the history of the Roman sumptuary laws, see Aulus Gellius 2.24 and Macrobius *Saturnalia* 3.17; on their enforcement, see for instance Suetonius *Julius* 43, an account of Caesar's severe measures against the sale of imported luxuries.

29 informer] At Rome, this occurred particularly in cases of *maiestas* 'treason,' when a quarter of the condemned man's property might be allotted to the informer. The system was much abused by some emperors, particularly Domitian; see Suetonius *Domitian* 12.

269

30 Plato] *Laws* 9.854D–855C and 862

31 severe] The biblical penalty was of course stoning (cf Deut 22:24 and John 8:5), as Erasmus recalls in the *Institutio christiani matrimonii* (LB v 648–9) where he again contrasts the punishments for adultery and theft. In Rome the *lex Iulia de adulteriis coercendis* passed by Augustus also prescribed the death penalty; see the *Institutes* of Justinian 4.18.4 and Tacitus *Annals* 3.24; this was confirmed by the emperors Constantius ii and Constans in AD 342: Justinian *Codex* 9.9.30 (31)

32 exemplary] *Laws* 9.854E

33 ills of the state] Cf Plato *Laws* 7.798B.

34 circumstances of the state] Cf Aristotle *Politics* 2.5.12 (1269a8–11).

270

35 practice] A case of this kind is described by Cicero *De oratore* 1.39.177.

36 law] Probably a reference to the practice of *vindicatio*, in which the victim of theft would sue for the restoration of his property, an action separate from the prosecution of the thief himself; see the *Digest* of Justinian 6.1.9ff.

37 customs duties] An example drawn from personal experience; see Ep 119:9n

on Erasmus' unfortunate experience at the hands of the English customs at Dover. See also the adage *A mortuo tributum exigere* (I ix 12; Phillips 227).

38 shipwreck] Roman law regarded those who took property washed ashore as no better than robbers (Justinian *Digest* 47.9.3) and the action itself as theft (Justinian *Institutes* 2.1.48). But in medieval England, for instance, although in theory the proceeds of wreck belonged to the crown and their collection was entrusted to the sheriffs, in practice, royal charters often permitted the owner of the foreshore to take the wreck if no claimant came forward within a prescribed period; see S.A. Moore *A History of the Foreshore and the Law Relating Thereto* 3rd ed (London 1888) 31 and 689. It is possible that Erasmus had in mind a scandal of this kind which happened in Holland in this very year, 1516; see Preserved Smith *A Key to the Colloquies of Erasmus* (Cambridge, Mass and London 1927) 18–20.

271

39 Greek philosopher] Anacharsis, quoted by Plutarch *Solon* 5.2; cf *Adagia* I iv 47.

40 vengeance] Perhaps a reminiscence of Neh 9:17; cf also Plutarch *Moralia* 550E: God's mildness and delay in inflicting punishment should be an example to human judges.

41 lèse-majesté] The crime of *maiestas minuta* 'treason' was originally an offence against the majesty of the Roman people (Cicero *De inventione* 2.17.53); under the empire its scope was broadened by the *lex Iulia maiestatis* (Justinian *Digest* 48.4) to take account of the existence of the prince; it was much abused by later emperors, particularly Domitian (Suetonius *Domitian* 12). Cf *Panegyricus* 44.

42 Hadrian] Hist Aug *Hadrianus* 18.4–5

43 Nero] Suetonius *Nero* 39

44 'In a free state ... free'] Suetonius *Tiberius* 28, the source for Erasmus' *Apophthegmata* 6 Tiberius 4 (LB IV 273B); although charges of *maiestas* were frequently brought during Tiberius' reign, Tacitus too suggests that the emperor himself bore little responsibility for the abuse of the law (*Annals* 1.73).

272

45 Augustus Caesar] The story is told in Seneca *De clementia* 1.9; Cinna, son of the conspirator against Julius Caesar, plotted to assassinate Augustus during a sacrifice; the Emperor, swayed towards mercy by his wife Livia, inflicted no sterner punishment on him than a two-hour rebuke. Cinna was later elected consul, and made Augustus his heir.

273

46 'guardians of the law'] In Greek in the text; Plato *Laws* 6.755A etc. They must be distinguished from the famous 'guardians of the state' (*Republic* 4.421A–B etc); Erasmus is thinking here of the law alone.

47 Ancients] Probably a reference to the Twelve Tables, the earliest Roman code of laws, which were published in the Forum on tablets of bronze or wood; see Livy 3.34. Plato (*Laws* 11.917) mentions that in Greece the rules of the market were written down and displayed in the market-place.

48 complications] Cf Isocrates *Ad Nicoclem* 17.
49 advocates] On the rapacity of lawyers, a favourite subject of contemporary
   satire, see for example the adages *Scarabeus aquilam quaerit* (III vii 1; Phillips
   239) and *Dulce bellum inexpertis* (IV i 1; Phillips 342), and two passages in the
   Moria, 107 and 125.
50 Plato says] *Laws* 3.690–1

7 / Magistrates and their duties

1 Magistrates] To avoid confusion, we have generally translated *magistratus* by
   'magistrate'; it should be remembered, however, that the Latin word often
   has the broader meaning of 'officer of the state' and is used of both senior
   administrators and judges.
2 Aristotle] *Politics* 4.6.3 (1294a3–4)

274
3 Plato forbids] *Laws* 6.755A; see also *Republic* 3.409 on the value of experience in
   a judge.
4 parts of the mind] Cf Aristotle *Politics* 1.5.5 (1260a) and Plato *Republic* 4.435ff.
5 extortion] The Latin is *actio repetundarum*, a reference to the Roman *lex repetundarum rerum* 'law of restoration of property,' first formalized in 149 BC
   and an important weapon against the excesses of provincial governors in
   particular; see Cicero *De officiis* 2.21.75.

275
6 business deal] Cf Aristotle *Politics* 2.8.7 (1273b2–3).
7 laws of the Caesars] See Dio Cassius 52.23 and 53.15, on edicts promulgated
   by Augustus Caesar. Previously Roman magistrates had received only their
   expenses.
8 Aristotle] *Politics* 5.7.9 (1308b33–4)

8 / Treaties

1 no state] Cf Plato *Laws* 4.715A–B and *Republic* 8.551D.
2 bits of paper] The Latin word is *syngrapha*, a bond or written agreement, often
   a promissory note; Erasmus gives examples of its use in a pejorative sense
   in *Adagia* IV vii 78: *Ex syngrapha agere*.

276
3 at fault] Compare Erasmus' remarks on the League of Cambrai in *Julius exclusus*
   173, and see Tracy *Politics* 23–6 for a brief account of the shifting alliances
   of the previous decade.
4 too literally] *Adagia* II iv 13: *Ad vivum resecare*, literally 'to cut to the quick'
5 friendly] Cf Hesiod *Works and Days* 346.
6 Certain nations] In the adage *Spartam nactus es, hanc orna* (II v 1; Phillips 302)

Erasmus gives as an example of this the Spaniards and the Germans; it was perhaps impolitic to repeat this in a work addressed to the future Charles v, who had hereditary rights among both nations.

277
7 Ulysses] A reminiscence of Horace *Epistles* 1.2.17–22
8 Italy] In the adage *Spartam nactus es, hanc orna* (II v 1; Phillips 302–4) Erasmus describes Italy as 'isolated ... both by the sea and the massive chain of the Alps,' and goes on to deplore the fruitless Italian adventures of the French kings Charles VIII and Louis XII (since 1494). See also Ep 288:121–4.

9 / The marriage alliances of princes

1 marriage alliances] For the background to this chapter, see E. V. Telle 'Erasme et les mariages dynastiques' *Bibliothèque d'Humanisme et Renaissance* 12 (1950) 7–13; compare also the colloquy Ἰχθυοφαγία (Thompson *Colloquies* 325).
2 near neighbours] Cf *Querela pacis* 312 on absurdly distant matches.
3 king's son] Perhaps an allusion to the scandal caused by the secret marriage of Mary Tudor and Charles Brandon, duke of Suffolk, in 1515; see Ep 287:15–16 and n. Mary's sister Margaret, widow of James IV of Scotland, had also caused consternation recently by her sudden marriage with the earl of Angus (August 1514).
4 Helen] On Helen of Troy as a proverbial source of discord, see *Adagia* I iii 69: *Haec Helena.*
5 common fatherland] Cf Tracy *Politics* 74 on the difficulties of Charles' grandfather, the Emperor Maximilian, as a 'foreigner' in the Netherlands; see also below 278 n8 on Philip of Burgundy's Spanish marriage.

278
6 iron chains] Literally 'adamantine chains': cf *Adagia* I vii 43 and also *Querela pacis* 320.
7 James] James IV married Henry VII's daughter Margaret in 1503 and was killed at Flodden in 1513; see Epp 280 and 325, and especially the emotional passage on the death in the battle of Erasmus' former pupil Alexander Stewart in the adage *Spartam nactus es, hanc orna* (II v 1; Phillips 304–5).
8 to avoid offending anyone] Erasmus' caution is understandable, since the Hapsburgs were notorious for the use of diplomatic betrothal. Maximilian's campaigns against the French had been justified on the sort of pretexts condemned in this chapter; see Tracy *Politics* 90. Erasmus was inclined to suggest that the premature death of Philip the Handsome was in part attributable to his Spanish marriage: see above 256, Ep 205, and the adage *Spartam nactus es, hanc orna* (II v 1; Phillips 303–4). Philip's son Charles, to whom the *Institutio* was dedicated, had been betrothed to Claude de France in 1501, then to Mary Tudor from 1507 to 1514; the latter finally married Claude's father Louis XII, and Charles was betrothed to other French princesses in 1515 and 1516. See Epp 252 and 287, and Tracy *Politics* 49–50 and 134 n9.

10 / The business of princes in peacetime

279

1 Scipio] Cicero *De officiis* 3.1 and Plutarch *Moralia* 196B; quoted also in Erasmus' *Apophthegmata* 5 Scipio Maior 1 (LB IV 257A)
2 Aeneas] Virgil *Aeneid* 1.305
3 The man ... sleep] *Iliad* 2.24–5 (and 61–2); Erasmus quotes the Greek and then translates it.
4 Wise men] For example Xenophon *Agesilaus* 8.8–9.2

280

5 bishops] Compare the contrasting views of the episcopal office represented by Peter and Julius in *Julius exclusus*. See also below 286, and passages in the *Moria* 137 and in the adage *Sileni Alcibiadis* (III iii 1; Phillips 281–96). On the true political role of bishops, as arbitrators, see below 284.
6 Mithridates] Cf above 256.
7 Alexander] Plutarch *Alexander* 42.2
8 proverb] *Adagia* II ii 82, found in Aristophanes *Wasps* 1431 and Cicero *Tusculanae disputationes* 1.18.41
9 Homer] Cf above 279.
10 swamps] Cf a passage in the adage *Spartam nactus es, hanc orna* (II v 1; Phillips 308), where a still stronger contrast is made between the theoretical duties of the prince and actual contemporary practice. Many of the duties described here would seem to be particularly relevant to Erasmus' low-lying native land.

281

11 frugal and restrained] Cf Isocrates *Ad Nicoclem* 32, on public splendour and private frugality in the ruler.
12 Theopompus' words] Plutarch *Moralia* 779E, based on Aristotle *Politics* 5.9.1 (1313a26), and included in Erasmus' *Apophthegmata* 1 Theopompus 98 (LB IV 118A)
13 proverb] This famous adage meaning 'Make the best of what you have' was one of those which was given a long commentary in the 1515 edition of the *Adagia* (II v 1; Phillips 300–8; many of its themes reappear in this chapter of the *Institutio*.
14 Epaminondas] Valerius Maximus 3.7 ext 5, the source for Erasmus' *Apophthegmata* 5 Epaminondas 33 (LB IV 253C)

282

15 eclipses of sun and moon] Erasmus did not perhaps take such portents as seriously as many of his contemporaries; see his remarks on a consultation with astrologers in Allen Ep 948:15–27 and the jocular references in Allen Ep 1005:1–14 and in the *Moria* 125.
16 Julius] See *Julius exclusus* 184–5.

11 / On starting war

1 On starting war] As Erasmus says at the end of this chapter, he had already written a good deal on the evils of war; in the *Apologia contra Stunicam* of 1522 (LB IX 370D), however, Erasmus cited this chapter as evidence that he was not opposed to all wars, since in it he had given rules for the conduct of war. But in fact this chapter clearly reflects Erasmus' pacific views: many parallels can be pointed out between it and, in particular, the adage *Dulce bellum inexpertis* (IV i 1; Phillips 308–353), published in 1515, and the *Querela pacis*, published in 1517. We have indicated only the most important of them. On the general attitude of Erasmus and his humanist colleagues, see R.P. Adams *The Better Part of Valor: More, Erasmus, Colet and Vives on Humanism, War and Peace 1496–1535* (Seattle 1962).

2 War breeds war] A favourite aphorism of Erasmus: cf *Dulce bellum inexpertis* (Phillips 314), *Panegyricus* 55, and *Querela pacis* 321.

3 creature] This comparison, a commonplace of pacific writing expounded originally in the prologue to Book 7 of Pliny's *Naturalis historia*, is developed at length in *Dulce bellum inexpertis* (Phillips 310–14).

4 just] On the 'just war,' a concept stretching back into antiquity but given shape by St Augustine, see J.A. Fernandez 'Erasmus on the Just War' *Journal of the History of Ideas* 34 (1973) 209–226.

283

5 mercenaries] For other portraits of mercenary soldiers see *Panegyricus* 54–5, *Dulce bellum inexpertis* (Phillips 334–5), and the colloquy *Militaria* (Thompson *Colloquies* 12–15). Mercenaries had played a large part in recent campaigns in the Hapsburg lands, and Erasmus actually crossed the path of one band of them in May 1516; see Tracy *Politics* 88–90.

6 Plato] *Republic* 5.470C–D, frequently cited by Erasmus and other humanists denouncing war between Christians; it may be noted that the passage in Plato is by no means as condemnatory of war as the humanists tended to suggest.

7 papal laws] The twelfth-century *Decretum* of Gratian c 23 brought together the most important papal rulings on the church's attitude to violence: see S. Chodorow *Christian Political Theory and Church Politics in the Mid-Twelfth Century: the Ecclesiology of Gratian's Decretum* (Berkeley, Los Angeles, London 1972) 223–46.

8 Augustine] For example in *De civitate Dei* 4.15 and 19.7

284

9 St Bernard] Bernard of Clairvaux 'praised warriors, but in such terms as to condemn all our soldiering' (*Dulce bellum inexpertis*, Phillips 339); the reference is to the *De laude novae militiae: ad milites Templi liber*, a panegyric of the militant but pious Knights Templar. Erasmus used the same examples in the same way in *Dulce bellum inexpertis* (Phillips 339) and in the *De bello turcico* of 1530 (LB V 354).

10 Christ] See for example Matt 5:9 and especially 26:52, the cornerstone of evan-

gelical pacificism, discussed in *Dulce bellum inexpertis* (Phillips 336–7, 344, and 347).

11 Peter] 1 Pet 3:11 and 2 Pet 3:14, for example
12 Paul] 2 Cor 13:11 and Heb 12:14, for example
13 astrology] For Erasmus' view, see above 282 n15.
14 alchemy] Erasmus tended to regard alchemy as charlatanry and its victims as fools; see the colloquies *Alcumistica* and Πτωχολογία in Thompson *Colloquies* 238–45 and 248–54.
15 arbitration] Cf Ep 288:91–7, *Dulce bellum inexpertis* (Phillips 343–4), and *Querela pacis* below 310. For a bibliography of arbitration in the medieval period, see R.H. Bainton *Christian Attitudes towards War and Peace* (London 1961) 116–17; see also his *Erasmus of Christendom* 152.

285
16 monarchy] Erasmus had little time for the pretensions of various princes to the inheritance of the Roman empire; in Ep 586 he points out the ignoble origins of that empire, and doubts whether its restoration is a practical proposition; in 1527 he seems to have refused Gattinara's request that he edit Dante's *De monarchia* to assist Charles v in his approaching confrontation with the papacy (Allen Ep 1790A). In Erasmus' often repeated view, the 'monarch of all the world' was God. See also Tracy *Politics* 8 and 16–17.
17 to the letter] *Adagia* II iv 13; cf above 276 n4.
18 calamities] A point made with some force in the 1515 adage *Testa collisa testae* (III vii 29; Phillips 297)
19 before Christ] Cf *Panegyricus* 55.
20 Virgil] *Eclogues* 1.70 *impius*
21 demolish one] Cf passages in *Dulce bellum inexpertis* (Phillips 326–7) and *Querela pacis* 318.

286
22 fleeting] A Stoic theme developed in *Dulce bellum inexpertis* (Phillips 324–5).
23 French] Cf *Querela pacis* 315. An addition in the Basel edition of 1518 makes this hatred mutual.
24 Bishops] Cf *Dulce bellum inexpertis* (Phillips 321–2) and *Querela pacis* 309.
25 Hebrews] Cf *Dulce bellum inexpertis* (Phillips 335–6) and *Querela pacis* 299–300. Origen had laid down that the Israelites' physical battles prefigured the spiritual struggles of the Christian church (PG 12 897), but this view was disputed by medieval canonists, among them Gratian (PL 187 1161), who maintained that the right to wage physical war had been transferred to Christians intact; see H. de Lubac *Exégèse médiévale: les quatre sens de l'Ecriture* (Paris 1959–64) II i 450–2.
26 David] See 1 Chron 22:7–11; cf *Querela pacis* 300.

287
27 on earth] Col 1:20
28 Turks] Cf Ep 335:170–92 and *Dulce bellum inexpertis* (Phillips 344–5); Erasmus clung to this opinion, in far less propitious times, in the *De bello turcico* of

1530 (LB V 345–68). See M.J. Heath 'Erasmus and War against the Turks' in
J.-C. Margolin ed *Acta Conventus Neo-Latini Turonensis* (Paris 1980) 991–9.
29 fleece the Christian people] An allusion to the scandal of Crusade indulgences, against which Luther was to launch his protest in the following year

288
30 Prince of Peace] Isa 9:6

COMPLAINT OF PEACE / *QUERELA PACIS*

Introductory note

290
1 Cf the letter to John Botzheim of 30 January 1523 (Allen I 29–36).
2 Tracy *Politics* 56

291
3 Cf R.H. Bainton 'The *Querela Pacis* of Erasmus' *Archiv für Reformationsgeschichte*
42 (1951) 32.
4 Ed W.J. Hirten (New York 1946)
5 José Chapiro *Erasmus and our Struggle for Peace* (Boston 1950)
6 See especially J. Hutton 'Erasmus and France: The Propaganda for Peace'
Studies in the Renaissance 8 (1961) 107–12; J.-C. Margolin *Guerre et paix
dans la pensée d'Erasme* (Paris 1973); C.R. Thompson 'Erasmus as Internation-
alist and Cosmopolitan' *Archiv für Reformationsgeschichte* 46 (1955) 167–95.

Dedicatory letter

292
1 Philip] Of Burgundy (1464–1524) one of the many natural sons of Philip the
Good; succeeded his brother David as bishop of Utrecht in 1517. This
dedicatory preface is Ep 603.
2 Prince Charles] Of Burgundy, son of Philip the Handsome, later the emperor
Charles V
3 Plato] *Republic* 7.520D
4 brother ... succeed] David, an elder natural son of Philip the Good, bishop of
Utrecht 1455–96; he had ordained Erasmus in 1492. Cf Ep 28:22n.
5 father ... sprung] Philip the Good, duke of Burgundy (1419–67), who had
worked for peace with France
6 recently] Erasmus had recently been at court (Allen Ep 596 introduction),
perhaps in his capacity as councillor, and may have noticed that there was
still opposition there to the policy of reconciliation with France. Cf Allen I 36f.

Complaint of Peace

293

1 Peace speaks] Added in *1529*; not in ASD
2 sea of disasters] *Adagia* I iii 28
3 morass] Latin *lerna*, the swamp where Hercules killed the hydra; cf *Moria* n310 and *Adagia* I iii 27.
4 Furies] Avenging spirits pursuing murderers
5 ocean of all the evils] *Adagia* I iii 28 (*mare malorum*)

294

6 concord] The Stoic concept of *concordia*; cf R.H. Bainton 'The *Querela pacis* of Erasmus' *Archiv für Reformationsgeschichte* 42 (1951) 32–48 and *Erasmus of Christendom* 142.
7 Storks ... loyalty] Cf *Panegyricus* 49. The family affection (*pietas*) of the stork was emphasized from antiquity onwards. It was believed that older storks were fed by the offspring they had hatched and reared: Aristophanes *Birds* 1355–7; Plato *Alcibiades* 1 135E; Aristotle *Historia animalium* 615b33ff. See also the *Hieroglyphica* of Giovanni Piero Valeriano (Basel 1556) bk 17, and *The Hieroglyphics of Horapollo* tr George Boas (New York 1950) 81–2 and 97.
8 dolphins ... services] Well known in antiquity for their friendliness to man, dolphins were also symbolic of helpfulness between parents and their young and *pietas* in general; Aristotle *Historia animalium* 566b2ff; Pliny *Naturalis historia* 9.24 and 33; A. Henkel and A. Schöne *Emblemata, Handbuch zur Sinnbildkunst des XVI und XVII Jahrhunderts* (Stuttgart 1967) cols 686–7.
9 harmony ... well known] St Augustine *De civitate Dei* 19.12 and Dio Chrysostom *Orationes* 40.35. The well-ordered social life of ants and bees was a popular Renaissance topos.
10 a male nearby] Pliny speaks of male trees in *Naturalis historia* 24.37 and 18.179.
11 magnet ... attracted] Pliny *Naturalis historia* 36.127
12 lions ... each other] Pliny *Naturalis historia* 7.5; Juvenal 15.160ff
13 murderous tusks] Ovid *Fasti* 2.232 (*fulmineo ore*); Phaedrus 1.21.5
14 concord between wolves ... proverbs] Cf *Adagia* II iii 63 (*Furemque fur cognoscit et lupum lupus*)

295

15 to man alone] The passage on the difference between man and beast is modelled on Cicero *De officiis* 1.4.11 and *De legibus* 1.6.27.
16 potions] The sorceress Circe changed Odysseus' men to pigs; see *Odyssey* 10.235ff.
17 tears] Pliny *Naturalis historia* 7.2; Juvenal 15.131–2
18 need ... another] Cf the myth of Epimetheus told in Plato *Protagoras* 320cff, especially 321c.
19 mutual affection] ἀντιπελάργωσις, a very rare word meaning love between parents and children; Kock *Comicorum Atticorum Fragmenta* III 9.39; *Adagia* I x 1

296

20 godhead] A Neoplatonic tenet which appealed to the humanists
21 confound ... profane] *Adagia* I iii 82
22 the mind of their subjects] For this concept see Aristotle *Politics* 1295a40 and Isocrates *Panathenaicus* 138.

297

23 counterfeit] Cf *Institutio principis christiani* 287 'trumped-up claims and spurious pretexts.'
24 Peripatetic] Ie Aristotelian
25 goat's wool] One of Erasmus' favourite expressions for trivial subjects of debate; Horace *Epistles* 1.18.15; *Moria* 84 and n22; *Adagia* I iii 53. For disputes between philosophers cf *Moria* 125–6.
26 barbed wit] *Adagia* III vi 87 (*Dentata charta*)
27 sheet-anchor] *Adagia* I i 29
28 All Christians ... faith] The 'philosophy of Christ' preached by Erasmus

298

29 Paul] 1 Cor 6:1
30 property] Cf the attack in *Moria* 137–8.
31 loggerheads amongst themselves] See *Moria* 131 for dissension amongst the religious orders. Bernardines are the Cistercians, called after St Bernard of Clairvaux.
32 Observants ... Colettines] The branch of the Franciscans which 'observed' the primitive rule of the founder and the section of the second order of St Francis (the Poor Clares) further reformed by St Colette (1381–1447)
33 third lot] The Conventuals, a branch of the Franciscan order favouring the accumulation and common holding of property
34 strife] Hesiod *Theogony* 225–6

299

35 passions] Cf Seneca *De ira* 1.7–8.
36 mutual love] Cf Seneca *De ira* 1.5.
37 prince of peace] Isa 9:6
38 Silius] Silius Italicus, *Punica* 11.592
39 psalmist] David, in Ps 76:2; explained in Heb 7:2 (king of Salem, which is, king of peace). The text translated is that of the Vulgate (Ps 75:3).
40 Isaiah] 32:17
41 gifts of the Holy Spirit] 1 Cor 13:13
42 God of peace] Rom 15:33; Heb 13:20
43 peace of God] Phil 4:7; Col 3:15
44 'messengers of peace'] Isa 33:7
45 Lord of hosts] 1 Kings 19:14; Isa 1:24
46 vengeance] Ps 94:1
47 correction of vices] Cf Isa 1.25ff

300

48 out of the heart] Cf *Institutio principis christiani* 252 for allegorical interpretation of the Old Testament.

49 'my people ... peace' Isaiah] 32:18
50 'peace ... Israel'] Ps 125:5
51 Isaiah marvels ... prosperity] Isa 52:7
52 opposite of Christ] Ie the devil
53 with the Father] 2 Cor 5:18
54 friend] John 15:14ff
55 'man of peace'] 1 Chron 22:9
56 not permitted ... Lord] 1 Chron 22:8
57 wage war] Cf below 306 and *Institutio principis christiani* 286.
58 proclaim] Luke 2:14
59 'Peace be with you'] John 20:19

301
60 greeting] Matt 10: 12–13
61 words of peace] Eg Rom 1:7; 1 Cor 1:3
62 good health] The classical Roman greeting *Salve* means 'Be in good health.'
63 'Love one another'] John 13:34; 15:17
64 'I give ... peace'] John 14:27
65 he asked] John 11:22, 42
66 'Holy Father ... we are one] John 17:11
67 'By this sign ... one another'] Cf John 13:35.
68 'As I ... loved you'] John 13:34; 15:12
69 without end] Cf St Augustine *De civitate dei* 18.41.1–3.
70 'This is ... one another'] John 15:12
71 'Our Father'] Matt 6:9
72 sheep] John 10:11, 14

302
73 branches] John 15:5
74 resist evil] Matt 5:39
75 good for evil] Matt 5:44
76 lilies] Matt 6:26, 28
77 excludes the rich ... heaven] Matt 19:23, 24
78 gentle in spirit] Matt 11:29
79 a gift ... brothers] Matt 5:23–4
80 chicks under her wings] Matt 23:37
81 cornerstone] Matt 21:42; Eph 2:20

303
82 Herod] Luke 23:12
83 sword] Matt 26:52; John 18:11
84 his dying words ... his death] Luke 23:24
85 to heaven] Acts 1:9
86 Holy Spirit] Acts 1:5
87 gathered together] Matt 18:20
88 fiery spirit] Acts 2:3
89 beneficial ... as fire] Cf Pliny *Naturalis historia* 36.200.
90 one soul] Acts 4:32
91 bringing together] The word *ecclesia* literally means 'assembly.'

304

92 reborn in Christ] Rom 6:4

93 same body] Rom 12:5; Eph 4:4; Ep 288:39–40; *Panegyricus* n213

94 free man] Gal 3:28

95 Scythians] Herodotus 4.70

96 Jerusalem] Gal 4:26; Heb 12:22; St Augustine *De civitate Dei* 19.11

97 evil men] *Adagia* II i 71; Euripides fragment 298 (Nauck); Aristotle *Eudemian Ethics* 1238a34 and 1239b22

305

98 past ten years] Cf 307 below 'wars fought during the last twelve years.' The period includes the war against Venice by the participants in the League of Cambrai – France, Spain, the empire, and the papacy in the person of Julius II – and then, after Venice had come to terms with the pope, the formation of the Holy League to expel the French from north Italy, in which England joined with Spain, the empire, Venice, and the pope; cf Ep 239:47. The French withdrew in 1512. Julius II was also leading his armies to recover papal lands in Italy, and after the League broke up, Francis I again invaded Italy, aided by Venice, and won his victory over the Swiss and Milanese at Marignano in 1515. As Erasmus' sympathies were with France he was generally uncritical of the flimsy pretexts on which the French invaded Italy.

99 river of sea] Horace *Odes* 2.1.29–36

100 God's command] Cf *Institutio principis christiani* 286.

101 Turks] Peace treaties with the Turks had been agreed in 1503 and 1514 and were renewed again on 8 September 1517.

102 victory] *Adagia* II vi 23

103 claim] This may be a reference to the French claim on Milan and Naples; Louis XII based his claims on the fact that his grandmother was a daughter of Filippo Maria, the 'last' Visconti of Milan who was, however, succeeded by Francesco Sforza in 1447; Charles VIII argued that Naples had been conquered by Charles d'Anjou in 1282.

104 interception ... spouse] Probably an allusion to Anne de Bretagne, officially betrothed to Maximilian, but married in 1491 to Charles VIII; see n160 below.

306

105 Dionysius] Tyrant of Syracuse (d 367 BC), often cited as a symbol of tyranny

106 Mezentius] King of Caere in Etruria and ally of Turnus in Virgil's *Aeneid*, where his cruelty is described in 8.485ff; cf *Institutio principis christiani* 223.

107 most prosperous of all powers] Cf Ep 549:14ff and *Panegyricus* 21.

108 Marraños] Spanish Jews baptized after Ferdinand's edict of 1492 but still adhering to Judaism. Many were expelled, and the pope Alexander VI had outraged Spanish orthodoxy by receiving them in Rome (perhaps the Jews in Italy referred to above). Cf Ep 549:12 *semiiudaei Marani*.

109 wild beasts] Ep 288:30 and Seneca *De ira* 2.83

110 said before] 294 above

111 armed them] *Adagia* IV i 1

307

112 despised populace] Latin *ignobile vulgus*; Virgil *Aeneid* 1.149
113 noble cities] *Institutio principis christiani* 233
114 helmet] Virgil *Aeneid* 9.612; Ovid *Tristia* 4.1.4. Erasmus never misses a chance to attack Julius II, who was over sixty when he started his ten-year campaign to recover and extend papal territories. Cf *Moria* 139.
115 shameful sight] Ovid *Amores* 1.9.4
116 cardinals] Eg the Swiss cardinal Matthaeus Schinner (1465–1522), who was not only active in negotiations against France but led armed troops

308

117 salvation] Isa 52:7; Rom 10:15
118 biographer] Suetonius *Titus* 9
119 Franciscans] Erasmus has in mind the English Franciscan Edmund Birkhead, according to Tracy *Politics* 170 n163; cf Allen Ep 1211:561, 602.
120 titles] Eg the 'Holy' League

309

121 Bellona] Roman goddess of war
122 Legate in the Field] Latin *campi legatus*, a title adopted by Cardinal Schinner
123 standard] The Swiss were given permission to use the cross as a standard by Julius II in return for their services in the Holy League.
124 both camps] Cf *Institutio principis christiani* 286.
125 'Our Father'] Matt 6:9

310

126 the evil one] Matt 6:13
127 Plato] *Republic* 5.470C–D; Erasmus transfers Plato's concept of Greek vs barbarian to Christian vs Turk.
128 sewn ... river] The Roman penalty for *parricidium* laid down by the Twelve Tables: the parricide was sewn into a sack with a dog, a cock, a snake, and a monkey and thrown into the Tiber. Cf Suetonius *Augustus* 33.
129 pretences] *fucos*; cf *Adagia* I v 52 (*Fucum facere*).
130 trappings] Ie. humbug, evasions; the phrase is taken from Persius *Satires* 3.30.
131 fooled] Gal 6:7
132 hear us] 'Te rogamus audi nos' is the common refrain in litanies of the Latin liturgy.
133 best overlooked] Cf *Moria* 98.
134 learned men] Cf *Institutio principis christiani* 284; Ep 288:90.

311

135 that may be] Cf Cicero *Ad familiares* 6.6.5. Cf also *Panegyricus* 55.
136 Leo's appeal ... concord] Leo X, a Medici pope, succeeded Julius II in 1513. He was active in arranging peace between England and France in 1514 and Erasmus hoped at this time that he would restore peace to Europe. Cf Ep 288:88–102 and Ep 335:79ff, addressed to Leo in 1515.
137 that of a father ... family] *Panegyricus* 44
138 think himself great] *Institutio principis christiani* 283

312

139 human and free] Cf *Institutio principis christiani* 234; Ep 288:103.

140 only Diocletian ... designs] Diocletian was Roman emperor from 254 until his abdication in 305. His policy was defensive, concentrated on reinforcing frontier defences and manning them by the legions, which he reduced in size while adding to their numbers. He also reformed army discipline and separated the civil from the military command; but he is generally remembered for his persecution of the Christians, and Erasmus' tribute here is a little surprising.

141 intermarriage ... king of Britain] As Philip the Handsome acquired Aragon and Castile through his marriage to Joanna; *Panegyricus* 10 and n5

313

142 'Better ... back of his head.'] *Panegyricus* 14 and n22 where the saying is traced back to Cato *Res rustica* 4.1

143 encourage courtesy] *Institutio principis christiani* 285

144 cost] *Institutio principis christiani* 285

314

145 largest number] Cf Virgil *Aeneid* 6.611.

146 common purpose] Latin *syncretismus; Adagia* I i 11

315

147 British] *Institutio principis christiani* 286. The hostility between the two recalls the Scottish march across the border and defeat at Flodden in 1513, when their king James IV was killed, along with his son Alexander Stewart, Erasmus' much-loved pupil.

148 Paul] 1 Cor 1:12 and 3:4

149 the French] A reference to the long dispute between France and the duchy of Gelderland; Martens' edition of 1518 and some later editions add 'Nunc Flandriam faciunt Germaniam.'

150 this common world ... homeland] Cf Ep 480:265ff.

151 if ... relationship] ASD punctuates differently, taking this clause as part of the next sentence.

316

152 in Homer ... reconciliation] *Iliad* 9.505; 19.91

153 mercenaries] Erasmus consistently attacks the use of mercenary armies; cf *Panegyricus* 55 and the colloquies *Militaria* (1522) and *Militis et Cartusiani* (1523). See also Tracy *Politics* 88ff.

154 'the law ... holds sway'] Cicero *Pro Milone* 4.11; cf *Panegyricus* n200.

317

155 housebreaker] Latin *parietum perfossor*; cf Plautus *Pseudolus* 980.

318

156 sham city] Bainton *Erasmus of Christendom* 121 refers this to the siege of Tournai by Wolsey.

157 accurately] Latin *ad verum calculum*; *Adagia* I v 55
158 Carians] Proverbial for treachery; Cicero *Pro Flacco* 65 and *Adagia* I vi 14; cf
Panegyricus n192.
159 realm] A reference to Maximilian's perpetual claim to the duchy of Gelderland
(Tracy *Politics* 90)
160 daughter] Margaret of Austria, Maximilian's daughter, was formally betrothed
to Charles VIII and repudiated by him in favour of Anne de Bretagne. This
gave Maximilian a lasting grievance against the French.
161 authority] Suetonius *Augustus* 28
162 emperors] Marcus Aurelius; Hist Aug *Avidius Cassius* 2.8

319
163 two of the Antonines ... target] Antoninus Pius, emperor 138–61 and Marcus
Aurelius, emperor 161–80, though in fact Vespasian also died a natural
death (Suetonius *Vespasian* 24).
164 that city ... man] Matt 5:14; 1 Cor 4:9
165 apostles] Bainton *Erasmus of Christendom* 121, 153; J.-C. Margolin *Guerre et paix
dans la pensée d'Erasme* (Paris 1973) 18. In 1512 twelve English cannons had
been named 'the twelve apostles.'
166 Homer] *Iliad* 13.636–9
167 shut] In times of peace; this took place only twice before the reign of Augustus
and three times during it, according to Suetonius *Augustus* 22; cf *Panegyricus* nn223–4.

320
168 smoke] Seneca *De ira* 3.42
169 Eternity] Ie the eternity of death; the 'everlasting home' of Ecclesiastes 12:5
170 Father] John 17:21
171 ended] The classical *Acta est fabula*; *Adagia* I viii 39
172 rope] Latin *vincula stuppea*; used in *Aeneid* 2.236 of the ropes which pulled the
Trojan horse into Troy
173 adamant] *Institutio principis christiani* 278; *Panegyricus* 65; *Adagia* I vii 43

321
174 human principle] Latin *humanitas*, the Stoic concept of man's innate magnanimity and rationality whereby he should respect his fellows and cultivate
the civilized virtues; cf Bainton *Erasmus of Christendom* 59–60.
175 Francis] King of France 1515–47; *Rex christianissimus* was one of his official
titles.
176 Prince Charles] See n2.
177 Maximilian] Emperor 1493–1519, grandfather of Prince Charles. Erasmus implies that he is less enthusiastic for peace than Francis, and evidently ex-
pects opposition to a peaceful settlement with France from him or from his
partisans in the Netherlands; Tracy *Politics* 56 and 162 n70.
178 King Henry] Ie Henry VIII

THE CICERONIAN: A DIALOGUE ON THE IDEAL LATIN STYLE / *DIALOGUS CICERONIANUS*

Introductory note

324

1 Allen Ep 1875:157 (1527)
2 See eg Allen Epp 1720:53, 2568:10ff, 2632:7.
3 For whom see Théophile Simar *Christophe de Longueil, humaniste, 1488–1522* Recueil de travaux publiés par les membres des conférences d'histoire et de philologie, fasc 31 (Louvain 1911).

325

4 This enabled Erasmus to claim him as a fellow-countryman: 'Longolius cum sit nostras' (Allen Ep 1026:5–6).
5 For whom see 435–6.
6 For details see 431ff.
7 See R. Aulotte 'Erasme et Longueil' *Bibliothèque d'Humanisme et Renaissance* 30 (1968).
8 See introduction to Allen Ep 914, the letter from Longueil to Lucas.
9 Ep 935, 1 April 1519

326

10 See 339 and 434, where Erasmus is recalling these criticisms ten or so years later.
11 The incident is recorded in Ep 1706, 6 May 1526.
12 The two speeches are discussed 431–4.
13 Epp 1675, 1706
14 See G. Vallese 'Erasme et Cicéron' and C. Bené 'Erasme et Cicéron' in *Colloquia Erasmiana Turonensia* ed J.-C. Margolin (Paris and Toronto 1972) 2 vols I 241ff and II 571ff.

327

15 See Allen Ep 1720:48. Other letters of that year (1701, 1713) contain thoughts eventually incorporated into the *Ciceronianus*.
16 See below text n703. Bade reissued the work in Paris in 1526.
17 Allen Ep 1595:130–2 from Lupset (August 1525)
18 See Ep 1791 from Olivar, 13 March 1527.
19 Allen Ep 1934:227–33

328

20 See below text n413.

330

21 See Allen Ep 2056:21, 1 October 1528. No edition of *Ciceronianus* was printed in Italy until Gambaro's of 1965 (for which see below n44).

331

22 For whom see 422.

23 In Ep 2021

24 In Ep 2021

24 See Allen Epp 2046:334ff and 2048:9ff.

25 For which see Budé's letter of April 1527, Ep 1812.

26 See Berquin's second letter, Ep 2066.

27 See Ep 2119. He was probably the author of the following: 'Desine mirari quare post ponat Erasmus / Budaeum Badio – plus favet ille pari' (Telle 191).

28 His skill in epigram is mentioned by Erasmus 416.

29 Ep 2048

30 Ep 2046

31 *Selectae epistolae* (Herwagen and Froben 1528), a volume filled out with three other long apologetic letters defending himself from various accusations, including the charges of heresy which he was facing at this time (Allen Ep 2021 introduction).

32 Ep 2047

33 See Allen Ep 2047 introduction.

34 For example, Johannes Köll (Brassicanus) (see Ep 2305) and Helius Eobanus (see Ep 2446)

35 Ep 2008, July 1528

332

36 See Allen Ep 2026:3n.

37 Ep 2040, September 1528

38 Ep 2061, October 1528

333

39 See Allen Ep 2008:28, where he admits to making 'some concessions' to affection.

40 Allen Epp 2008:11ff, 2446:97ff

41 See *Contemporaries of Erasmus: A Biographical Register of the Renaissance and Reformation* 3 vols (Toronto: University of Toronto Press 1984–   ) for complete information about the contemporaries of Erasmus referred to in the *Ciceronianus.*

42 ASD I-2 656

334

43 See Ep 2682 and text nn659, 664. Erasmus also for a time confused this *Oratio* with the *Della imitatione* which the Ciceronian Giulio Camillo (for whom see text n308) had written in Paris in 1530–1 as a reply to the *Ciceronianus,* and which was said to be circulating among Ciceronians in Italy in 1532. Erasmus had heard of this unpublished work through Wigle van Aytta (Ep 2632). Even after clarification on this point, Erasmus persisted in believing that Camillo had contributed in some measure to the *Oratio.* See CEBR sv Camillo.

44 For much detailed and valuable information concerning Longueil, Erasmus,

Ciceronianus, and the whole Ciceronian controversy, see Stephanus Dolet *Dialogus de Imitatione Ciceroniana, adversus Desiderium Erasmum Roterodamum, pro Christophoro Longolio* (Lyon: Gryphius 1535), facsimile text and edition in Telle, and Desiderio Erasmo da Rotterdam *Il Ciceroniano o Della stilo migliore*, testo critico, traduzione italiana, prefazione, introduzione et note a cura di Angiolo Gambaro (Brescia: La Scuola Editrice 1965). Translations or summaries of many of the documents mentioned in this introduction in connection with the controversy occasioned by Erasmus' dialogue, together with a complete translation of the *Ciceronianus*, may be found in Izora Scott *Controversies over the Imitation of Cicero* Columbia University Contributions to Education 35 (New York: Teachers College, Columbia University 1910).

45 Ep 3127 to Melanchthon, 6 June 1536
46 See below text n566 for the possible source for this antithesis.

335
47 For Vlatten's career, see Allen Ep 1390 introduction. The dedicatory letter is Ep 1948, 14 February 1528, translated 337–8.
48 Ep 1964, 8 March 1528
49 In Ep 1975, 19 March 1528
50 See ASD introduction to text.
51 See above 330, 333.
52 Ep 2088, translated 338–41. It was printed amidst the minor pieces at the end of the volume, before some epitaphs on Wimpfeling. The original dedicatory epistle was retained in its normal place.
53 I am indebted for this information to Sir Roger Mynors.

Dedicatory letters

337
1 My honourable friend] This dedicatory letter is Ep 1948.
2 Homer ... calls] Eg *Iliad* 1.144. See also *Adagia* II i 47 *Res sacra consultor*.
3 'Amidst ... a place'] Horace *Odes* 4.12.27
4 Horace again] *Ars poetica* 451

338
5 My dear Vlatten] This second dedicatory letter to Vlatten is Ep 2008. See above, introductory note 335.
6 on pronunciation] *The Right Way of Speaking Latin and Greek: A Dialogue* CWE 25 347–475
7 'The extras ... load'] *Adagia* IV ii 69

339
8 Euripus] A channel between the island of Euboea and Boeotia in mainland Greece, famous for its swift currents and tides
9 satirist] Persius 5.153

340

10 John] 1 John 5:19

11 Christoph von Utenheim] See Ep 598 introduction.

12 'flee ... nothing'] Thomas à Kempis *Imitation of Christ* 3.37. Wimpfeling, like Erasmus, had been influenced in youth by the ideals of the Brethren of the Common Life, who created the spiritual context from which the *Imitation of Christ* emerged.

13 bishop] Of Basel from 1502

14 somewhere] In *De integritate* (1505)

341

15 brother] Actually his step-brother

16 three letters] See text n260.

17 troublemaker] Allen Ep 2088:127n identifies him as Heinrich Eppendorf.

The Ciceronian: A Dialogue on the Ideal Latin Style

342

1 On the Ideal Latin Style] *De optimo dicendi genere*, a title recalling that of Cicero's treatise *De optimo genere dicendi*, better known as *Orator* (for the title, see Cicero *Ad Atticum* 14.20.3)

2 Bulephorus] For the Homeric word *boulephoros* and the value of the 'giver of counsel,' see the first dedicatory epistle, Ep 1948, above 337.

3 Unless ... sharpness] Terence *Phormio* 735

4 scab] Syphilis, which spread rapidly over Europe in the sixteenth century, was variously known as 'the Neopolitan scab' or 'the French disease.'

5 something with its source ... depths of the mind] Added 2nd ed

6 Davus] A slave in Terence *Andria* who makes fun of his old master in seemingly innocent conversation

343

7 understand medicine] Bulephorus 'the counsellor' is about to practise the therapy of the word. See 408 below, where Dr Word is introduced, and n495.

8 bull's horns growing on their heads] Like the daughters of Proteus, who imagined themselves to be cows; see Virgil *Eclogues* 6.48.

9 That ... going to do] Cf Celsus 3.18.11: 'It is often better to agree (with those who suffer from a delusion) rather than resist them, and so gradually and imperceptibly lead them from their foolish talk to a saner state of mind.'

10 Peitho] Persuasion; see Cicero *Brutus* 59.

11 charms away the soul] See *De oratore* 2.187, where Cicero quotes a line of the early Latin dramatist Pacuvius: 'Flexanima atque omnium regina rerum oratio' (Soul-charming power, queen of all things, speech). Pacuvius' line imitates Euripides *Hecuba* 816, a line referring to Peitho. Erasmus had published a translation of the *Hecuba* in 1506.

344

12 enraptured by a nymph] Erasmus puts in Bulephorus' mouth the Greek word
employed by Socrates in Plato *Phaedrus* 238D to indicate that he feels inspiration coming upon him. Nymphs were the semi-divine spirits of the wild
Greek countryside endowed with powers of prophecy, and a man who saw
them became enraptured or possessed, filled with prophetic or mad frenzy.

13 pushing at this rock] Terence *Eunuchus* 1085; the phrase refers to the punishment in hell of Sisyphus, condemned forever to push uphill a great stone
which constantly rolled down again.

14 suffer more from possessing] An echo of Terence *Phormio* 167, where Antipho,
having married his girl, is terrified at the prospect of his father's wrath

15 once said of Pericles] See Cicero *Brutus* 59; Pericles, the leader of Athens at the
height of its glory in the fifth century BC, was remembered as a powerful
and persuasive orator.

16 nothing fine comes easy] *Adagia* II i 12

17 particularly fond of you] Erasmus here gives Nosoponus' words a Ciceronian
cast; see 371 and eg Cicero *Ad familiares* 9.14.5.

345

18 mysteries] A term referring primarily to the rites of Demeter and Kore at El-
eusis near Athens, the Eleusinian mysteries, open only to those who had
passed through a ceremony of initiation and concealed from the uninitiated

19 Christophe de Longueil] D 1522; for details see introductory note 324-6.

20 Quintilian] 10.1.115; Quintilian adds 'assuming that he was going to develop
further.'

21 More than that ... as well.] It would be more in character if the first of these
remarks was assigned to Bulephorus and the second to Hypologus, whose
contributions tend to be facetious or said 'tongue in cheek.'

22 by Italians] Some Italians' arrogant dismissal of all northerners as 'barbarians'
incapable of writing good, ie Ciceronian, Latin and in particular the criticisms directed at his own style were particularly galling to Erasmus. He therefore presents the Italians' acceptance of Longueil as a Ciceronian as all the
more remarkable, and undercuts its value by his sarcastic tone.

23 had begun to study that] Longueil had begun Greek in Paris, and went to Italy
c 1515, accompanied by Lazare de Baïf, expressly to study under Lascaris.
He spent two years in Rome attending the classes of Musurus and Lascaris,
and began to write letters in Greek and to buy Greek manuscripts. He
continued his study of Greek literature during his last three years in Venice
and Padua (1519-22), though most of his time was devoted to Cicero (see
Théophile Simar *Christophe de Longueil, humaniste, 1488-1522* Recueil de travaux publiés par les membres des conférences d'histoire et de philologie,
fasc 31, Louvain 1911, 49-53, 81).

24 all things in common] Terence *Adelphi* 804; *Adagia* I i 1

346

25 into your brotherhood ... we will] Terence *Eunuchus* 1083-4

26 reveal the mysteries] The humorous depiction of Nosoponus' activities that
follows was interpreted as a vicious caricature of Longueil by his admirers.

After his conversion to Ciceronianism, Longueil spent five years reading chiefly Cicero (Pole's life of Longueil; see n703). In Erasmus' Colloquy *Echo* of 1526, the 'ass' has spent ten years reading Cicero only.

27 a Carthusian from meat] Perhaps another reference to Longueil, who practiced various asceticisms and was buried in Franciscan habit. The Carthusian rule enjoined total abstention from meat.

28 chapel] Nosoponus, avoiding any Christian word, uses *lararium* (a domestic shrine of the *Lares*, ancient household gods). The word is however non-Ciceronian, hardly even classical, occurring in Lampridius' life of the third-century Roman emperor Alexander Severus (see 410), who kept images of Cicero and Virgil in a *lararium*.

29 picture ... on all the doors too] Cf Cicero *De finibus* 5.3, where Epicureans are said to have their master represented not only in portraits but also on goblets and carved gems. In Erasmus' *Convivium reliogiosum*, the host's house is adorned everywhere with religious and edifying paintings.

30 carved on gems] Nosoponus is presumably referring to a portrait cameo in antique style, such as were produced in Italy from the end of the fifteenth century.

31 lexicon] Latin and Greek dictionaries, both monolingual and bilingual, were being produced in considerable numbers at this period. Shortly after the appearance of *Ciceronianus*, in 1535, Mario Nizzoli, a fanatical Ciceronian, was to produce the first version of his famous lexicon, *Observationes in M.T. Ciceronem*, designed as a handbook for Latin composition. He says in the preface he had spent nine years on it. See n308 for Camillo's eccentric Cicero lexicon.

347

32 periods] Period, the technical term for an utterance in which at least two units are organized into a logically, aesthetically, and rythmically pleasing whole; the complex period enclosing several units is characteristic of Cicero's mature style. For a discussion and analysis of Cicero's sentence structure endeavouring to identify the essential of his style, see Harold C. Gotoff *Cicero's Elegant Style: An Analysis of the Pro Archia* (Urbana: University of Illinois Press 1979).

33 Marcus Tullius] Cicero's full name was Marcus Tullius Cicero. In earlier centuries he was frequently referred to as 'Tully,' though 'Cicero' is usual nowadays. Cicero is named constantly in this dialogue, and Erasmus uses both 'Cicero' and 'Marcus Tullius.' This variation has been preserved to some extent in the translation in order to avoid monotonous repetition of the word 'Cicero.'

34 recto or verso] After page numbering was adopted in printed books, it was usual at first not to number the two sides of a leaf separately but to distinguish them as *recto* and *verso* of the single sheet numbered on the *recto*. This practice survived until the middle of the sixteenth century, though numbering on both sides begins to appear fairly early in the century.

348

35 *amo, lego, scribo*] Three common verbs used as paradigms in Latin grammars.

The famous Donatus of the fourth century AD, whose grammars were used throughout the Middle Ages, lists every possible form of *lego*, whether used or not (see below).

36 It's no great thing] This sentence was added in the 3rd ed.

37 Ciceronially] Erasmus borrows the adverb *Tulliane*, coined by St Augustine *Contra Pelagium* 2.10.37.

38 *amabam*] Changed in 2nd ed to *amabo* 'I shall love,' which Cicero uses frequently, especially in his letters in its colloquial sense 'please,' but *amabam* also occurs.

39 *amaras ... amasti*] Contracted forms of *amaveras, amavisti*

40 *scriptor*] Changed in the 2nd ed to *scriptoribus* (dative and ablative plural). Both *scriptoribus* and *scriptor* occur in Cicero. A few of the other rejected forms occur also. Nosoponus of course does not have to be right, and it is more amusing if he is not, but Erasmus' details, especially if based on memory rather than on a lexicon, are mostly impressively correct.

41 *stultitias ... ambituum*] Various nouns, mainly abstracts, quoted in case forms which occur rarely or not at all in classical Latin literature, where abstract nouns are often restricted in usage to the singular number; these forms are all plural.

349

42 'Slight the theme ... on his name we call.'] Virgil *Georgics* 4.6–7

43 I would say *nasutus*] He would be ill advised, as it is not Ciceronian, any more than *laudatissimus*. *Ornatior* and *laudatior* do occur in Cicero.

44 *lectiuncula*] This unusual word is actually used once by Cicero, *Ad familiares* 7.1.1 (and was so recorded by Nizzoli), and Erasmus has presumably remembered it from Cicero, but he seems to have invented *scriptorculus*. These two words are derivatives formed with a diminutive suffix. See *De copia* CWE 24 338–9 for Erasmus' views on the validity of new formations; for his predilection for diminutives, see D.F.S. Thomson 'The Latinity of Erasmus' in *Erasmus* 125–6.

45 not *dispicio*] He could allow himself both this and *transcribo* (see below), as both are Ciceronian.

46 Terence] The early Latin dramatist, c 195–159 BC, praised as the exemplar of correct Latinity by all critics, the most famed judgment being that of Julius Caesar who described him as *puri sermonis amator*. Terence was often included in the school curriculum as a source from which to learn sound Latin usage. He was one of Erasmus' favourite authors, and is frequently quoted by him (six times already in this text).

350

47 Draconian code] Drawn up by the Athenian lawgiver Dracon in the seventh century BC and notorious for the severity of its penalties; see Aulus Gellius 11.18.

48 epiphonemata] Exclamations or other striking expressions used to provide a resounding conclusion to an argument or an exposition of facts; see Quintilian 8.5.11.

49 wagon-load] Too big for man or beast to carry; *Adagia* I vii 74
50 it was truly said] Cicero *De oratore* 1.150; Quintilian 10.3.1
51 or ... out of Virgil] Added 3rd ed
52 When weary ... still] Aeneid 4.522–5 (first line altered)
53 Pythagoras] A Greek from Samos who c 531 BC established a religious-philosophical community in Croton in southern Italy. He taught that the soul was condemned to a cycle of reincarnation as man, animal, or plant, and that if it was not to sink to an existence lower than that of man it must strive to resist the contaminating effects of the flesh by purification of mind and body through study and mental and physical discipline (including strict dietary regulations). His studies in numerical ratios as revealed in the musical scale led him to interpret the order to be seen in the physical universe as a manifestation of universal number, which he spoke of as a harmony or disciplined relation. The 'music of the spheres' was the inaudible harmony created by the ordered revolutions of the heavenly bodies in their proportionally spaced concentric orbits.

351
54 'the crowd with its envy'] Horace *Odes* 2.16.39–40
55 Ovid] *Fasti* 6.5
56 shrine of the Muses] Nosoponus is scrupulously doing what the Ancients recommended: Pliny had a sound-proof room in his villa (see *Epistles* 2.17.24); Demosthenes used an underground room (see Plutarch *Demosthenes* 7); Quintilian 10.3.22–8 lists conditions conducive to study.
57 blacksmiths] See Seneca *Epistulae morales* 56.4.
58 what shall we gain] Seneca ibidem 5
59 people who suffer from love] See Quintilian 12.1.4ff on the need for the student of oratory to be free from vice and from all mental preoccupations.

352
60 warning from others' peril] *Adagia* II iii 39
61 'nails to earth ... of God'] Horace *Satires* 2.2.79, a humorous reference to Pythagoras' teachings on the effect of undisciplined eating habits on the soul. See above n53.
62 Hesiod] The early Greek didactic poet, writing somewhat later than Homer
63 the Muses spoke with him] On Mount Helicon, as he records in *Theogony* 22–5, a scene symbolizing his inspiration and commissioning as a poet
64 'Great ... to arms'] Horace *Epistles* 1.19.8 citing Ennius, the father of Latin poetry (239–169 BC) together with other poets known as drinkers, in support of a proposition that poetic inspiration is enhanced by alcohol
65 'Horace was full ... Dionysus!''] Juvenal 7.62, referring to Horace *Odes* 2.19, where the poet celebrates the exultant power of the god of wine

353
66 fires that don't smoke] Nosoponus uses the word *acapnus* 'smokeless,' borrowed from Greek and recorded in Columella, the Elder Pliny, and Martial. While Erasmus can happily use such a word, as his stylistic criteria allow him

to employ any available Latin word in the appropriate context (see *De copia* CWE 24 308), it is not for the Ciceronian Nosoponus. See n72.

67 John Doe or Richard Roe] In Latin, Titius, the general name used by Roman lawyers

354

68 period] See n32.

69 put it aside] See Quintilian 10.4.2.

70 Areopagite] A member of the Areopagus, the upper council at Athens, a body of great antiquity, moral authority, and incorruptibility, whose jurisdiction included trial for murder; *Adagia* I ix 41

355

71 they tell us] See Cicero *De oratore* 1.150; *Adagia* I vi 30.

72 in this very conversation] Except for the occasional Ciceronian phrase, Nosoponus has indeed been talking the same kind of eclectic Latin as the others. The very boxes (*scrinia*, 346 above) in which he has shut up his books are unciceronian.

356

73 Demosthenes] The Athenian orator and politician (384–322 BC), considered by ancient critics the greatest of Greek speakers. Cicero was often compared with him.

74 was never willing to rise] Plutarch *Demosthenes* 8.3

75 stank of lamp-oil] As was said of Demosthenes by his opponent Pytheas; see Plutarch ibidem; *Adagia* I vii 71.

76 dust and ashes] *Adagia* I ix 30

77 freely share] An echo of Horace *Epistles* 1.6.67–8

78 *Apelles*] The most famous painter of antiquity, living in the fourth century BC. See Pliny *Naturalis historia* 35.79–97 for an account of the man and his work. Analogies are drawn between the development of oratory and of the visual arts in Cicero *Brutus* 70ff and in Quintilian 12.10.1–12.

357

79 Zeuxis] Another famous painter of the period fifth/fourth century BC, active c 435–390; see Pliny *Naturalis historia* 35.61–6.

80 picture of Helen ... masterpiece] See Cicero *De inventione* 2.1–2; Erasmus follows Cicero in using the story of Zeuxis as an analogy for imitation in the literary sphere. Croton was a Greek colony founded on the coast of Bruttium in the toe of Italy c 710 BC. The inhabitants presumably invited the famous Zeuxis to come from Athens when commissioning their painting.

81 Brutus] Marcus Junius Brutus, the most famous of Julius Caesar's murderers, the philosopher, orator, and friend of Cicero. For Brutus' reception of the views put forward by Cicero in *Orator*, a treatise on the best style of speaking dedicated to him, see Cicero *Ad Atticum* 14.20.3; see also Tacitus *Dialogus de oratoribus* 18.5.

82 *Pro Milone*] Cicero was the final speaker for the defence when Milo was charged with the murder of Clodius, a political rival, killed in a fracas between

the followers of the two men in the violent disturbances of 53 BC. Cicero was too nervous in the hostile situation to deliver the speech as he had intended it, and Milo, anticipating condemnation, retired into exile. The speech we have is the written version of what Cicero could have said. Quintus Asconius Pedianus (9 BC–76 AD), who wrote commentaries, of which fragments survive, on a number of Cicero's speeches, thought *Pro Milone* his finest. See Asconius *Commentarius in Milonianam* 36.

358

83 treated the same case] As a rhetorical exercise; see Quintilian 3.6.93, 10.1.23. The speech is not extant.

84 Atticus] Titus Pomponius Atticus, Cicero's friend, correspondent, literary critic, and publisher

85 nail-marks] See Cicero *Ad Atticum* 15.14.4, 16.11.1.

86 Cato] Marcus Porcius Cato of Utica, the Younger Cato (95–46 BC), a man of high principle and intransigent character

87 called Cicero a comic] During the trial of Lucius Murena; Cicero, consul at the time, spoke for the defence and made jokes at the expense of the Stoics, since Cato, one of the speakers for the prosecution, was a well-known member of the Stoic sect. Cato is said to have smiled and remarked, 'What a funny man we have for consul!'; see Plutarch *Cato minor* 21, *Demosthenes and Cicero* 1.4.

88 Gallus] Gaius Asinius Gallus (d 33 AD) was the son of Asinius Pollio (below n92). He compared his father with Cicero to Cicero's disadvantage; see Aulus Gellius 17.1.1, Pliny *Epistles* 7.4.3ff, and Quintilian 12.1.22.

89 Lartius, Licinius] A Larcius or Largius Licinus (a first century AD jurist and advocate) wrote *Ciceromastix* attacking Cicero's Latinity. See Aulus Gellius ibidem. (The manuscripts of Gellius fluctuate between Licinus and Licinius, and Licinius seems to have been the reading of printed texts in Erasmus' day.) This is presumably the person meant here; the name may have been accidentally divided by the printer.

90 Cestius] Lucius Pius Cestius, a popular teacher of rhetoric in the Augustan age and a violent detractor of Cicero as a speaker. He wrote replies to a number of Cicero's famous speeches; see Quintilian 10.5.20.

91 Calvus] The orator and poet Gaius Licinius Calvus (d 47 BC). He and Cicero were totally opposed on the question of style; see Quintilian 12.1.22, Tacitus *Dialogus de oratoribus* 18.5.

92 Asinius] Gaius Asinius Pollio (d 5 AD), writer, orator, patron of the arts, a notoriously censorious literary critic, and an implacable anti-Ciceronian; see Quintilian 12.1.22, Elder Seneca *Suasoriae* 6.14.

93 Caelius] If this is Marcus Caelius Rufus, Cicero's protégé, friend, and correspondent, who is not noted as a critic of Cicero, Erasmus may have listed him here on the basis of Tacitus *Dialogus de oratoribus* 17.1, where Calvus and Caelius are associated. But the person intended could be Caecilius, a Greek teacher of rhetoric of the Augustan age, who compared Demosthenes and Cicero and criticized Cicero (see Plutarch *Demosthenes* 3 and Quintilian 9.3.47).

94 Seneca] Lucius Annaeus Seneca (5/4 BC–AD 65), the most distinguished orator

and literary figure of the period AD 35–65, author mainly of essays on moral and philosophical topics. (See further n222.) For his criticisms of Cicero see *Epistulae morales* 114.16 and Aulus Gellius 12.2.

95 Some of them called him] See Quintilian 12.10.12–14 and Tacitus *Dialogus de oratoribus* 18.5.

96 Asiatic] See 377.

97 the envious] See Quintilian 12.10.13.

98 the proscriptions] Lists of names of persons considered as public enemies and outlaws, who could therefore be killed by anyone with impunity.

99 the triumvirate] A coalition (established November 43 BC) consisting of Octavian (later the emperor Augustus), Mark Antony, and Lepidus. Octavian callously abandoned Cicero to Antony's vengeance in December 43; see n487.

100 to write so much on the subject] Eg Cicero *De oratore* 2.217–90; Quintilian 6.3.1ff, 37ff

101 Demosthenes lacked facility] Quintilian 6.3.2

102 Tiro] Marcus Tullius Tiro, Cicero's devoted freedman, secretary, and friend, who wrote a life of his former master, collected his letters, and was possibly responsible for a collection of his witticisms in three books; see Quintilian 6.3.5.

103 Dorians ... Athenians] Cicero *De oratore* 2.217; *Adagia* I ii 57

104 pastoral poetry and comedy] The invention of comedy was claimed by the Dorian Greeks (see Aristotle *Poetics* 3); fifth-century Athenian dramatists (of whom Aristophanes is the chief surviving representative) developed it into a sophisticated literary form. The development of pastoral poetry, which has much in common with the mime, a form of comedy, is associated with various persons of Dorian background, notably Theocritus.

105 never came anywhere near] Cf Quintilian 10.1.100.

359

106 Cicero's ... Augustus'] Various witticisms of these persons were recorded eg in the lives written by Suetonius and Plutarch. Macrobius (see n539) gives a selection in *Saturnalia* 2.3–4 of Cicero's and Augustus'.

107 Seneca preferred] *Epistulae morales* 8.8; *De tranquillitate animi* 11.6

108 the mime writer Publius] Known as Publius Syrus until the nineteenth century, when his true name Publilius Syrus was restored. Various moral sayings extracted from the mimes were transmitted as part of the corpus of Senecan writings; they were assigned to their true author in Erasmus' edition of Publilius (combined with *Disticha Catonis* and *Septem sapientum celebria dicta* in *Opuscula aliquot Erasmo Roterodamo castigatore* [Louvain: Th. Martens 1514]).

109 voiced by Quintilian] His assessment of Seneca's style is given at 10.1.125ff. For Erasmus' views on Seneca, see the reference at n222.

110 Aulus Gellius' strictures] *Noctes Atticae* 12.2

111 does admit] Ibidem 12.2.13–14

112 Sallust] Gaius Sallustius Crispus, the historian (86–c 34 BC) renowned for his condensed style; see Quintilian 10.1.32, 4.2.45.

113 Brutus] See n81; except for fragments, none of his speeches or writings has survived; information on his style is given by Quintilian 9.4.76, 10.1.123, 12.10.11; see also Tacitus *Dialogus de oratoribus* 25.

114 admired for its forcefulness] Quintilian 12.10.23
115 Brutus] For the severity of his style, see Quintilian 9.4.76, 12.10.11.
116 Pollio] See n92. Only fragments of his speeches and other writings have survived; his style is discussed in Quintilian 10.1.113 and Seneca *Epistulae*
   morales 100.7

360

117 division into heads] A rhetorical term, indicating the procedure by which a
   speaker sets out the points at issue in a lawsuit, and indicates in summary
   form the line of argument he is going to take
118 Hortensius] Quintus Hortensius Hortalus, Cicero's slightly older contemporary (114–50 BC), the leading Roman orator until about 69 BC when Cicero
   took precedence. Cicero discusses his style in *Brutus* 301–3, 317, and 320–6,
   mentioning his particular skill in division at 302.
119 credibility] See Cicero *De inventione* 1.25, and below 368.
120 Quintilian] 12.1.14ff
121 indulges more in boasting] See Quintilian 11.1.17.
122 acknowledged by Quintilian] 10.1.115, 12.10.11. Quintilian attributes this
   quality to Calvus. Erasmus has confused Calvus with Caelius, mentioned
   by Quintilian shortly before.
123 Aristides, Phocion] See 385. Both were distinguished for honesty and
   integrity.
124 Ixion's] See eg Pindar *Pythians* 2.
125 stratagem of the gods] See Euripides *Helena*.
126 his own disclaimers] Eg *Orator* 104ff, where Cicero says he is not the perfect
   orator and has not achieved perfection in every sphere of oratory; see also
   Quintilian 11.1.17ff.

361

127 what mortal man ... excel everyone else] See Cicero *De inventione* 2.2.
128 all the other disciplines together] Cicero *De oratore* 1.20
129 Trachalus] Galerius Trachalus, an orator distinguished for his fine delivery
   and beauty of tone; see Quintilian 10.1.119, 12.10.11.
130 Crassus] Lucius Licinius Crassus, the most distinguished orator of the period
   immediately before Hortensius and Cicero. Cicero speaks admiringly of him
   in *Brutus* passim; for his control, see ibidem 158.
131 Quintilian ... tells the student] 10.2.24ff
132 Quintilian awards Cicero first place] 2.5.20

362

133 *De republica*] Almost the only part known in Erasmus' day was the last section,
   the so-called *Somnium Scipionis*, modelled on the vision introduced by
   Plato in the last book of his *Republic*. It was preserved because of the Platonic
   doctrines it contained. Other portions of the work were recovered in 1820.
134 the proverb] *Adagia* I ix 34
135 Tiro, we are told] Quintilian 6.3.5
136 Elysian fields] One of the names for the happy abode of good souls after
   death; cf n207.

137 Horace] *Ars poetica* 19ff; the second part of the story, which became proverbial, is not in Horace, but is taken by Erasmus from the ancient commentators. The point is that the artist could only paint cypress trees.

363
138 rejected *De inventione*] Cicero *De oratore* 1.5; see also Quintilian 3.6.60. *Orator*
is a slip for *De oratore*.
139 a flimsy piece of work] In *Ad familiares* 9.12.2
140 *De legibus*] Probably not published until after Cicero's death, and therefore
unpolished
141 Lysippus] A distinguished Greek sculptor of the fourth century BC, working
mainly if not entirely in bronze; see Pliny *Naturalis historia* 34.61–5.
142 a candid and outspoken person] As suggested by the incident recorded in
Pliny ibidem 35.85
143 left without the finishing touches] A famous incomplete work in antiquity was
Apelles' painting of Venus Anadyomene, which no one was skilled enough to complete; see Cicero *De officiis* 3.10; Pliny *Naturalis historia* 35.91.
144 saying] Terence *Andria* 805
145 Poliziano] In a letter to Bartolomeo Scala (*Politiani epistolae* 5.1) he attributes
much textual corruption to the German practitioners of the new art of
printing. For Poliziano see below 416, and for Scala, see 418, 443.

364
146 *Rhetorica ad Herennium*] Four books on rhetoric addressed to one Herennius,
and ascribed to Cicero from Jerome's time onwards. After Lorenzo Valla
raised doubts as to Cicero's authorship, the work's authenticity remained a
moot point: for example, Longueil explicitly rejected it in his *Defensio* (for
which see 431ff), whereas Nizzoli used it for his Cicero lexicon. It is not
accepted as Ciceronian today, though the identity of the writer has not
been definitely established.
147 but ... compared with Cicero.] Added 3rd ed
148 A speech *Pro Marco Valerio*] In 54 BC Cicero was contemplating the defence of
Marcus Valerius Messala on a charge of bribery (see *Ad Quintum fratrem*
3.3.2), but no genuine speech survives, if indeed one was ever delivered. A
few tiny fragments of doubtful authenticity are known.
149 Porcius Latro's] A distinguished teacher of rhetoric in the first century BC. The
speech attributed to him was in the fifteenth and sixteenth centuries often
printed together with Sallust's account of Catiline's conspiracy and Cicero's
four Catilinarian speeches.
150 more than one such farce] Eg Fausto Andrelini was tricked into taking as
classical a distich of Pietro Santeramo; see Reedijk *Poems* 62; Gianfrancesco
Pico in his letter on imitation to Bembo (see n260) tells of a man who ascribed
to Cicero letters of his own and sent out genuine letters of Cicero over his
own name, to the great confusion of the critics.
151 Aulus Gellius] A slip for bk 15, ch 6. The *De gloria* did not survive into the
Middle Ages.
152 literary testimony] Aulus Gellius 1.7

153 *in potestatem esse*] *In* followed by accusative case, usually meaning 'into,' instead of the expected ablative case, a reading discussed ibidem 1.7.16–17

365

154 on another occasion] *Philippics* 13.43
155 picks on Antony] In *Philippics* 3.22
156 Thais] Terence *Eunuchus* 865–6
157 Cicero avoided] Aulus Gellius 10.21
158 *novissimus*] The standing of the word had been discussed by Italian scholars of the fifteenth century. Pietro Crinito (see 418), writing to Alexander Sartius (text in *Politiani epistolae* 12.22), says on Poliziano's authority that it does occur in Cicero, and that he personally has seen it in *Orator*, in a letter from Cicero to Octavian, and in *Pro Roscio Comoedo* (where it does occur in 30).
159 Cato and Sallust] See Aulus Gellius 10.21. This is the Elder Cato (234–149 BC), the earliest extant Latin prose writer and orator, whose style the historian Sallust imitated to some extent.
160 Gellius] Ibidem
161 *caussa, visse, remissi*] Quintilian 1.7.20. This was the accepted spelling in the time of Cicero.
162 the warts on the beloved] Cf Horace *Satires* 1.3.39–40
163 'breathed no Muse or Apollo'] Martial 2.89.3–4: 'carmina quod scribis Musis et Apolline nullo / laudari debes: hoc Ciceronis habes' (You're a poet over whom breathed no Muse or Apollo; / you can be proud of that – it's Cicero you follow).
164 the verse, where he is altogether inferior] Quintilian 11.1.24. The Elder Seneca remarks (*Controversiae* 3 preface 8) that Cicero's eloquence deserted him when he wrote verse. See 367.

366

165 Ennius ... Lucilius] For these early poets see 392, where this material is used again. Cicero greatly appreciated the early Latin poets, and many of the surviving fragments are preserved only in his quotations. For Seneca's criticism of Cicero's fondness for quoting Ennius, whom he admired above all others, see Aulus Gellius 12.2.3. See also Quintilian 1.8.11 and Tacitus *Dialogus de oratoribus* 20.5.
166 Virgil ... Persius] Poets writing later than Cicero in the period c 40 BC–60AD. The first four are major classical poets (see 410); Aulus Persius Flaccus, the Stoic satirist (AD 34–62), has been out of favour in more recent times because of his obscure and contorted style, but this was no obstacle to the appreciation and quotation of him in previous ages.
167 easier to surpass] See Quintilian 10.2.10.
168 Heracles!] The Greek hero who performed the famous labours, Hercules in Latin. His name was used as an exclamation of surprise, anger, or disgust. Erasmus writes it in Greek here.
169 Asconius] See n82.
170 Seneca] *De brevitate vitae* 5; see also Quintilian 11.1.18ff and Plutarch *Cicero* 24.1–2.

171 if the teachers of rhetoric ... good man] Eg Quintilian 1 preface 9: 'oratorem autem instituimus illum perfectum qui esse nisi vir bonus non potest'; ibidem 12.1.1: 'sit ergo nobis orator ... is qui a M. Catone finitur: vir bonus dicendi peritus'; see also Elder Seneca *Controversiae* 1 preface 10. The view became a commonplace of rhetorical teaching.

172 a faulty arrangement] See Quintilian 9.4.41.

367

173 *per imperitos scribas scribas*] Erasmus added a refinement in the 2nd ed, substituting *Basso* at the end for *mihi* (... write right to Wright).

174 *O fortunatem ... Romam*] Quoted in Quintilian 9.4.41, ridiculed in Juvenal 10.122

175 quoted by Quintilian] 9.4.41, from a letter now lost

176 double molossus] The molossus was a metrical unit containing three long (heavy) syllables; a double molossus was an extremely heavy closing cadence.

177 not to nod] Quintilian 10.1.24–5

178 Didn't Virgil imitate Homer ... Hesiod] Aulus Gellius 9.9.3

179 Greek lyric poets] 'Greek' added in 2nd ed

368

180 as he says] *Odes* 4.2.27–32

181 Lucilius] Horace's most important predecessor in satire; see Horace *Satires* 1.10.46ff.

182 from one single source] Cicero often stresses the need for the orator to be, like himself, widely read in all disciplines; see eg *De oratore* 1.158–9; *Brutus* 322.

183 Didn't Cicero himself teach] Eg *De oratore* 2.156, 177; *Partitiones oratoriae* 19

184 artifice ... a hold over our minds] Cf Aristotle *Rhetoric* 3.2 (1404b18–20) and *Ad Herennium* 1.10.17. For similar sentiments see Giovanni Pico della Mirandola to Ermolao Barbaro (*Politiani epistolae* 9.4) Garin (see n872) 808.

185 Plato ... lisp] Plutarch *Moralia* 53c 'How to Tell a Flatterer from a Friend'

186 patchwork poems] Centos, in which lines, half-lines, and phrases from an earlier poet (Virgil was the chief source in Latin, Homer in Greek) were combined to construct an entirely new poem, an activity popular with Christian versifiers in late antiquity and the Middle Ages. The best known is probably a Virgilian cento on the life of Christ produced by Proba, a fourth-century woman of Roman aristocratic family; it was published in 1489, edited by Jacob Canter of Groningen (see Ep 32).

187 impart information ... action] The three functions of oratory: *docere, movere, suadere*; see Cicero *Brutus* 276; *Orator* 69.

369

188 and if he isn't] Quintilian 12.1.3. See n171.

189 don't occur all at once] Cf Seneca *Epistulae morales* 33.1–2

190 that point again] See 363.

191 vanity he mentions] *Ad Atticum* 2.17.2

192 that habit of stroking the chin] Plutarch *Cicero* 48

193 long and scraggy neck] *Brutus* 313

194 tendency to shout] Ibidem
195 nervousness when starting to speak] See Plutarch *Cicero* 35.3; and Asconius *Commentarius in Milonianam* 36 for Cicero's nervousness when delivering the *Pro Milone*.
196 excessive indulgence in humorous remarks] Plutarch ibidem 25–7
197 concealed the faults] See 378.
198 Ciceronian apes] The first occurrence in the dialogue of this famous phrase, not originating with Poliziano but first used by him in a derogatory sense, *Politiani epistolae* 8.16. See n872.
199 Attic style] A straightforward, unadorned, deceptively easy style favoured by certain Athenian orators of the fourth century BC and emulated in both Greek and Latin at various periods in succeeding centuries.

370
200 the great teacher] Quintilian 12.10.21
201 Quintilian] 10.2.17–18
202 *esse videatur*] A phrase that Cicero uses quite often as it generates one of his favoured closing rhythms (– ‿ ‿ ‿ – –), sometimes employing it pleonastically in place of *sit* 'would be,' apparently to produce the desired cadence
203 *Ad Herennium*] See n146.
204 *Somnium Scipionis … Pro Rabirio*] Both accidentally misquoted. The speech here referred to is *Pro Rabirio Postumo*, the one mentioned above *Pro Rabirio perduellionis reo*.

371
205 speech he made to the knights] Now considered spurious
206 *P.C.*] Ie *patres conscripti* 'conscript fathers'; see n289.
207 Homer gave to Lucian] Lucian *Vera historia* 2.20; the 'Islands of the Blest' or the 'Fortunate Isles' were a place of happy rest for the souls of heroes and good men, situated somewhere in the far west.
208 *ante hac dilexisse*] Nosoponus uses phrases reminiscent of these at 344.

372
209 Codro Urceo] Presumably a joke, as Charles v was born in 1500, in which year Urceo died. For Urceo see 416.
210 *S.D.*] Ie *salutem dicit*. Cicero does add plain titles, such as *imperator, propraetore*. See n214.
211 Ferdinand] Of Austria, who became king of Hungary and Bohemia in 1526
212 Velius] See 428.
213 *suus*] Cicero uses this only when writing to his immediate family.
214 *salutem plurimam dicit*] The usual practice of Cicero and his correspondents is to write *x s(alutem) d(icit)* combined with a name in the dative case at the head of formal letters, in less formal ones *x s(alutem)* only plus the name, eg M. Cicero imp(erator) s(alutem) d(icit) Q. Thermo propraet(ore); Caelius Ciceroni s(alutem). The more effusive *S.P.D.* is used occasionally by Cicero.
215 Bertholf] Of Ledeberg, between Aalst and Ghent, an assistant of Erasmus' from 1520 to 25

216 Algoet] Levinus Panagathus of Ghent, also an assistant of Erasmus', from 1519 to 26

217 'Grace, peace, and mercy ... Christ] 1 Tim 1:2; 2 Tim 1:2

218 'Keep well'] *Cura ut recte valeas*, a phrase frequently employed as a closing formula for familiar letters by Cicero

373

219 fitting and appropriate] *Decorum et aptum*, a standard part of ancient rhetorical doctrine, discussed by Cicero *De oratore* 3.210 and *Orator* 123

220 as we said earlier] See 360.

221 Quintilian] 10.1.125ff

222 This is the point ... other persons] Added 2nd ed, March 1529. Erasmus' second and much improved edition of Seneca appeared the same month. In the dedicatory epistle, 2091, he gives an extended treatment of Seneca's style, quoting ancient opinions. Quintilian's censures tended to prejudice other critics. (In Erasmus' time, it was not generally recognized that there were two Senecas, and Erasmus, like other scholars, attributes the rhetorical works of the father, the Elder Seneca or Seneca Rhetor, to the son.)

374

223 doctors] For the worthy and unworthy imitators of a great doctor see Galen *Exhortatio ad bonas artes* 643, and *Quod optimus medicus idem sit et philosophus* 665, 667, 669, in Erasmus' translation (Basel: Froben, May 1526), made from the Aldine *editio princeps* of Galen (April–August 1525), and available in ASD I-1, ed J.H. Waszink.

224 'irrelevant to Dionysus'] Ie nothing to do with the matter in hand; *Adagia* II iv 57; also the title of the colloquy Ἀπροσδιόνυσα sive *Absurda*

225 But if you'll allow ... to our subject] Added in the 2nd ed

226 apes ... sons] Admiration of a person should make us resemble him like sons, not like a picture or an ape: Seneca *Epistulae morales* 84.8, Petrarch *Epistolae de rebus familiaribus* 23.19. For Ciceronian apes see n198.

227 Crassus] See 361.

375

228 physiognomist] See Pliny *Naturalis historia* 35.88. Theories concerning the interrelationship of body and soul were developed particularly in the period after Aristotle, and had an increasing influence on writers, painters, and orators. The study was popular in the Renaissance also.

229 Zeuxis was able ... skin] See Pliny *Naturalis historia* 35.63, 98 for Zeuxis' ability to indicate character, and for Aristides of Thebes, who expressed mind, feeling, emotions.

230 attempt to reproduce an effect] Quintilian 10.1.82.

231 Murius] The name is presumably meant to suggest that of Erasmus – contemporary puns on his name included plays on Latin *mus, muris* 'mouse'; see L.-E. Halkin 'Nomen Erasmi' *Erasmus in English* 6 (1973) 14 and John R.C. Martyn 'Nomen Erasmi, tertio' ibidem 7 (1975) 7. In Ep 584 (1517) Erasmus records that sittings for the portrait of himself painted for More by Quentin Matsys had to be temporarily abandoned after he took some liver pills on

the advice of his doctor. Erasmus felt also that Dürer's engraving failed to represent him adequately because of his ill health at the time (see Ep 1729, 30 July 1526).

376

232 Horace] *Epistles* 1.19.19–20, misquoted presumably from memory. Horace says 'was infuriated' rather than 'laughed at.'

233 propositions] Ie the main heads of the argument

234 Bulephorus] The last speaker started off as Hypologus but has gradually moved into the style and attitudes of Bulephorus.

235 the giants] The giants' impious and inevitably unsuccessful attack on heaven, which they endeavoured to scale by piling 'Pelion upon Ossa,' is a favourite Renaissance example of lost endeavor, misdirected by presumption; see *Adagia* III x 93.

236 were destroyed by their desire] Like Semele, for example, who presumed to ask her lover Zeus to appear in his full majesty and was destroyed by the ensuing lightning (Ovid *Metamorphoses* 3.288ff). See n432.

237 'a task ... fraught'] Horace *Odes* 2.1.6

377

238 his virtues ... approximate to faults] See Quintilian 8.3.7.

239 doctors hold the theory] Hippocrates (*Aphorisms* 1.3) said this about the over-developed health of athletes; quoted in Galen *Exhortatio ad bonas artes* 651–2 (n223).

240 Horace] *Ars poetica* 25–7

241 become bald] Quintilian 10.2.17

242 Attic style ... Rhodian ... Asiatic] The plain, intermediate, and florid styles of oratory

243 in Sallust's case] Quintilian 4.2.45

244 So Quintilian thought] 10.1.76

245 Isocrates] 436–338 BC, an Athenian orator, teacher of rhetoric, and educational and political theorist. For his smoothness and rhythm see Cicero *Orator* 151, 174–6; see also a further discussion of his style in Quintilian 9.3.74, 10.1.79.

378

246 Seneca is praised] Quintilian 12.10.11

247 Brutus' seriousness] See 359.

248 The feature praised in Crispus] Quintilian ibidem

249 impassioned presentation] *Dinosis*, for which see Quintilian 6.2.24 and Cicero *Orator* 97–9, *Brutus* 279.

250 Seneca ... is characterized] See Quintilian 10.1.125ff.

379

251 His style ... sterner minds] See 358.

252 Quintilian] 10.2.12.

253 rises superior] Pliny *Naturalis historia* preface 7. See also Younger Pliny *Epistles* 4.8.6: to emulate Cicero successfully is not something that lies easily within men's grasp: it is a gift of the gods.

254 Horace] *Odes* 4.2.1–4: Icarus ambitiously flew too near the sun on his wings of
    feathers and wax, which disintegrated and plunged him into the sea –
    another example of aiming too high. For Pindar see nn401, 407.
255 by approximating to faults] See n238.
256 get the credit of writing good stuff] This echoes a remark of Longueil's in
    Longolii epistolae 4.29.
257 distinguish imitation from emulation] A distinction already made by Quintilian
    10.2.10ff

380

258 singing a song] A fault censured by several ancient critics, eg Quintilian
    11.3.57–9
259 What was said about him] Quintilian 10.1.106
260 Yet Quintilian says ... see the danger, Nosoponus.] An insertion, made in the
    2nd ed, in which Erasmus picks up several points made by Pietro Bembo in
    a letter replying to one of Gianfrancesco Pico della Mirandola on the subject of
    the imitation of Cicero. Pico had taken an eclectic stand on the choice of a
    stylistic model, desiring scope for individuality, whereas Bembo advocated
    imitation of the best only, ie Cicero, agreeing however with Pico that one
    should not be content with mere imitation but should always press on to
    surpass one's model(s); the successful imitation of Cicero was in any case
    open only to persons of ability and stylistic sensitivity, so that possible con-
    tenders were very few in number. The putting of these views of Bembo into
    the mouth of Nosoponus may have been the reason why some Italians inter-
    preted Nosoponus as a caricature of Bembo (see n813).
    The letters between Pico and Bembo were exchanged in 1512–13, but Erasmus
    says in Ep 2088 (see 341) that he became aware of them only after the
    publication of the first edition of *Ciceronianus*. The text is available in Bembo
    Opera III (Basel 1556); for a modern edition see *Le epistole 'De imitatione' di
    Giovanfrancesco Pico della Mirandola e di Pietro Bembo* a cura di Giorgio Santang-
    elo (Florence 1954). A translation into English may be found in Izora Scott
    Controversies over the Imitation of Cicero Columbia University Contributions to
    Education 35 (New York: Teachers College, Columbia University 1910).
261 Stoic paradoxes] Philosophical doctrines expressed in extreme and at first
    sight unacceptable form, for which the Stoics were famous, eg, all sins are
    equal
262 Chrysippus'] A Stoic philosopher (c 280–207 BC) renowned for his skill in
    analysing and refuting fallacies, but also criticized for involved and tedious
    argument. See Cicero *De oratore* 1.50.
263 court of the Areopagus] See n70.
264 Atellan farce] A form of Roman drama of a rather improvised nature, contain-
    ing stock clownish characters, and marked by farcical plots and coarse
    dialogue, as Roman writers tell us. Only fragments survive.
265 gave a cat a saffron robe] *Adagia* I ii 87
266 royal purple to an ape] *Adagia* I vii 10
267 dressed Bacchus] As Aristophanes did in *Frogs*
268 Sardanapalus] A king of Assyria who became a byword for luxury and effemi-
    nacy; *Adagia* III vii 27

381

269 Cato the Censor] Marcus Porcius Cato (234–149 BC), the Elder Cato, great-grandfather of Cicero's contemporary, the Younger Cato

270 Scipio] Scipio Africanus Maior (236–184 BC) the conqueror of Hannibal in the second Punic war

271 Ennius] The father of Latin poetry (239–169 BC)

272 language is a sort of dress] Cicero in several places uses the metaphor of style as a garment, eg *Brutus* 274.

273 a kind of painting] A common metaphor in ancient literary criticism

274 Apelles] See n78. Alexander would allow none but Apelles to paint him and none but Lysippus to make a statue of him; see Cicero *Ad familiares* 5.12.7.

275 If someone painted] Michelangelo, Raphael, Botticelli, and Dürer, for example, were representing Christian figures in classical form.

382

276 Apelles ... portrayed Diana] Diana in the midst of a group of maidens was one of his most admired paintings; see Pliny *Naturalis historia* 35.96.

277 Agnes] A young virgin, martyred at Rome in the fourth century AD

278 Anadyomene] Rising from the sea; see Pliny *Naturalis historia* 35.91 and n143.

279 St Thecla] Supposedly a disciple of St Paul, who suffered much persecution for her vow of virginity

280 Lais] The younger Lais, like the elder Lais, was a famous Corinthian courtesan of the fourth century BC.

281 Lysippus] See n141.

282 the object as it actually is] Cf Plutarch *Moralia* 17F–18D (*Quomodo adolescens poetas audire debeat* 3).

283 your rhetorical theorists] See eg Quintilian 12.1.33ff.

284 'nothing to do with Dionysus'] See n224.

285 Socratic introduction] Referring to Socrates' method of philosophic enquiry by asking questions on apparently unrelated topics; the answers to these prepared the way for the right answer to the real question. The next section of question and answer recalls Socrates' method of getting the other person to admit various premises which then commit him to a particular conclusion.

383

286 speak appositely] See Cicero *De oratore* 3.37.

287 senate] The oligarchic governing body of republican Rome, as in Cicero's time. A number of Cicero's surviving speeches were delivered before it.

288 curia] A building in which meetings of the senate were often held

289 conscript fathers] The traditional form of address used when speaking to the assembled senate

290 equestrian order] The second social class in ancient Rome, consisting of the moneyed business men, often mentioned in Cicero's speeches

291 tribes and centuries] Rome had a variety of assemblies for voting purposes, one of which was divided into tribes and another into centuries.

292 augurs and haruspices] Two colleges of religious functionaries, expert in the interpretation of omens, ie signs of various sorts indicating the approval or disapproval of the gods

293 pontifices maximi] The priests (*pontifices*), supervised all religious observance in the Roman state, and had at their head the pontifex maximus.

294 flamens] A lesser priesthood of great antiquity, consisting of fifteen *flamines*, each dedicated to the service of a different divinity; see n349.

295 vestals] A venerable order of six celibate women, primarily serving Vesta, goddess of the hearth, but fulfilling other important and archaic religious duties

296 aediles ... dictators] The chief magistrates of republican Rome; see 433.

297 Caesars] The title born by the emperors of Rome; it originated with Julius Caesar, with whom it was a family name, not a title.

298 comitium] The place where elections and some other political business took place

299 statues ... ovations] Honours awarded to victorious generals and leading public figures; for triumph, see n325; an ovation was similar to a triumph, but much less spectacular.

300 supplications] National days of prayer, either of intercession or thanksgiving

301 feasts of couches] Pulvinaria, a religious ceremony in which a splendid banquet was held in honour of various divinities whose presence was symbolized by their images laid on richly adorned couches

302 Capitol] The chief of Rome's seven hills, which came to represent all that was most inviolable in the city; it was crowned with the temple of Jupiter Optimus Maximus.

303 sacred fire] Of Vesta; it symbolized the continuing existence of Rome: see Horace *Odes* 3.30.8: 'dum Capitolium scandet cum tacita virgine pontifex' (while priest and silent vestal shall the Capitol ascend).

304 provinces ... allies] Peoples and communities in carefully differentiated relationships with Rome

305 Tarpeian height] A cliff on one face of the Capitoline hill, here used for the hill itself. The temple of Jupiter on the hill was, like other temples, used on occasion for meetings of the senate.

384

306 I saw with my own eyes] This incident, which Erasmus claims to have witnessed, may have occurred on 6 April 1509, during his visit to Rome that year. The account provides support for his charge of paganism, directed at the Roman Ciceronians (see n413). But for the generally Christian nature of sermons preached at the papal court at this period see John W. O'Malley *Praise and Blame in Renaissance Rome: Rhetoric, Doctrine and Reform in the Sacred Orators of the Papal Court, c 1451–1521* (Durham, North Carolina: Duke University Press 1979).

307 Pietro Fedra] Tommaso Fedra Inghirami of Volterra, 1470–1516, canon of the Lateran 1503, Vatican librarian 1505. He was called the Cicero of his age, see Allen Ep 1347:271. (Erasmus is mistaken in the Christian name.)

308 Camillo] Giulio Camillo Delminio of Friuli (1480–1544), a classicist and orientalist, poet and orator, and an extreme Ciceronian. See the letters from Wigle van Aytta of Zwichem (Epp 2632 and 2657 of 1532) for an amusing description of his strange 'Amphitheatre,' apparently a room lined with multiple pigeon-holes containing among other things entries making up a vast

lexicon, phrase inventory, and subject index to the works of Cicero. Zwichem compares his activities with those of Nosoponus (described 346–50).

Though admired by many, Camillo was by some considered an impostor.

309 Day of Parasceve] The Preparation (of the Passover), ie Good Friday; see John 19:14.

310 because of his health] No doubt a sarcastic comment, as Erasmus was no lover of the worldly, militant Julius II

385

311 impassioned presentation ... he chose] *Dinosis*; see n249.

312 the rhetoricians] Eg Quintilian 6.2.7, 20ff

313 Decii] According to Roman tradition, Publius Decius Mus and his son of the same name both (in 340 and 295 BC respectively) brought Rome victory in battle by the rite of *devotio*: they vowed themselves together with the enemy army to the powers of the world of the dead and then ensured their own deaths by charging into the midst of the enemy ranks. This automatically entailed the destruction of the foe.

314 Quintus Curtius] In 362 BC a young noble, Marcus Curtius, leaped fully armed with his horse into a vast cleft which had opened up in the Roman Forum, vowing himself to the powers below to ensure the perpetuity of Rome. Erasmus is mistaken in the praenomen.

315 Cecrops] A mistake for Codrus, an early king of Athens who sacrificed his own life to ensure Athenian victory over the Spartans

316 Menoeceus] Sacrificed himself for Thebes in Boeotia in the war of the Seven against Thebes.

317 Iphigenia] The daughter of Agamemnon, willingly (according to some accounts) sacrificed to Artemis at Aulis to enable the Greek fleet to make the crossing to Troy. These are all stock examples of self-sacrifice, often mentioned together in Latin literature.

318 Socrates] The thinker put to death by the Athenians in 399 BC

319 Phocion] An Athenian statesman and general wrongly put to death for treachery in 317 BC (see Plutarch *Phocion* 33–8). In both these cases, the Athenians soon repented of the executions and raised statues to the victims. A draught of hemlock was the normal mode of execution with the Athenians.

320 Epaminondas] In the course of delivering his native city Thebes from Spartan domination, Epaminondas retained his military command beyond the legal date (a capital offence) and was impeached, but honorably acquitted, in 369 BC (see Plutarch *Pelopidas* 24–5).

321 Scipio] The great Scipio Africanus (the Elder Scipio), conqueror of Hannibal, the Romans' most dangerous opponent in the second Punic war, and deliverer of Rome from the Carthaginian threat. Political opposition generated attacks on his personal integrity, his influence was undermined, and he left Rome to live in exile where he soon died (in 184 BC).

322 Aristides] An Athenian statesman and soldier who did much to establish the supremacy of Athens in the fifth century BC. His honesty became proverbial.

323 ostracism] A procedure at Athens by which political leaders could be sent into exile for ten years, so called because the voters wrote the names of those

they wished exiled on *ostraka* (potsherds). The famous story of the illiterate citizen who wanted to vote for Aristides' ostracism because he was tired of hearing him called 'the Just' is found in Plutarch *Aristides* 7.

324 to die with Christ ... rise with him again] Rom 6:8; Col 2:12

386

325 triumphs] After a particularly resounding victory, the successful Roman commander was granted the right of processing through the streets of Rome together with his army; these processions became increasingly spectacular – the ones named are three of the most famous.

326 Scipio] See n321; he triumphed after the defeat of Hannibal.

327 Aemilius Paulus] Defeated King Perseus of Macedon in the third Macedonian war in 168 BC; his triumph was remarkable at the time for lasting three days and for the richness of the spoils displayed.

328 Julius Caesar] In 46 BC he celebrated the defeat of four enemies in a combined triumph longer-lasting and more splendid than any previous one.

329 apotheosis] Most Roman emperors were on their deaths deemed to have ascended to heaven and become divine (*divus*), an event celebrated by splendid rites and rich offerings.

330 Paul] Eg 1 Cor 1:18ff; Gal 6:14; Col 2:14–15

331 the shadow of a mighty name] An echo of Quintilian 12.10.15

332 the name of the man] The author of the sermon was possibly Tommaso Fedra (n307 above). See ASD I-2 639 n17. If so, Erasmus perhaps refrains from identifying him explicitly because he liked the man when he met him (see Allen Ep 1347:263–4).

333 Sardanapalus] See n268.

334 Benedict ... Francis ... Augustine] Erasmus is here attacking three of the four major monastic orders, the Benedictines who lived by the Rule of St Benedict of Nursia (c 480–c 553), the Franciscans founded by St Francis of Assissi (1181–1226), and the Augustinians who followed the Rule of St Augustine, based on the teachings of St Augustine of Hippo (354–430).

387

335 Thomas] Aquinas; see n587.

336 Scotus] Duns Scotus (c 1274–1308) wrote commentaries on the Bible and on Aristotle, and on the *Sentences* of Peter Lombard, the basic textbook of Medieval scholastic philosophy.

337 Durandus] Gulielmus Durandus (c 1270/75–1334). He also produced a commentary on the *Sentences*. (See Ep 396:101n). Erasmus, like other humanists, found distasteful the technical, complex Latin evolved as a tool to expound scholastic philosophy. He usually speaks disparagingly of the schoolmen and their Latin; see 414. His remarks here are intended to be provocative.

338 monstrous] A phrase from Terence *Phormio* 954

339 Horace] *Ars poetica* 309–16

340 Quintilian] 12.2

388

341 'symbol'] *Symbolum*, 'creed,' a usage established by the time of Cyprian

342 'Jupiter Optimus Maximus'] The title given by the Romans to the chief deity of their pantheon

343 'Apollo' or 'Aesculapius'] Two Greek divinities particularly associated with healing and called on as saviours by ancient pagans; Apollo was the son of Jupiter, Aesculapius of Apollo.

344 'Diana'] Apollo's sister, the virgin goddess of wild nature

345 'foeman'] Erasmus uses an archaic word for 'enemy,' *perduellis*, which he quite often uses in place of the normal *hostis*. The word *perduellis* occurs in Cicero in specialized contexts.

346 'proscription'] Ie declaring an outlaw. See n98.

347 'consign to the spirits of dread'] The formula for a curse eg on an enemy army, ensuring their destruction in battle. See above n313.

348 'debar from fire and water'] The customary legal formula by which a person was outlawed at Rome

349 'flamen Dialis'] The most important of the flamens, serving Jupiter. See nn294, 342.

350 'conscript fathers'] See n289.

351 'senate and people of the Christian republic'] s.p.q. *reipublicae christianae*, modelled on *senatus populusque Romanus* (s.p.q.r.), the formal phrase for the full sovereign authority of the Roman state

352 'comitia'] The term for the voting assemblies of ancient Rome, which were sometimes held in the comitium

353 'denouncer'] Erasmus uses the Greek word *sycophantes*, meaning 'informer,' as *diabolus* (devil) means 'accuser.'

354 for the consecration ... 'sanctifying cake'] Further examples added 2nd edition

355 'curio'] A kind of minor priest

356 'manumission'] The act of setting free a slave from bondage. Erasmus possibly derived some of his Ciceronian equivalents for Christian terms from the *Sententiarum quattuor* of Paolo Cortesi (see 418). See CEBR sv Cortesi.

389

357 Peitho] See 343.

358 just what Cicero does] Such inserts appear in the text of various of Cicero's lawcourt speeches, indicating pauses in the procedure while written or verbal evidence was taken. The evidence itself is not recorded in the text.

390

359 Thomas and Scotus] See 387.

360 Varro] Marcus Terentius Varro, the scholar, antiquarian, and encyclopaedist contemporary with Cicero, author of a vast number of books, few of which have survived. Quintilian in 10.1.95 speaks of Varro's thorough cognizance of the Latin language.

361 Caesar ranks higher] Quintilian 10.1.114

362 Nor ... begetter of the Roman tongue] Erasmus deliberately rejects the title *parens linguae latinae* so often applied to Cicero, both in antiquity and in the Renaissance.

363 Aristotle] He treats marriage in *Politics* 2.2ff, 7.16.

364 Xenophon] The historian and disciple of Socrates, c 430–354 BC. His works cover a diversity of topics; the training of a wife is discussed in *Oeconomicus*.

365 Plutarch] C 46–120 AD; a favourite source for Erasmus, who draws extensively on his wide range of philosophical essays, as well as the popular lives of famous Greeks and Romans. Marriage is treated in *Praecepta coniugalia*.

366 Tertullian] The vehement Christian apologist, (c 160–225 AD), a priest who later joined the extreme and heretical sect of the Montanists. For his views on marriage, see *Ad uxorem*, *De monogamia*, and *Exhortatio ad castitatem*.

367 Jerome] St Jerome (c 348–420 AD). For his views on marriage see eg *Letter* 123 *De monogamia*.

368 Augustine] St Augustine (354–430 AD). For his views on marriage see eg *De nuptiis et concupiscentia* and *De bono viduitatis*.

369 Virgil] In *Georgics*, a didactic poem in four books on various farming activities and country life

370 Cato] Ie the Elder Cato (see n269) in *De re rustica*, a practical manual mainly on the running of a farm

371 Varro] See n360. His only complete surviving work is *De re rustica*, three books on various types of animal and crop farming.

372 Columella] Wrote in 60 AD nine prose books on farming, plus one in verse modelled on Virgil's *Georgics*

373 *beatitas, beatitudo*] Words invented by Cicero and used in *De natura deorum* 1.95, commented on in Quintilian 8.3.32

374 *finis bonorum*] Cicero wrote five books *De finibus bonorum et malorum*, discussing theories and definitions of the supreme good and evil in life; for the term *finis*, see *De finibus* 3.26, 5.23.

375 *visum, visio, species*] Words used by Cicero to translate Greek philosophical terms employed in discussing the theory of knowledge

376 *praepositum ... reiectum*] Two of Cicero's words for the Greek terms used by the Stoics in the exposition of their theory of relative good and bad. The remaining terms (*occupatio ... acclamatio*) belong to rhetorical theory, and occur in *Rhetorica ad Herennium*, Cicero's rhetorical works, and Quintilian, passim.

391

377 admitted ... words to Roman citizenship] An expression used by Seneca *Epistulae morales* 120.4

378 Every sphere of human activity is allowed] Cf Cicero *De finibus* 3.3–4.

379 'three over two' ... 'five over three'] Sesquialtera, superbipartiens, terms explained by Boethius *De arithmetica* 1.28

380 bringing the sky down] Virgil *Aeneid* 5.790–1; *Adagia* I iii 81

381 symbol] See n341.

382 'Sweet oils on lentils'] Used of something out of place; *Adagia* I vii 23

392

383 Romulus ... Decius] Heroes of the early Roman republic constantly cited as examples in Latin literature: Romulus was the founder and first king of

Rome; for Scipio Africanus, see n321; for Quintus Curtius and Marcus Decius see nn313–14. (Erasmus has misremembered the praenomen in both cases).

384 conscript fathers] See n289.

385 Quirites] Centuries-old name used to address the assembled citizens of Rome

386 senate and people of Rome] See n351.

387 in the *Philippics*] Eg 1.26: 'Consules populum iure rogaverunt populusque iure scivit' (The consuls did duly apply to the people for decision and the people did duly take cognizance).

388 in the *Topica*] Eg 15: 'Si aedes eae corruerunt vitiumve fecerunt quarum ususfructus legatus est, heres restituere non debet nec reficere non magis quam servum restituere, si is cuius ususfructus legatus est deperisset' (If the dwelling collapses or suffers damage, that is, the dwelling the usufruct of which has been bequeathed, no obligation is incumbent upon the heir to replace or rebuild it, in the same way as there is no obligation to replace a slave if the slave of whom the usufruct is bequeathed should have died).

389 Homer] The poets here listed (Homer ... Naevius) are quoted by Cicero, especially in his philosophical works; for the Greek writers he provided his own verse translation. See 365–6.

390 Euripides] Greek tragedian, c 485–406 BC

391 Sophocles] Greek tragedian, c 496–406 BC

392 Ennius] See n271.

393 Lucilius] A satirist, died 102/1 BC

394 Accius] A tragedian of the second century BC

395 Pacuvius] A tragedian, c 220–130 BC

396 Naevius] A dramatist and epic poet of the third century BC

397 Virgil] These poets (Virgil ... Martial) all wrote later than Cicero's lifetime (d 43 BC). See 366.

398 Seneca] Primarily a prose writer, but presumably included here for his verse tragedies. See however 409.

399 Lucan] Seneca's nephew, an epic poet (39–65 AD)

400 Martial] The epigrammatist, 40–104 AD

393

401 Pindar] A Greek lyric poet of the fifth century BC, writing in a powerful, impetuous style much admired by Horace; see below n407.

402 Herodotus] The fifth-century BC Greek writer, 'the father of history.' His account of the eastern Mediterranean, the first real historical work, for all its merits, does include numerous fabulous and unlikely anecdotes to which Erasmus here refers. Vives called Herodotus 'the father of lies.'

403 Diodorus] Diodorus Siculus, a first-century BC Greek historian, who wrote a world history in forty books starting with the legendary period

404 Livy] The Roman historian (59 BC–c 17 AD) who wrote a history of Rome in 142 books covering events from the foundation of the city up to his own time. His account of the early history of Rome, telling of kings, wars, and folk heroes, has certain similarities with the historical books of the Old Testament.

405 Socrates' 'irony'] His method of philosophic enquiry was to feign ignorance,

and to reach philosophic positions by debate rather than by dogmatic statement. See Cicero *De oratore* 2.269–70; Quintilian 9.2.46.
406 compare the Psalms] The Psalms were favourably compared with Pindar and
Horace by Jerome in his version of Eusebius' *Chronicle* bk 2 preface.
407 Pindar's flatteries] His epinician odes (choral poems of elaborate structure and
metre in an exalted style) eulogized victors at Greek athletic festivals.
408 Theocritus' trifles] Theocritus, a Greek poet of the third century BC, established pastoral poetry as a literary genre. Pastoral was traditionally considered light weight. One of its themes was the passion of love in its various
aspects.
409 'Thessalian Tempe'] A famous Greek beauty spot; Horace *Odes* 1.7.4
410 Is 'the gift ... God the Father'] Added 2nd ed
411 Hannibal] Considered by the Romans their most dangerous enemy; his brilliant generalship almost brought about their defeat in the second Punic war
(against Carthage) 218–201 BC.

394
412 You've hit the nail on the head] Plautus *Rudens* 1306
413 paganism] This charge of paganism aroused bitter resentment amongst the
Italian Ciceronians. Erasmus had long been accusing the members of the
Roman Academy of being particularly guilty; see Epp 1111 (1521), 1479, 1489,
1496 (1524), and 1805, 1885 (1527). Though this was true of the Roman
Academy in the time of Pomponio Leto (for whom see n630), it is doubtful
whether Erasmus was justified in continuing to attribute paganism to the
contemporary Academy.
414 Hannibal] See above n411.
415 Camillus] A hero of the early Roman republic, most famous for his victory over
the invading Gauls in 367 BC

395
416 Ennius' and Accius'] See 392.
417 Theocritus] *Idylls* 6.18–19
418 'vetch among the vegetables'] *Adagia* I vii 21
419 'Saul among the prophets'] 1 Kings 19:24
420 'sweet oils on lentils'] *Adagia* I vii 23
421 'gold ring in a pig's snout'] Prov 11:22
422 'Put your ... sheet-anchor'] *Adagia* I i 24
423 'Stand ... solid rock] Luke 6:48
424 the Aspendian lyre-player] Cicero *Verrines* 2.1.53: he played so quietly that no
one could enjoy his music but himself.
425 Paul's epistle] 1 Cor 6:12
426 the Twelve Tables] A Roman code of law written down in the fifth century BC.
Fragments of the text were preserved through quotation by grammarians,
lawyers etc, but there are no material remains of the original.
427 laws written on tables] Exod 32:15–16; Deut 9:10

396
428 museums] Erasmus is referring to the collections of antiquities made by many

Renaissance Italians as ancient works of art and material remains began to come to light in increasing quantities. The house of Pietro Bembo (see 435) at Padua was famed for such a collection.

429 into Danaë's lap] See Horace *Odes* 3.16: after Jupiter visited Danaë in the form of a shower of gold, she conceived and bore Perseus.

430 Gabriel announcing] Luke 1:26–38

431 Ganymede] A boy whom Jove, in the form of an eagle, carried up to heaven to serve as cupbearer at the feast of the gods

432 festivals of Bacchus] Bacchanalia, an originally Greek festival in honour of Dionysus/Bacchus, the god of wine. The rites, open only to initiates who were thereby assured of life after death, were generally considered by outsiders to be violent and obscene. In art the god was often depicted leading a riotous train of drunken revellers. His myth embodies a kind of resurrection and baptism, in that he was taken by Zeus from his mother's womb after she was consumed by the fires of a thunderbolt and there after cared for by nymphs who bathed him.

433 festivals of ... Terminus] Terminalia, the Roman festival at which boundary stones were ceremonially authenticated and sanctified by libation and blood sacrifice followed by a feast. The festival does not seem to have been regarded as particularly vicious or obscene in ancient times. See Ovid *Fasti* 3.639ff.

434 Lazarus] John 11

435 Christ baptized] Matt 3:13; Mark 1:9; Luke 3:21

397

436 battling with the gods] Referring particularly to the giants in their assault on Olympus; see n235.

437 Quintilian] 10.2.19, 2.8.1

438 unremmitting toil] Virgil *Georgics* 1.145–6

439 meddle in vain] See Quintilian 10.2.20

440 ox to the wrestling school] *Adagia* I iv 62

441 Water possibly ... fire to water] For possible classical sources see Aristotle *De generatione et corruptione* 2.3, 4, 5, 8; Seneca *Naturales quaestiones* 3.10.

442 Virgil holds first place] Quintilian 10.1.85–6

443 he's the greatest in that branch] Quintilian 10.1.96.

398

444 Still, what's to prevent us ... means not being like him at all.] Added 2nd ed. Erasmus is again taking up statements made by Bembo in his letter to Gianfrancesco Pico (see n260). Bembo had said that Cicero's style could be adapted to deal with any subject in prose, whereas Virgil was an appropriate model for epic, but not for elegy, lyric, or drama. The insertion fits somewhat uncomfortably in its context.

445 bray with the ass] Apuleius' (see n544) style in *The Golden Ass* was likened to the braying of an ass by Lorenzo Valla and others; see E. Norden *Die Antike Kunstprosa* (Leipzig and Berlin 1909) II 778. For Apuleius as a stylistic model and the conflict of Apuleianism with Ciceronianism, see John F. D'Amico 'The Progress of Renaissance Latin Prose: The Case of Apuleianism' *Renaissance Quarterly* 37 (1984) 351–92.

399

446 Petronius] Presumably Bulephorus thinks this sophisticated, dissolute, and witty character, author of the *Satyricon* and member of the emperor Nero's inner circle, is the person that Nosoponus least resembles.

447 Apelles] See n78.

448 Sphinx] The monster that terrorized Thebes, tearing apart approaching travellers who could not answer the riddle it put to them; Oedipus solved the riddle and destroyed the Sphinx.

449 Hermogenes] Tigellius Hermogenes, a singer, Horace's contemporary, who gave music lessons to young ladies; see Horace *Satires* 1.2.3, 1.10.90.

450 high court of the Areopagus] See n70.

451 Roscius] A leading Roman actor and friend of Cicero's; Roman acting involved a great deal of gesture and miming, and oratory too had its recognized postures and movements.

452 he found in every great orator] See Quintilian 10.1.109.

400

453 leading Roman families] His friend Atticus researched this subject (Nepos *Atticus* 18).

454 from some experts] From Roscius the comic actor (see above) and from Aesopus the tragic actor; see Plutarch *Cicero* 5.3.

455 Some people have indeed suggested] Quintilian 6.5.11

456 *Partitiones*] 79

401

457 that most acute of critics] Horace *Ars poetica* 309

458 'thumb ... by day'] Horace ibidem 269

459 a neat observation ... when they go] Seneca *Epistulae morales* 108.4, speaking of the effect of contact with philosophy; Cicero *De oratore* 2.60 had already used the first of these similes for the effect of leisure reading on style.

460 If he settled down to reading a single author] Added on the authority of LB. The text in ASD does not make sense as it stands.

402

461 first take care of what to say] Compare the famous remark of the Elder Cato: 'rem tene, verba sequentur,' preserved by the rhetorician Julius Victor (*M. Catonis fragmenta* ed H. Jordan, Leipzig 1860, 80).

462 sticks to the realms of probability] See Quintilian 2.10.2ff.

463 Cicero] *Brutus* 94. Gaius Laelius Minor was a cultured and eloquent Roman statesman living at the turn of the third century BC, whose speeches were still extant in Cicero's time.

464 must be thoroughly digested ... contributory elements] See Seneca *Epistulae morales* 84.6–7 and 3–5 and Quintilian 10.1.19 for these metaphors of digestion and honey production used to illustrate the idea of constructive imitation.

403

465 Yew makes the honey poisonous] See eg Virgil *Eclogues* 9.30–1.

466 Apelles and Zeuxis] See 356–7.

467 points out to you] Cf Quintilian 10.2.27

468 propositions] Ie the main heads to be developed in the argument

469 the two types of emotion] πάθη and ἤθη, violent and gentle; see Quintilian 6.2.8ff and Cicero *Orator* 128ff.

470 No one was a more felicitous exponent] See Quintilian 3.1.20

404

471 material ... omitted] Quintilian ibidem. Quintilian deals with emotion at 6.2.7, 20ff; aphorism 8.5; amplification 8.4.1; propositions 4.4.5ff; basis or ground 3.6; reading, imitating, composing 10.1–3.

472 do without theory] Cf Quintilian 2.11.1ff.

473 Cato the Censor] See 381.

474 Cato of Utica, Brutus, and Asinius Pollio] See above 358.

475 the jury expected] See Quintilian 4.1.57, Tacitus *Dialogus de oratoribus* 20.2.

476 of the advocates] Added 3rd ed, with minor alterations in the text

405

477 Phocion ... than Demosthenes] For Phocion see n319 and for Demosthenes n73. Phocion's effectiveness in persuading the Athenian assembly to reject Demosthenes' proposals in favour of his own caused Demosthenes to call him 'the pruning knife' of his eloquence (Plutarch *Phocion* 5.2–3).

478 Aristides than Themistocles] For Aristides see 385. Themistocles (528–462 BC), was contemporary with and often opposed to Aristides; for their rivalry see Plutarch *Aristides* 3.

479 Cato than Cicero] See Plutarch *Cato minor* for various occasions on which Cato successfully opposed Cicero. Plutarch seems to prefer Phocion to Demosthenes and Cato to Cicero.

480 made things worse ... prosecution] Possibly a confused memory of Plutarch *Cicero* 26.4

481 finer thing to be a Phidias] See Cicero *Brutus* 257. Phidias was the fifth-century BC Athenian sculptor who designed the Parthenon sculptures.

482 put up with Cicero orating] See Tacitus *Dialogus de oratoribus* 20.

483 against Verres] Only the first of the Verrine orations, *actio prima*, was actually delivered: in it Cicero demonstrated Verres' guilt so convincingly that Verres took himself into exile, and the case was closed. Cicero wrote up the rest of the evidence he had assembled as the long *actio secunda* in five books.

484 Catiline] Four speeches

485 Clodius] A personal enemy of Cicero's (see n82) frequently assailed eg in the speeches *Pro Milone, De domo sua, Pro Sestio*

486 Vatinius] *In Publium Vatinium testem interrogatio*, not a particulary long speech, but, like the others, full of invective

487 against Antony] The fourteen so-called 'Philippic Orations' in which Cicero attacked Antony in 44–43 BC, in the months just before he was murdered by Antony at the age of sixty-three. Tacitus in *Dialogus de oratoribus* 37.6 gives the speeches on which Cicero's greatness as an orator rested as *In Catilinam, Pro Milone, In Verrem,* and *Philippics.*

406

488 To four Italians] Possibly Baldesar Castiglione, Andrea Navagero, Alessandro
D'Andrea, and Bendetto Tagliacarne, cited as critics of Erasmus in Ep 1791
from Olivar, written from Valladolid, March 1527, though being mostly about
fifty years old in 1528 they were hardly young enough to qualify for the
contemptuous reference a few lines further on to 'four silly young Italians.'

489 Marcus Tullius does not insist] *De finibus* 1.15; *De oratore* 3.142

407

490 This cannot be said too often] Added 3rd ed

491 was rightly twitted] Quintilian 10.3.12–14

408

492 Aesculapius] The son of Apollo the god of healing, and, after Apollo, the most
important healing divinity of antiquity

493 Hippocrates] The most celebrated physician of antiquity (probably fifth century BC), to whose name was attached much of the corpus of Greek medical
writings

494 Word ... reasonable words] Literally 'Logos treated me with logos.' Logos
means both 'word/speech' and 'reason.'

495 'The word ... sickness of the soul'] For the therapeutic power of the word see
the quotations assembled in *Adagia* III i 99. Erasmus here quotes (in Greek)
Plutarch *Consolatio ad Apollonium* 102B. See further Marjorie O'Rourke Boyle
'Erasmus' Prescription for Henry VIII: Logotherapy' *Renaissance Quarterly*
31 (1978) 161–72.

496 bout of false shame] Horace *Satires* 2.3.39

497 the *Brutus*] A survey of earlier Roman orators dedicated to Brutus (see n81),
which probably gave Erasmus the idea for the catalogue of writers in Latin
that follows. It had already provided a model for Paolo Cortesi's *De hominibus
doctis dialogus* (c 1490).

498 Julius Caesar] Almost an exact contemporary of Cicero's, 102–44 BC

499 in correct and appropriate Latin] Cicero *Brutus* 261

409

500 no very great achievement] Cicero ibidem 140, 261

501 authorship] Aulus Hirtius, one of Caesar's officers, and others, added bk 8 to
Caesar's *Bellum Gallicum* and *Bellum Alexandrinum, Bellum Africum, Bellum
Hispaniense* to his *Bellum civile*. See Suetonius *Julius* 56. *Bellum civile* itself was
left in an unfinished state, and various parts of it have been attributed to
other hands.

502 Caelius] See n93; seventeen of his vivid, racy letters to Cicero are preserved.

503 Plancus] Lucius Munatius Plancus. Thirteen of his letters are preserved; his
style was adjudged by J.J. Scaliger to be particularly elegant and finished.

504 Decius Brutus] Now known as Decimus Junius Brutus; not to be confused with
Marcus Junius Brutus (mentioned below; see also n81) but, like him, in the
plot to assassinate Caesar. Twelve of his letters are preserved.

505 Tiro] See n102.

506 Bithynicus] The text offers *Auli Cecinnae Bithynii*, presumably an error, as Cicero's correspondents include Aulus Caecina (one letter) and Pompeius Bithynicus (one letter).

507 Pompey ... Caesar] These correspondents are represented by one or two letters, at most six, preserved, like those of the above correspondents, in the fourteen books of *Epistulae ad familiares*. The correspondence with Marcus Brutus is however partially preserved in a separate book, *Epistulae ad Brutum*. As members of the senate, magistrates, judges, advocates, and holders of governorships, all Cicero's correspondents here mentioned must have had occasion to make many speeches. Though some of these were written down and survived for a time (see Tacitus *Dialogus ἀe oratoribus* 37) they disappeared eventually.

508 Caelius a Ciceronian] Caelius is perhaps picked out because of the lively style revealed in the extant letters and discussed in Quintilian (passim) and Tacitus *Dialogus de oratoribus* 21.

509 Sallust] See n112. Sallust employed a style deliberately recalling that of the Elder Cato a hundred years earlier.

510 Seneca] See nn94, 222, 398.

511 tragedies] Much read and praised in the Renaissance. Erasmus expressed doubts as to Seneca's authorship in the preface to his 1529 edition of Seneca's works (see n222). Nowadays Seneca's authorship is generally accepted, except for the *Octavia*.

512 Valerius Maximus] He wrote c 32 AD *Facta ac dicta memorabilia*, a collection of anecdotes and examples for the use of rhetoricians, dedicated to the reigning emperor Tiberius.

513 African] The extravagant and mannered Latin style employed by writers from the Roman province of Africa, notably Apuleius (see 411), but also the Christian writers to a considerable extent (especially Tertullian; see 413), gave rise in the sixteenth century to a theory of *Africus tumor*, an exuberance of language supposedly reflecting the character of the North African; see E. Norden *Die antike Kunstprosa* II 590ff, where the theory is demolished.

514 Suetonius] Gaius Suetonius Tranquillus (c 69–140 AD), chiefly known for his *Lives of the Caesars*, of which Erasmus prepared an edition printed with the *Historiae Augustae scriptores* (Basel: Froben 1518), for whom see n523.

515 Livy] See n404.

516 several people said] Ie Asinius Pollio (see n92), information found in Quintilian 8.1.3. Quintilian himself attributed to Livy the quality of *lactea ubertas* (10.1.32), a rich style that remained wholesome, and thought him suitable for schoolboys (2.5.19).

517 Tacitus] Cornelius Tacitus, c 55–120 AD. He wrote in fairly Ciceronian Latin a work on oratory, *Dialogus de oratoribus*, from which Erasmus has derived some of his information, also historical works, *Agricola*, *Germania*, *Histories*, and *Annals*, displaying an increasingly individualistic and unciceronian style.

518 Quintilian] Marcus Fabius Quintilianus (c 35–c 100 AD), teacher of rhetoric and author of the *Institutio oratoria*, which Erasmus quotes so often. Quintilian makes clear his admiration for Cicero, whom he considered the supreme Roman orator, but he does not write his textbook in Ciceronian Latin.

410

519 the *Declamationes* we have] The so-called *Declamationes minores* and *maiores* attached to Quintilian's name. No genuine declamation or speech of Quintilian has survived, so his style of oratory cannot be judged.

520 Quintus Curtius] Quintus Curtius Rufus, probably first century AD. He wrote a romantic account of Alexander's exploits in rhetorical style, which Erasmus edited in 1518 (Strasburg: A. Schürer).

521 as the proverb goes] Added 3rd ed

522 not a patch on Parmeno's pig] Plutarch *Moralia* 674B–C, *Adagia* I i 10: Parmeno's imitation of pigs and other animals was so realistic that people preferred it to the genuine thing. The proverb was used of anything that falls short.

523 Aelius Spartianus ... Flavius Vopiscus] The names of six historians (known collectively as the *Historiae Augustae scriptores*), who profess to have written between 284 and 337 AD the *Lives* of thirty Roman emperors from Hadrian to Numerian. (According to modern views, the work is probably a deception.)

524 Aurelius Victor] A writer of the fourth century AD who wrote *Caesares*, lives of Roman emperors from Augustus to Constantius

525 Aemilius Probus] For long accredited with the authorship of the *Lives* of famous Greeks and Romans written by Cornelius Nepos, Cicero's friend. Nepos' authorship was recognized in an edition of 1569 by Dionysius Lambinus. Erasmus forgets to comment on the style, which is inelegant and oddly unclassical.

526 Ammianus Marcellinus] A historical writer of the fourth century AD, whose narrative covers the years 96–378 AD

527 Velleius Paterculus] C 19 BC–31 AD. He wrote an outline of Roman history from the beginning to AD 30 in two books, in rather poor style. The manuscript was discovered in 1515 and published in 1520 by Beatus Rhenanus.

528 epitomes] Condensed versions of longer works, popular in the later Roman empire; the *Epitome* of Livy's vast history caused the loss of most of the original.

529 Florus] Lucius Annaeus Florus, second century AD, author of a history in two books intended to glorify Rome, based on various earlier writers, especially Livy

530 Eutropius] Fourth century AD; he wrote a survey of Roman history up to 364 AD in ten books, based in part upon the *Epitome* of Livy.

531 Solinus] Gaius Iulius Solinus (c 200 AD), who wrote a geographical and historical summary of various parts of the world, largely based on the *Naturalis historia* of the Elder Pliny

532 the two Plinys] The Elder Pliny (23–79 AD), was the author of a considerable range of works, of which only the *Naturalis historia* in thirty-six books has survived; the style is not elegant. The Younger Pliny, his nephew, (61–c 113 AD) is chiefly famous as the author of prose literary epistles on miscellaneous topics (see 430). His style is closer to Cicero's than that of many of his contemporaries, but is deliberately simpler and much less spontaneous.

533 the speech he wrote] *Panegyricus*, the written version of a speech delivered in 100 AD; on its influence on Erasmus' *Panegyricus*, see CWE 27 3.

534 Virgil ... Martial] It is surprising at first sight to have poets compared at all with Cicero, but ancient critics found the three styles, grand, middle, and plain, exemplified in verse writers as much as prose writers. See Aulus Gellius 6.14. In Allen Ep 2695:17ff Erasmus remarks that there is more connection between the styles of prose and poetry in Latin than there is in Greek.

411

535 more like an orator] Lucan's epic on the civil war between Caesar and Pompey is highly rhetorical, full of speeches and elaborate descriptions; see Quintilian 10.1.90.

536 Lucretius] Titus Lucretius Carus, a major classical poet belonging to an earlier age (c 94–55 BC), author of *De rerum natura*, a poem in six books of hexameter verse expounding the Epicurean philosophy, especially its physical theories. Erasmus seem to quote him only rarely, perhaps finding his subject-matter uncongenial. Lucretius' verse has often, as here, been judged to be rugged and old-fashioned in comparison with his successors in hexameter verse, especially Virgil

537 Ennius ... Lucilius] See 392.

538 Aulus Gellius] Erasmus now returns to post-Ciceronian prose writers with Gellius, an author of the second century AD, who wrote *Noctes Atticae* in twenty books, a prose miscellany of anecdotes and odd bits of information, literary, historical, grammatical, etc. He had the contemporary taste for linguistic archaism. See *Adagia* I iv 37.

539 Macrobius] Ambrosius Theodosius Macrobius (fourth/fifth centuries AD), author of *Saturnalia* in seven books, another derivative miscellany, which includes a considerable amount of Virgilian criticism.

540 Aesop's silly crow] See Aesop *Fables* 162 (Chambry) and Phaedrus *Fables* 1.3, the tale of the jackdaw in borrowed peacock's plumes. Erasmus' crow comes from the version in Horace *Epistles* 1.3.19.

541 Greek stammering in Latin] Macrobius was not Italian, possibly African, and his native language was probably Greek; see Macrobius' own remarks in the preface to *Saturnalia*.

542 commentary on the *Somnium Scipionis*] 2.10.11. This is his two-book Neoplatonic commentary on Cicero's *Somnium Scipionis* (see n133). This commentary was much read at times in the Middle Ages and Renaissance and aided the survival of Cicero's work.

543 Symmachus'] Quintus Aurelius Symmachus, fourth century AD. He wrote ten books of letters modelled on the Younger Pliny's.

544 Apuleius] An African of the second century AD, writing in a mannered, bizarre style, especially in *The Golden Ass* (a picaresque novel retailing the adventures of a man bewitched into an ass) and *Florida*, a collection of extracts from his exhibition speeches. This style is characterized by short units whose elaborate balance is underlined by sound patterning and word-play, and by a heterogeneous vocabulary containing archaisms, colloquialisms, poeticisms, rarities, and neologisms. The more straightforward *Apology* was the speech he made in his own defence when charged with winning his wife's affections and fortune by witchcraft.

545 Martianus Capella] Another African, of the fifth century AD, who wrote an

allegory in mixed prose and verse, *De nuptiis Mercurii et Philologiae*, in a style similar to Apuleius'

546 Boethius] Anicius Manlius Severinus Boethius (fifth/sixth centuries AD), mainly known for *Consolatio philosophiae*, a dialogue between himself and Philosophy written in a mixture of prose and verse, a work containing pagan imagery although the author was a Christian. He also wrote among other things theological treatises and translations of and commentaries on Greek philosophical works.

547 Ausonius] Decimus Magnus Ausonius (fourth century AD), tutor to the emperor Gratian and professor of rhetoric at Bordeaux. He produced a considerable corpus of poetry in the classical tradition, in which his Christian faith, though sincerely expressed, is not proclaimed with fervour. On his elevation to the consulship he offered a tediously fulsome speech of thanks to the emperor.

412

548 Lactantius] Caecilius Firmianus Lactantius (fourth century AD), a teacher of rhetoric who wrote a number of Christian works after his conversion, the best known being *Divinae institutiones* in seven books. He was called 'the Christian Cicero' for his classical and mellifluous style, modelled on Cicero's, by Gianfrancesco Pico della Mirandola (the nephew of the more famous Giovanni Pico della Mirandola, see 416) in *De studio divinae et humanae philosophiae* bk 1 ch 7. Erasmus ascribes the remark to Rodolphus Agricola (see 425) in Ep 49:116.

549 was said to flow] By Jerome, *Letters* 58.10: 'quasi quidam fluvius eloquentiae Tullianae.' Erasmus adds the adjective *lacteus*, applied to Livy by Quintilian (see n516) and repeated by Jerome with reference to Livy at *Epistles* 53.1: 'lacteo eloquentiae fonte.' Erasmus perhaps unconciously conflated the two passages, but he probably wants a pun on the name Lactantius, as in Ep 2103. Lactantius receives remarkably extended treatment. Possibly Erasmus had been thinking about him recently while reading over his notes on the text of Lactantius' *De opificio Dei* (published March 1529; see Allen Ep 2103), but no doubt he felt that the title 'Christian Cicero' required examination in the present context.

550 not a Ciceronian] See n566.

551 introduction] *Divinae institutiones* 1.1.5

552 aeternae] ASD corrects *aeternae*, the reading of the 1528 edition and of LB, to *aeterna*, but *aeternae* is the only reading given for the text of Lactantius here in *Corpus scriptorum ecclesiasticorum latinorum* (Vienna-Leipzig 1866–   ) XIX 2 and is also the reading of Aldus' edition of 1515 (ed Giambattista Egnazio).

553 scazon] A metrical unit consisting of a light syllable followed by three heavy ones. Cicero was criticized for his use of *balneatori* (sic) and *archipiratae* (sic) in this position; see Quintilian 9.4.63–4. All the Latin phrases from *balneatore* to *reliquerunt* end in a scazon.

554 again and again] Erasmus uses a Greek phrase of a type occurring in drama.

555 double trochee] Syllables arranged in the pattern heavy, light, heavy, light

556 *quaesisse videatur*] See n202.

557 Cyprian] A teacher of rhetoric who became bishop of Carthage and was even-
    tually martyred 258 AD. He was the author of a considerable number of
    Christian works, apologetic and instructional. Erasmus' edition of his *Opera*
    appeared in 1520 (Basel: Froben). In the dedicatory epistle (Ep 1000) Eras-
    mus attributes to him persuasive power combined with clarity and purity of
    diction.

413
558 Christian ... Ciceronian] See below n566 for the antithesis.
559 Hilary] A highly educated man (fourth century AD), who became bishop of
    Poitiers. Erasmus edited his works in 1523 (Basel: Froben). See the dedica-
    tory epistle, Ep 1334, in which Erasmus says more about Hilary's elaborate,
    theatrical style.
560 as the great man says] Jerome *Letters* 58.10. He remarks that Hilary is too
    difficult stylistically for the inexperienced to read.
561 string of words] Erasmus gives some samples in Allen Ep 1334:842ff: eg *intim-
    are, disproficit*.
562 Sulpicius] Severus (fourth/fifth centuries AD), a lawyer who embraced the
    ascetic life after the death of his wife; his most famous work was the *Life* of
    St Martin of Tours.
563 Gallic] In Allen Ep 1334:275 Erasmus says grandiloquent rhetoric is character-
    istic of the Gallic nation, Budé (see 421) included.
564 Tertullian] See n366. Like Apuleius he was African, and was roughly his
    contemporary. He exhibits similar stylistic features, but his Latin is notori-
    ously difficult because of its abruptness, idiosyncratic syntax, and a vocabu-
    lary even more marked than Apuleius' by new creations and unprecedent-
    ed meanings.
565 Apuleius] See 411.
566 flogging he received] In his famous dream (see *Letter* 22 Ad *Eustochium* 30) he
    appeared before the judgment seat of God and was flogged for being not a
    Christian but a Ciceronian, possibly the earliest occurrence of the word 'Cice-
    ronian' in this sense. Erasmus' edition of Jerome's letters, included in the
    complete works published by Froben in 1516, was interpreted by some as
    expressing strictures on the saint's style (see Ep 2045). Erasmus remarked
    in his life of Jerome that Jerome's style was such that the flogging was unjusti-
    fied, a sentiment earlier expressed by Theodorus Gaza (recorded by Scala
    in a letter to Poliziano, *Politiani epistolae* 5.2).
567 an enormous ... reproduce] Changed in the 2nd ed to read: 'an enormous
    drawn-out period, so that he often has to get himself back on course from
    the byway he's taken. But he doesn't mark out his lengthy stretch of speech
    into subordinate units and sections like Cicero, and he doesn't reproduce
    ...' Erasmus' edition of Augustine's works was completed by May 1529, a little
    later than the 2nd ed of *Ciceronianus*. Erasmus complains Allen Ep 1000:65
    and elsewhere of Augustine's involved and obscure manner of expression.
568 Paulinus] Of Nola (fourth century AD), the brilliant pupil of Ausonius (see
    411) and a distinguished figure in society and the literary world until he
    embraced the ascetic life. His poetry, in classical style, expresses an intense
    Christian faith. Erasmus is presumably referring here to his prose letters in

an obscure and inflated style interspersed with frequent biblical citations.

569 Ambrose] C 334–97 AD, a man of consular rank and a provincial governor before his sudden elevation to the bishopric of Milan. Erasmus' edition of Ambrose's extensive writings was published in 1527 (Basel: Froben). In the dedicatory epistle (Ep 1855) Erasmus characterizes Ambrose's style as mellifluous, pleasing rather than forceful; he thinks more of him as a personality than as a writer.

570 the Roman Gregory] Gregory the Great (pope 590–604), along with Jerome, Augustine, and Ambrose, one of the four Fathers of the Latin church. As he was born in the city of Rome he might well be expected to attain the stylistic ideal: see 384.

571 his style is turbid] Cf Horace *Satires* 1.4.11, saying the same thing of Lucilius.

572 Isocratean canons] For Isocrates' style see n245.

573 Leo the Tuscan] Leo the Great of Volterre in Tuscany (pope 440–61), one of the Doctors of the western church, significant for his formulation of Christian doctrine and his conception of the role of the papacy. His letters and sermons show him as a competent Latin stylist.

414

574 Bernard] St Bernard of Clairvaux (1090–1153), born of a noble family at Fontaines, near Dijon in Burgundy. He wrote a considerable number of ascetic and mystical treatises, which made a great impact at the time, in no small measure due to their rhythmical, affective style in the tradition of St Augustine.

575 part of being an orator] See n171.

576 Bede] The Venerable Bede (c 673–735), the Anglo-Saxon scholar and the most learned man of his age, a prolific writer best known today for his *Historia ecclesiastica gentis Anglorum*; Erasmus regarded him mainly as a biblical commentator, like other writers in this group (see Allen Ep 2771:11).

577 Remigius] Of Auxerre (c 841–c 908), author of many philosophical and theological works

578 Claudius] Bishop of Turin (d c 830). He wrote commentaries on the Psalms, Gospels, and Pauline Epistles.

579 Hesychius] Fifth-century priest of Jerusalem. His seven books of commentaries on Leviticus were published in a Latin version in 1527 (Basel: Cratander); see Ep 2008. He also wrote a commentary on the Psalms used by Sadoleto; see Ep 2385.

580 Anselm] C 1033–1109, archbishop of Canterbury 1093. The most important of his works is *Cur Deus homo*, on the necessity of the atonement.

581 Isidore] Bishop of Seville 602–36. He wrote a vast amount, including history, but is known best for his *Etymologiae*, an encyclopedia which transmitted much ancient knowledge to the Middle Ages. See Ep 260, where Erasmus condemns his Latin.

582 choppers and mutilators] Erasmus invents a Greek word derived from the verb 'to dock, curtail.' LB has an explanatory note: 'qui decurtat syllabas, adeoque male pronuntiat.'

583 Alexander of Hales] The 'Irrefragable Doctor' (c 1180–1245), a theologian who taught at Paris; his pupils included Bonaventure.

584 Peter of Ghent] Erasmus seems to be mistaken in the name, and probably means Henry of Ghent, a secular scholastic philosopher and theologian (c 1217–93). His *Quodlibeta* and *Disputationes* had been published fairly recently in Paris (1518 and 1520 respectively).

585 of the same kidney] *Adagia* III v 44. Erasmus means here scholastic theologians, with whom in general he had little patience; see eg *Antibarbari* CWE 23 67.

586 Bonaventure] 1221–74, Minister General of the Franciscans, a theologian and mystic known as the 'Seraphic Doctor'

587 Thomas] Aquinas (c 1225–74), Dominican philosopher and scholastic theologian, the 'Angelic Doctor.' He wrote a vast range of works, culminating in the *Summa theologiae*; his *Quaestiones* rehandle certain sections of the *Summa*.

588 Poems] He wrote a sequence and hymns for the feast of Corpus Christi which are still in use today.

589 nearer to our own time] The identification in the notes that follow of writers contemporary with Erasmus has been kept brief, as full information on almost all of them can be found in CEBR.

590 Petrarch] 1304–74, called 'the father of humanism.' Many classical works were rediscovered as a result of his zealous searches, most notably Cicero's *Epistulae ad Atticum* in 1345. He was remarkable in his age for his appreciation of Cicero as a stylist, and himself wrote in a style which to some extent looked to classical rather than medieval standards. His best-known Latin works are probably his *Epistolae de rebus familiaribus*, inspired by Cicero's private correspondence.

591 Biondo] Flavio Biondo of Forli, 1392–1463, an important and active humanist whose later years were devoted largely to historical and antiquarian writings that were of immense importance in the developing study of the material remains of ancient Rome

592 Boccaccio] Giovanni Boccaccio of Florence (1313–75). He first won fame as a writer in Italian – love sonnets, romances, and the famous *Decameron*. Influenced by Petrarch, he dedicated his later years to humanist studies and his subsequent writings were in Latin, the best known being the encyclopaedic *Genealogia deorum* in fifteen books.

415

593 Giovanni Tortelli] Of Arezzo (c 1400–66), mainly known for his *De orthographia*, a huge miscellany of philology, history, geography, and antiquities.

594 Francesco Filelfo] Of Tolentino (1398–1481), who taught rhetoric in various places in Italy, but whose insolence and invective made him many enemies. His Latin writings include speeches, polemical and educational works, poems, and letters.

595 Leonardo of Arezzo] Leonardo Bruni (1370–1444), a distinguished humanist who served the city of Florence as its chancellor and historian. He translated many Greek works into Latin – his Plutarch's *Lives* was particularly influential. His letters, famed for their Latinity, were published in eight books in 1472. He wrote a life of Cicero, whose style he studied and admired.

596 Guarino] Guarino Guarini of Verona (1374–1460), the most famous teacher of the fifteenth century. His vast output in Latin included manuals of Latin

grammar and syntax (he was one of the originators of Ciceronianism), textual criticism, editions of texts, orations and lectures. He translated from Greek some Lucian and Isocrates, fifteen *Lives* of Plutarch, and Strabo.

597 Lapo] Lapo da Castiglionchio the Younger (1405–38), renowned for his accurate and elegant translations from Greek. He Latinized many *Lives* of Plutarch, some speeches of Demosthenes and Isocrates, and the *Characters* of Theophrastus. He contributed Xenophon's *Oeconomicus* to Nicholas v's project for the translation of Greek literature into Latin.

598 Acciaiuoli] Donato Acciaiuoli of Florence (1429–78), who combined scholarship with administration and public life. He wrote a Latin commentary on Aristotle's *Ethics*, *Politics* and *Physics*, and translated the *Politics*, together with some *Lives* of Plutarch.

599 Antonio Beccaria] Of Verona (1400–74), humanist and churchman. His translations include various works of Athanasius and Plutarch.

600 Francesco Barbato] The text offers Franciscus Barbatius: if this is Poggio's friend Francesco Barbato of Sulmona (c 1300–63), the jurist and poet who was famous for his translations from Greek, he seems somewhat out of place here in Erasmus' list, which is more or less chronological. Possibly we have an error for Francesco Barbaro, a noble of Venice (1390–1454), grandfather of Ermolao Barbaro (see 416) and translator of Plutarch *Aristides* and *Elder Cato*, also author of a treatise *De re uxoria*.

601 Antonio Pasini of Todi] Antonius Tudertinus (d 1466). He translated some of Plutarch's *Lives*.

602 Leonardo Giustiniani] Of Venice (1388–1446), a statesman of culture who assembled a considerable library of Greek, Latin, and Italian texts. He translated Plutarch's *Cinna* and *Lucullus*, and wrote various Latin works, including poetry and letters.

603 Achille Bocchi] Of Bologna (1488–1562) gained fame by his *Apologia in Plautum, cui accedit vita Ciceronis auctore Plutarcho nuper inventa* (Bologna 1508).

604 invention … a major part of eloquence] See Quintilian 10.2.1: 'invenire primum fuit estque praecipuum.'

605 Poggio] Poggio Bracciolini (1380–1459), chancellor of Florence from 1453. He wrote extensively in a vigorous but non-classical Latin style; Erasmus did not think much of it, nor of Poggio's reaction to the criticisms of Valla (see below) in their famous and scurrilous dispute on the question of Latin style in 1452–3 (see Epp 23:78n and 26:88).

606 disgustingly incorrect] In the course of the dispute, Valla wrote two *Libelli in dialogo conscripti*, in the first of which Guarino's cook, a German, declares that Poggio uses 'kitchen Latin' worse than his own; see Valla *Opera* (Basel 1540, reprinted Turin 1962) 368ff; see also R. Pfeiffer 'Küchenlatein' *Philologus* 86 (1931).

607 Valla] 1406–57. In his *Elegantiae linguae latinae* (c 1440) on Latin idiom and style, he set out classical usage as the model for Latin prose writing. His aggressive tone, here and elsewhere, and his untempered criticism of the style of his contemporaries won him many enemies. Personally he preferred Quintilian's style to Cicero's; see Gambaro (above, introductory note n44), xxxiii.

416

608 Ermolao Barbaro] Of Venice (c 1453–1493). Together with Pico and Poliziano, who follow in Erasmus' list, Barbaro represented a great age of Italian intellectual achievement, and Erasmus here salutes all three together, as he does elsewhere. Barbaro's most famous work was the authoritative *Castigationes Plinianae* (1492–3), a discussion of the Elder Pliny's *Naturalis historia*. His studies in Pliny supplied him with many strange Latin words for use in his own writing.

609 Pico] Giovanni Pico della Mirandola (1463–94), the precocious young philosopher who, after a meteoric career as a student of literature, became associated with Ficino's (see n615) circle in Florence. To his thorough knowledge of scholastic Aristotelianism acquired in Paris he added Platonism, Neoplatonism, Hermetic philosophy, and the Kabbalah.

610 languages ... theology] He learned Hebrew, Old Persian, and Arabic in order to further his understanding of the Scriptures and of Aristotle, and at the age of twenty-four promulgated 900 theses, a number of which were condemned as heretical.

611 Gianfrancesco Pico della Mirandola] c 1469–1533, nephew of the above. His chief works were *De studio divinae et humanae philosophiae* and *Examen doctrinae vanitatis gentilium*, criticizing Plato and Aristotle.

612 Pietro Bembo] See 435.

613 though otherwise ... running for this prize] Added 3rd ed. See n260 for Gianfrancesco Pico's correspondence with Bembo on the subject of imitation. Although Erasmus became aware of the correspondence in the period between the first and second editions of *Ciceronianus* and had made some adjustments in the second edition, this insertion was not made until the third edition. The words 'a philosopher and' were inserted in the 2nd ed: at the end of his letter, Pico makes the conventional apology for his Latinity, saying that he has spent too long reading the barbaric Latin of recent Italian theologians and philosophers.

614 Angelo Poliziano] Angelo Ambrogini of Montepulciano (1454–94), the most distinguished humanist of his time, and tutor to the sons of Lorenzo de' Medici; his fame attracted to Florence scholars from all parts of Europe. Erasmus approved of his eclectic Latin style (see 444), and in Ep 126:157 speaks of its 'Attic loveliness.'

615 Marsilio Ficino] Of Figline (1433–99), the distinguished Renaissance Platonist and inaugurator of the Florentine Platonic Academy. He wrote original works in Latin, as well as translating Greek philosophical texts.

616 angelic gifts] A pun on the name Angelo

617 Codro Urceo ... Marullus] Erasmus now lists a group of scholars of Greek origin who had moved to Italy and contributed much to the Italian Renaissance.

618 Lascaris] Janus or Johannes Lascaris of Rhyndacus (1445–1535), the only one of the group still living. He taught Greek first in Florence, where he was responsible for the *editio princeps* (1494–6, printed in a splendid font of Greek capitals) of four plays of Euripides, Callimachus, Apollonius Rhodius, Lucian, and the Greek Anthology. While ambassador to Venice for Louis XII (1503–8) he joined the Greek scholars in the Aldine circle and met Erasmus.

In 1513–18 he was in Rome as a member of Leo x's Greek cóllege, and succeeded Musurus (see below) as its director in 1517. He visited Paris on three occasions between 1495 and 1534. This was particularly important for the dissemination of Greek studies in France, and his students included Budé (see 421). His *Epigrammata greco-latina* were published in Paris (Bade, 1 July 1527). He was accredited with the authorship of an epigram attacking Erasmus which circulated in Paris after the publication of the first edition of *Ciceronianus* (see introductory note 331 and Ep 2027 from Gervasius Wain, 16 August 1528).

619 the nobility of his birth] He was related to the Byzantine imperial family.
620 Codro] Antonio Codro Urceo of Ravenna (1446–1500). He held the chair of grammar and rhetoric at Bologna and wrote numerous works in Latin prose and verse (published Bologna: de Benedictis 1502).
621 Epicurus] The founder of the Epicurean school of philosophy, which posited pleasure as the goal of existence. Epicurus meant by this the true pleasure of the mind, which entailed a high degree of abstinence and sobriety. To this end he recommended a quiet life, untroubled by obligation or ambition. (This is probably the point here.) Epicurus in his own writings deliberately used a straightforward, naturalistic, even crude style. His doctrine of pleasure was often misunderstood, but various patristic and medieval writers had appreciated his real intentions. A number of fifteenth-century humanists (Valla, Bruni, Filelfo, and others) studied and rehabilitated his teaching. Erasmus generally treats 'Epicurean' as a term of praise (see the colloquy *Epicureus*; Thompson *Colloquies* 535–51). Urceo seems to have acquired his name Codro (Codrus was a proverbial poor man) from his modest way of life.

417
622 George of Trebizond] Born in Crete (1395–c 1472). He came to Venice in 1417, and subsequently taught Greek in Vicenza, Venice and Florence. He contributed to Nicholas v's translation of Greek literature inaccurate versions of Aristotle's *Rhetoric* and *Historia animalium*, Plato's *Laws* and *Parmenides*, and various Greek Fathers. He also wrote a Latin grammar (1471) and a *Rhetoric* (1434).
623 Theodorus Gaza] Of Salonika (1398–1475). He taught at Ferrara for several years, and was the first professor of Greek there. In 1451 he was summoned to Rome to contribute to Nicholas v's translation project, for which he provided Aristotle's *Problemata* and an improved version of the *Historia animalium*, and Theophrastus' *Historia plantarum*. He further translated Aelian *Tactica*, Dionysius of Halicarnassus *De compositione verborum*, and five Homilies of Chrysostom. He also translated Cicero's *De senectute*, *De amicitia*, and *Somnium Scipionis* into Greek. Erasmus used his Greek grammar when teaching at Cambridge in 1511 (see Ep 233), and subsequently translated bk 1 (1516) and bk 2 (1518).
624 Britons and Frisians] See 422 and 425.
625 Georgio Merula] Giorgio Merlani of Alessandria near Milan (c 1430–94). He translated into Latin parts of Dio Cassius.
626 Marullus] Michael Marullus Tarchaniota of Constantinople, (c 1445–1500). He composed a considerable amount of fine Latin verse in various metres,

written in classical idiom, full of classical imagery and phraseology, with no admixture of Christianity; in particular his *Hymni naturales* celebrated the pagan gods of antiquity.

627 Marcus Musurus] Of Retimo, Crete (1470–1517). Erasmus knew him in Venice, where, together with Lascaris, Egnazio, and Aleandro (see nn618, 654, 659) he helped Erasmus in the preparation of the Aldine *Adagia* of 1508 by the loan of manuscripts (see Ep 269:55n). The prefaces mentioned may be the Latin prefaces accompanying the first editions of Greek authors which Musurus produced for Aldus, though these were actually written by Aldus himself.

628 summoned to Rome] By Pope Leo x

629 archbishop] Of Monemvasia in south-eastern Greece c 1516. He died in the following year.

630 Pomponio Leto] Julius Pomponius Laetus of Diano (1428–97), a pupil of Lorenzo Valla, and founder c 1460 of the Roman Academy. The Academy was dissolved in 1467 on suspicion of paganism, but later restored. Pomponio had a great reputation among his contemporaries, but Erasmus seems unimpressed.

631 Sacchi] Bartolomeo Sacchi of Piadena (Bartolomeo Platina), 1421–81. Of his many works, the best known is his *Lives of the Popes* (1479). *De optimo cive* and *Panegyricus* (in praise of Cardinal Bessarion) were published in 1504.

632 if I am not mistaken] Added 2nd ed

633 Filippo Beroaldo the Elder] Of Bologna (1453–1505), professor of rhetoric at Bologna 1472–6 and 1479–1505. He was a prolific editor and commentator on classical texts, noted especially for his extensive edition of Apuleius (Bologna 1500), whose archaizing style he made his model in a consciously anti-Ciceronian stance.

418

634 Filippo Beroaldo the Younger] Of Bologna (1472–1518), nephew of Filippo Beroaldo the Elder. Erasmus and he became friends when they met in Rome in 1509.

635 Giorgio Valla] Of Piacenza (c 1447–99). He taught at Milan, Pavia, and Venice, and was widely read in natural sciences as well as literature.

636 Cristoforo Landino] Of Florence (1424–1504), a famous teacher and member of the Florentine Academy.

637 Mancinelli] Antonio Mancinelli of Velletri (1452–1505), a teacher who wrote a considerable number of grammatical treatises, commentaries on Latin authors, and poetry

638 Pietro Marso] Of Rome, (1442–1512). Erasmus, who met him in Rome, thought him honest and industrious but not distinguished (see Ep 152:23n).

639 Battista Pio] Giovanni Battista Pio of Bologna (c 1460–1540), a pupil of the Elder Beroaldo. His Latin style, like his teacher's, was characterized by archaism, and c 1513 he was considered the leader of the Roman anti-Ciceronian archaizing movement; see D'Amico (n445) 378.

640 Cornelio Vitelli] Of Cortona (d c 1509). He was the earliest teacher of Greek at Oxford (c 1475), and also taught briefly in Paris. His chief published work dealt with the *Letters* of the Younger Pliny.

641 Leoniceno] Niccolò Leoniceno of Vicenza (1428–1524), a scholar, philosopher, and physician who taught at Ferrara for sixty years. He published Latin translations of Greek medical works. Erasmus met him once in 1508 and had a great respect for him.

642 Leonico] Niccolò Tomeo Leonico of Venice (1456–1531), a Platonist who taught at Padua, lecturing on Plato and Aristotle from the Greek text. Erasmus met him during his stay in Venice, and he also taught a number of Erasmus' English acquaintances. He made numerous translations from Greek. His *Dialogi* were published in 1524 (see Allen Ep 1479:180n).

643 Bartolomeo Scala] Of Colle di Val d'Elsa in Tuscany (1430–1491), a scholar and administrator in the service of the Medici in Florence, where he was chancellor 1465–97. He disputed violently with Poliziano on Latin language and style (see further 443ff).

644 Paolo Cortesi] Of San Gimignano (c 1465–1510), a scholar and churchman who served in the curia 1481–1503. He too disputed with Poliziano on the question of stylistic imitation. He was a leading Roman Ciceronian and wrote in a strict Ciceronian style for which he was generally admired.

645 Pietro Crinito] Of Florence (1475–1505). He did a considerable amount of teaching, and wrote a number of miscellaneous works on classical subjects. He had a reputation as a writer of Latin verse.

646 Jacopo Antiquario] Of Perugia (1444–1512), a churchman in the employ of various rulers of Milan. He was a scholar who gave encouragement to other scholars, notably Poliziano, but did not write much himself.

647 say something about Paolo Cortesi later] See 444ff.

648 Domizio Calderini] Of Verona (1446–1478). He went to Rome c 1466, and died there of plague at the age of thirty-two.

649 Scipione Fortiguerra] Scipio Carteromachus of Pistoia (1466–1515). A distinguished Greek scholar, who was a member of the Aldine circle and produced for Aldus an edition of Demosthenes (1504). Erasmus got to know him well in 1508 during his visit to Italy, and was helped by him in the interpretation of Greek manuscripts. See Ep 217:4n.

650 Girolamo Donato] Of Venice (c 1457–1511). He was much engaged in government, embassies, and negotiations, such as those between Venice and Julius II in 1509–10, and Erasmus met him once in Rome in 1509. He had written one or two things apart from letters.

651 Antonio Sabellico] Marcantonio Coccio Sabellico of Vicovaro near Rome (1436–1506). He was a member of Leto's Roman Academy; later he taught rhetoric at Venice, where the much younger Egnazio (see below) opposed and challenged him. His writings were mainly historical.

419

652 proverb] See Cicero *De finibus* 5.3; *Adagia* I ii 52.

653 Paolo Emilio] Of Verona (c 1460–1529), an Italian humanist who helped to promote the revival of classical studies in France. He lived in Paris from 1483, where Erasmus probably met him, and wrote an official history of France, *De rebus gestis Francorum*, in ten books, which won him the title of 'the French Livy.'

654 Giovanni Battista Egnazio] Giambattista Egnazio Cipelli of Venice (1478–

1553). He was a distinguished member of the Aldine circle and famous as an orator. Erasmus got to know him in Venice, and counted him a friend.

655 Paolo Bombace] Of Bologna (1476–1527), a friend of long standing of Erasmus', who enjoyed his hospitality in Bologna 1506–7 (see Ep 210). He worked on the Latin elegiac poets, but seems to have published little.

656 people who wanted to replace him] They gave his Greek lectureship at Bologna to another man while he was away at Siena taking the baths for the sake of his health in 1510–1511. Shortly after, he resigned his other lectureship in rhetoric and poetry and went to Venice (see Ep 251). From 1518 he was in Rome in the employ of the curia, becoming secretary to Clement VII (5 September 1524); he died in the sack of Rome in 1527.

657 Andrea Alciati] Of Milan (1492–1550), the most famous legal scholar of his generation. He reformed legal studies by applying to the texts of civil law the humanistic principles of historical and philological investigation, eg in *Annotationes* on the Justinian Codex (1515), and (his most famous work) *De verborum significatione libri iv* (1530). He had literary interests as well: his *Notes* on Tacitus were published in 1517; he also translated poems from the Greek Anthology and wrote Latin verse; a four-line epitaph of his on Johann Froben was included in the second, third, and fourth editions of *Ciceronianus*; above all his *Emblemata* (short Latin verses explaining accompanying allegorical woodcuts) were much admired and translated.

658 Cicero] *Brutus* 145

659 Girolamo Aleandro] Hieronymus Aleander of Motta, Friuli (1480–1542), a scholar and teacher of Greek and Latin, who also knew Hebrew and Syriac. In his earlier years he taught very successfully in Venice, Paris and Orléans and published works on Greek grammar and literature. He was appointed Vatican librarian in 1519, but later gave up literary studies for administration and diplomacy, and rose steadily in the service of the Church. His friendship with Erasmus was begun during Erasmus' stay in Venice 1507–8, but later their relationship changed to antagonism over the Lutheran question. Erasmus subsequently on several occasions accused Aleandro of attacking him anonymously or under cover of others' names. See Ep 256.

660 archbishop of Brindisi] In 1524

420

661 Prince of Carpi] Alberto Pio (c 1475–1531), nephew of Pico della Mirandola

662 as far as I know] Added 2nd ed

663 a very long letter] Pio propounded the view that Erasmus was in sympathy with Luther's teaching, and in Ep 1634 (Basel 10 October 1525) Erasmus wrote to him to disclaim this. In reply, Pio sent from Rome *Responsio paraenetica* in the form of a letter (15 May 1526) attacking the heresies of Luther and charging Erasmus with being the root and cause of the whole Lutheran business. Erasmus was slow in replying, and Pio, having meantime fled to France after the sack of Rome in 1527, circulated his *Responsio* in Paris and then had it printed by Bade (7 January 1529). By 13 February, Erasmus had completed and got printed his own *Responsio*. Pio continued the controversy with a huge volume, *In locos lucubrationum Erasmi*, where he listed passages in Erasmus' writings which he held to support Lutheran doctrines, but he

died in 1531 before the printing was completed (Paris: Bade, 9 March 1531, also Venice: Giunta 1531). Erasmus called the work a Parthian shot and pursued the matter after Pio's death with another *Apologia* (1531).

664 written in response ... by another's hand] Added (together with 'whoever he is' in Nosoponus' reply) in the 3rd ed, ie October 1529, between Pio's *Responsio* and *In locos lucubrationum*. In a number of letters (eg Allen 2379:110, 2411:50, 2466:98) Erasmus suggests that material had been supplied to Pio by his erstwhile friend Aleandro (see n659), as well as by the Franciscans of Paris. Aleandro denied the charge (Ep 2572). Erasmus also asserted (eg Allen Ep 2329:100) that the Spaniard Ginès de Sepúlveda (see n756) was responsible for the Latin. Ginès published in 1532 *Antapologia pro Alberto Pio Comite Carpensi in Erasmum Roterodamum* (Rome: Bladus).

665 with theology and philosophy] See Allen Ep 1804:254 (1527), where Erasmus calls Pio a layman with theological ambitions who fancied himself as an Aristotelian.

666 Ricchieri] Lodovico Ricchieri (Caelius Rhodiginus) of Rovigo (1469–1525), a not very distinguished teacher of classics, who had a fancy for archaic vocabulary (see Telle 315).

667 Calcagnini] Of Ferrara (1479–1541). He spent most of his life in Ferrara, where he met Erasmus once in 1508. His most notable work was *Quod caelum stet, terra moveatur* (Ferrara c 1520). In Ep 2869 (17 September 1533), he thanks Erasmus for his remarks here, and agrees that no one has ever attained the Ciceronian ideal in every respect.

668 our discussion will bring us back] See 435 for Sadoleto and Bembo, 436 for Giambattista Casali and Pontano, 437 for Sannazaro.

669 Gaguin] Robertus Gaguinus of Calonne, Artois (1433–1501), General of the Trinitarian order in Paris. He wrote in both French and Latin, including a Latin history of France (1495), which won him a considerable reputation. Some of his orations were published with his letters and various minor works in 1498.

670 the two brothers Fernand] Charles (d 1517) and Jean Fernand of Bruges, members of the Parisian literary circle associated with Gaguin, in which connection Erasmus presumably met them

671 Gui Jouvenneaux] Guido Juvenalis (c 1460–1505). At first he taught in Paris, producing commentaries on Terence (1492) and on Valla's *Elegantiae* (1494). He then entered the religious life, and was elected abbot of St Sulpice at Bourges (1497). His *Letters* were published in 1499; his subsequent writings were religious.

672 Josse Bade] Jodocus Badius of Assche in Brabant (c 1461–1535), scholar-printer in Paris from 1499, and publisher of many of Erasmus' books from c 1505 onwards, until Erasmus transferred his business to Froben c 1517. Bade felt free thereafter to publish works by Erasmus' opponents (see eg n663).

421

673 Budé] Guillaume Budé (Gulielmus Budaeus) of Paris (1468–1540), the most learned Frenchman of the time, with a wide knowledge of many subjects, but especially admired as the finest Greek scholar in France.

674 domestic worries] Bade had a large family.

675 making money] For his exactness in money matters see Ep 263 to Erasmus.

676 I would allow … compel our admiration] This passage caused a furore in Paris
on the first publication of the *Ciceronianus*: Nosoponus' rating of Bade as a
better Ciceronian than Budé, the glory of French scholarship, was taken as a
deliberate insult to both to Budé himself and to French learning in general.
Erasmus was induced by the representations of his friends (see introductory
note 331) to modify it in the second edition, and it then read as follows:
Nosoponus I would allow him to compete for this glorious title sooner than
Apuleius. On the whole, Bade's endeavours have met with considerable
success – his style displays both fluency and scholarship – though they would
have met with more if domestic worries and his commitment to making
money hadn't interfered with the quiet detachment that accords with literary
studies, which any candidate in this competition must be able to enjoy.
Bulephorus Perhaps you will grant the honour of this title to Guillaume Budé,
the man who is the glory of all France? **Nosoponus** How can I grant him
something for which he has no ambition and would not acknowledge if I did?
Though otherwise his exceptional and manifold gifts of intellect compel our
admiration.
Erasmus presumably substituted Apuleius for Budé in some annoyance, as
being perhaps the least Ciceronian of all ancient writers (see nn 544, 445).
Budé's relations with Erasmus had long been discordant, though the two
remained outwardly polite (see Ep 2061 from Vives), and Budé took offence
at what was said here in the first edition, and was not appeased by the change
in the second. He did not write to Erasmus again. In his *Commentarii* he
took the opportunity of reasserting Cicero's title as 'begetter of the Roman
tongue,' rejected by Erasmus in this dialogue (see 390), but continued
nonetheless to express views on fanatical Ciceronianism which were in accord
with Erasmus', and which he had communicated to Erasmus in Ep 1812 (22
April 1527), his last letter to him before this incident.
Bade too must have read these words with very mixed feelings, but he made
no direct rejoinder, only an indirect one in the preface to his edition of
Cicero's *Philippics*, (6 October 1529); see Telle 411.

677 Jacques Lefèvre] Jacobus Faber d'Etaples (c 1460–1536). He published several
commentaries on and editions of Greek philosophical and theological
works and later turned to Biblical criticism. His *Commentaries* on St Paul (1512)
occasioned violent disagreement with Erasmus in 1516–7, from which their
friendship did not recover.

678 Jean de Pins] Joannes Pinus of Toulouse (c 1470–1537). He studied in Italy
under Musurus and Beroaldo the Elder, where he met Erasmus. From 1507
onwards he was involved in diplomacy and administration, and was variously
ambassador to Venice and Rome 1515–23; nonetheless he wrote biogra-
phies and miscellaneous minor works. To other scholars he was a generous
patron (see Allen Ep 928:36n). He admired Longueil, and as ambassador
tried to protect him from the attacks of his enemies in Rome (see introductory
note 325).

679 when he celebrated … than his status] Added 2nd ed; de Pins had become
bishop of Rieux in 1523. In the 3rd ed Erasmus inserted 'and his high
ecclesiastical office.'

680 Nicolas Bérault] Of Orléans (c 1470–c 1545), a close friend of Budé and a Greek scholar. He was a teacher first in Orléans, later in Paris, with many distinguished pupils, including Longueil. Erasmus stayed with him in Orléans in 1506, and their relations remained friendly.

681 François Deloynes] Of Beaugency near Orléans (c 1468–1524). Deloynes was a great friend of Budé, with whom he studied law at Orléans; he taught law there until 1500, when he became a member of the Parlement of Paris. Erasmus met him in Orléans and Paris, and they corresponded to some extent. Erasmus speaks of him with respect as a scholar, and calls him a great patron of literature (Allen Ep 1603:110), but he does not seem to have published anything.

682 authors like Accorso, Bartolo, and Baldo] Three distinguished medieval jurists, authors of standard commentaries on legal teaching texts; Francesco Accorso (1182–1260), Bartolo da Sassoferrato (1313–56); and Baldo degli Ubaldi (1327–1400). Their style was generally despised by the humanists.

683 Lazare de Baïf] Of La Flèche (c 1496–1547). He was in Rome with Longueil c 1517, working at Greek under Lascaris (see n618). He translated Sophocles *Electra* and Euripides *Hecuba* into French verse, but was best known for three archaeological treatises: *De re vestiaria* already published (Basel: J. Bebel, March 1526), *De vasculis* (Basel: Froben 1531, with the second edition of *De re vestiaria*), and *De re navali* (Paris: R. Stephanus 1536). From 1525 he held various diplomatic appointments.

684 Claudius Cantiuncula] Claude Chansonette of Metz (c 1490–1560). He became professor of civil law at Basel in 1518, and rector of the university the following year. He returned to Metz in 1523, and thereafter was constantly travelling about Europe in the service of various rulers. His opinion on points of law was highly valued. He believed in combining the study of law with that of literature, and was a voracious reader of books of all kinds. Erasmus praises him again in Allen Ep 1841:10–19.

422

685 can sing] *Canit*: Erasmus is punning on the name Cantiuncula in an affectionately teasing manner, as Cantiuncula wrote only, albeit elegantly, on topics connected with the law, and does not seem to have written poetry. His writings to date were *Topica per exempla legum illustrata* (Basel: Cratander 1520), *Paraenesis de ratione studii legalis* (1522), and *Oratio apologetica* (1522) in which he defends the study of civil law from the charge of incompatibility with Christianity. See A. Rivier 'Claude Chansonette, jurisconsulte messin et ses lettres inédites' *Mémoires couronnés de L'Académie Royale des Sciences, des Lettres et des Beaux-Arts de Belgique* 29 (1880).

686 de Schepper] Cornelis de Schepper (Cornelius Duplicius) of Nieuwpoort (1503–55). While at the university of Paris he studied philosophy, medicine, history, mathematics, and astronomy. Thereafter he spent a short time in the colleges of Louvain (he had left by 1520), and presumably Erasmus knew him there. In 1523 he published an attack on astrologers which established him as a writer of repute. Soon after, he entered on his career as roving ambassador in the service successively of the exiled Christiern II of Denmark, of Charles V and Ferdinand I. He added to his reputation with

the *Defensio* of King Christiern written in 1524, and in 1526 wrote a verse epitaph on the death of the the king's wife Isabella.

687 Another ... roles in life] This section on Cantiuncula and de Schepper was added in the 3rd ed. Cantiuncula wrote to his friend Boniface Amerbach, 3 November 1529, requesting a copy of this edition; see Rivier (n685 above) 52.

688 du Ruel] Jean du Ruel (1479–1537), dean of the medical faculty at Paris and physician to Francis I. He translated Dioscorides *De medicinali materia* in 1516 and (subsequent to this mention in the first ed) *Veterinaria medicina* 1530, *De natura stirpium* 1536.

689 Petrus Mosellanus] Peter Schade (c 1493–1524). He taught Greek and Latin at Leipzig from 1515 until his early death.

690 Where shall I put ... recently entered the lists] This section on Mosellanus was added in the 3rd ed.

691 Germain de Brie] Germanus Brixius of Auxerre (c 1490–1538). He was distinguished for his knowledge of Greek, which he had studied under Lascaris in Venice and Musurus in Padua. His friendship with Erasmus dates from their meeting in Venice in 1508. De Brie was one of the friends who wrote to tell Erasmus of the stir caused in Paris by the *Ciceronianus* on its first appearance (Ep 2021). He reported at the same time that persons had attempted to stir up ill will between himself and Erasmus by interpreting Nosoponus' remarks here as uncomplimentary. De Brie knew Longueil, and wrote poems (two Latin, one Greek) concerning his death, for publication in Bade's 1526 edition of Longueil's works. His fourteen lines of Latin elegiacs on the death of Maarten van Dorp were included in the first edition of *Ciceronianus*. His considerable fame as a poet was established by *Chordigerae navis conflagratio* (Paris: Bade 1513).

692 William Grocyn] Together with his friends Linacre and Latimer, Grocyn (d 1519) was a member of the scholarly group round More which welcomed Erasmus during his sojourns in England, and to which Erasmus here pays tribute. Erasmus' relations with Grocyn and Linacre were, however, not always entirely harmonious. See Ep 350.

693 one little letter] Whether or not Grocyn wrote anything else, the only thing to be printed was a letter written to Aldus, which, because if its elegant Latinity, Aldus printed together with Linacre's edition of Proclus *Sphaera*.

423

694 And he didn't favour ... laconically as well.] Added 3rd ed

695 Thomas Linacre] Primarily a medical man, physician to King Henry VIII from 1509, Linacre (c 1460–1524) was also a scholar with a profound knowledge of Greek and Latin, well read in ancient scientific and medical writers.

696 Richard Pace] Pace (c 1482–1536) met Erasmus in 1508 while studying in Ferrara. He was later employed by Henry VIII as royal secretary and diplomat, and held various ecclesiastical appointments in England.

697 Thomas More] Erasmus' lifelong friend, More (1478–1535) was at this time one of Henry VIII's chief advisers but was not yet chancellor of England or involved in the conflict with the king which led to his execution in 1535.

698 his parents' authority ... study the law] His father was a judge, eventually promoted to the King's Bench in 1523. More had two years at the Universi-

ty of Oxford, and then transferred to the Inns of Court (New Inn 1494, Lincoln's Inn 1496); he was called to the bar before 1503, and was also appointed reader in law at Furnival's Inn.

699 public office] Under sheriff of London in 1510, in which office he won popularity for his expedition and fairness

700 royal and state business] Reluctantly, More joined Henry VIII's council with the position of master of requests in 1518, an office which obliged him to reside with the court. In 1521 he became under-treasurer, and in 1525 chancellor of the duchy of Lancaster. Henry did not appoint him chancellor of England until after the 2nd ed of *Ciceronianus,* ie in October 1529.

701 poetry] In 1504 he translated epigrams from the Greek Anthology into Latin with Lily. He also wrote original epigrams in Latin (1512) and some English verse.

424

702 William Latimer] Latimer (c 1460–1545) was a classical scholar, Fellow of All Souls', Oxford, and tutor to Reginald Pole; of his writings, none are known except some letters to Erasmus.

703 Reginald Pole] A gifted and learned young man (1500–58), who was a protégé of Henry VIII. He had a very chequered career, in part due to the stand he took over the king's divorce. He became a prominent figure in the Catholic reform movement, and in spite of suspicions as to his orthodoxy, came near to being elected pope in December 1549. He was eventually appointed archbishop of Canterbury in 1556. While studying in Italy, he became a close friend of Longueil, who died in his house in Padua in 1522. In accordance with Longueil's last wishes, he published an edition of Longueil's works (Florence: Giunta 1524), containing the two speeches in his own defence (see 431ff), one speech addressed to the Lutheran party (see 434), and his letters (see 430), anything else being suppressed. The life of Longueil which Pole wrote for inclusion in this volume was anonymous, composed, according to the title-page 'by a very close friend.'

704 the king himself] Henry VIII (1509–47), whose reign at first appeared to usher in a golden age of literature, scholarship, and the arts, until the king's attention and resources were diverted to foreign wars. Erasmus had great hopes of him as a Christian prince when he first ascended the throne; moreover his promises of favour had drawn Erasmus to England in 1511.

705 two little books] *Assertio septem sacramentorum adversus Martinum Lutherum* (London: Pynson 12 July 1521); *Literarum quibus ... Henricus octavus ... respondit ad quandam epistolam Martini Lutheri exemplum* (London: Pynson 2 December 1526). It was rumoured that Erasmus had a considerable hand in the Latinity of the first (see Epp 1298, 1313). Henry received the title 'Defender of the Faith' in October 1521.

706 if I knew of anyone] Erasmus might have recalled at least Hector Boece of Dundee (c 1465–1536), principal of King's College, Aberdeen, whom he had known well in Paris, and to whom he had dedicated *Carmen de casa natalitia Jesu* (see Epp 47, 1495). Boece's *Historiae Scotorum* had been published in 1527 (Paris: Bade).

707 Saxo Grammaticus] C 1158–1220. His *Danorum regum heroumque historiae* (which contains the Hamlet story) was published in Paris in 1514.

708 Cornelissen] Adrianus Cornelii Barlandus (1486–1538). He held the first Latin chair in the Collegium Trilingue 1518–9 (see n726). His Latin writings were considerable: he annotated several Greek and Latin authors, including some works of Cicero; he also wrote history. His prose epitaph on the death of Maarten van Dorp was included in the first edition of *Ciceronianus*. He wrote to thank Erasmus for his remarks here (Ep 2025, Louvain, 14 August 1528).

425

709 prolific writers] *Polygraphi* (in Greek script); Erasmus calls himself *Polygraphus* in several places, eg the colloquy *Charon*. The word was used by Cicero *Ad Atticum* 13.18 of Varro, the polymath, reputedly the author of about 500 books (see n360). Erasmus uses it with reference to Jerome in Allen Ep 1451:69.

710 tares] Latin *zizania*, one of the biblical words favoured by Erasmus; see D.F.S. Thomson 'The Latinity of Erasmus' in *Erasmus* 125.

711 in a hurry] Erasmus several times admits to his practice of rushing books into print, see Allen Ep 1352:92n. In Allen Ep 1885: 146–50 he says he writes too fast for Ciceronian polishing.

712 'balanced on one foot'] Ie without any trouble, as Horace said disparagingly of Lucilius, *Satires* 1.4.10. Etienne Dolet in his *Ciceronianus* takes up these self-criticisms and constantly refers to Erasmus' garrulity and slapdash methods (see eg 17, 19, 48, 50, 179, 183 of the text in Telle) and calls him (11) *Batavus ille scriptor* 'that Dutch scribbler.' Cf n805.

713 Willem Hermans] Gulielmus Gaudanus of Gouda (1466–1510), an intimate friend of Erasmus' youth, a pupil of Hegius, and a fellow monk at Steyn.

714 Gillis van Delft] Aegidius Delphus (d 1524), a scholar and poet of Erasmus' acquaintance who studied and taught mainly in Paris. His verse included metrical paraphrases from the Bible.

715 Maarten van Dorp] Of Naaldwijk (1485–1525). He at first taught Latin and philosophy at Louvain, but later turned to theology and became professor of divinity there (1515). See Allen Ep 1646 for Erasmus' verse epitaph on his death, included with 12 other verse and prose epitaphs by various hands in the first edition only of *Ciceronianus*.

716 others' judgments] Erasmus considered Dorp inconstant and easily influenced. There is perhaps a reference to the famous misunderstanding when Dorp was instigated by the theologians of Louvain to take issue with Erasmus in 1514 over *The Praise of Folly* and the projected *New Testament*. The two men were reconciled largely through Thomas More, and since then Dorp had remained a friend and supporter of Erasmus, though with some uneasy passages.

717 Jacob Teyng] Jacobus Ceratinus of Hoorn (d 1530), a man with a chequered career, moving about from place to place as a teacher.

718 Comus] The spirit of revelry and licence; Erasmus considered the Germans as a nation prone to indulgence, especially in drink; see eg *Adagia* I ix 44 and IV viii 2.

719 Langens and Canters] Rudolf von Langen of Everswinkel (d 1519), was a

Westphalian humanist, a friend of Agricola and Hegius, and important as an educationalist. The Canters were a family famous for learning, who reputedly used only Latin within the household. Erasmus corresponded with the son Jacob Canter. Erasmus again speaks of Langens and Canters together with Agricola as representative examples of Frisian learning in Epp 1237 and 2073.

720 Rodolphus Agricola] Rudolf Huusman or Huisman of Baflo, Friesland (1444–85). After studying in Germany and at Louvain, Agricola spent several years in Italy, where he met with a number of the distinguished humanists of the day, improving his Greek with Theodorus Gaza. He transmitted this humanistic learning to Germany after his return there in 1479, and was greatly esteemed as one of the chief pioneers of the Renaissance in the north.

426

721 Haio Herman] Of Emden (d c 1540). In Ep 2091 (1529) Erasmus speaks of him as a successor to Agricola, and in Ep 1978 (1528) had urged him to edit Agricola's works, but it seems Herman published neither these nor anything of his own.

722 There is ... his natural gifts] This section on Herman was added in the 2nd ed. For the circumstances see Ep 2056 (1 October 1528) to Herman: Erasmus reports that Ursinus Velius (see 428, n759) had written to take him to task for failing to mention various scholars, including Herman; Erasmus defended himself by saying there was not much point in mentioning those who had not published anything. None the less, he inserted this passage in the 2nd ed, and wrote again to Herman (Ep 2108, 25 February 1529) telling him the omission had been repaired.

723 Alexander Hegius] Of Heck, near Horstmar (1433–98), a friend of Agricola's (see 425) and rector of the school of St Lebuin at Deventer 1483–98.

724 Hermann von dem Busche] Hermannus Buschius (c 1468–1534), a pupil of Hegius and Agricola, which no doubt suggested his name to Erasmus here. Hitherto he had had a disappointing and unsettled career, but had published quite a number of works, mainly poems. Erasmus met him once or twice and seems to have liked him and thought well of his abilities.

725 Conradus Goclenius] Konrad Wackers of Meneringhausen (c 1489–1539). He became professor of Latin in the Collegium Trilingue at Louvain in 1519 in succession to Cornelissen (see n708), and held the chair until his death. It is not clear whether Erasmus knew him earlier than 1519, but he was one of Erasmus' closest friends in Louvain. He was primarily a teacher and did not write for publication, but he did translate Lucian's *Hermotimus* into Latin, and fourteen lines of Latin elegiacs composed by him on the death of Maarten van Dorp were included in the first edition of *Ciceronianus*.

726 Collegium Trilingue] Endowed by Jérôme de Busleyden to be founded in the University of Louvain for the study of the three biblical languages, Hebrew, Greek, and Latin. Erasmus was much involved in realizing Busleyden's intentions, and in seeing through its establishment in 1517 (see Ep 205 introduction).

727 We're told that Cicero] See 369.

427

728 Christoph von Carlowitz] Christophorus Carlebitzius of Hermsdorf near Dresden (c 1507–78), a young scholar who had recently (1527) come to visit Erasmus in Basel with a recommendation from Goclenius.

729 'still in green leaf'] Ovid *Heroides* 17.263

730 Reuchlin] Johann Capnio of Pforzheim (1455–1522), the distinguished Hebrew scholar and first German teacher of Greek, who became the centre of a violent controversy between the Dominicans of Cologne and the representatives of the new learning.

731 Jakob Wimpfeling] Of Sélestat (1450–1528), a devout teacher of conservative attitudes who wrote a considerable number of polemical pieces in support of his strongly held views. Erasmus had been fêted by the literary society of Strasbourg under Wimpfeling's presidency in 1514 (see Ep 302 introduction).

732 Wimpfeling is experiencing] This sentence was added in the 2nd ed. Wimpfeling had died in November 1528, shortly after the first edition, and the 2nd (and subsequent) editions of *Ciceronianus* included three epitaphs on his death. The dedicatory epistle to this 2nd ed includes an encomium of Wimpfeling and a further mention of Spiegel, who had been tutored by his uncle. See 339–40 where the passage is translated.

733 Jakob Spiegel] Of Sélestat (c 1483–c 1547), a lawyer who taught for a time at Vienna, and was counsellor to Maximilian I, Charles V, and the archduke Ferdinand. He republished his uncle's autobiographical *Expurgatio contra detractores* in 1514. His own main work was a frequently reprinted *Lexicon iuris civilis*.

734 Philippus Melanchthon] Philipp Schwarzerd of Bretten near Pforzheim (1497–1560), Reuchlin's great-nephew and an infant prodigy, early acquiring a great reputation as a Greek scholar.

735 other pursuits] Referring to his involvement with Luther and the reform movement.

736 Ulrich von Hutten] A German knight and humanist (1488–1523) who espoused the cause of Lutheranism; his original friendship with Erasmus turned to antagonism, largely because of Erasmus' refusal to come out firmly on the side of Luther (see Ep 2088, above 339, where Erasmus claims to have given him his fair due here in spite of this enmity).

737 Willibald] Pirckheimer of Eichstätt (1470–1530), a gifted, generous nobleman of wide culture, a friend and frequent correspondent of Erasmus'. He was also a learned jurist and practical statesman, a councillor of Nürnberg for twenty-five years, and adviser to the emperors Maximilian I and Charles V. In his last years he devoted himself to literature and produced voluminous Latin writings.

738 He certainly ... reach it.] Modified in the second edition to read 'Whether he pursues the goal I do not know, certainly he doesn't reach it.'

739 administrative duties and poor health] He resigned his position as councillor of Nürnberg in 1522, partly because of continual attacks from enemies, but also because of ill health – he suffered from gout and kidneystones (see Allen Ep 2493:21).

740 though he ... exerted his powers] Added 2nd ed

741 Ulrich Zasius] Ulrich Zäsi of Constance (1461–1536), a practising lawyer and
    eventually professor of law at Freiburg, author of extensive legal writings,
    and a close friend of Erasmus' since 1514.

428

742 The whole of Germany ... than Cicero] The section on Zasius was added in the
    3rd ed.

743 Well then] Changed in 2nd ed to read 'All right then, but I offer you from not
    far away Bruno Amerbach ...'

744 Bruno Amerbach] Eldest son (1484–1519) of the Basel printer Johann, closely
    involved with the press after his father's death in 1513. He had died of
    plague, quickly following his wife, and Erasmus' six-line verse epitaph, men-
    tioning his knowledge of Greek, Latin, and Hebrew, was included in the
    first and subsequent editions of *Ciceronianus*.

745 Henricus Glareanus] Heinrich Loriti of Canton Glarus, (1488–1563), the direc-
    tor of boys' schools in Basel and Freiburg. A man of wide learning, he
    produced editions of Latin historians and poets, and was particularly interest-
    ed in chronology, geography, and music; his most important work was
    Dodecachordon (1547) on ancient musical theories. He was also a poet and his
    verse epitaph on Johann Froben was included in all four editions of
    Ciceronianus.

746 Ursinus Velius] Caspar Bernhard of Schwiednitz (c 1493–1539), who lived
    much of the time after 1518 in Vienna. He met Erasmus on a visit to Basel in
    1521. His *Poemata* were published in 1522.

747 an account of the campaigns] Erasmus had learned of Ursinus' projected his-
    torical work when Ursinus wrote (Ep 1917, December 1527) to report his
    appointment as historian to King Ferdinand, to whose children he had earlier
    been tutor. Ursinus was displeased at having his plans thus made public
    (Allen Ep 2008:6–10). The history, dealing with the war in Hungary 1526–31,
    was never completed.

748 Jacobus Piso] Of Medgyes (d 1527). He was Hungarian ambassador to Rome in
    1509 and met Erasmus there. He returned to Hungary in 1516, and later
    served on various embassies. He lost all his possessions after the battle of
    Mohacs in the war with the Turks, and Ursinus wrote to tell Erasmus of his
    death, which occurred in March 1527 (Ep 1917, 10 December 1527).

749 Yes ... I was sorry] Added 2nd ed

750 Andreas Critius] Andrzej Krzycki (1482–1537). He held various high adminis-
    trative and ecclesiastical offices in Poland. He had come to Erasmus' knowl-
    edge in 1525 via his *In Lutherum oratio* and thereafter they exchanged letters
    and gifts. They seem to have taken to each other immediately, and Eras-
    mus' letters to him are very frank. The only one of Critius' letters to survive
    (Ep 1652) supports Erasmus' comments here.

751 abilities all in ready money] As the emperor Augustus said of Lucius Vinicius,
    a fluent extempore speaker; see Elder Seneca *Controversiae* 2.5.20; Quin-
    tilian 6.3.111.

752 to bloom again and recover] The Renaissance in Spain developed comparative-

ly late and slowly, and Erasmus included only three Spanish scholars in the first edition: Nebrija, Zúñiga, and Sancho Carranza. There were, however, others he could have named. Alfonso Valdés wrote (Ep 2163, 15 May 1529) to report an enthusiastic reception for *Ciceronianus* in Spain and a Spanish printing to meet demand for copies, but he commented on the small number of Spanish scholars named, and like Velius (see n759) was surprised at the omission of Vives.

429

753 Nebrija] Elio Antonio (Antoninus Nebrissensis) of Nebrija (1444–1522), a humanist with a knowledge of Hebrew, Greek, and Latin. He produced editions of classical Latin and of Christian poets, a Latin grammar (1485), the first Spanish grammar (1492), a Latin-Spanish lexicon (1492), and a pioneering work on correct pronunciation of classical Greek (1486).

754 López] Diego López Zúñiga (Lopis) of the University of Alcalá (d 1531), a bitter enemy of Erasmus', and the leader of the theological opposition to him in Spain. Erasmus claims in the preface to the second edition of *Ciceronianus* (see page 339) to have given him fair mention in spite of this enmity. Their antagonism seems to have become less bitter after 1527. See Allen IV 621–2.

755 Sancho] Sancho Carranza (Sanctius) of Miranda in Navarre (d 1531), a theologian teaching for a time at Alcalá, where Juan Ginès de Sepúlveda was among his pupils. Erasmus had been annoyed by his polite criticisms of the New Testament in 1522, but by this time had come to see him as a friend and supporter in Spain.

756 Ginès] Juan Ginès de Sepúlveda (Genesius) of Pozoblanco (1491–1573), a Castilian at this time living in Rome. He was a very prolific writer; much of his work was later than the *Ciceronianus*, but he had already written several treatises, and translated a number of Aristotle's works into Latin. In Italy he was a protégé of Alberto Pio (see n664), with whom he endured the sack of Rome. This reference to Ginès was removed in the second edition and replaced by one below in the section on Portuguese writers (see n761).

757 Vives] Juan Luis Vives of Valencia (1492–1540). He met Erasmus in Brussels c 1516–17, and later knew him well in Louvain, where Vives was teaching from c 1518. He was one of his regular correspondents. He had published a number of works before *Ciceronianus*, but the ones that confirmed his reputation belong to the period after 1529. His two prose epitaphs on the Louvain theologian Maarten van Dorp were included in the first edition of *Ciceronianus*.

758 way of Mandrabulus] Ie get steadily worse (Mandrabulus' promised annual sacrifices to Juno became smaller each successive year). See Lucian *De iis qui mercede conducti degunt* 21, a dialogue translated by Erasmus; also *Adagia* I ii 58.

759 I shall be surprised ... its flexibility] Added 2nd ed. Ursinus Velius wrote from Prague, c 28 June 1528, criticizing *Ciceronianus*, and especially remarking on the omission of Vives, supposedly a friend of Erasmus'. Erasmus replied to Velius (Ep 2008), and also wrote to Vives apologizing for his oversight (Ep

2040, 2 September 1528); Vives accepted his apology (Ep 2061), though he was clearly hurt by the omission. Erasmus then made this insertion in the second edition.

760 Caiado] Henrique Caiado (Hermicus) of Lisbon (d 1509), a Portuguese poet who spent several years in Italy and made the acquaintance of many eminent scholars. He had a reputation as drinker and wit. Erasmus seems to have met him in Rome, and describes his death in *Adagia* IV viii 2; he also wrote a verse epitaph on his end (Reedijk *Poems* 291).

761 in his talk] In the 2nd ed an insertion follows (see n756): 'and Ginès, who recently published a booklet in Rome, and inspired great hopes for his future.' The booklet is possibly *De fide et libero arbitrio* (against Luther) of 1525. The change assigns Ginès to Portugal instead of to Spain, and in Ep 2938 (23 May 1534) he complained to Erasmus of being thus made Portuguese. Erasmus apologized, explaining not very convincingly (Ep 2951) that he had confused him with another person of a similar name. Ginès was not particularly pleased with this slightly expanded comment of the second edition, as he felt that his reputation was already sufficiently established by his writings and translations to merit appreciation of himself as an actual rather than as a potential scholar, and wrote to Alfonso de Valdés to say so; see Marcel Bataillon *Erasme et l'Espagne: Recherches sur l'histoire spirituelle du XVIe siècle* (Paris : E. Droz 1937) 407 (also tr Antonio Alatorre *Erasmo y España: Estudias sobre la historia espiritual del siglo XVI* [Mexico: Fondo di Cultura Económica 1950/1966]).

430

762 Christophe de Longueil] See introductory note 324ff.

763 matters of serious import] Cf Tacitus *Dialogus* 37.4–8, where the speaker says that great themes are necessary for great oratory.

764 Longueil wrote *Letters*] See n703.

765 a good many of the Younger Pliny's] Eg 1.6, on a day's hunting, or 8.8, on the source of the Clitumnus, the elaborate description of a beauty spot

766 the comments] See Cicero's remarks at *Ad familiares* 15.14.2–3.

431

767 two speeches ... supposedly delivered] *Orationes duae pro defensione sua in crimen laesae maiestatis*; see n796.

768 so often put back on the anvil] Cf Horace *Ars poetica* 441. According to the title-page of the printed edition, Longueil had revised the speeches carefully for publication.

769 fault of the times he lived in] Seneca said the same of Cicero (Aulus Gellius 12.2.7), meaning that Cicero had to make concessions to contemporary taste.

770 conscript fathers ... citizens] As well as using Ciceronian phraseology, Longueil's two speeches constantly refer to these and other institutions of the Ciceronian period as if they were a contemporary reality, and so give the effect of being delivered by Cicero in his own setting. See 383.

771 Octavius Caesar] Ie the emperor Augustus; his reign, the Augustan age,

which succeeded to the republican government by senate and people, was particularly splendid materially and culturally.

432

772 'mistress ... the toga'] Virgil *Aeneid* 1.282 (altered)

773 club of people] Presumably Erasmus means the Roman Academy.

774 more generous persons] Bembo, Sadoleto, and Mariano Castellano, who gave him hospitality in Rome; see Théophile Simar *Christophe de Longueil, humaniste, 1488–1522* Recueil de travaux publiés par les membres des conférences d'histoire et de philologie, fasc 31 (Louvain 1911) 62.

775 nowadays] Especially after the sack of Rome in 1527

776 Basel] A tribute to the city in which Erasmus had been living since October 1521. He moved to Freiburg in April 1529.

777 'barbarian'] Ie Longueil; his name was added in the 2nd ed.

778 Capitol] At the time of Longueil's 'trial,' after centuries of siege, destruction, and neglect, there was very little left of the impressive buildings that covered the Capitoline hill in classical and post-classical times; large scattered fragments of the huge temple of Jupiter Optimus Maximus were still to be seen, but most of the area was derelict or occupied by more recent buildings: the Gothic church of Santa Maria in Ara Coeli belonging to the Franciscans, the fifteenth-century Palazzo dei Conservatori, and the Palazzo Senatorio or Palazzo della Ragione, built on the remains of the ancient *tabularium* or record office. After being several times fortified, dismantled, ruined, and reconstructed during the Middle Ages, this palazzo was now a castellated brick building, associated with four irregular towers, used by the civic administration of Rome and by lawyers (see Flavio Biondo *Roma instaurata* I). The name Capitol had apparently been transferred from the hill to this building, which played such an important part in the medieval and Renaissance history of the city of Rome. The reconstruction of the Capitol area after Michaelangelo's designs was not started until 1538.

779 speech of accusation] By Celso Mellini; see Simar (above, n774) 62–72. It was delivered in the great hall of the Capitol before Pope Leo x (who enjoyed literary debate and favoured the Ciceronians) and a great crowd of distinguished Romans. The speech survives in manuscript in the Vatican library.

780 speech in praise of France] The *Panegyric* on St Louis ix of France, delivered at Poitiers 1508–9, where Longueil was studying law. Longueil gave himself out to have been about eighteen at the time. His enemies reproduced the speech, which had been published in Paris in 1510 (Henricus Stephanus), and circulated it in Rome.

781 a barbarian ... barbarians] Added 3rd ed. The arrogant Italian attitude which dismissed all northern men of letters, Erasmus included, as barbarians, obviously continued to rankle.

433

782 *Batrachomyomachia*] *The Battle of the Frogs and Mice*, a parody of the Homeric manner, probably written in the third century BC

783 peril to his life] The situation depicted in Cicero's first Philippic oration. For the Philippics see n487.

784 Romulus, with his Quirites] See nn383, 385.

785 conscript fathers] See n289.

786 classes and tribes] The citizen body of Rome was in two of its various voting assemblies subdivided into classes according to wealth, and into tribes according to domicile.

787 praetors] Praetors held the second highest magistracy, and controlled the administration of justice.

788 veto] The tribunes were representatives of the common people, and one of their powers was the right of vetoing motions put before the senate or assemblies of the whole people.

789 provinces ... allies] See n304.

790 'passions'] See 385.

791 rousing them from their tombs] Added 2nd ed. Erasmus is probably thinking of Cicero's evocation of Appius Claudius Caecus in *Pro Caelio* 33.

792 Quintilian] 2.10.2ff, 10.5.14

434

793 spoke without inhibition ... death removed] Antony and his troops left Rome after the first Philippic was delivered (see above n783), so that Cicero then had a free field, and his next speech attacking Anthony (the second Philippic) was a supreme example of invective.

794 may I be forgiven for saying so] Added 3rd ed, an ironic placatory gesture

795 ill-disposed towards me] See 325–6.

796 the speeches are available] They were not actually delivered. The long-standing animosity towards Longueil had become very intense in the preceding two months, being brought to a head by honours which the pope bestowed on him at Bembo's instance. Longueil began to fear assassination and retreated from Rome, but he had prepared these two speeches in his own defence and left them in the hands of his friends. Soon after his departure his 'trial' took place (16 June 1519), and the accuser's speech was received with such acclaim that Longueil's supporters feared to read out the speeches entrusted to them. They did however publish them in Rome some weeks later (see n814), and their obvious merit vindicated Longueil and temporarily at least discomfited the opposition. News of the victory followed Longueil to Venice, but he proceeded to visit northern Europe before returning to an excited Rome. The speeches were also rushed into print by Aldus in 1519, and by de Gourmont and Bade in Paris 1520. They were included in Pole's 1524 edition of Longueil's works (see n703).

797 to prove ... truth.] Added 3rd ed

798 five speeches in praise of Rome] These, delivered in the presence of Gian Matteo Giberti 5–9 August 1518, were not printed, but are preserved in manuscript in the Vatican library.

799 leaving unsaid] Erasmus by implication again accuses the Roman Academy of irreligion.

800 barbarous tongue] Dante (*De Vulgari eloquentia* 1.11.2) called the speech of Rome the worst of all Italian dialects.

801 speech against Martin Luther] Longueil undertook to write five speeches against the Lutherans at the request of Leo x. Only one was complete at the time of his death, and this was published by Reginald Pole in his 1524 edition of Longueil's works.

435

802 earlier] See 388, 391.

803 'those they ... other things.'] Martial 4.49.10

804 *Colloquia*] These, with other works, had given particular offence to orthodox churchmen in several countries, and in May 1526 had been condemned by the theology faculty of Paris (see Ep 2037).

805 Dutch word-spinner] *Orator Batavus*, as Longueil called Erasmus; see Allen Ep 1595:133n and the second dedicatory epistle above 339. Erasmus was disparagingly referred to by Italians as *Germanus, Batavus*.

806 Greek word] Meaning 'applauded,' or possibly 'well-wrought'; cf n768.

807 those who fired] Bembo chiefly; also Sadoleto. These two distinguished churchmen and literary figures were leaders of the Ciceronian movement in Italy.

808 Jacopo Sadoleto] Of Modena (1477–1547), papal secretary to Leo x, and a member of the reformed Roman Academy. He was later made cardinal in 1536.

809 Pietro Bembo] Of Venice (1470–1547), a noble and (like Sadoleto) papal secretary to Leo x and a member of the Roman Academy, but of greater literary eminence. He too was made cardinal, in 1539.

810 nothing of Bembo's available] Bembo wrote both prose and poetry in Latin and Italian, as well as editing Virgil's *Culex* and the plays of Terence (1530). Some of his Latin and Italian works had appeared by this time, but Erasmus seems not to know of them. The letters Longueil received from Bembo and Sadoleto had been published as the fifth book of *Longolii epistulae* in Pole's edition of Longueil's works of 1524, a text Erasmus had obviously read. The sixteen books of letters written by Bembo as papal secretary received the *editio princeps* in 1536, and the collected letters appeared in 1550–2. Bembo revised his official letters into more Ciceronian Latin before publication; see H. Hauser 'Deux Brefs inédits de Leon x à Ferdinand au lendemain de Marignan' *Revue Historique* 100 (1909) 329–30, 332–4.

436

811 Bembo's equal] He wrote Latin poems, the most notable celebrating the discovery of the Laocoön in 1506. In later life he wrote numerous prose treatises covering education, philosophy, and theology. He also composed Latin orations. His letters, other than those to Longueil (see above) were published later than *Ciceronianus*. His commentary on Psalm 50 (Vulgate) *Miserere mei* was already published (1525).

812 bishop of Carpentras] Near Avignon. He was appointed in 1517 by Leo x, but his duties as papal secretary and, later, diplomatic missions kept him from his see until he moved there from Rome just before the sack of 1527.

813 on Christian topics ... best possible way] Added 3rd ed and no doubt intended to dispel the suspicion in some quarters that Erasmus had been attack-

ing Bembo in his pillorying of the Ciceronians. Erasmus was by this time better acquainted with Bembo, and found that he could agree with much in Bembo's modified form of Ciceronianism. Later, in Ep 2453 to Ursinus Velius (1531), he made a point of praising Bembo and Sadoleto as stylists.

814 Battista Casali] Baptista Casalius (d 1525), canon of the Lateran, a renowned orator and an admirer of Longueil, whose *Defensio* he edited in 1519 in conjunction with Mariano Castellano and Flaminio Tomarozzo, writing the prefatory epistle. See n796 and Allen Ep 1479:30n.

815 *De lege agraria*] Addressed to Clement vii (1524); the title recalls three speeches of Cicero, similarly named.

816 Pontano] Giovanni Pontano (1426–1503), president of the Academy at Naples, a prolific writer of Latin prose including history and political philosophy, and of light and occasional verse. In Ep 531 (1517) Erasmus had censured him as almost a 'Ciceronian ape.' He receives extended notice here no doubt because some Italians had expressly preferred him as a stylist to Erasmus (see n488).

817 general topics] The prose treatises *De fortitudine* and *De oboedientia* were published in 1490, *De splendore* in 1498.

818 treatise *De principe*] Published 1490

819 dialogues] *Charon* (with the same title as one of Lucian's) and *Antonius* published in 1491; *Asinus, Actius, Aegidius* in 1507

437

820 *Meteora* and *Urania*] Poems on meteorological and astrological topics composed c 1476–80

821 those barbs] Cf Cicero *De oratore* 3.138, where Cicero says something similar of Pericles.

822 Sannazaro] Jacopo Sannazaro (Actius Syncerus) 1456–1530. A close friend of Pontano and a member of the Neapolitan Academy, Sannazaro was known as 'the Christian Virgil' for his Latin poetry after classical models, the best known being *De partu virginis libri iii* (1526), and *Eclogae piscatoriae* (c 1520), 'pastoral' poems set among fisherfolk. He was author also of the famous *Arcadia*, in Italian (1504).

823 briefs ... of Leo and Clement] Briefs were private letters sent out in the name of the pope, which the papal secretaries were responsible for drafting. Both the practice and the name went back to about 1490. Leo's (6 August 1521) was written by Bembo, Clement's (5 August 1527) by Sadoleto.

824 Cardinal Egidio] Egidio Antonini da Viterbo (1469–1532), appointed General of the Augustinian order in 1507, created cardinal by Leo x in 1517. He was famous as an orator, his opening speech at the fifth Lateran Council (1512) being much admired. Many years before the publication of the poems, he had recommended Sannazaro to Bembo as a talented Christian poet: see the letter of Bembo to Sannazaro of 1 April 1505 (in Bembo *Epistolae familiares* vol 4).

825 Baptista Mantuanus] Battista Spagnoli of Mantua (1448–1516), Shakespeare's 'good old Mantuan,' a Carmelite friar and a prolific writer of verse published in three volumes by Bade in 1513

826 didn't go so far wrong] See Ep 49 (1496), where Erasmus had praised Mantuanus as a Christian Virgil, a man using discretion in his application of classical material to Christian subjects. Colet thought Mantuanus a suitable Christian author for reading by the boys of St Paul's school.

827 sibylline oracles] A collection of miscellaneous prophecies, attributed to various pagan prophetesses known collectively as sibyls, which apparently foretold the birth of Christ. Belief in the existence of such prophecies was based on Virgil's 'Messianic' *Ecologue* 4, and texts were produced to substantiate it in the early Christian centuries. Lactantius *Divinae institutiones* 1.6 names ten such sibyls. Filippo di Barberi, in a treatise published in 1481, listed twelve sibyls to parallel the twelve major prophets.

828 Proteus] The Old Man of the Sea, who could be made to reveal answers to questions (ie. prophesy) if he could be held down through multifarious transformations

829 nymphs, hamadryads, and nereids] Nymphs were semi-divine beings personifying for the Greeks the beneficient forces of nature, and various species were believed to inhabit different parts of the living world: hamadryads dwelt in trees, nereids in the sea. They were represented in art as beautiful maidens, often unclothed.

830 to the Virgin Mother] *De partu virginis* 1.19

831 *divorum*] Divus was used in classical Latin for men such as emperors who had been divinized after their deaths (see n329), and the word was later used by Christians as a title for saints.

832 the one hymn ... birth of Jesus] *Cathemerinon* 11 *Hymnus natalis domini*; Erasmus published a commentary on *Cathemerinon* 11 and 12 (hymns for Christmas and Epiphany) in 1524 (Basel: Froben).

833 Goliath] Used as a symbol of Antichrist in the Middle Ages and later. The poem is praised in these terms in Bembo's brief (see n823).

438

834 which ... in its praise.] Added 3rd ed

835 no reason for rejecting] Cf Seneca *Epistulae morales* 40.12.14.

836 patchwork poem] See n186.

837 Quintilian] 6.2.1–17

838 break up a mosaic] The construction of continuous discourse from recombined fragments of classical writers was known as the *stile a mosaico*.

839 rape of Ganymede] See n431.

439

840 Horace] *Ars poetica* 12–13.

841 in his pocket – and in his heart] *In sinu*, used both literally and metaphorically

842 Phocion ... Marcus Tullius] See 385.

440

843 Greek proverb] *Adagia* III ix 43

844 Apicius] A Roman gourmet of the first century AD. The cookery book that goes under his name was given its *editio princeps* in 1498.

441

845 if God gave them the chance] Cf Horace *Satires* 1.1.15.

846 jump the barrier] *Adagia* I x 93

847 components of the art of speaking] *Ad Herennium* 1.1.3

848 giants fighting against the gods] See n235.

849 or at least from the most outstanding] Added 2nd ed

442

850 Pallas from the brain of Jove] Terence *Heautontimorumenos* 1035–6

851 A certain amount ... no shame to a man] See Cicero *De officiis* 1.130, an aspect of decorum.

852 controlling the features ... corresponds to the face] Cf Cicero *De oratore* 3.221, *Orator* 60 and Quintilian 11.3.80–1 on the avoidance of grimacing in oratory. Cicero remarks in both places *imago animi vultus* 'the face is the image of the mind.'

853 your Peitho] See 343.

854 Quintilian] See 409–10.

855 *Rhetorica ad Herennium*] See 364.

856 Sallust] See 409.

857 Quintus Curtius] See 410.

443

858 Leonardo of Arezzo] See 415.

859 Lorenzo Valla] See 415.

860 Ermolao Barbaro] See 416.

861 Cristophoro Landino] See 418.

862 Poliziano] See 416.

863 Paolo Cortesi] See 418.

864 Tertullian] See 413.

865 Bede] See 414.

866 Jerome] See 413.

867 Lactantius] See 412.

868 and yet all be Atticists] Quintilian 12.10.20

869 without any support from grammar] Dolet took exception to this charge that Ciceronians wrote ungrammatical Latin (Telle, text 62ff).

870 'have it in their prayers'] Horace *Satires* 2.6.1

871 Scala, who found ... unciceronian] See the correspondence of 1493 between Scala and Poliziano, in *Politiani epistolae* 5.

444

872 his letter] See the two letters exchanged by Poliziano and Cortesi, which Erasmus here summarizes. The text of the letters, published in *Politiani epistolae* 8. 16 and 17, is available with Italian translation in *Prosatori latini del quattrocentro* ed Eugenio Garin (Milan and Naples 1952) 902–10; an English translation, together with a translation of Poliziano's letter to Scala (see n871 above) is provided in Izora Scott *Controversies over the Imitation of Cicero* Columbia University Contributions to Education 35 (New York: Teachers College, Columbia University 1910).

873 somebody else's footprints] Quintilian 10.2.10; *Adagia* IV x 32
874 'worn ... digested them'] Poliziano ibidem

445
875 prolix] Three times as long as Poliziano's
876 though ... I do not know] Added 2nd ed
877 Hyponosus] 'One who feels a bit sick'; perhaps also he does not now know which side he is on, and feels more aligned with Nosoponus.
878 read and esteemed] Latin *habendum in sinu*, see n841.
879 Latin poets] 'Latin' added 2nd ed. The sentiment is expanded in Ep 2695 (1532), where Erasmus says the situation is different in Greek.
880 serious] Added 2nd ed

446
881 someone else's footprints] See n873.
882 his float] *Adagia* III vi 26. The phrase is used in Poliziano's letter.
883 Aristotle] Here probably referring to his school's considerable output of scientific writings on cosmology, meteorology, zoology, and plants, but Aristotle's own writings could not be described as stylish.
884 Theophrastus] Aristotle's successor, particularly important for his development of the scientific work of the school; he wrote on winds, weather, fire, plants, and odours, as well as the famous *Characters* and works on logic and rhetoric.
885 Pliny] The Elder Pliny, author of the thirty-six books of the *Naturalis historia*, in a not very elegant style
886 his native genius is against it] *Repugnante Minerva*: see Cicero *De officiis* 1.110: 'invita ut aiunt Minerva, id est adversante et repugnante natura.'
887 will cost him far too dear] For a similar sentiment see Seneca *Epistulae morales* 88.38.
888 Ovid] *Amores* 2.4

447
889 heresies ... paganism] See Ep 541:149ff (26 February 1517), where Erasmus is already warning against a humanism that is only nominally Christian; see above 393–4.
890 He does not ... own day and age] See 387.

448
891 pursue something you cannot achieve] Cicero *De officiis* 1.110

WORKS FREQUENTLY CITED

SHORT-TITLE FORMS
FOR ERASMUS' WORKS

INDEX

WORKS FREQUENTLY CITED

This list provides bibliographical information for publications referred to in short-title form in introductions and notes. For Erasmus' writings see the short-title list following (pages 609–12).

Allen   P.S. Allen, H.M. Allen, and H.W. Garrod eds *Opus epistolarum Des. Erasmi Roterodami* (Oxford 1906–58) 11 vols and index

ASD   *Opera omnia Desiderii Erasmi Roterodami* (Amsterdam 1969–)

Bainton 'Erasmus and Luther' R.H. Bainton 'Erasmus and Luther and the Dialog *Julius exclusus' Vierhundertfünfzig Jahre lutterische Reformation 1517–1967: Festschrift für Franz Lau* (Göttingen 1967) 17–26

Bainton *Erasmus of Christendom* R.H. Bainton *Erasmus of Christendom* (London 1970)

Born   Lester K. Born ed and trans *The Education of a Christian Prince by Desiderius Erasmus* (New York 1936; reissued in paperback in the series Records of Civilization 1968)

Brosch   M. Brosch *Papst Julius II und die Gründung des Kirchenstaates* (Gotha 1878)

CEBR   *Contemporaries of Erasmus: A Biographical Register of the Renaissance and Reformation* ed P.G. Bietenholz and T.B. Deutscher (Toronto 1985–) 3 vols

CWE   *Collected Works of Erasmus* (Toronto 1974–)

Chambers   D.S. Chambers *Cardinal Bainbridge in the Court of Rome 1509–1514* (Oxford 1965)

Creighton   M. Creighton *A History of the Papacy during the Period of the Reformation* (London 1882–94)

Erasmus   T.A. Dorey ed *Erasmus* (London 1970)

Gregorovius   F. Gregorovius *History of the City of Rome in the Middle Ages* trans A. Hamilton (London 1900–2)

Hauser   H. Hauser 'Le *Julius* est-il d'Erasme?' *Revue de littérature comparée* 7 (1927) 605–18

Hefele   J. Hefele *Histoire des conciles d'après les documents originaux*
                        trans H. Leclercq (Paris 1907–   )

Isnardi Parente   M. Isnardi Parente ed and trans *L'Educazione del principe
                        cristiano* (Naples 1977)

LB   J. Leclerc ed *Desiderii Erasmi Roterodami opera omnia* (Leiden
                        1703–6) 10 vols

Lemaire de Belges   Lemaire de Belges *Oeuvres* ed J. Stecher (Louvain 1882–91)

McConica   J.K. McConica 'Erasmus and the "Julius": A Humanist
                        Reflects on the Church' in C. Trinkaus and H.A. Oberman
                        eds *The Pursuit of Holiness in Late Medieval and Renaissance
                        Religion* (Leiden 1974) 444–71

Opuscula   W.K. Ferguson ed *Erasmi opuscula: A Supplement to the
                        Opera omnia* (The Hague 1933)

Oulmont   C. Oulmont *Pierre Gringoire* (Paris 1911)

Pascal   P. Pascal trans J.K. Sowards ed *The 'Julius Exclusus' of
                        Erasmus* (Bloomington 1968)

Pastor   L. Pastor *The History of the Popes from the Close of the Middle
                        Ages* ed and trans R.F. Kerr et al, 3rd ed (London 1938–53)
                        40 vols

PG   J.P. Migne ed *Patrologiae cursus completus ... series graeca*
                        (Paris 1857–1912) 162 vols

Phillips   Margaret Mann Phillips *The 'Adages' of Erasmus* (Cambridge
                        1964)

Pineau *Erasme*   B. Pineau *Erasme et la papauté: étude critique du Julius exclusus*
                        (Paris 1924)

PL   J.P. Migne ed *Patrologiae cursus completus ... series latina*
                        (Paris 1844–1902) 221 vols

Reedijk *Poems*   C. Reedijk *The Poems of Desiderius Erasmus* (Leiden 1956)

Rodocanachi   E. Rodocanachi *Histoire de Rome: le pontificat de Jules II
                        (1503–1513)* (Paris 1928)

Rogers   Elizabeth Frances Rogers ed *The Correspondence of Sir Thomas
                        More* (Princeton 1947)

Stange   C. Stange *Erasmus und Julius II: eine Legende* (Berlin 1937)

Telle   E. Telle ed and comm *L'Erasmianus sive Ciceronianus d'Etienne
                        Dolet (1535)* Travaux d'Humanisme et Renaissance 138
                        (Geneva 1974)

Thompson *Colloquies*   Craig R. Thompson ed and trans *The Colloquies of Erasmus*
                        (Chicago and London 1965)

Thompson *Under*   G. Thompson *Under Pretext of Praise: Satiric Mode in Erasmus'*
  Pretext of Praise   *Fiction* (Toronto 1973)

Tracy *Growth of a Mind* James D. Tracy *Erasmus: The Growth of a Mind* (Geneva 1972)

Tracy *Politics*   James D. Tracy *The Politics of Erasmus: A Pacifist Intellectual
                        and His Political Milieu* (Toronto 1978)

SHORT-TITLE FORMS FOR ERASMUS' WORKS

Titles following colons are longer versions of the same, or are alternative titles.
Items entirely enclosed in square brackets are of doubtful authorship. For abbreviations, see Works Frequently Cited, pages 606–8.

Adagia: Adagiorum chiliades 1508 (Adagiorum collectanea for the primitive form,
    when required) LB II / ASD II-5, 6 / CWE 30–6
Admonitio adversus mendacium: Admonitio adversus mendacium et obtrectationem
    LB X
Annotationes in Novum Testamentum LB VI
Antibarbari LB X / ASD I-1 / CWE 23
Apologia ad Fabrum: Apologia ad Iacobum Fabrum Stapulensem LB IX
Apologia ad Caranzam: Apologia ad Sanctium Caranzam, or Apologia de tribus
    locis, or Responsio ad annotationem Stunicae ... a Sanctio Caranza defensam
    LB IX
Apologia ad viginti et quattuor libros A. Pii LB IX
Apologia adversus Petrum Sutorem: Apologia adversus debacchationes Petri Sut-
    oris LB IX
Apologia adversus monachos: Apologia adversus monachos quosdam hispanos LB
    IX
Apologia adversus rhapsodias Alberti Pii LB IX
Apologia contra Latomi dialogum: Apologia contra Iacobi Latomi dialogum de tribus
    linguis LB IX
Apologiae contra Stunicam: Apologiae contra Lopidem Stunicam LB IX / ASD IX-2
Apologia de 'In principio erat sermo' LB IX
Apologia de laude matrimonii: Apologia pro declamatione de laude matrimonii LB IX
Apologia de loco 'Omnes quidem': Apologia de loco 'Omnes quidem resurgemus' LB
    IX
Apologia invectivis Lei: Apologia qua respondet duabus invectivis Eduardi Lei
    Opuscula
Apophthegmata LB IV
Appendix respondens ad Sutorem LB IX
Argumenta: Argumenta in omnes epistolas apostolicas nova (with Paraphrases)
Axiomata pro causa Lutheri: Axiomata pro causa Martini Lutheri Opuscula

Carmina varia LB VIII
Catalogus lucubrationum LB I
Christiani hominis institutum, carmen LB V
Ciceronianus: Dialogus Ciceronianus LB I / ASD I-2 / CWE 28
Colloquia LB I / ASD I-3
Compendium vitae Allen I / CWE 4
[Consilium: Consilium cuiusdam ex animo cupientis esse consultum Opuscula]

De bello turcico: Consultatio de bello turcico LB V
De civilitate: De civilitate morum puerilium LB I / CWE 25
De concordia: De sarcienda ecclesiae concordia LB V
De conscribendis epistolis LB I / ASD I-2 / CWE 25

De constructione: De constructione octo partium orationis, or Syntaxis LB I / ASD I-4
De contemptu mundi: Epistola de contemptu mundi LB V / ASD V-1
De copia: De duplici copia verborum ac rerum LB I / CWE 24
De immensa Dei misericordia: Concio de immensa Dei misericordia LB V
De libero arbitrio: De libero arbitrio diatribe LB IX
De praeparatione: De praeparatione ad mortem LB V / ASD V-1
De pueris instituendis: De pueris statim ac liberaliter instituendis LB I / ASD I-2 / CWE 26
De puero Iesu: Concio de puero Iesu LB V
De ratione studii LB I / ASD I-2 / CWE 24
De recta pronuntiatione: De recta latini graecique sermonis pronuntiatione LB I / ASD I-4 / CWE 26
De tedio Iesu: Disputatiuncula de tedio, pavore, tristicia Iesu LB V
De virtute amplectenda: Oratio de virtute amplectenda LB V
Declamatio de morte LB IV
Declamatiuncula LB IV
Declarationes ad censuras Lutetiae vulgatas: Declarationes ad censuras Lutetiae vulgatas sub nomine facultatis theologiae Parisiensis LB IX
Detectio praestigiarum: Detectio praestigiarum cuiusdam libelli germanice scripti LB X / ASD IX-1
[Dialogus bilinguium ac trilinguium: Chonradi Nastadiensis dialogus bilinguium ac trilinguium *Opuscula*] / CWE 7
Dilutio: Dilutio eorum quae Iodocus Clithoveus scripsit adversus declamationem suasoriam matrimonii
Divinationes ad notata Bedae LB IX

Ecclesiastes: Ecclesiastes sive de ratione concionandi LB V
Elenchus in N. Bedae censuras LB IX
Enchiridion: Enchiridion militis christiani LB V
Encomium matrimonii (in De conscribendis epistolis)
Encomium medicinae: Declamatio in laudem artis medicae LB I / asd i-4
Epigrammata LB I
Epistola ad Dorpium LB IX / CWE 3
Epistola ad fratres Inferioris Germaniae: Responsio ad fratres Germaniae Inferioris ad epistolam apologeticam incerto autore proditam LB X
Epistola ad graculos: Epistola ad quosdam imprudentissimos graculos LB X
Epistola apologetica de Termino LB X
Epistola consolatoria: Epistola consolatoria virginibus sacris LB V
Epistola contra pseudevangelicos: Epistola contra quosdam qui se falso iactant evangelicos LB X / ASD IX-1
Epistola de esu carnium: Epistola apologetica ad Christophorum episcopum Basiliensem de interdicto esu carnium LB IX / ASD IX-1
Exomologesis: Exomologesis sive modus confitendi LB V
Explanatio symboli: Explanatio symboli apostolorum sive catechismus LB V / ASD V-1
Expostulatio Iesu LB V

Formula: Conficiendarum epistolarum formula (see De conscribendis epistolis)

Hymni varii LB V
Hyperaspistes LB X

Institutio christiani matrimonii LB V
Institutio principis christiani LB IV / ASD IV-1 / CWE 27

[Julius exclusus: Dialogus Julius exclusus e coelis *Opuscula*] / CWE 27

Lingua LB IV / ASD IV-1
Liturgia Virginis Matris: Virginis Matris apud Lauretum cultae liturgia LB V / ASD V-1

Methodus: Ratio verae theologiae LB V
Modus orandi Deum LB V / ASD V-1
Moria: Moriae encomium LB IV / ASD IV-3 / CWE 27

Novum Testamentum: Novum Testamentum 1519 and later (Novum instrumentum
    for the first edition, 1516, when required) LB VI
Obsecratio ad Virginem Mariam: Obsecratio sive oratio ad Virginem Mariam in re-
    bus adversis LB V
Oratio de pace: Oratio de pace et discordia LB VIII
Oratio funebris: Oratio funebris Berthae de Heyen LB VIII

Paean Virgini Matri: Paean Virgini Matri dicendus LB V
Panegyricus: Panegyricus ad Philippum Austriae ducem LB IV / ASD IV-1 / CWE 27
Parabolae: Parabolae sive similia LB I / ASD I-5 / CWE 23
Paraclesis LB V, VI
Paraphrasis in Elegantias Vallae: Paraphrasis in Elegantias Laurentii Vallae LB I /
    ASD I-4
Paraphrasis in Matthaeum, etc (in Paraphrasis in Novum Testamentum)
Paraphrasis in Novum Testamentum LB VII / CWE 42–50
Peregrinatio apostolorum: Peregrinatio apostolorum Petri et Pauli LB VI, VII
Precatio ad Virginis filium Iesum (in Precatio pro pace)
Precatio dominica LB V
Precationes LB V
Precatio pro pace ecclesiae: Precatio ad Iesum pro pace ecclesiae LB IV, V
Progymnasmata: Progymnasmata quaedam primae adolescentiae Erasmi LB VIII
Psalmi: Psalmi, or Enarrationes sive commentarii in psalmos LB V
Purgatio adversus epistolam Lutheri: Purgatio adversus epistolam non sobriam
    Lutheri LB IX

Querela pacis LB IV / ASD IV-2 / CWE 27

Ratio verae theologiae: Methodus LB V
Responsio ad annotationes Lei: Liber quo respondet annotationibus Lei LB IX
Responsio ad collationes: Responsio ad collationes cuiusdam iuvenis gerontodidas-
    cali LB IX

Responsio ad disputationem de divortio: Responsio ad disputationem cuiusdam
  Phimostomi de divortio LB IX
Responsio ad epistolam Pii: Responsio ad epistolam paraeneticam Alberti Pii, or
  Responsio ad exhortationem Pii LB IX
Responsio ad notulas Bedaicas LB X
Responsio ad Petri Cursii defensionem: Epistola de apologia Cursii LB X
Responsio adversus febricitantis libellum: Apologia monasticae religionis LB X

Spongia: Spongia adversus aspergines Hutteni LB X / ASD IX-1
Supputatio: Supputatio calumniarum Natalis Bedae LB IX

Vidua christiana LB V
Virginis et martyris comparatio LB V
Vita Hieronymi: Vita divi Hieronymi Stridonensis *Opuscula*

Index